Reflections on Translation Theory

Benjamins Translation Library (BTL)

ISSN 0929-7316

The Benjamins Translation Library (BTL) aims to stimulate research and training in Translation & Interpreting Studies – taken very broadly to encompass the many different forms and manifestations of translational phenomena, among them cultural translation, localization, adaptation, literary translation, specialized translation, audiovisual translation, audio-description, transcreation, transediting, conference interpreting, and interpreting in community settings in the spoken and signed modalities.

For an overview of all books published in this series, please see
www.benjamins.com/catalog/btl

General Editor

Yves Gambier
University of Turku &
Immanuel Kant Baltic
Federal University (IKBFU),
Kaliningrad, Russia

Associate Editor

Franz Pöchhacker
University of Vienna

Honorary Editor

Gideon Toury†
Tel Aviv University

Advisory Board

Rosemary Arrojo
Binghamton University

Michael Cronin
Dublin City University

Dirk Delabastita
University of Namur

Daniel Gile
Université Paris 3 - Sorbonne
Nouvelle

Amparo Hurtado Albir
Universitat Autònoma de
Barcelona

Zuzana Jettmarová
Charles University of Prague

Alet Kruger
UNISA, South Africa

John Milton
University of São Paulo

Anthony Pym
University of Melbourne and
Universitat Rovira i Virgili

Rosa Rabadán
University of León

Sherry Simon
Concordia University

Şehnaz Tahir Gürçaglar
Bogaziçi University

Maria Tymoczko
University of Massachusetts
Amherst

Lawrence Venuti
Temple University

Michaela Wolf
University of Graz

Volume 132

Reflections on Translation Theory. Selected papers 1993–2014
by Andrew Chesterman

Reflections on Translation Theory

Selected papers 1993–2014

Andrew Chesterman
University of Helsinki

John Benjamins Publishing Company
Amsterdam / Philadelphia

The paper used in this publication meets the minimum requirements of the American National Standard for Information Sciences – Permanence of Paper for Printed Library Materials, ANSI z39.48-1984.

DOI 10.1075/btl.132

Cataloging-in-Publication Data available from Library of Congress:
LCCN 2017001379 (PRINT) / 2017016300 (E-BOOK)

ISBN 978 90 272 5878 6 (HB)
ISBN 978 90 272 5879 3 (PB)
ISBN 978 90 272 6576 0 (E-BOOK)

© 2017 – John Benjamins B.V.
No part of this book may be reproduced in any form, by print, photoprint, microfilm, or any other means, without written permission from the publisher.

John Benjamins Publishing Company · https://benjamins.com

Table of contents

Preface	IX
Section I. Some general issues	1
PAPER 1 On the idea of a theory (2007)	3
PAPER 2 Shared ground in Translation Studies (2000) *With Rosemary Arrojo*	17
PAPER 3 What constitutes "progress" in Translation Studies? (2000)	25
PAPER 4 Towards consilience? (2005)	35
Section II. Descriptive and prescriptive	43
PAPER 5 The empirical status of prescriptivism (1999)	45
PAPER 6 Skopos theory: A retrospective assessment (2010)	55
PAPER 7 Catford revisited (2012)	71
PAPER 8 The descriptive paradox, or how theory can affect practice (2013)	81
Section III. Causality and explanation	95
PAPER 9 Causes, translations, effects (1998)	97
PAPER 10 A causal model for Translation Studies (2000)	123
PAPER 11 Semiotic modalities in translation causality (2002)	137

PAPER 12
On explanation (2008)   **147**

Section IV. Norms   **165**

PAPER 13
From 'is' to 'ought': Laws, norms and strategies in Translation Studies (1993)   **167**

PAPER 14
A note on norms and evidence (2006)   **185**

Section V. Similarities and differences   **193**

PAPER 15
On similarity (1996)   **195**

PAPER 16
Problems with strategies (2005)   **201**

PAPER 17
The unbearable lightness of English words (2007)   **213**

Section VI. Hypotheses   **223**

PAPER 18
The status of interpretive hypotheses (2008)   **225**

PAPER 19
Reflections on the literal translation hypothesis (2011)   **237**

Section VII. "Universals"   **251**

PAPER 20
Beyond the particular (2004)   **253**

PAPER 21
What is a unique item? (2007)   **269**

PAPER 22
Kundera's sentence (2004)   **281**

PAPER 23
Universalism in Translation Studies (2014)   **295**

Section VIII. The sociological turn   **305**

PAPER 24
Questions in the sociology of translation (2006)   **307**

PAPER 25
The name and nature of Translator Studies (2009)   323

PAPER 26
Models of what processes? (2013)   331

Section IX. Translation ethics   345

PAPER 27
Proposal for a Hieronymic Oath (2001)   347

PAPER 28
An ethical decision (2009)   363

References   369

Name index   391

Subject index   395

Preface

These selected papers all have to do with conceptual analysis; alongside textual analysis, this is one of the oldest methods used in Translation Studies (hereafter: TS). In most cases, the articles do not represent empirical research and are not data-driven. When there are examples these are usually only illustrative, to indicate how I interpret a concept, or to show that something is at least possible, or to elucidate a point. No empirical research is possible without some conceptual analysis, of course, since (for instance) hypothesis formation and data analysis involve categorization and categories represent concepts. I therefore hope that the conceptual work and arguments represented here can contribute to empirical research, as well as to greater understanding of the phenomenon of translation.

One of the repeated themes is my concern about the increasing fragmentation of TS. Several papers explore the possibility of establishing some shared conceptual and/or methodological ground between different branches of the field. Aspects of this theme include the relation between prescriptive and descriptive approaches and between theory and practice, different kinds of hypothesis and explanation, bridge concepts such as causality, and the notion of consilience. The papers are grouped into thematic sections, and each section has a short introduction, putting the papers into context. The selection reflects my thinking over the past couple of decades or so, on a variety of topics in translation theory and translation research methodology. The methodological topics derive mainly from my work in supervising MA and PhD theses, and participating in international graduate schools and seminars.

A general rhetorical caveat should be made here. Like other scholars, I am not always careful enough to distinguish clearly, by textual means, between factual claims and conceptual or interpretive ones. That is, a clause like "there are two kinds of norms" is of course not an empirical claim, although it may syntactically look like one, but an interpretive one. It should be glossed: 'I argue/suggest that it is useful to conceptualize norms as falling into two categories'. The nature of such conceptual claims is discussed in some detail in Paper 18.

The papers are mostly reproduced unchanged, with the original source indicated in a footnote, together with copyright permission acknowledgement where necessary. Abstracts and keywords have been added for papers which originally did not include them. Some texts have been slightly revised, with minor corrections and updated references and links, and a few cuts have been made in order to minimize overlaps with other papers included here, although some repetition inevitably remains. Changes are indicated in introductory footnotes and/or square brackets. Misprints have been corrected. Format features, such as the numbering of sections and use of italics, have been made consistent. All references have been collected into one list, at the end of the volume. In cases where this list then contains references to publications by the same author in the same year (e.g. referred to in different papers), the necessary editorial additions or revisions have been made in the texts as well (e.g. 2001*a*, 2001*b*). Numbered *end*notes belong to the original texts. Asterisked *foot*notes have been added in this volume, and so has most text within square brackets.

For fruitful discussions, insightful comments and critical feedback, I owe enormous debts of gratitude to colleagues, friends and students – in MonAKO (the acronym of our Helsinki University Translation Studies unit during most of the period covered by these papers), in Finland's wonderful nationwide KäTu (translation research) community, and further afield at CETRA (KU Leuven), EST (the European Society for Translation Studies), the Tarragona Intercultural Studies Group, and others. I cannot list them all, so I will just mention one. Gideon Toury's work has been a lasting inspiration to me, as to so many others; he first got me interested in norms and explanations, and a certain way of thinking about translation, and insofar as I have felt part of a "school" in Translation Studies, it is Descriptive TS. I learned of his death as I was preparing this volume, and dedicate it to his memory.

For encouragement and advice on this volume, my warm thanks go to Yves Gambier, the editor of the Benjamins Translation Library, and to Isja Conen, Patricia Leplae and the efficient team at Benjamins.

Helsinki, October 2016
AC

SECTION I

Some general issues

This opening section deals first with the notion of a theory, in a wide sense: what a theory – including a theory of translation – can be. Some of the topics mentioned in Paper 1 are discussed in more detail in other papers in this volume: topics such as explanation, models, hypotheses, metaphors, universals and causality. In this paper, there is a section on models as a kind of theory: I suggest three basic kinds of model. However, I have later recognized that there also seems to be a fourth type, a network (nexus) or agent model, such as used in some sociological research on translation. Using such a model, the researcher constructs a network of the agents involved in a translation event or practice and plots the various relations between them. This type of model was particularly brought to my attention by the work of Kaisa Koskinen (e.g. 2008).

The second paper, written jointly with Rosemary Arrojo, was the opening contribution to a Forum debate in *Target*, about the extent to which TS scholars from different academic or philosophical backgrounds might think it possible to agree on fundamentals in our very heterogeneous interdiscipline. At a lively conference at Vic in 1999, it was clear that there were very different views of TS around, represented for instance by Gideon Toury, Laurence Venuti and Theo Hermans. Rosemary and I, with very different initial positions, were both motivated to see how much "shared ground" we could find. I remember proposing the idea of a joint paper to Gideon Toury in a taxi after the conference, and he said *Target* (which he edited) would welcome a Forum debate on the subject. Our opening salvo was followed by responses in the following issues of Target, with concluding comments by both of us in *Target* 14, 1 (2002). At the end of the exercise, neither of us felt that much shared ground had been found, although the exchange of views had been most interesting. Perhaps TS scholars can only agree to disagree... I am most grateful to Rosemary for agreeing to have our piece reprinted here.

Paper 3, on the notion of progress in TS, started as a conference paper in Stockholm. It appears here in a slightly revised version, with some cuts concerning topics (kinds of explanations and hypotheses) which are treated in more detail elsewhere in this volume. The difference discussed here between the views of TS as an empirical or hermeneutic discipline have also been addressed by Daniel Gile, who sees a division between TS scholars coming from a humanities background and those coming from an empirical science one. This division is reflected in different research conventions. (Early summary statements of Gile's argument, and some responses to it, can be found on the website of the European Society for Translation Studies, at www.est-translationstudies.org/ > Resources > Research issues.) With respect to the clash between the views of scholars and professional translators on what TS should be doing, see further Cross (1998) and Chesterman and Wagner (2002), and also Paper 5 in this volume. The importance of the "hermeneutic *as*" is illustrated in some detail in Paper 18.

Paper 4 also started at a conference. It represents a second attempt to map out some "shared ground", this time around the notion of consilience. Following E. O. Wilson, I interpret this term as referring to the ideal of uniting different fields of knowledge. One way of doing this within TS is to look for "bridge concepts" which connect different aspects of our field. This paper also touches on the sociological turn, causality, translation models and strategies, all of which topics are discussed in more detail in other papers in this volume.

These four papers all reflect my concern with the increasing fragmentation of TS, into more and more subfields that often seem to have little connection with one other. Different theoretical assumptions, and different conceptions of what TS is as a discipline or interdiscipline, are reflected in different research aims, methodologies, and areas of interest. A major reason for this fragmentation is of course the nature of translation itself: the concept is so wide and fuzzy, comprising so much heterogeneity and so much cultural and temporal variation, that it is not surprising we have no single overarching theoretical framework. Translation does not sit easily into the confines of a natural category, as evidenced by the abundance of definitions that have been proposed for the concept and by the lack of a standardized terminology. As the field continues to develop, the tension continues between, on one hand, an expansive centrifugal drive to explore ever new aspects of this rich cultural phenomenon, and, on the other, a consolidating centripetal drive to establish and strengthen at least some shared ground. This continued tension is itself one reason why the field is so fascinating – and also why I believe conceptual analysis continues to have a significant role.

PAPER 1

On the idea of a theory[*]

This article is based on a lecture that has been given to several groups of doctoral students at various times and in various places. It outlines five notions of what has been taken to constitute a "theory": myth, metaphor, model, hypothesis and structured research programme. The most fundamental of these is the hypothesis. These different ideas of what a theory can be are illustrated with examples from Translation Studies. Any theory aims at description and explanation, and these two concepts are also discussed. A final comment takes up the idea that translations themselves are theories, and that a translator is thus a theorist or *theoros*.

Keywords: theory, description, explanation, myth, metaphor, hypothesis, structured research programme

1. A way of seeing

The etymology of the word "theory" goes back to the Greek θεωρία 'theoria', meaning 'a way of looking at something', in order to contemplate it and understand it better. In this broad sense, we can say that a theory is a helpful point of view. I take (better) understanding to be the general goal of any theory. A theory of translation is thus a view of translation – or some part or aspect of it – which helps us to understand it better.

This is an instrumental notion of "theory": a theory is an instrument of understanding. Good theories are useful instruments; bad ones are eventually discarded in favour of better ones. But theories are also goals or ends in their own right, in the sense that they are conceptual structures that need to be designed, formulated and tested. In other words, theories themselves are also *forms* of understanding. If understanding is the final goal, constructing a theory is an intermediate goal which can then serve as an instrument to that end, at the same time as it gives this understanding a form. In this context, it is useful to compare the notion of a

---

[*] First published in 2007 in *Across Languages and Cultures* 8, 1:1–16. Reprinted here by kind permission of the publisher, Akadémiai Kiadó. This version is slightly revised. The keywords have been added.

method, from Greek *meta hodos* 'after the way'. Methodology is, etymologically, the business of proceeding along the way (*hodos*) to do something or to reach a goal. If a theory represents a form of understanding, methods are the ways in which one actually uses, develops, applies and tests a theory in order to reach the understanding it offers.

2. Description, explanation

The general goal of understanding a phenomenon means that we need access to appropriate concepts, an ability to describe and explain, and often also the ability to predict. Appropriate concepts need to be defined, and justified in preference to other "shadow" concepts that might have been used instead but were not: i.e. the choice of concepts needs to be justified. (Compare the notion of "shadow translations", used e.g. by Johansson 2004.) The concepts also need to be related to each other, as illustrated e.g. in the concept diagrams used in terminology. There are a great many concepts in Translation Studies (TS) which have been given competing definitions: we do not have a consistent terminology, in any language. Consider the variety of available definitions of the key concepts of "translation", "equivalence" and "strategy", for instance; or the different typologies of these concepts that have been proposed (on strategies, see e.g. Chesterman 2005[*]).

A description can be done from many perspectives. The linguist Kenneth Pike (1959) suggested trying at least three such perspectives: seeing the phenomenon as a particle (in isolation; and in comparison with similar particles); as a wave (in which the phenomenon is seen as merging with other phenomena in space and time; this perspective also includes the historical, diachronic view); and as a field (where the phenomenon is related to its surrounding context). We could also look at it from a functional perspective: what use is it, what is its value? (Cf. Booth et al. 1995:40.)

Explanations also come in many forms. We can explain for instance how something is possible (what are the necessary conditions?), or why it had to happen (what are the sufficient conditions?). Explanations work by showing relations of generalization, causality, or unification with other patterns of phenomena. Hypotheses about translation universals, for instance, aim to explain the occurrence of, say, explicitation in a given translation by positing a *generalization*: all (or most) translations manifest some explicitation, and this makes it easier to understand why this particular translation does as well, if there is indeed a

---

[*] Paper 16 in this volume.

general tendency. If the generalization is true, we are not surprised when we find explicitation, because the generalization offers an explanation of a kind. *Causal* explanations also increase our understanding of why something happened, or why the form of something is as it is. And if we can show the relations between the *explanandum* (that which needs to be explained) and other phenomena, if we see it in the context of a more general pattern, we also feel we have found some kind of explanation. For instance, we can better understand why there have been several different German translations of the classic Finnish novel *Seitsemän veljestä* ('Seven brothers', by Alexis Kivi) if we look at the context of the different social and political conditions at different periods in Germany, different translators with different intentions and ideologies, different publishers, different translation norms, different German images of Finland at different times, and so on (Kujamäki 1998, 2001). These conditioning factors are all weakly causal, but, as is often the case in the human sciences, our sense of understanding here comes more from seeing the broad picture than from evidence of causality in a strict sense. To the extent that we can relate these factors within a single model, we can arrive at an explanation via *unification*. (On explanation via unification, see Salmon 1998.)

Predictions can be used to test explanations. But not all explanations imply the corresponding ability to predict. However, even if precise predictions are not possible, an explanation reduces our surprise that the phenomenon in question has occurred, and perhaps allows us at least to anticipate other occurrences in future. An explanation thus allows us to "make sense" of something. (For further discussion of this general theme, see e.g. Chalmers 1999.)

3. Kinds of theory

It is helpful, I suggest, to distinguish five types or notions of theory. I outline them here. Examples from Translation Studies follow below.

Some of the first theories were *myths*: they were symbolic narratives which offered some way of "making sense" of something mysterious. "We are meaning-seeking creatures," writes Karen Armstrong (2005: 2); "[...] from the very beginning we invented stories that enabled us to place our lives in a larger setting, that revealed an underlying pattern [...]". Think of the many myths of creation, in different cultures, for instance. Or the 20th-century Gaia myth which invites us to see our planet as a living organism. A myth can have enormous effects on a person or a society.

Theories can also take the form of *metaphors* or similes. To see something strange *as* something more familiar (or as being *like* something more familiar, or as a *kind* of something more familiar) is one way of making sense of it. Physicists have learned to see light, for instance, as particles; or as waves; or, nowadays, as both at the same time. "Metaphor is one of our most important tools for trying to comprehend partially what cannot be comprehended totally," say Lakoff and Johnson (1980: 193). But a metaphor only sheds light on one side of a phenomenon: every metaphor also hides what it does not highlight. We do not see the dark side of the moon.

Myths and metaphors are often said to represent the kind of knowledge which Plato called *mythos*, as opposed to *logos*. Mythos is the form of knowledge that is symbolic, intuitive, figurative, imaginative; logos is rational, explicit.

Scientific theories often involve metaphors and myths, but they typically aim to be more explicit, based on evidence, and empirically testable. One kind of scientific theory is a *model*, which seeks a relation of similarity with whatever it is a model of. Models represent what are taken to be the main elements of a phenomenon, their main functions, and the main relations between the elements. Think of models of our planetary system, before and after Copernicus. Or models of the brain (like the model of the brain as a black box, with input and output); or models of cognitive processes (decision-making, for instance, is sometimes represented as an algorithm of yes/no choices, a view which is implicitly based on the metaphor of the mind as a computer).

For some philosophers, theories are seen as *hypotheses*. A hypothesis is, roughly speaking, an educated guess at the best answer to a question, based on the most reliable facts available. Popper's general model (sic!) of scientific progress centres around the idea of generating and testing hypotheses (e.g. Popper 1959). To solve an initial problem, a tentative theory (a hypothesis) is proposed, then this is tested (the stage of error elimination), and the result is usually a new problem; and so the process continues. The original invention of the idea of a hypothesis has been a major step in the development of the scientific method, because it means that empirical claims need to be tested against evidence rather than believed on the basis of the authority of the claimer, or on tradition, or on intuition alone.

There are various basic types of hypothesis (illustrations coming below).

Descriptive hypotheses:	all Xs have feature F / belong to class Y.
Explanatory hypotheses:	X is caused by / made possible by, Y; Y explains X.
Predictive hypotheses:	in conditions ABC, X will (tend to) occur.
Interpretive hypotheses:	X can be (usefully) interpreted as Y.

The first three types are self-explanatory; they are all empirical hypotheses. Predictive hypotheses are used to test (some) explanatory ones.

Interpretive hypotheses have a different status from the other types, because they are not tested directly against empirical evidence (are they true?) but against pragmatic criteria (are they conceptually useful, insightful?). My claim that there are five types of theory, for instance, is this kind of hypothesis. I find it useful, as a way of clarifying the picture. But if someone proposes a competing hypothesis – say, that it makes more sense to classify types of theory into seven, or seventeen groups – we simply have to see which classification seems more useful, which "catches on", which gives rise to better research. Interpretive hypotheses are nevertheless an integral part of doing science. All definitions and classifications, for instance, are based on them, not to speak of data interpretation. If birds and dinosaurs are classified as belonging to the same zoological class, we shall probably "see" them rather differently than we would otherwise. Do you define a tomato as being a fruit or a vegetable? Is Pluto a planet nowadays or not? Alternative classifications illustrate the enormous variety of ways in which we human beings can conceptualize our world (for a classic study, see Lakoff 1987).

My fifth type of theory is the *structured research programme*. This view is argued for especially by Lakatos (e.g. 1970). Such a theory has two main components. At the centre, there is a "hard core" of fundamental principles and assumptions which are not questioned within the programme but taken for granted (although they may be questioned by people outside the programme). Outside this core, there is a "protective belt" of supplementary assumptions and hypotheses to be tested, protecting the hard core.

Of these five types of theory, the hypothesis is the fundamental one. Myths and metaphors can be seen as interpretive hypotheses, to be tested in use. Models are hypotheses too, to be tested against evidence; and the same can be said of the cluster of hypotheses and assumptions which make up a research programme: you try them out, and if they do not work adequately, you eventually try something else.

Let us now look at how these kinds of theories are represented in Translation Studies.

4. Myths of translation

In the West, the dominant myth of translation is the Babel myth (Genesis 11). This myth has had major consequences for our perception of translation. We see it as tainted by the Fall from the Paradise of perfect communication, by failure; it is always second-best, never as good as the original; and so on.

But we do not have to see translation through the eyes of this pessimistic myth. In the East, apparently, translation can be seen in terms of the myth of metempsychosis, or the transmigration of souls (Devy 1999). It can thus be associated with the idea of rebirth, spiritual progress: as a soul returns to live again in a new body, so a text may be born again in a new language, and perhaps in a form that is in some way better than its previous existence. This is rather a more optimistic view, looking not at what is lost in translation but what might be gained. Traces of this alternative myth can also be found in Renaissance writings on translation in the west, as when translators are described as having some spiritual affinity with their authors, as if the two had a shared soul (Hermans 1985c: 127).

5. Metaphors of translation

The history of Translation Studies is full of metaphors and images of translation. Here is a selection from the Renaissance period in Europe, all having to do specifically with literary translation (paraphrased from Hermans 1985c, where exact sources are given).

Translation is (like) imitation.
The translator is like a painter who shows a person's body but not his soul.
The translator digests the original, turning it into blood and food.
To translate is to follow in the footsteps of the original.
A translation is the rival of the original, striving to beat it at its own game.
The translator is the servant or slave of the original.
A translator is a magpie among peacocks (i.e. trying to look like a peacock but failing).
The translator is like Phaeton, who wanted to drive the chariot of the sun and was punished for his presumption (i.e. if he dares to challenge the mastery of the original).
A translation is the echo of a song.
A translation offers false pearls in place of diamonds.
A translation is like the reverse side of a tapestry.
A translation is a plain garment (whereas the original is a rich cloth).
A translation is like candlelight compared with the sun.
Translations are shadows of beautiful bodies.
Translation opens windows to let in the light.
The translator brings treasures which were hidden in the earth.
A translation is a jewel in the rough casket of language.
Translating is like pouring a precious liquid from one vessel into another.

Such conceptualizations reveal implicit theories about translatability, the relation between meaning and form, translation equivalence and translation quality.

My own preferred metaphor is from memetics (Chesterman 1997a). I find it interesting to see translations as ways of carrying the evolution of ideas (memes) from one culture to another, like biological organisms carry the evolution of genes. Translations help memes to survive and spread. This metaphor thus allows me to see translation within the framework of cultural evolution.

Translation has also been seen as *a kind of* something else which is more familiar: as a kind of rewriting, for instance (Lefevere 1992a). This placing of translation under the more general term highlights its similarities with other kinds of rewriting, such as paraphrasing, summarizing, or anthologizing (and correspondingly downplays other kinds of similarities). Sometimes there are serious disagreements about these hierarchies. There is currently some debate about whether translation is a kind of localization, or whether localization is a kind of translation (see e.g. Pym 2004). To some extent such interpretive hypotheses are expressions of power and status: if translation is the higher term, it seems to be more important, and localization is demoted to being a mere type of translation. And vice versa. So the debate is partly an institutional, territorial one, with consequences concerning research funds, jobs, salary levels and so on.

6. Models of translation

I have elsewhere (Chesterman 2000a[*]) distinguished three types of models used in Translation Studies.
Comparative models show translations in a relation to other texts, which may be

- source texts (> the equivalence relation),
- non-translated comparable texts in the target language (> the naturalness relation),
- other translations (> research on translation universals), or
- non-native texts, learners' texts.

Examples of comparative models are those developed by e.g. Catford, Koller, Vinay and Darbelnet; those based on contrastive research; and corpus-based work on translation universals. Catford's model (1965) is based on an analysis of the various kinds of relations holding between source texts and translations, on his theory of equivalence and his classification of types of shift. An equivalence typology also lies at the centre of Koller's model (1979); he distinguishes denotative, connotative, text-type, pragmatic and formal types of equivalence. Vinay and Darbelnet (1958) were primarily interested in the contrastive syntactic and rhetorical differences between English and French, and proposed a number of "procedures" as ways of conceptualizing the kinds of changes that translators make when moving from one language to another. For instance, the procedure of "transposition", which involves changing the word class. Although Vinay and Darbelnet framed their procedures in dynamic terms, these are usually seen as ways of conceptualizing the results of these various procedures. What we see, empirically, is the result of a change of word class, for instance, when a verb in English is translated as a noun in French.

---

[*] Paper 10 in this volume.

With the advent of corpus methodology, scholars began looking empirically at other kinds of relations. Translations into, say, English can be compared to matched (i.e. with same subject matter and text type, etc.) non-translated texts originally written in English, in order to see whether there are systematic differences between the two corpora. In other words, we can measure the naturalness of the translations. We can also compare translations into English with translations into other languages, from a variety of source languages, and see whether we find evidence of recurrent features (universals?) of the translations, regardless of language or text-type, which might therefore be due to the translation process itself. (Examples will be given below of some claims that have been made as a result of such research.) We might also want to compare translations to texts produced by non-native speakers: perhaps the effect of the extra constraint of the translation situation is similar to that of having to produce a text in a non-native language.

In all versions of these comparative models, then, we are dealing with two sets of texts and looking at the relations between them. The relations are basically static and contrastive.

Process models, on the other hand, represent the temporal sequence of stages in the translation process, either at the cognitive level of translation decisions, or the sociological level of working procedures. An early and influential process model was the one proposed by Nida (e.g. 1969). He suggested that translation was like crossing a river (note the image!), but added that a translator does not actually cross at the point where the source text is. The translator first analyses the source text (reduces it to a simplified form, i.e. looks for an easier place to cross the river), then makes the transfer to the target language, and then "restructures" the translation, which means stylistically polishing it so that it corresponds to the stylistic profile of the original and/or to the expectations of the audience. He thus modelled the translation process in terms of the three stages of analysis, transfer and restructuring.

Other scholars have modelled the process differently. Sager (1994) bases his analysis on four working procedures: specification (understanding the client's instructions, checking that the brief is appropriate and feasible); preparation (finding the necessary resources, terminology, and so on); translation; and evaluation (revision). Nord (1991a: 32f) argues for what she calls a looping model. Here, step one is analysis of the translation skopos; step two is analysis of the source text; and step three is the production of the target text. Nord calls this model a looping one, because it illustrates the way in which the translator continually loops back and forth between the three elements of the model: skopos, source text analysis and target text synthesis. This model is thus more complex than a linear one going directly from source to target.

Process models are also evident in cognitive research using think-aloud protocols (TAPs), where the aim is to model the translator's decision-making process (for surveys, see e.g. the special issues of *Across Languages and Cultures* 3, 1, 2002; and *Meta* 50, 2, 2005). Work using the Translog program also tracks the translation process: here, the computer records the translator's every key-stroke against a clock, producing a time record of the translator's typing actions. When this is combined with a think-aloud protocol and perhaps a video recording, and a retrospective interview, we can arrive at a fairly detailed picture of the observable translation process and make some inferences about what happens at the cognitive level. (For some recent Translog work, see Hansen 2002 and other papers in the same volume; and Hansen 2005.)

On a much larger time-scale, a process model also underlies work on translation history. Here, though (as also with some of the cognitive research) there is an overlap with causal models, in which the focus is not only on the temporal relation of what came before or after what, but on the cause-and-effect relation.

Causal models, in their simplest form, look like this:

Causal conditions > Translations > Effects

Translations themselves are both the result of preceding causal conditions and themselves the cause of consequences. These consequences may range from acceptance or rejection of the text by the client, or feedback from critics, to major cultural developments. Think of the role played by translation in the history of science, for instance. In the human sciences, however, causality can seldom if ever be represented as a simple linear chain. What we usually find is a whole complex of factors and contributory conditions, some of which are more powerful than others, and many of which also affect each other. In a very broad sense, the causal conditions of translations range from the cognitive to the socio-cultural. The immediate cause of a given word in a translation, for instance, must be that the translator decided to write that word: the proximate cause is cognitive. But we can continue asking "why?". Perhaps he made that decision because of his working conditions (a bad dictionary? not enough time?). Why were the conditions like that? (The client didn't care? The client chose a poorly qualified, cheap translator?) What are the norms for that kind of translation task in that culture? What are the underlying values and ideologies? And so on – the questions never end, but answers to them can contribute something to our wish to understand "why" something occurred in this translation. Similar lists of questions can be made for other starting-points. Why, for instance, did a given translation have such-and-such an effect on the client / on the readers / on society / on cultural development as a whole?

Causal models are used explicitly in several current theories. Skopos theory, for instance, assumes as axiomatic that the single most important cause of the form of a given translation is (or should be) its skopos, its purpose. (See e.g. Vermeer 1996, Nord 1997.)

Scholars who have applied relevance theory to translation, on the other hand, propose that the fundamental explanatory cause is the principle of relevance itself. Roughly speaking, this is defined as the cost-benefit relation between the reader's effort to understand (= cost) and the cognitive effects the message has (= benefit): the more benefit and less cost, the more relevance; and speakers are assumed to aim for optimal relevance. Relevance theory claims to offer a cognitive explanation for why people communicate as they do (and also why they translate as they do, since translation is seen here as being simply one form of the interpretive use of language, i.e. like reported speech). (See Gutt 2000.)

Norm theory takes a different view of causation, looking more broadly at the socio-cultural conditions and norms, including for instance the translation tradition in a given culture, which affect translator's decisions. (A classic source is Toury 1995.) In translation training, translators are typically socialized into the current norms in their society; but not all translators receive formal training, and need to pick up the norms in other ways. Norms are based on values, which in turn lead us to translation ethics: a translator's professional ethics also affect his decisions about how to act as a translator. Reception studies (also represented in Kujamäki 1998, cited above) also use a causal model to analyse why a given translation had a given effect.

From this point of view, it is evident that all work on translation quality has an underlying causal model, too. This is apparent in translation quality control, where checking and documentation of procedures aim at assuring the quality of the various stages of the translation process, on the assumption that if the process is OK the resulting product will also be OK. (See e.g. the CEN standard for translation services, EN 15038: 2006, e.g. via www.cen.eu [and now (2016) the ISO 17100 standard, issued in 2015].) It is also apparent in quality assessment, whether during training or in working life. A given translation fails, or is rejected by the client, because it has given defects; in other words, it causes a negative effect on someone. One could even say that research on machine translation uses an implicit causal model: if the aim is to produce a better automatic translation program, the focus is on adjusting the program to produce an optimal-quality result – you vary the causal conditions and check the effects.

7. Hypotheses of translation

Interpretive hypotheses abound, of course. All operationalization decisions are based on them. An example might be a decision to interpret the concept of translation quality, in a given research project, as "grades from 1 to 5 given by translation trainers using a matrix of defined error types and weightings"; as opposed for instance to "impressionistic grading by peers" or "acceptance or rejection by the client".

Descriptive hypotheses have come much more to the fore with the interest in corpus studies on translation universals, mentioned earlier. All claims about universals are descriptive hypotheses. A well-known example is the explicitation hypothesis, that translators tend to make explicit what was only implicit in the source (originating from Blum-Kulka 1986). Another is the law of increasing standardization, that translations tend to use a more unmarked style than their source texts (Toury 1995). A third example is the claim that translators tend to reduce repetition. (For a recent selection of work on these hypotheses, see Mauranen and Kujamäki 2004.) Yet another well-tested example is the retranslation hypothesis, that later translations of a given text into a given target language tend to be closer to the source than its first or earlier translations. This hypothesis does not seem to be finding much confirmation (see most recently Brownlie 2006).

Explanatory hypotheses are also common, but have so far tended to refer to individual case studies. A given translation, it is argued, has particular features *because of* a number of given factors. Brownlie (2003), for instance, proposes the following factors which seem to explain much of her material: the individual situation and context of production, including the translator's attitudes; the conditions determining the textuality of a translation, the way it is subject to different textual and intertextual constraints; translators' norms; and the effects of intersecting fields such as publishing and academia (in the case of academic texts). An example of a more general explanatory hypothesis is the claim that translators tend to start their mental processing with a literal translation: the literal translation hypothesis. This would explain the progression from more literal towards freer versions evidenced in studies of the revision process, where the analysis focuses on sequences of interim draft solutions (e.g. Englund Dimitrova 2005). Another explanatory hypothesis has emerged from TAP research: that the quality of a translation can (sometimes) be (partly) explained by the translator's mood and emotional state (see e.g. Jääskeläinen 1999).

Predictive hypotheses are less common in Translation Studies, where experimental research is not widespread. (It is more usual in Interpreting Studies: see e.g. Pöchhacker 2004.) One example is the claim (or assumption?) that if a translator has more time the translation will be of a better quality. This is an idea that has been challenged at least by Hansen (2002). Implicitly, of course, every translator proposes a predictive hypothesis when he or she delivers a translation: the prediction is that the client will accept it as a good (or at least adequate) translation; and the test is the reaction of the client.

Formulating a hypothesis explicitly is crucial. There is a big difference between e.g. "translation shapes the formation of cultural identity" and "translation reflects the formation of cultural identity". The first is an explanatory, cause-and-effect hypothesis, which suggests that translation is a (presumably contributory) condition of cultural identity formation. It is presumably not a necessary or sufficient cause, however. And precisely when translation would be a contributory condition is not made explicit in this formulation. The second formulation is an interpretive hypothesis: translation can be interpreted as reflecting cultural identity formation. Anyone wishing to disagree would need to counter-argue that, in their view, translations are more usefully regarded as signs of something else, or that some other signs of cultural identity formation are more important.

Good empirical hypotheses are testable against evidence; they are internally coherent, simpler or more powerful than competing hypotheses, bring added value, and raise new questions and hypotheses.

It is a good idea either to start a research project with a hypothesis (better: a pair of contrasting hypotheses), or else end with a claim that can function as a hypothesis to be tested in a future research project.

8. Structured research programmes (?)

We can find some examples in TS which seem to be structured research programmes in Lakatos' sense, but perhaps only to some extent. Polysystem theory, for instance, has a set of "hard-core" assumptions, including the following (from Hermans 1985b). We can analyse cultures in terms of polysystems, i.e. systems of systems. A system is a structured complex of elements that can be distinguished from its environment. Systems can be identified, but they are not static; each system has a centre (e.g. of canonized forms) and a periphery, and it has conservative and innovatory elements, which are in a constant state of flux. Within a polysystem, different systems and subsystems struggle for central status. One such system is that of literature, which itself contains other systems, such as genres. Translations show what can happen at the interface of systems; they can be part of the centre or of the periphery. Perhaps the most innovative and provocative assumption in polysystem theory is that all translation involves some manipulation, for a given purpose, such as the intended function of a translation in the target system. – Research based on these assumptions has given rise to a large number of descriptive case studies, but general empirical hypotheses have not been much in evidence, with the exception of general claims about the ubiquity of interference.

Corpus research on translation universals could also be said to share some basic assumptions, such as the idea that features specific to translations are worth seeking in their own right, not as evidence of poor translations; that translations constitute a text-type of their own, a "third code", neither source nor wholly target; that we have a (potentially) universal concept of translation available which can apply to all cultures and all ages; and that there is some reliable way of deciding what translations to include in a corpus and what to exclude (for instance on the parameters of professional vs. amateur, native vs. non-native, or even good vs. bad: after all, a bad translation is still a translation, of a kind…). (For some criticism of these assumptions, see Tymoczko 1998.) The empirical hypotheses are then the various claims about possible universal features, referred to above.

One lesson we can draw from this view of a theory is the importance of distinguishing between what is assumed, what is being asked or tested, and what is finally being claimed. Assumptions can be challenged, and hidden assumptions can be exposed. Hypothesis-testing procedures and operationalization decisions can also be challenged. And claims may be met with counter-evidence and counter-claims, or suspected of being illogical. The difference between assumptions, hypotheses and claims is thus a question of their status in a given research project, not of their propositional content as such.

But there is certainly not one shared paradigm in TS, which would allow the development of a single research programme covering the whole field. (See the *Target* debate, starting with Chesterman and Arrojo 2000*) We share very general aims – to understand translation and the significance of the work of translators – but we do not all work with the same sets of concepts, nor even the same types of data. The lack of a single shared paradigm is also reflected in our heterogeneous methodologies. (See Gile's provocative division between the Empirical Science Paradigm and the Liberal Arts Paradigm, on the EST website at <http://www.est-translationstudies.org/ > Research issues.)

9. Contributing to theory

The five types of theory I have outlined are not mutually exclusive. By this I mean that a given research project may make use of different types. It might use a causal model and propose or test an explanatory hypothesis, within a broader structural framework of other assumptions and hypotheses, for instance. Or it might focus on a descriptive hypothesis framed in a comparative model and formulated in terms of a striking metaphor. One way of contributing to theory is indeed to show the relations between different existing theories and theory-types, and thus try to develop a still more general theory.

One can also contribute to theory in other ways. By providing new data (in order to test existing theories), for instance. Or by offering a better interpretation of existing data; by clarifying and relating concepts and assumptions. Or by

---

* Paper 2, below.

proposing a better model or a new hypothesis. Or by testing or refining a given hypothesis, or proposing a new way of testing one, a new methodology. In other words: one can contribute by suggesting a new or better answer to an interesting question, by pointing out a new path which might lead to a better answer, or by raising a new interesting question or problem.

Ultimately, the aim (as I see it) is to link various substantiated claims in terms of more general laws, in the same field or in other fields, in steps towards the possible unification of knowledge: consilience.

10. A translation is itself a theory

This final comment is really only a footnote. I suggest that a translation itself can be seen as a theory of how the source text can be translated, in all the five senses outlined above.

It usually represents the source text as a linear narrative, like a myth.

It is usually taken "to be" metaphorically the source text (etymologically *translate* = *meta-phor*). When I say 'I have read Tolstoy' (albeit in English translation), I am not lying, for my *War and Peace* "is" the Tolstoy novel.

A translation usually models the source text isomorphically, both holistically and in terms of its parts.

It constitutes a hypothesis about the source text, about how it can be interpreted, usually about its meaning. A translator implicitly makes a claim that his translation is equivalent in some relevant way to the source text, a claim that is tested by the reception of the translation by clients, readers and perhaps critics (cf. Pym 1995).

And the whole process of translating is like a structured research programme, with a clearly defined problem to be solved, a set of assumptions (such as translation norms), and a multitude of individual hypotheses to be tested, for each segment of the text.

So translators theorize all the time (see also Pym 1992a). But they theorize also in a deeper sense. As Carol Maier (2006) suggests, the translator is a *theoros*, i.e. a person who makes a "journey" in order to seek knowledge, a better way of seeing; perhaps even wisdom. Maier writes (168–9): "the traveller witnessed things and events with which he was unfamiliar. To see, then, in this context was to theorize. [...] Moreover, to theorize those unfamiliar things was to be affected by them, to be moved to wonder." This wondering contemplation takes us to the very roots of philosophical enquiry.

PAPER 2

Shared ground in Translation Studies*

With Rosemary Arrojo, Universidade Estadual de Campinas, Brazil

The authors propose thirty "theses" concerning translation that might be accepted by scholars coming from different philosophical and research backgrounds. The "theses" have to do with the definition of 'translation', where we might look for causal explanations, and assumptions about translation effects.

Keywords: essentialism, definition, explanation, translation effects, meaning

One of the themes that came up for debate at the Vic Forum on "Training Translators and Interpreters: New Directions for the Millennium" in May 1999 was the apparent conceptual or theoretical gap between those who approach translation studies from the perspective of postmodern cultural studies and textual theories and those who see it more as an empirical, descriptive field.

The debate between these different approaches is sometimes couched in terms of essentialism vs. non-essentialism. In general, essentialism claims that meanings are objective and stable, that the translator's job is to find and transfer these and hence to remain as invisible as possible. Non-essentialism, on the other hand, basically claims that meanings (including the meaning of the concept of "translation") are inherently non-stable, that they have to be interpreted in each individual instance, and hence that the translator is inevitably visible.

We (RA and AC) thought it would be interesting and constructive to see how far these two approaches to translation studies can be reconciled. RA has earlier argued for a non-essentialist approach to research and training (e.g. Arrojo 1998), and AC has argued for an empirical one (e.g. Chesterman 1998a[†]).

What follows below is first of all a set of 30 "theses" which represent our shared ground; we have written them together, and both of us accept the formulations

---

* First published in 2000 in *Target* 12, 1: 151–160 (10.1075/target.12.1.08che). Reprinted with kind permission from John Benjamins Publishing Company, Amsterdam/Philadelphia (www.benjamins.com). The abstract and keywords have been added.

† Paper 9 in this volume.

used. Any of these theses could be expanded at some length, but we have tried to be brief. This shared list is followed by two "codas", in which each of us comments on the shared ground and expands on selected points.

What is translation?

1. Translation Studies (TS) – or any research on translation – seeks to understand the phenomenon of translation, however this is defined and practised.
2. Any definition of anything is theory-bound, so there is no such thing as a totally objective definition of "translation" that we can take for granted before we start studying it, as there will never be any definition of translation that will be all-inclusive. We start with a preliminary working definition, and refine it as we go along. Different scholars, with different research aims, tend to start (and end up) with different definitions. We should aim to be as aware as possible of why we choose or accept a particular definition and/or conception of translation.
3. There is no such thing as absolutely "raw" data. Data are ultimately taken, not given. We can recognize this, but we cannot escape it. But since we cannot manage with no data at all, we must select something to study. We should aim to be as aware as possible of why we choose the data we choose.
4. One aim of TS is to discover which kinds of texts (in certain cultures at certain times) have been labelled "translations", as compared with texts that are not called translations. This aim includes the study of who labels the texts, and for what reasons, and whether such attributions change over time.
5. The English word *translation* might not necessarily denote exactly the same thing as some other word that approximately means 'translation' in another language (such as *Übersetzung*). TS is interested in mapping these different conceptions, and how they change over time. Even within English (which just happens to be the language we are both using here), people's concepts of what constitutes a "translation" may vary widely. A valid research goal is to examine the extent to which these various conceptions of translation overlap, both within and across cultures.
6. TS also studies what gets translated (at a given period, in a given culture) and what does not, as part of the movement of ideas between cultures.
7. TS studies the people and groups of people who actually do the translating, too: who they are (were), what kind of cultural background they have, etc.
8. Another research goal is to study the discourse on translation in a particular culture at a particular time – e.g. the discourse engaged in by translators themselves, by clients, by society at large, and by translation scholars. This is one way of exploring the question "what is translation" – what do people say about

it? Even if people do not actually say much about translation, this in itself is an interesting finding: cf. the debate about the translator's invisibility etc.
9. People (including translation scholars) often express their concept of translation as a metaphor. Any metaphor of translation presents it in a certain light, rather than in some other light. We cannot manage without such metaphors.
10. All metaphors carry implications about meaning. The metaphor "translation is transfer", for instance, implies that something is indeed transferred, something that presumably remains constant throughout the process and is thus objectively "there". This something is often thought to be the meaning (or the message, or the sense, or the *vouloir dire*, or…).
11. Other metaphors have different implications. The metaphor "translation is performance" reflects a conception according to which translation is a form of interpretation and re-creation. The metaphor "translating is cannibalism" reflects a conception of translation which advocates the translator's alleged right to exploit the source text for whatever purpose seems appropriate.
12. The concept of "translation" might be described as a prototype concept: the centre of the concept is represented by (kinds of) texts which most people, in a given culture and period, accept as translations, but at the periphery we find less typical examples, which some people accept and others do not. TS seeks to discover what features seem to be part of the central area, and which seem more peripheral (both in a given culture/period, and also more generally) – and also why these features are thus distributed.
13. We can distinguish many different kinds of translations, some more frequently found than others, some more typical than others. TS seeks to establish a typology of translation types (both within a culture/period and more generally).
14. The question "What is a translation?" is closely linked to the question "What is a good translation?". TS is interested in studying how opinions and criteria concerning translation quality vary within and across cultures and periods. It is also interested in seeing whether there are quality criteria that are shared across cultures and periods.

Why is this (kind of) translation like this?

15. Understanding a phenomenon also means being able to explain why it is as it is, and why it exists at all. TS is interested in exploring the various enabling conditions / reasons / influences / causes of translatorial behaviour.
16. There are many different senses of explanation. Some causes seem more deterministic than others; some seem no more than influences or contributory factors. Some factors may only explain in the sense that they increase understanding by reducing surprise when something happens or is found.

17. TS looks at many different kinds of influences / causal conditions: the translator's personality, gender, cognitive state, personal experience, decision processes; the influence of the client, of the skopos, of features of the translation situation itself, the source text, the source and target languages, the implied readers; socio-cultural and historical factors, ideological factors, values, ethical considerations…
18. One way of explaining why translations (in a given culture/period etc.) are as they are is to try to describe the norms in the source and target cultures which have influenced the translators in question. Such influence might be positive (translators follow them) or negative (translators react against them).
19. Everyone is different, and every act of translation takes place in unique circumstances, if we analyse it in enough detail. Every translation is thus in some sense unique and cannot be explained by reference to any other translation.
20. Translating is a human activity (excluding machines here). To some extent, we all behave in similar ways. Different instances of whatever we call translating behaviour will manifest some similarities – by definition, if they fall within whatever preliminary definition we are using for the object of study. In other words, there are patterns of translatorial behaviour, manifested as observable patterns in translations themselves.
21. Patterns of behaviour and text can be studied. The study of such patterns may enable scholars to make statements about regularities, such as: in certain circumstances, translators often seem to do this kind of thing; or: in certain circumstances, translations often seem to have these kinds of features.

What consequences do translations have?

22. TS also seeks to study the effects of translations: in general, and also during particular cultures and periods etc. In the first place, are translations read actually as translations or as texts of the target culture? TS aims to develop explanatory hypotheses which account for the effects of translations, for instance in terms of translation features. For instance, if people do not laugh at a translated joke, or laugh at an unexpected place in the text, this may be because of some feature in the translation itself. Among other things, TS studies the claims below (23–30).
23. Like originals, translations can change the state of mind of the reader.
24. Like originals, translations can affect the subsequent behaviour of the reader.
25. Like originals, translations can affect whole cultures, including the (typical / prevalent) perception of one culture by another culture. Cultures of course include languages.

26. In some readers, some translations trigger quality judgements. Some readers, such as clients in particular, react positively or negatively to the perceived quality of a translation.
27. Some readers are paid to react in this way (critics, teachers). They might not be typical / representative readers.
28. Some people express their quality expectations as prescriptive statements of the form "translators (under these conditions, faced with this problem, etc.) should / should not do this". TS studies such prescriptive statements, e.g. as part of the discourse on translation.
29. Information about the enabling conditions which tend to lead to translations with desirable effects is useful to trainee translators and their teachers, as is information about the features of these translations which tend to have desirable effects. (Desirable to whom? Yes, also a relevant question.)
30. Studying the causes and effects of translations raises major questions of ethics. For instance, in what sense might the effects of a decision to translate, of a translation, or of a particular translatorial decision, be "good"?

Coda by AC

Ad 9–11: Statements that translation can (or should) be seen or interpreted in a given way (*as* something) are, I think, to be understood as interpretive hypotheses. That is, they are hypotheses which claim that it is useful (in some way) to interpret translation in this way. Such hypotheses can be evaluated in terms of the added value they bring to TS, and perhaps also in terms of their possible consequences, e.g. for translators' self-image or translatorial decision-making. More generally, interpretive hypotheses underlie any conceptual analysis. An argument that there are five kinds of equivalence, for instance, can be rephrased thus: I hypothesize (for these reasons…) that it is useful to interpret the concept of equivalence as consisting of five sub-concepts. All descriptive research is based on some kind of conceptual analysis. We need initial interpretive hypotheses, for instance, about which features of the total environment it seems relevant or useful to isolate and label, for a particular purpose.

Ad 10: I would want to add that some meanings (in certain contexts) seem more stable than others. Compare e.g. proper names like the *University of Vic*, or the denotation of a phrase such as *350 milligrams*, and abstract nouns like *democracy* or *translation*. All meanings are context-bound, but some seem more context-bound than others. Sometimes an essentialist position seems less well justified than at other times.

Ad 18: Norms are by definition prescriptive, that is, they exert prescriptive force. People can either conform to such prescriptions or resist them. But *statements* of norms are not in themselves prescriptive but descriptive: they simply say what the norms in question appear to be.*

Ad 21: For me, a statement about a regularity is first of all a descriptive hypothesis, of the following general form: all translations (of a given type) tend to have such-and-such a feature; or: all translators (under given conditions) tend to do this kind of thing. (Cf. the study of alleged translation universals such as explicitation.) Some scholars seek to formulate very general descriptive hypotheses in terms of laws. These laws are not intrinsically prescriptive: they merely describe behavioural regularities, patterns, at a very general level. True, they may be *felt* (e.g. by some translators) to be prescriptive. Statements about translation universals or regularities, to the extent that they are corroborated by empirical evidence, can function as explanations: translator T did this (partly) *because* translators in general do this, and T is indeed a translator. In other words, such statements function as explanatory hypotheses; the same is true of descriptions of norms.

Ad 28: I think these prescriptive statements are really predictive hypotheses: if you, the translator, do not do this, I predict that the result will be that someone (myself, the client, reader…) will not like your translation. Such predictive hypotheses can obviously be tested against empirical evidence.

Ad 29: Applications of translation theory in translator training are implicitly based on the ability of the theory to make predictions, to propose good predictive hypotheses. We can try to predict from conditions to translation features; and also from translation features to translation effects. We can use predictive hypotheses to test explanatory hypotheses. Predictive hypotheses are not prescriptive in any way, they do not impinge on the translator's freedom to make choices.

Finally: what would a translation theory look like, then? For me, a theory of translation would be a logically linked set of well-corroborated hypotheses (interpretive, descriptive, explanatory and predictive hypotheses). These hypotheses would account for the ways translations (of various types) tend to be related to various kinds of conditions and consequences (historical / cultural / ideological / situational / personal / linguistic etc.). Such a theory would be always open to new refinements etc., and it would always be vulnerable to be replaced by some other theory which better suited some particular purpose.

---

* This was not well expressed. The term *norms* throughout this volume is interpreted in the sense of shared correctness notions, not in the sense of what is "normally" done. *Descriptive* statements about norms, e.g. by people in a given community, or by scholars, should not be confused with *prescriptive* "norm statements": in norm theory a "norm statement" is a technical term denoting the official codification of a norm by a norm authority. See Paper 14, below.

Coda by RA

Ad 9–11: If, as we have agreed, "there is no such thing as a totally objective definition of 'translation' that we can take for granted before we start studying it, as there will never be any definition of translation that will be all-inclusive", it necessarily follows that any research on the area will be ideologically and historically marked and will, thus, reflect the circumstances and the interests of those who produce it. If all research is necessarily mediated by the subjects and the circumstances that produce it, no study of translation can claim to be purely "objective", neutral or even "descriptive". Moreover, if "interpretive hypotheses underlie any conceptual analysis", and if "all descriptive research is based on some kind of conceptual analysis", as Chesterman says, we cannot by any means claim to clearly separate the descriptive from the interpretive. And, if we cannot do so, we will never have a general theory of translation that could be universally acceptable once and for all.

Ad 10: Meanings are always context-bound. Depending on our viewpoint and our circumstances, we may perceive them to be either "more" or "less" stable but all of them are always equally dependent on a certain context. A proper name such as *the University of Vic*, for example, only makes sense to those who are familiar with the explicit and implicit context to which it belongs and which makes it meaningful. The same certainly applies to notions such as *democracy*, which may be perceived by some to be less stable. If we ask Fidel Castro, or Augusto Pinochet, for instance, what "democracy" is, their answers will certainly indicate that there is nothing "unstable" about their definitions of the concept, no matter how different they may end up to be. Both Castro and Pinochet will be sure that each of them has the right, true "definition" and that the other one is wrong. The implications of such statements for translation are certainly essential and far-reaching and they may be summarized as follows: no translation will ever be definite or universally acceptable, no translation will ever escape ideology or perspectivism. If original meanings are not "objectively there", no translation will ever be able to be absolutely faithful to the so-called "original", even though it may be perceived as such by some at a certain time, under certain circumstances.

Ad 15–16: It must be added, however, that "understanding a phenomenon", for me, necessarily implies mediation. In other words, the subject who "understands a phenomenon" is inevitably implicated in such an understanding. Consequently, any explanation will also bear the mark of the one doing the explanations and his or her circumstances.

Ad 18: Surely, statements of norms are not in themselves prescriptive but they are not merely "descriptive" either. They will inevitably reflect the viewpoint, the interests, and the perspective of those who elaborate or "describe" them and will not by any means be universally valid or applicable.

Ad 21/28: Again, considering that descriptive statements or hypotheses cannot be objectively distinguished from the interpretive perspectives which produce and make them possible, it follows that whatever is considered, for example, as a "regularity" will reflect the interests of a certain translation specialist, or research group, at a certain time, in a certain context. When a specialist proposes a statement, or a "descriptive hypothesis" such as "all translations (of a given type) tend to have such-and-such a feature" or "all translators (under given conditions) tend to do this kind of thing", supposedly relying on "empirical evidence", he or she is inevitably speaking from a certain viewpoint informed by certain circumstances and ideological and cultural interests. What he or she considers as "empirical evidence" will certainly be perceived as something else by other specialists theorizing from different viewpoints. From such a perspective, any claim to transform such statements or hypotheses into "universals" is basically authoritarian to the extent that it not only attempts to impose its own local, historically and ideologically determined conclusions into general, neutral "laws" but also disregards other (inescapably) local statements or hypotheses. Another authoritarian trait of this kind of research is the relationship that it explicitly and implicitly tends to establish with translators in general. In other words, while the specialist seems to be entitled to formulate and to establish laws, whether intended to be prescriptive or not, translators are mere objects of study.

Ad *29*: Applications of translation theory in translator training should emphasize a reflection on the many implications and consequences of translation as a form of writing. Instead of trying to make predictions, a theory of translation should attempt to empower translators-to-be and raise their conscience as writers concerning the responsibility they will face in the seminal role they will play in the establishment of all sorts of relationships between cultures.

We hereby invite other scholars to respond…

PAPER 3

What constitutes "progress" in Translation Studies?*

Translation Studies is sometimes taken to be an applied science, sometimes a hermeneutic discipline, and sometimes an empirical human science. Each of these views has a different idea of what would be understood as progress: different criteria. We do not have a shared paradigm in TS, but we might one day arrive at one by bringing together different kinds of explanation.

Keywords: progress, applied science, hermeneutic discipline, empirical science, paradigm, explanation

Notions of progress in Translation Studies depend largely on what kind of academic discipline you think TS is. There seem to be three basic views, each of which is based on certain philosophical assumptions. These different assumptions give rise to a good deal of misunderstanding, as well as disagreement. Individual scholars are not necessarily to be associated exclusively with one or another of these views, but I find the three positions useful in drawing up a map of the current state of affairs.

1. Applied science

First, there is the view that TS is an applied science, like engineering or technology, or perhaps economics. On this view, the goal of the discipline is to solve practical problems: specifically, problems that are seen by society as being important. Seen in this light, the discipline has an agenda that is set by external needs: the need for a high-quality machine translation system, for instance; or the need for good translators that can be trained rapidly and at low cost; or the need for a multilingual

---

* First published in 2000 In Birgitta Englund Dimitrova (ed.), *Översättning och tolkning. Rapport från ASLA:s höstsymposium, Stockholm, 5–6 november 1998*. Uppsala: ASLA, 33–49. Permission to reprint is gratefully acknowledged. This version is revised and shortened. The abstract and keywords have been added.

term bank of financial and banking terminology. The keyword of this view is *for*: TS is *for* society, *for* translators, *for* international communicators.

This is the view held by most professional translators I know. The kinds of questions that interest them are, for instance: How to translate faster without sacrificing quality? How to improve translation quality? How to improve source-text quality? How to educate clients, so that they have a more realistic idea of what translating involves? How to train future translators more effectively? How to set up a translation typology that can be used to specify translation contracts more realistically? Where are the guidelines or principles that professionals can turn to in order to get ideas about how to solve particular kinds of recurrent translation problems?

In other words, these professionals assume that TS is there to help them. They want to "look up" to theoretical work, to find solutions there to their own problems. To some extent, however, their concerns conflict with one of the recent developments that is seen by many as a sign of progress: the change from prescriptive to descriptive work. Descriptive scholars do not see it as part of their job to hand down useful guidelines; for them, professional translators and their products are the *object* of research, that which is to be described and explained.

Applied TS has of course addressed some of the issues that professionals are interested in – much has been written on training methods, on practical problem-solving, on assessment criteria, etc. There are even general national and international guidelines on good translation practice, too (if these can be counted as applied TS). Skopos theory can also be mentioned here: it aims (or appears to aim – see Chesterman 1998b [and Paper 6 in this volume]) to describe the factors leading to an optimum translation, one that satisfies the skopos, and the theory thus preserves an inherent prescriptive aspect that is invaluable for instance in teaching. In principle this could be invaluable for practising translators, too.

The whole of the machine translation project, with all its by-products, also deserves to be mentioned. Whether it is fair to include this work under TS – it was not originally developed by translation scholars but by mathematicians and computer engineers – is a point I will not discuss here, except to note that it certainly plays a role on the contemporary translation conference scene.

2. Hermeneutic discipline

The second view sees TS as a hermeneutic discipline, one of the humanities, like literary theory or philosophical conceptual analysis. To the extent that this kind of discipline is also conceptualized as "problem-solving", its problems mainly originate not in external society but within the discipline itself; they are problems that are deemed scientifically interesting for their own sake. Examples are: How to define translation? How to define equivalence? What do we gain, or lose, if we see translation as cannibalism, or as manipulation, or as performance, or as decoding? What insights does postmodernism bring to our understanding of translation? How do certain types of translations betray the Other? (For a representative example, see Bassnett and Lefevere 1998.) The keyword symbolizing this view is *as*: translation, or the translator, is seen *as* something. This hermeneutic *as* lies of course at the root of many theories of understanding: one understands an unknown by seeing it, or framing it, as a known: thus we understand (or think we understand) light by conceiving of it as a wave, or as particles.

The cultural turn taken by many TS scholars in the 1980s, with its interest in translators, clients and patrons as manipulators of power, also brought with it a line of research with an explicit ideological agenda. Studying the relations between translation and culture meant not only exploring the patterns of these relations, but also empirical research aimed at uncovering their hidden causes and effects (e.g. Baker 1996). Critical cultural studies in TS seek to reveal the mechanisms of translatorial manipulation, of bias, in order to increase people's awareness and hence prevent such manipulation in future. Feminist scholars, for instance, want not just to increase knowledge but to change society (for a survey, see von Flotow 1991). Venuti (e.g. 1995) wishes to change translation practices and thus change the ways in which one culture perceives another.

These latter, critical scholars thus share one particular feature with my first group, those for whom TS is an applied science. For both, TS is a means to an end – an end that may be practical (better quality translations, better translators) or ideological (more emancipated citizens, a better kind of society). However, very few professional translators are concerned with translating the kinds of texts that these scholars tend to study; and they are not primarily worried about *as* questions, although they may well be motivated by a desire to facilitate intercultural relations more generally.

With respect to practising translators, proponents of this view seem to be mostly interested in such themes as the translator's self-image, and also the translator's image in society. The scholars themselves tend to see their role as that of interpreters, interpreting translators to themselves and to society at large, interpreting the causes and effects of various kinds of translations, for instance in terms of prevailing ideologies or ideological conflicts.

3. Empirical human science

The third view is that TS is an empirical human science, like sociology or psychology; a behavioural science, whose object of study is a particular kind of human behaviour. On this view, TS has the same kinds of aims as any other science: to describe, explain, and predict. Here is the classical statement by Hempel (1952: 1, cited in Toury 1995: 9):

> Empirical science has two major objectives: to describe particular phenomena in the world of our experience and to establish general principles by means of which they can be explained and predicted. The explanatory and predictive principles of a scientific discipline are stated in its hypothetical generalizations and its theories; they characterize general patterns or regularities to which the individual phenomena conform and by virtue of which their occurrence can be systematically anticipated.

On this view, TS proceeds by proposing well-justified hypotheses and testing them against empirical data. Interrelated and corroborated hypotheses may then lead to theoretical laws. A recent example of this approach is Toury's work on descriptive translation studies, norms, and laws of translational behaviour (1995). My keyword for this view of TS is *if*: this kind of research seeks to establish the *conditions* under which particular kinds of translations are produced, or under which translations have particular kinds of effects.

Scholars working along these lines do not see themselves as people to be "looked up to" by practising translators; on the contrary, these scholars are trying to describe and explain the wonderful and extraordinary things that translators do. Their job is not to suggest guidelines, to prescribe. They have in fact been nearly unanimous in rejecting prescriptivism – understood as the focus on what translators should do, what translations should be like – because they see such a focus as unscientific. Applied translation studies are accepted within this approach, but kept distinct from descriptive or theoretical studies proper (recall Holmes' map, in Holmes 1988a). However, the rejection of prescriptivism has widened the distance between translation theorists and professional translators.

[…] [The use of the term "translation laws" by some empirical scholars has sometimes led to misinterpretation. These "laws" are not prescriptive, like those laid down by a parliament; they are general formulations, like the law of gravity in physics. The term itself is perhaps unfortunate, as it may imply a more universally "nomic" concept than is appropriate for a human science.] […]

4. Notions and criteria of progress

External progress (or social progress) refers to the institutional status of a discipline, as measured for instance by the number of academic posts, conferences, journals, publications, scientific associations, etc. All these factors reflect (to some extent) the status of the academic field in society, and also (to some extent) the status of professional translators. Measured in this way, the external progress of Translation Studies over the past couple of decades has been remarkable; but I shall not examine this aspect further here.

Internal progress, on the other hand, is evaluated by the members of the academic discipline concerned, or by neighbouring disciplines; it is measured as scientific progress, progress towards greater understanding, or the like. Our question is: how is this internal progress to be understood? Progress might be thought of as gradual approximation towards a goal – but what goal? Each of our three basic positions frames its goal in a different way, and thus has a different notion of progress.

For our first group, the applied scientists, progress is a *pragmatic* issue, concerning product quality. Basic questions here are: Is this product better than the previous one? Does this new tool work well enough? Does it have more applications? Is this process better? Is the client more satisfied? Is the translator more satisfied? Is there a saving of time and/or money? Is the process now more ecologically viable? Does this way of training translators make for better translators? Progress is something better *for* someone, or something better *for* more people.

What progress has TS made in this respect? Actually, quite a lot, especially if you accept the machine translation project as being part of TS. We have many useful computer aids, term banks etc. Our translator training curricula are developing all the time. However, there are still too many poor translations around, still too many clients who do not understand the translator's job. Many translators suffer from stress and frustration, and are far from satisfied with their conditions of work. There is still ample room both for translation quality improvement and for establishing better and more realistic methods of assessment.

If you see the field more as a hermeneutic discipline, progress means more understanding, more awareness, more self-awareness; more understanding of historical and cultural influences; a more critical attitude to prevailing ideology; ethically better practices. Progress means a bigger picture of the whole, more abstraction, more generality; but it also means a closer view of the details, more elaboration, more specialization, more articulation. Theoretical progress means a better *representation* of the object of research, in macrocontext and microdetail. Progress is a better *as*.

Signs of this progress? Well, we have an ever-increasing accumulation of metaphors and images for translation. We have a greater understanding of the translator's historical role, and of the ideological and other pressures constraining translators' choices. We can see something of the causes and effects of particular translations or kinds of translations. We can see that certain kinds of translation may conceal hidden agendas, of which the translators themselves may or may not have been conscious. And we can see something of the whole web of power relations amid which the translator sits. So we now have a much broader view of our object of study than scholars did, say, thirty years ago – including ethical aspects. On the other hand, the "we" in these conclusions refers mainly to the scholarly community itself; less so to society at large, to clients, or even to translators. Also, it is not always clear what the added value is of a new metaphor for translation, or whether the adoption of such a metaphor would have any empirical consequences.

For those who see TS as an empirical human science, progress means better hypotheses: those that are more general, more productive of other testable hypotheses, better corroborated; those that suggest empirically justified laws; those that appear to approximate more closely to the truth. It therefore also means more valid explanations and closer predictions; and of course better theories. It also means more facts, upon which hypotheses and laws can be based. In sum, progress is more accurate links between conditions and associated translational phenomena.

Progress? Well, we have lots of empirical case studies, both historical and contemporary. We have a number of empirical research methods that have been well tested, ranging from descriptive analysis to protocol studies. We have lots of significant facts, and lots of apparent interconnections between translations and surrounding conditions of various kinds. And we have several ways of getting at the causes of translational features, notably the concept of norms. But we have relatively few explicit hypotheses or laws, very little research that is so explicitly reported that it can be replicated, and more interest in generating hypotheses than testing them. We have not yet made much progress towards building a general empirical theory of translation, in the empirical sense of "theory" as an explicit body of related axioms and laws. We do not even have a generally accepted translation typology, having to make do with a confusing mass of overlapping terms. Here too, the professional translator is disappointed.

5. Theories and paradigms

All in all, it is perhaps the applied science approach that has made most visible progress so far, on its own criteria. This is somewhat paradoxical, as it seems that we have been rather less successful in creating anything much to "apply". The second and third approaches have not yet made much progress towards creating a general *theory* of translation. True, there are some "theories" in TS: we do use the term "theory" as a countable noun, but in rather restricted senses. Current in TS are at least the following:

- Catford's linguistic theory of translation
- the interpretive theory of sense
- skopos theory / the functionalist school / translatorial action
- polysystem theory / the manipulation school

Catford's linguistic theory (1965) aims to be a description of the translator's potential textual solutions, based on interlinguistic comparison. It is really a taxonomy of textual replacement, accompanied by a translation typology that may be of interest of linguists but is largely irrelevant to the needs of real-world clients. His notion of conditioned equivalence is important – and obviously relevant to machine translation – but the theory itself proposes no hypotheses that can be tested and takes little account of non-textual cause or effect.

The theory of sense, based on the notion of deverbalization, proposes an answer to the question: how do interpreters interpret? It has been much applied at ESIT in Paris, in interpreter training (e.g. Seleskovitch and Lederer 1984). However, its main tenet does not appear to be directly testable empirically. In essence, it remains descriptive, and largely speculative.

Skopos theory (e.g. Reiß and Vermeer 1984) also centres around a single idea. And it too appears most relevant to the applied science view, as a pedagogical tool. By focusing on one particular kind of cause, it usefully detaches translator trainees from staring too exclusively at the source text; and it also serves to loosen the narrow concern with equivalence. Its empirical status is less clear, as is its testability. Its focus on one kind of cause may also mean that other causes are neglected. It has so far paid less attention to effects, except in the sense that translations can be usefully assessed in terms of how well they meet their intended skopos. The functional approach as a whole has taken as its starting-point the position of the translator faced with a source text to translate: how to do it? What factors to take into account? However, this approach has been less successful in pinpointing the effects of the skopos on the translator's actual textual choices, and in proposing testable generalizations about the relationship between skopos and translation-text.

Polysystem theory (e.g. in Toury's work) has been concerned with the causes and the effects of mainly literary translations, at the level of whole cultures rather than specific clients or readers. It has perhaps been most successful in outlining the various major socio-cultural forces that impinge upon a translator's textual choices, forces that exist mainly in the target culture but also include the client and aspects of the source text and culture. The starting point has been the target text itself, not the position of the translator. Toury (1995) has proposed two hypothetical laws (of interference and growing standardization), accompanied by a number of variants in empirically testable form. With respect to our three basic views of TS, polysystem theory represents a blend between literary studies and empirical science, but the latter approach has become more prominent in recent work.

Other "theories" have appeared occasionally, but have remained isolated cases not taken up by many other scholars. In addition, other concepts such as "model" or "school" have been used to label particular approaches, perhaps with more modesty. None of the theories mentioned above, nor other models or schools, have yet attained the status of a general paradigm. All are partial in scope.

In terms of the progress of TS as a scientific discipline, then, we seem to be at what Kuhn (1970) called the pre-paradigmatic stage. We have competing "schools" or "approaches", sometimes known as "theories" and sometimes not. We have not yet arrived at a period of "normative" science, in which practitioners all share a basic methodology, a set of goals and an understanding of what constitutes an important and interesting problem. We do not even agree yet on what kind of thing might properly be called a theory of translation – in this sense, we do not seem even to be looking for the same kind of object. (Recall the title of Toury's 1980 book: *In search of a theory of translation*.)

We find ourselves in this pre-paradigmatic position partly because we have different ideas about what TS should be like as a discipline, as I have illustrated. But partly also because we are coming into Translation Studies from very different angles, with different philosophical backgrounds. Some of us come from literary or cultural studies, some from computer engineering, some from language teaching, some from linguistics, some from history, some from sociology or psychology, even some from professional translation or interpreting.

If Kuhn is right, the next stage will be the emergence of a shared paradigm that will hold sway for a while, before other competing paradigms appear to challenge it and the field shakes down to a new (temporary) consensus.

[...]

6. In conclusion

Some kind of shared paradigm might be arrived at via a broad research focus on explanation, on causes and effects of all kinds, as a way of relating our three initial positions. The applied scientists are interested in effects; in particular, effects that are perceived to be practical and positive: good quality translations, better tools, etc. Quality assessment itself is a kind of effect produced by the translation. So we need to know what kinds of conditions lead to translations that have desired positive effects, which are assessed as good. In fact, the best way in which pure theory can made relevant to professionals is surely this: if we can systematize a wide range of textual choices made by other translators both present and past, relating them to their background conditions, together with an analysis of the various effects of these choices, then we can provide information of great value to translators pondering their own choices and imagining their potential effects.

We need to know more about useful ways of analysing the effects of translations in general, too. The literary scholars are interested in such matters as the socio-cultural and ideological causes of the form (profile) of a translation, and in its reception (i.e. effects) in the target culture. And the empirical scholars are interested (among other things) in norms and general tendencies that are observed under different kinds of translation conditions; in how translatorial decision-making affects translation quality; and in how translatorial decision-making is itself affected by a variety of factors. On a more general level, we can explore the ways all kinds of translation-related decisions, concerning both the translation process and translation policy, affect society as a whole, including not only the status and image of the translators themselves but also intercultural relations in the widest sense.

It seems that many of us are looking at the same elephant, but talking different languages. Maybe what we need is some mutual translation between our different frames of reference.

Translation Studies is a multifaceted interdiscipline, drawing on different research traditions. Because of this, and because of the very nature of translation as a complex human (and machine) activity, we need, for instance, broader and more differentiated concepts of explanation and causality than those prevailing in narrower fields. This broadening may enable us to build a general empirical theory of translation that is both rich and robust, one that can make the best use of all three of our initial positions. And that will be real progress.

PAPER 4

Towards consilience?[*]

Since Translation Studies is an interdiscipline, there is a risk that it will become fragmented into separate subfields with no connections between them. The paper proposes that in order to prevent this development, we could focus on bridge concepts such as causality, which can show links between textual, cognitive, cultural and sociological approaches to translation. This might promote the ideal of consilience, the unity of all knowledge.

Keywords: interdiscipline, causality, bridge concept, brief, strategy, norm, effect, consilience

1. Pros and cons of interdisciplinarity

Translation Studies is an interdiscipline. This is now widely recognized, at least since Snell-Hornby et al. (1994). This status has both advantages and drawbacks (see e.g. Chesterman 2002).

On the plus side, interdisciplines mark the growth of knowledge, as new fields emerge on the borders of existing ones. They allow us to pose new kinds of questions, and to seek solutions to complex problems. They thus rejuvenate the overall field of knowledge, preventing it from stagnating. Each new interdiscipline asks us to look at reality from a new perspective. In so doing, interdisciplines remind us of the exploratory nature of much research, especially of research into complex and heterogeneous phenomena (Klein 1990). As McCarty (1999) points out, any interdiscipline actually "translates" between neighbouring fields, makes communication and exchange between them possible, and thus adds value. This is an unusually apt metaphor for a field whose very object of study is translation: the interdisciplinary nature of our field is an iconic reflection of its object.

---

[*] First published in 2005 in Karin Aijmer and Cecilia Alvstad (eds), *New Tendencies in Translation Studies*. Göteborg: Göteborg University, Department of English, 19–27. Editorial permission to reprint is gratefully acknowledged. The text here is slightly revised and shortened. A fuller version of this paper appeared later in 2005, in *Revista Canaria de Estudios Ingleses* 51, 19–32. The abstract and keywords have been added.

Interdisciplinarity also has its negative sides. One is the fragmentation of a new field, which makes it difficult to develop an overall coherent theory. A more serious problem is the risk that, in borrowing theoretical concepts and methods from more established disciplines, we actually do no more than transfer labels, and our borrowing remains at a superficial level. This may lead to misunderstandings, when key terms are given different interpretations. Consider for instance the concept of the norm, which came into translation research from sociology and sociolinguistics. Translation scholars still disagree how the concept should be defined and interpreted in our field (see Schäffner 1999). And we still cannot agree how to define equivalence, a term which comes originally from mathematics and logic – or even if we need the concept at all. With respect to the "limited borrowing" of concepts or tools, Malmkjær (2000) emphasizes the problem of not knowing enough about the background context, assumptions and implications of the borrowed concepts. Klein (1990: 88) further points out that borrowed concepts may already be out of date in their original discipline, or may be less reliable than the borrower assumes.

One good way to counter these risks would be via collaboration, with research done in teams whose members have different backgrounds and different expertise. Unfortunately, most research in translation studies is still done by individuals.

2. Four levels of translation research

Ten or fifteen years ago it was customary to see Translation Studies as being divided into two camps: linguistic approaches and cultural approaches. This dichotomy arose (in the West) from a reaction against text-bound research methods which traditionally took as central the relation between translations themselves and their source texts, the relation of equivalence. (See e.g. Bassnett and Lefevere 1996.) But to present translation studies as thus split into two does us all a disservice. For one thing, it obscures the fact that both these approaches need each other: we need both perspectives – both the micro, textual one and the macro, cultural one – for each sheds light on the other (see e.g. Baker 1996, Pym 1999, Tymoczko 2002). A second reason to criticize this oversimplified picture is the amount of research it actually leaves out. It leaves out the study of translation as a cognitive phenomenon, such as research using think-aloud protocols. (See e.g. the special issue of *Across* 3, 1, 2002.) And it also omits mention of research on the sociology of translation. (See e.g. Hermans 1999 or the special issue of *Actes de la recherche en sciences sociales*, no. 144, 2002.)

In fact, rather than classify translation research as falling into two opposing camps, we could better think of our field as consisting of four complementary levels or approaches. These are: the textual, the cognitive, the sociological and the cultural.

The textual level focuses on texts themselves, as linguistic data in written or oral form; textual research looks at the relations between translations, their source texts, and parallel non-translated texts in the target language. It is thus interested in concepts such as equivalence, naturalness and fluency, and in the possibility of finding universal or very general features of translations as texts of a distinctive kind.

Research on the cognitive dimension is interested in the decision-making processes in the translator's mind, in the influence of such factors as the translator's emotions and attitudes, the amount of professional experience, the time available, the routine or non-routine quality of the translation task. The focus is on the cognitive processing, which is inferred from observation.

Sociological research looks at such topics as the translation market, the role played by the publishing industry and other patrons or agents, the social status and roles of translators and the translator's profession, translating as a social practice, and what Toury (1995: 249) has called the translation event. This can be defined as starting with the client's request for a translation and ending with payment of the fee. Between these two come many different work phases involving interaction with both human and non-human resources (see e.g. Mossop 2000). The sociological focus is thus on people and their observable actions.

On the cultural level, finally, the focus is on ideas, on the transfer of cultural capital between different repertoires or polysystems. Central issues are questions of ideology, cultural identity and perception, values, relations between centre and periphery, power, and ethics.

Although these four areas of translation studies can thus be roughly separated, there is of course much research that cannot be placed easily into one box or another, and overlaps are common. As I shall illustrate below, overlaps can in fact be significant, in that they explicitly make links between different spheres.

3. Causality

One productive way of forging links between these different areas of research is via the notion of causality. It is only relatively recently that causality has played an explicit role in translation research, although it has of course been present implicitly for much longer (Chesterman 1998a).

The models of translation that are used in linguistic, text-based approaches are not explicitly causal. Most of them are static, comparative models. On one side we have a source text (or sentence, or item) and on the other a target text, and we study the relations between the two. We look for similarities and differences, and see what tends to correspond to what. We are in fact looking for correlations between two sets of textual data. The same basic kind of model is used in corpus studies comparing translations and parallel texts, in the search for translation universals. (See e.g. the special issue of *Meta* 43, 4, 1998 [and Papers 20 and 21 in this volume].)

Some linguistic models, and most cognitive and sociological models, are process models. They conceptualize translation – or rather translating – as a process taking place over time. Examples are the various proposals concerning the typical phases of the translation process (e.g. Sager 1994); the phases of cognitive problem-solving, and the phases of the sociological translation event that I mentioned briefly above. These dynamic models might be called implicitly causal, for they obviously assume a causal relationship between the process and the final product.

It is only the causal models proper, however, that allow, and indeed require, an explicit linkage between different levels. Causal models provide an explicit framework for investigating the causes and effects of translations. Causal models usually relate textual features of translations to some features outside the translation. For instance: this translation is like this, it contains these particular features, because of the way this translator worked and the decisions that she took; the translator worked like that because of the client's instructions and the ridiculously short deadline; the client specified these conditions because of the norms governing translation work of this kind in this society at this time, which are themselves determined e.g. by commercial values. Similar causal chains can be set up for the effects that translations themselves cause: first on the cognitive states of readers, then perhaps on the observable behaviour of readers or groups of readers, and then even on readers' perceptions of their cultural identity, on their native language, on the spread of an ideology, whatever. (For more on types of theoretical models, see e.g. Chesterman 2000a; Williams and Chesterman 2002, Chapter 3.)

4. Bridge concepts

Causality is thus a "bridge concept", in that it enables us to see connections between phenomena at different levels. Indeed, it forces us to see these connections, and thus provides one way of moving towards consilience. Let us take a look now at some other bridge concepts.

A good example is the concept of the *norm*. Norms entered translation studies via Even-Zohar's work on cultural transfer, but they are also central notions in sociology. As ideas, they exist in the cultural sphere, but their prescriptive force, their causal influence, is seen in social behaviour and in the results of this behaviour.

In translation studies, we see evidence of norms in the ways translators work, in how they keep to deadlines, in their general translation strategies and methods, i.e. in the social sphere. But we also see evidence in the textual sphere, in the translations themselves. It is thus significant, with respect to consilience, that norms have become such a central concept in descriptive translation studies over the past few decades.

Another example: between the sociological and the cognitive, we have, for instance, the client's specification, the translation *brief*, the instructions. The specification (presumably) affects the way the translator thinks about a particular task, the way in which decisions are made during the process. Skopos theory has made the task specification a central notion, but much remains to be discovered about the precise nature of the relation between given features of a specification, given features of the cognitive process of translating, and given features of the resulting translation.

Another bridge concept, mediating between the cognitive and the textual, is that of the translation *strategy*. Strategies are problem-solving plans or standard procedures, i.e. cognitive routines, conceptual tools; as such, they are not directly observable. But we can of course observe their manifestations, as textual solutions, as target-text features corresponding to source-text features. Some strategies are general ones, pertaining to the task as a whole: e.g. whether to translate freely or not, what to do with names, whether to use footnotes, whether to foreignize or not; others are specific to particular problems or items. Some scholars study these solutions as "procedures", others as "shifts" or "techniques" (cf. Molina and Hurtado Albir 2002).

So far, I have mentioned three bridge concepts that mediate the causal conditions under which translations are done. But translations themselves also act as causes; as I hinted at above, they have effects in all three non-textual spheres: cognitive, social and cultural. We do not yet have any established terminology here, so perhaps I can suggest some. To refer to the effects of the textual (i.e. translations themselves) on the cognitive (i.e. the mental and emotional reactions of readers), we might use the term "*reactions*". To refer to the effects of translations on individual or group behaviour, i.e. on the social level, we might speak of "*responses*". Responses would include critical ones, such as writing a translation review or giving feedback as an editor. So a reaction is what a reader thinks or feels, and a response is what a reader actually does. To describe the effects of translations at the cultural level, we might then speak of "*repercussions*". Examples of repercussions might be the canonization of a literary work, changes in the evolution of the target language, changes in norms, changes in the perception of cultural stereotypes. Thus defined, reactions, responses and repercussions are also bridge concepts, linking the textual to other spheres.

On one hand, then, we seem to need conceptual borders, because without them, in other words without categories, we cannot think at all. But at the same time we can try to overcome or at least challenge these categorical borders, by exploiting notions that set up alternative categories, such as these suggested bridge concepts between levels, schematically illustrated as follows. (The arrows are an initial indication of the assumed direction of causation, but the true picture must be far more complex.)

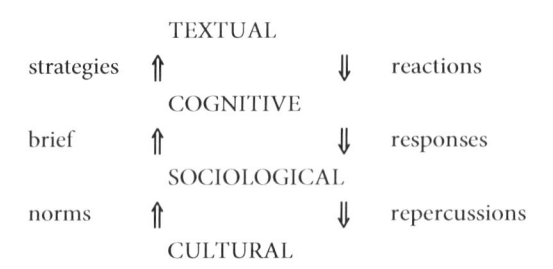

		TEXTUAL		
strategies	⇑		⇓	reactions
		COGNITIVE		
brief	⇑		⇓	responses
		SOCIOLOGICAL		
norms	⇑		⇓	repercussions
		CULTURAL		

[...]

5. Consilience?

Consilience literally means 'jumping together'. Its first use in English apparently dates back to the 19th century, but the roots of the concept it represents are older, going back to Ancient Greece. Underlying the word is the notion of the unity of all knowledge. This notion was particularly to the fore during the Enlightenment period in Europe, in the 18th century: a period marked by both humanism and optimism, a belief in the possibility of human and scientific progress.

Edward O. Wilson's book on the subject, entitled *Consilience*, appeared in 1998. Wilson is perhaps most famous today as the founder of the science of sociobiology, which uses ideas and hypotheses derived from biology to examine and explain the social behaviour of human beings. In particular, Wilson has sought to apply Darwin's theory of evolution to social and cultural change. (He is not responsible for the rise of so-called social darwinism, which is actually based on a misunderstanding of Darwin's ideas. See e.g. Dennett 1995, Segerstråle 2000.) Wilson's attempt to sketch out the ways in which different sciences can be linked, not only with each other but also with the humanities, is of amazing scope and vision.

It is significant that Wilson's own field, sociobiology, emerged as an interdiscipline, sitting astride the border between biology and sociology. Consilience is all about interdisciplines (or transdisciplines or pluridisciplines…), about crossing boundaries between traditional fields. As Wilson points out, the most powerful explanations are often those that relate different fields.

From the consilience point of view, modern translation studies thus announces itself as a new attempt to cut across boundaries in the search for a deeper understanding of the relations between texts, societies and cultures.

One way of moving towards consilience might be by embedding Translation Studies into memetics, the study of memes (see Chesterman [1997a] 2016 and 2000b). Memes are elements of culture; in particular, of cultural transfer. The term was proposed and first used by Richard Dawkins, in his book *The Selfish Gene* (1976). This was a popular book about genetics, about how the behaviour of organisms is influenced by the way genes seek to promote their own survival. Towards the end of the book, Dawkins introduced the notion of a meme as the cultural equivalent of the gene. (Actually the notion itself has an older pedigree, although the term is new. See Laland and Brown 2002 for the general background to memetics.) The term has since been taken up by many scholars. The philosopher Daniel Dennett uses it in his attempts to explain consciousness (1991), and in his defence of modern Darwinism (1995). Edward O. Wilson uses it in his theory of gene-culture coevolution, in his book on consilience that I mentioned earlier. (See also Blackmore 1999, and for more varied views Aunger 2000.) Memes were explictly brought into Translation Studies by Chesterman (1996, 1997a), and independently by Vermeer (1997).

If we see translations as carriers of memes, and Translation Studies as part of memetics, we may be able to embed our field more readily into the study of evolution more generally. By exploring the parallels between biological and cultural evolution, we may perhaps make a few constructive steps in the direction of consilience.

SECTION II

Descriptive and prescriptive

This section brings together four papers dealing with aspects of the relation between descriptive and prescriptive approaches.

Paper 5, on prescriptivism, shares some ground with the previous section, such as the Hempel quotation and the relation between translation research and translation practice. It also touches on the themes of causality and the study of effects that are given more attention in a later section in this volume (Papers 9–12). Research on revision procedures has certainly grown since the paper was first published: see for instance Mossop ([2001] 2007) and Englund Dimitrova (2005) and the work cited there. There has also been more research on reception: for a survey, see Brems and Ramos Pinto (2013).

Paper 6 is a critical review of skopos theory, a project that was sparked initially by an interview with Hans Vermeer (Chesterman 2001a). One of the key points is the unclear status of the theory: is it descriptive or prescriptive?

Paper 7 reviews another well-known translation theory – Catford's – which is purely descriptive.

Paper 8, on what I have called the descriptive paradox, can be read in relation to the so-called "descriptive fallacy" of logical positivism, according to which speech acts are treated as descriptive logical propositions that can only be true or false (see e.g. Austin 1962). In my paper, however, I am not concerned with logic or with performative speech acts, but with potential empirical consequences of a descriptivist approach.

PAPER 5

The empirical status of prescriptivism[*]

Many translators evidently think that translation theory has little to contribute to translation practice. One reason for this view may be the shift to a descriptive approach in recent decades, aiming to describe and explain translations but not directly tell translators how to translate. However, traditional prescriptive guidelines can easily be seen as predictive hypotheses concerning translation effects: translate like this, because otherwise I predict that the client will not like it! Descriptive empirical research on the effects of different kinds of translation choices can produce relevant information for translators.

Keywords: prescriptivism, descriptivism, empiricism, hypothesis, effect

1. The gap between theory and practice

Translation Studies studies translation, translations, and increasingly also the process of translating. There is therefore some cause for concern when the people who actually do the translating seem to find Translation Studies irrelevant, metaphysical nonsense.

This, for instance, is the view of Lars Berglund, an industrial translator working in Germany (1990). He is especially critical of the German academic tradition of Übersetzungswissenschaft, which he describes as "an irrelevance, a discipline without much significance to translators and the people they serve" (145). According to Berglund, this is mainly because academic theoretical studies have an idealized view of source texts and because "they reflect an inadequate and misguided view of the translator's obligations and loyalties, and seem to ignore the practical requirements that arise from these obligations" (146). For practising translators, this is a serious legitimacy problem.

---

[*] First published in 1999 in *Folia Translatologica* 6, 9–19. Editorial permission to reprint is gratefully acknowledged. The article is based on a paper read at the EST Congress in Granada, 23–26.9.1998. This text contains some minor revision and a couple of reference updates. The abstract and keywords have been added.

Or consider the critical response among professional translators to the recently published *Routledge Encyclopedia of Translation Studies* (1998), which is surely a reasonable attempt to crystallize the current state of the art. A review in *Language International* (10, 1, 1998) comments: "language professionals involved in the day-to-day business of translation will find it largely irrelevant to their immediate concerns" (39). The work lacks entries on e.g. dictionaries, translation tools, LISA (the Localization Industry Standards Association), translation markets or quality certification.

Or this, from a review of the same work in the ITI Bulletin (Cross 1998): "What [the Encyclopedia] does not include at all is any reference to the largest body of translation work being done in the world today, that is "technical" translation. [...] Will it help one become a better translator? I doubt it. [...] Does it help to give the translation profession a feeling of self-esteem and worth? Hardly. [...] From the point of view of my working life, it is interesting but irrelevant."

There are several possible reasons for reactions such as these. One is that practising translators have particular expectations about what kind of a discipline Translation Studies is supposed to be, expectations that are very different from the assumptions held by many translation scholars. Translators (and many translation teachers too) expect it to be an applied science; some scholars might agree, but others would see their field very differently, either as a hermeneutic humanistic discipline like literary theory or culture studies, or as a human science like psychology or sociology or linguistics. Different conceptions of the field are also reflected in the kinds of translations that tend to be studied: predominantly literary ones or not, for instance.

2. To describe and explain

I suggest that a further reason for this gap between theory and practice is, paradoxically, the stress given in much recent work to a descriptive approach, as opposed to a prescriptive one. I say "paradoxically", because the whole point of inaugurating a descriptive approach (see e.g. Toury's early work, summarized in Toury 1995: see especially pp. 7–19) was to push the discipline onto a proper scientific basis, a basis formed of empirical facts about what translations are actually like, not wishful speculative thinking about what they should be like. We study the norms, descriptively; it is the norms that prescribe, not the scholar.

Toury (1995: 9) cites Hempel (1952: 1) on the fundamental aims of any empirical science:

Empirical science has two major objectives: to describe particular phenomena in the world of our experience and to establish general principles by means of which they can be explained and predicted. The explanatory and predictive principles of a scientific discipline are stated in its hypothetical generalizations and its theories; they characterize general patterns or regularities to which the individual phenomena conform and by virtue of which their occurrence can be systematically anticipated.

At this point, some scholars might object that Hempel's philosophy of science is more suited to the natural sciences than to a humanistic discipline like translation, in which (these scholars might say) the aim is not to explain and predict phenomena in the way that this is done in, say, physics, but to simply to understand them. I shall not discuss this philosophical objection here, except to say that the borderline between explaining and understanding is very fuzzy, and that "predicting" can also cover a weaker sense of "not being surprised at". I shall assume that Hempel's basic view can also be extended and/or adapted to cover hermeneutic approaches. At its core is simply the observation that scientists and scholars in general seek to describe and explain – and hence to understand – and that they do this by means of proposing, testing and refining or rejecting hypotheses, or generalizations of different kinds (not necessarily explicitly, it is true).

The bulk of Toury's book focuses on the aim and methodology of describing what translations are like, but it also encompasses the explanatory aim: why are they like that? – Hence the need to study norms. Norms can be studied descriptively, but they have prescriptive and thus explanatory force. Recall Toury's statement of the issues that Translation Studies must tackle (1995: 15): all that translation *can* involve; what it *does* involve (not: should!) and the *reasons* for this (explanation); and what it is *likely* to involve under given conditions (i.e. prediction). The ultimate theoretical aim is then to propose hypotheses which can be tested, and which may become established as laws (not prescriptive laws, but abstract explanatory generalizations concerning the behaviour of translators).

The rejection of prescriptivism, explicitly stated in many contexts by descriptive translation scholars, has not been taken on board by everyone. Scholars who see Translation Studies in more applied terms have continued to be concerned with issues of translation quality, translator training, the improvement of translator aids, etc. Newmark (e.g. 1988) continues to hand down prescriptive common sense, and Viaggio (e.g. 1994) has insisted that concepts of quality are inherent in a community's concept of translation itself. Says Viaggio (1994: 97): "prescriptivism is inescapable. If there is no right, or at least better way of translating, then we are all wasting time, breath and money: there is nothing but language to teach."

Viaggio's view here can be interestingly linked to the philosopher Alasdair MacIntyre's discussion of virtue (1981). MacIntyre argues that the classical concept of virtue can be best understood as relating to a practice: virtue is (or was understood to be, in classical antiquity) excellence in a social practice. Practices are things like carpentry, soldiering… translating. One of MacIntyre's points is that functional concepts which describe practices naturally imply a qualitative, ethical aspect. To say (my example) that "X is a translator", for instance, implies "X ought to do what a translator ought to do", and furthermore that "X must know what a good translator is like, i.e. one who does what he/she ought to do". At least, these implications hold under the default reading of the utterance "X is a translator". If the implications are known not to hold for X (a non-default reading), we would probably rather say "X is a bad translator" or "X is a translator, but I would not recommend him" or the like. (Thus does MacIntyre derive "ought" from "is" – cf. Chesterman 1993[*].)

3. Hypotheses of cause and effect

Translations are not merely phenomena that are determined or caused or influenced by other phenomena; they are also phenomena that have effects, they themselves are the determining causes of other phenomena. Translations change things, and so translators themselves are also agents of change, not just of preservation. Translations affect readers in multiple ways, they affect target and also source cultures, and they affect intercultural relations and perceptions. Indeed, the cultural turn in Translation Studies has given quite some attention to these issues (consider Venuti's arguments about the causes *and effects* of a domesticating translation strategy, for instance: see e.g. Venuti 1995, *passim*).

Toury's approach includes effects implicitly, in several ways. This is evident for instance in notions such as norms themselves, tolerance of interference, or degree of conformity to a norm. Because norms have prescriptive power, norm-breaking may lead to sanctions, which are one obvious kind of effect. We can also seek to explain effects (such as sanctions) by appealing to aspects of a translator's decisions, or aspects of the commission, or aspects of the sociocultural conditions (norms) prevailing in the source or target cultures.

It might nevertheless be worth setting the aims of empirical translation studies more broadly than Toury's formulation, with a more explicit inclusion of translation effects. Let us say that empirical translation studies aim to discover

---

[*] Paper 13 in this volume.

a. what translations are, what characteristics they have;
b. why they are like that; and
c. what effects they have on readers and cultures.

The first aim is descriptive: we describe the features that translations of various kinds have, e.g. in linguistic terms, and/or in terms of translation strategies, shifts or procedures, and/or in terms of a translation typology; such a description gives us a *translation profile*. The second aim is explanatory: why do we have this profile, why these features etc.? We can look for reasons in the translator's state of mind, in the decision-making process (at the level of what Toury calls the translation act); and we can look for causes in the external circumstances of production (at the level of the translation event: Toury 1995: 249), or further afield in the sociocultural conditions of the source and target languages. The third aim can also be understood descriptively: we can describe (roughly) what effects translations actually appear to have on various kinds of readers and cultures, and we can then try to interpret these effects. (Defining precisely what an effect is, of course, is not easy; nor is an effect something that is always easy to measure.) We can also try to predict certain broad effects: we can propose hypotheses about what effects will follow from a translation that has such-and-such features. If our predictive hypotheses are corroborated, we are then in a position to explain these effects. Let us consider how such predictions fit in with empirical translation research as a whole.

In Translation Studies, various kinds of explanatory and predictive hypotheses can be broadly classified into four classes. Each of these classes has to do with a relation between a particular translation profile, i.e. features or strategies evident in a given translation (or type of translation), and either its antecedent conditions or its effects. These relations may be causal, such that the translation itself is either determined (the dependent variable) or determining (an independent variable). But the relation may also turn out to be a weaker one, of correlation only; or it may of course even be coincidental. The four classes of hypotheses can be illustrated as follows (where causes, profile and effects obviously represent no more than labels for complex systems and hierarchies):

Conditions (causes)

(i) ⇓   (ii) ⇑

Translation profile

(iii) ⇓   (iv) ⇑

Effects

i. Given certain antecedent conditions concerning the translator and the circumstances of translation, we can hypothesize (predict) that these will give rise to particular translation profiles, features, strategies or even general laws (in the sense of patterns, tendencies) of translation behaviour. Example: if literary texts are translated from small (dominated) cultures into big (hegemonic) cultures, translators will tend to use a domesticating strategy (cf. Venuti, *passim*). Or: if a given literary work is translated successively at different periods into a given target culture, the first translation will be plain prose, then later there will be a free translation, then later still a closer translation (inferred from Goethe, see e.g. Lefevere 1992b: 75–77; cf. also Gambier 1994). Or: if the translator is a first-year student on a translator training course, the translation will be more literal than if the translator is a more advanced student (inferred from personal experience).

ii. Given certain features of a translation profile, we can propose hypotheses about their causes (or, more weakly, about correlations with their conditions of production). Example: given certain shifts in Desfontaines' translation (in 1743) of Fielding's novel *Joseph Andrews*, we can hypothesize that these were because of the translator's explicitly stated desire to make the translation conform to French stylistic and rhetorical norms, and to make the novel morally more uplifting (Taivalkoski-Shilov 2006).

iii. Given certain translational features, we can propose hypotheses about their effects. Example: if a translation of a children's story uses a lot of complicated syntactic constructions, it will be less appreciated by adults reading the story to children than a translation that uses simpler constructions, and the simpler translation will be easier for the children to understand (cf. Puurtinen 1995). Or: if texts are translated with a domesticating strategy, the result will be an increase in cultural prejudice and the suppression of difference (Venuti) – not so easy to test, this one! Or: if EU translations have certain features (partly because of the constraints of certain regulations), the effect on EU citizens reading these texts will be a distancing or alienating one, inducing a critical attitude to EU bureaucracy, as evidenced e.g. in irritated letters to newspapers.

iv. Given certain effects, we can make hypotheses about the translational features that caused them. Example: if a play that does well in one country is a flop when translated into another culture, the nature of the translation itself may be the cause (Leppihalme 2000a). Or: if a translation is rejected by the client, we can hypothesize that this is because it had such-and-such features.

Hypotheses of types (i) and (iii) are thus predictive, and those of types (ii) and (iv) are explanatory. Comprehensive research structures can obviously link both causes (e.g. client's goals in commissioning the translation) and effects (are the client's goals realized? are there unintended or undesirable side-effects?). The immediate effect of given translation conditions is certain features of the translation profile; but these in turn then have their own effects – the chain of causation continues forwards. Similarly, the immediate cause of observed effects is of course the translation profile itself, but this profile is itself determined by the conditions in which the translation was done, at the levels of translation act and translation event, and the chain also extends further back: one can always continue asking "why?" Ultimately, the extensions are presumably infinite, in both directions: think of the much-cited example from chaos theory, of a butterfly flapping its wings and causing a hurricane on the other side of the world...

So where does prescriptivism come in? Precisely here: prescriptive statements are none other than hypotheses about translation effects. They fall into class (iii) above, as one kind of predictive hypothesis. True, they are not often presented explicitly as hypotheses, but that is what they are. Statements like "In principle, in authoritative and expressive texts, [original metaphors] should be translated literally" (Newmark 1988: 112), or "translations should aim to have the same effect on their target readers as the source texts had on the source readers", or "translators should translate transgressively, not fluently", can be paraphrased approximately like this: "I predict that if translators do *not* translate in the way I prescribe, the effect will be that readers will not like their translations / that the publisher will reject the text / that intercultural relations will deteriorate" or the like.

4. Problems with hypotheses of effect

The main methodological problem here is this: often, implicit hypotheses of effect are not tested. It is simply assumed that they hold good, that they are common sense or that they follow logically from a given argument. In terms of research methodology, such statements are incomplete, for if they have not been tested they remain speculative, however plausible they may seem, and they cannot contribute to empirical progress.

The good news is that there is ample scope for useful research here. We might first test prescriptive claims by checking them against what (professional) translators actually do: do they actually translate original metaphors in the way Newmark prescribes? All such metaphors or just some of them? Which ones? Do all translators seem to do this, or only some of them? Which ones? And we can then try to test the implicit claim concerning the assumed effects of *not* translating metaphors in this way: an experimental study might be able to show how clients, or publisher's readers, or indeed any other kind of readers, react to other kinds of translation.

A related methodological problem has to do with sampling. Prescriptive pronouncements (i.e. implicit hypotheses of effect) are usually made by teachers, translation scholars, critics, sometimes by clients: figures who have, or assume they have, some authority. These authority figures thus predict that unless the translation is like this, the effect will be undesirable. But: undesirable to whom? To what readers? To the teacher, scholar or critic? – Yes, presumably, at least to the people making the pronouncements. What about other readers, the readers for whom the translation was actually intended, or the client? Can we assume that the teacher, scholar or critic is a typical reader? I.e. is this sample (usually of a single reader) representative? Obviously not. So on what grounds can a teacher, scholar or critic implicitly claim to represent other readers, to be a valid test-case? Presumably, on the grounds of experience, acquired expertise and imagination, they can put themselves empathetically in the position of other, more typical readers to some extent. But this is no substitute for empirical research testing their prescriptive claims.

Translation effect analysis is still in its infancy. Skopos theory may have a contribution to make here: after all, the skopos of a translation could be understood in terms of its intended effect on its intended readers. The intended effect is thus a condition, existing (in the form of an intention) prior to the translation process, which then regulates (or should regulate) this process. Skopos theory has not yet focused on ways of assessing actual effects after the translation has been delivered, published and read (see e.g. Vermeer 1996). Vermeer (1998: 52) actually appears to have grave doubts about the feasibility of studying concrete effects in any detail; however, some kinds of general effects are easy enough to observe, and might be studied with the aid of simple parameters such as intended vs. unintended (see Chesterman 1998a[*]). The relevance-theoretical approach advocated by Gutt (1991) also seems a fruitful one here.

In this context, it is surprising that studies of translation quality often rely on the kinds of highly untypical readers I have mentioned. There has been less research on the reactions of real-life clients, of real-life, typical, intended readers.

5. Narrowing the gap between theory and practice

If we include the empirical study of translation effects in our research field, prescriptive approaches thus fall naturally into place as one form of normal hypothesis formation and testing: they do not need to be banned. A second advantage would be that this would narrow the gap between Translation Studies and the quality concerns of practising translators, of clients, of translation teachers, and of society at large.

---

[*] Paper 9 in this volume.

Empirical research of any kind often starts with a problem. What, then, are the problems which Translation Studies might be expected at least to tackle, if not to solve? Here are some, grouped in terms of cause and effect.

Studying causes in general
- Why is this particular translation like this? Why did the translator use these strategies?
- Why do translations of a particular type, at a particular period, tend to be of such-and-such a kind?
- Why do translators (of a given kind) tend to translate as they do? These questions (like several of the others in this list) obviously presuppose that we have an adequate descriptive apparatus available, allowing us to specify the characteristics of a given translation (type) with respect to all relevant parameters.

Studying effects in general
- How do translations of certain kinds affect cultural relations? How do they affect readers of different kinds?
- How can translation effects actually be described and studied? With what conceptual and empirical tools?
- How do we test the validity of a scholar's or critic's assessment of a translation? After all, an assessment is itself (the result of) an effect of a kind: it represents the effect which the translation had on the assessor; but the latter is usually not a typical reader.

Searching for causes of, or conditions favouring, or strategies leading to, "undesired" effects
- Why are there so many bad translations around? As receivers of translations we note that they have a certain effect on us, often an undesired effect: we are irritated by errors and defects. Who produces such translations, under what conditions, for what pay, with what qualifications and training, for clients with what kinds of expectations? The need for sociological fieldwork here is evident.
- Why are source texts often so badly written? What can we discover about the people or committees that produce such texts, how can we influence them? (Cf. the "Fight the Fog" campaign within the EU.[*]) This question thus focuses on one of the assumed causes of bad translations.

---

[*] This campaign is now (2016) no longer current, but has been followed by several initiatives including one promoting Clear Writing. See <http://ec.europa.eu/dgs/translation/publications/magazines/languagestranslation/documents/issue_01_en.pdf>

- Why are (covert) translations often nevertheless recognised to be translations? What can we learn from corpus studies of parallel texts about translationese?
- What are the causes of translation errors and irritating features? Yes, we can make some guesses… Do we then test these guesses?

Searching for causes of, or conditions favouring, or strategies leading to, "desired" effects

- How to improve the quality of translations? Yes, we have a lot of research on training methods, and also a good deal on producing useful technical and other aids. There is less on, say, the optimal way of organizing a translation agency, or selecting candidates for a training course.
- How do competent translators improve on badly written source texts? What strategies do they use, what are their tricks of the trade? How do they organize their work processes? (Mossop 1998)
- How do translators successfully solve other kinds of problems, such as translating particularly long sentences, or allusions, or jokes?
- How to program machines to translate? Yes, much research and progress has been made here. The machine translation project has perhaps been the one that has kept closest to Hempel's empirical methodology: constructing a machine translation system means proposing hypotheses about what a machine will produce under given conditions; the translations produced are means of testing these hypotheses. Each machine-produced translation has an effect (on readers, also on the programmers): you find it intelligible, or not, you accept it, or you don't, you wonder how to fine-tune a subcomponent of the program in order to improve some aspect or other, then you test it again…
- How to educate clients and the general public, to change their attitudes and prejudices about how translators work and what translations can be? Would more enlightened clients contribute towards better translations? Not much research here yet…
- How to formulate ethical principles of translation that will improve intercultural relations? How then to test these principles, to see whether cultural relations are in fact improved?

So: let us by all means promote empirical research, let us continue to formulate hypotheses that can be empirically tested, let us seek descriptive and explanatory adequacy for our theories, looking at both causes and effects of translatorial action. But even if we aim to rid translation research of non-empirical bathwater, we do not have to throw out the prescriptive baby as well. The effect of doing so may be undesirable.

PAPER 6

Skopos theory
A retrospective assessment*

This is a critical assessment of skopos theory, looking at its basic assumptions, its problematic empirical and ontological status (descriptive or prescriptive?), and its conceptual and pedagogical contributions.

Keywords: skopos, metaphor, descriptive adequacy, explanatory adequacy, value-free science, action theory, relevance theory, prescriptive theory

1. Introduction

It is often said, especially by laymen, that translation does not really have a theory. Not true: it has lots! (Well, it depends what you want to call a theory; but still…) But at least it does not have a general theory, right? Translation Studies has produced at best only a mixture of fragmentary theories. – This claim is not quite true either: we have several candidates which present themselves as general theories of translation. One them is skopos theory.

It is now about a quarter of a century since the publication of Reiß and Vermeer's classic work, *Grundlegung einer allgemeinen Translationstheorie* (1984), and even longer since the earliest publications on a functional approach to translation. Skopos theory, as a particular type of general functional theory, seems fairly well established on the map of Translation Studies, and is duly mentioned in all the textbooks. But how well has it stood the test of time? My aim here is to offer a general retrospective assessment of the theory, also taking account of some more recent criticism.

---

* First published in 2010 in Werner Kallmeyer, Reuter Ewald and Jürgen Schopp (eds), *Perspektiven auf Kommunikation. Festschrift für Liisa Tiittula zum 60. Geburtstag.* Berlin: SAXA Verlag, 209–225. The abstract and keywords have been added.

2. Axiomatic assumptions

Any theory rests on basic assumptions that are not tested within a given research paradigm, but are taken as given, self-evident, based on common sense and logic. We must start from somewhere, after all. But of course we can always query these assumptions if we wish, standing outside the paradigm. Some of them may be only implicit, hidden. But good theories aim to make all the relevant assumptions as explicit as possible, for instance as axioms from which the rest of the theoretical claims can be deduced. Skopos theory is unusual among other theories of translation, in that it has this form of a deductive, "syntactic" theory based on a small number of explicit axioms. In the 1984 version, these are called "rules" (*Regeln*). I give them here in summarized form (in the original German, from Reiß and Vermeer 1984: 119), followed by some brief initial explications and comments.

1. Ein Translat ist skoposbedingt.
2. Ein Translat ist ein Informationsangebot in einer Zielkultur und -sprache über ein Informationsangebot in einer Ausgangskultur und -sprache.
3. Ein Translat bildet ein Informationsangebot nicht-umkehrbar eindeutig ab.
4. Ein Translat muß in sich kohärent sein.
5. Ein Translate muß mit dem Ausgangstext kohärent sein.
6. Die angeführten Regeln sind untereinander in der angegebenen Reihenfolge hierarchisch geordnet ("verkettet").

Ad 1: Skopos theory thus assumes that a translation always has a skopos (a purpose), even though this may not always be clear (*ibid.*: 21). This skopos may often differ from that of the source text (surely a useful point). The skopos is the highest determining factor influencing the translator's decisions. Elsewhere (*ibid.*: 96), the rule is phrased: "Die Dominante aller Translation is deren Zweck." The theory assumes that the skopos is oriented towards to the intended target recipients: all translations have such a readership; even if you cannot always specify them, there are always "there" (*ibid.*: 85). – I will return below to problems of definition.

Ad 2: The theory assumes that language is embedded in culture. Translation is seen as a subtype of more general cultural transfer (Reiß and Vermeer 1984: 13). The "information offer" concept relates to the underlying theory of communication, whereby a sender "offers" information to a receiver. This information is assumed by the sender to be "interesting" to the receiver (*ibid.*: 76, 103), and, if the communicative act is successful, it will be interpreted by the receiver in a way that is compatible with the sender's intention and does not give rise to a "protest" (*ibid.*: 67, 106).

Ad 3: Translations are not normally reversible; and a given source text has many possible translations.

Ad 4: Intratextual coherence is assumed to exist to the extent that the text makes sense to the receiver, that it is compatible with the receiver's cognitive context, as in any form of communication. Note that rules 4 and 5 have a clear prescriptive form, unlike the others.

Ad 5: This fidelity rule assumes that the translation represents the source text, in some way which is relevant to the skopos. The theory recognizes a range of equivalence types.

Ad 6: This rule is of a different status from the others, and, as part of a general theory, problematic. We might at least want to query the order of rules 4 and 5 as being universally valid.

Immediately after giving this summary, the authors claim that these rules are "probably" the *only* general rules of translation (*ibid*.: 120). All further development of the theory would then be filling in more detail, providing rules for the analysis of the target situation, establishing conditions for the selection of different translation strategies, and so on (*ibid*.: 85).

A last initial comment: at the very beginning of the book, the authors define "theory", quite reasonably, thus: "Unter 'Theorie' versteht man die Interpretation und Verknüpfung von 'Beobachtungsdaten'" (*ibid*.: vii). This definition nevertheless seems to be rather at odds with the way they actually present their theory. The argument of the book does not start with empirical observations or inductive generalizations, but proceeds deductively. Examples are given to support claims, but many of them seem to be invented.

In a later publication, Vermeer (1996: 12f) contextualizes skopos theory explicitly as a form of action theory. Here too he sets out a number of axioms (now called, in English, "theses"), as follows, ending at about the point where the previous list (above) began:

1. All acting presupposes a "point of departure", i.e. an actor's position in space and time, convictions, theories, etc., including their respective history.
2. All acting is goal-oriented.
3. From a variety of possibilities [...] that action will be chosen which one believes one has the best reasons for choosing under the prevailing circumstances. The reason(s) may not be conscious for the actor.
4. Given the prevailing circumstances, an actor tries to reach the intended goal by what seem to him the/an optimal way, i.e., for which he believes he has the best overall reason(s).

5. Translating is acting, i.e. a goal-oriented procedure carried out in such a way as the translator deems optimal under the prevailing circumstances.
6. Thesis 5 is a general thesis valid for all types of translating [including interpreting].
7. In translating, all potentially pertinent factors (including the source text on all its levels) are taken into consideration *as far as the skopos of translating allows and/or demands.* [Emphasis original]
8. The skopos of (translational) acting determines the strategy for reaching the intended goal.

One might wonder about the apparent underlying assumption here that human behaviour is necessarily always rational – *if* these axioms are supposed to be descriptive (on which more below). Another underlying assumption, to which we shall return, is the assumption of optimality: that the translator (always) acts in an optimal way.

3. Conceptual contribution

Quite apart from any other merits, a theory may contribute new concepts to a field. These may aid theoretical thinking in general, as well as description and explanation, and may be taken up and adapted by other theories. New theoretical concepts are interpretive hypotheses, to be tested pragmatically in use (see further e.g. Chesterman 2008a[*]). Two aspects of this potential conceptual contribution will be mentioned here, beginning with the central concepts themselves.

3.1 Key terms and conceptual distinctions

Some of the earliest criticism of skopos theory had to do with some of its definitions, or the lack of them (see Koller 1990, on functional theories more generally; Kelletat 1986; Hebenstreit 2007). We can also ask whether the relation between the set of terms and the set of necessary concepts is an appropriate one. Are there too many terms, or too few?

Skopos is said to be a synonym of *Zweck* (purpose) or *Funktion* (Reiß and Vermeer 1984: 96), but "function" itself is not explicitly defined in the same context. Perhaps it could be glossed as "intended effect". But: effect on whom? Intended receivers, or any and all receivers? And intended by whom? Is it only the client's intention that counts? What about the source author's? The publisher's? When does

---

[*] Paper 18 in this volume.

an effect begin, and end? What about heterogeneous effects? How do we actually measure effects? Furthermore, if skopos equals function, we may wonder why a new term is needed. Confusingly, the German term *Funktion* is used in several senses, including the mathematical one. Two of these senses do indicate an interesting distinction: "external function" is said to denote the translator's general objective of making a living, whereas "internal function" refers to the skopos of a given translation (or translation process) (*ibid*.: 4). This external function seems very close to the term *telos* proposed in Chesterman and Baker (2008), to describe a translator's ideological motivation for working as a translator, either generally as a career or on some specific, perhaps chosen, assignment.

Later, Vermeer (1996: 7–8) seeks to distinguish three related concepts as follows: the *intention* is what the client wants to do; the *skopos* is what the translation is for; and the *function* is the "text purpose as inferred, ascribed by recipient". But there remain problems here. Are these distinctions necessary? When might an intention clash with a skopos? *Function,* in particular, remains an unclear concept. Recipients are not a homogeneous set, and may well ascribe very different functions. Even a model reader may react differently on different occasions. And besides, actual reception should surely be distinguished from intended function. Both intentions and functions may be virtually impossible to access, particularly if the translations studied are distant in time or space. – The conceptual and terminological confusion here has not been resolved (see e.g. Nord 1997: 27f; Sunwoo 2007).

Another problematic term is that of *coherence*, used both to refer to the similarity relation of equivalence between source and target, and to the intratextual interpretability of the translation itself. These seem very different concepts, and one wonders why the theory uses the same term. Since we already have "equivalence", and this term is used in skopos theory too, why do we need a new term? We also already have "similarity", if something looser than "equivalence" is wanted.

A translation is defined in the second axiom as an *offer of information* about a source text (which is itself another such offer, about something else). This interpretation of the relation between source and target is much weaker than any notion of equivalence, weaker even than relevant similarity (although Reiß and Vermeer do refer occasionally to the offer as being a "simulating" one, e.g. p. 80, 105). It does not appear to constrain the "offer" in any way, except insofar as the offer is assumed to be "interesting" to the receivers and is "coherent" with the source text. Here again we can ask: does this term really earn its place?

Regarding the German term *Translation* itself, we can appreciate the way in which skopos theory (following a German tradition in Translation Studies) uses this to cover both written and oral translation: this is a neat solution we have not managed to imitate in English, and which has subsequently been widely accepted. There will, however, always be argument about the appropriate extension of the term. Kelletat (1986) and Koller (1990) think the skopos notion of translation is too broad because of the way it downgrades the importance of the source text and thus allows very free translations, adaptations etc., within the concept. Kelletat (1986: 15) even suggests the Reiß/Vermeer definition would include the whole of Latin literature! In my view, on the contrary, it is too narrow, if it is taken to exclude non-optimal translations.

The theory's use of the term "adequacy" (*Adäquatheit*) also merits a comment. The term was already familiar from other approaches, particularly Toury's (e.g. 1980). But skopos theory defines it differently, not as a retrospective relation of closeness between target and source but as a prospective one between the translation, the source text *and the skopos* (Reiß and Vermeer 1984: 139). This skopos-sense of adequacy is so easily confused with the Toury-sense that scholars now either have to specify which sense is intended or give up using the term altogether. It is risky to give a new sense to an already established term.

Skopos theory, like other functional approaches, has also contributed to a more differentiated conceptualization of the agents involved in the translation process. Instead of simply having a sender and a receiver, we have learned to distinguish between writer, client, translator, publisher, recipient, addressee and so on. In this sense, skopos theory has helped to shift the discipline towards a more sociological approach.

3.2 Underlying metaphorical structure

A good theory's concepts do not exist in isolation, but in a network of relations. This network may be more or less consistent in terms of its metaphorical structure. Martín de León (2008) has recently drawn attention to some interesting problems in the underlying metaphorical conceptualization of skopos theory. She argues that the theory combines two different metaphors: TRANSFER and TARGET. This suggests a lack of conceptual consistency, insofar as the metaphors are incompatible.

The TRANSFER metaphor describes the movement of an object from A to B, and assumes that the object (or some essence of it) does not change en route. This means assuming some kind of equivalence, of course. As an underlying metaphor for translation (visible in the etymology of this word), it normally needs to reify some notion of meaning (referred to as the message in Holz-Mänttäri 1984). The client's intention might also be regarded as an "object" that is to be preserved. However, the view of a translation as merely an "offer of information" about the source text appears to go against the TRANSFER metaphor.

The theory's notion of intertextual coherence also relates to this metaphor, albeit loosely. But how valid is this assumption that meaning is "there" in the text? Several contemporary models of cognition would argue that meaning always emerges via a process of interpretation, a process which depends on multiple variables and is not completely predictable (see e.g. Risku 2002). – In my view, both these positions are overstated. Surely some meanings are more obviously, objectively "there" in a text, while others are much less so and are open to interpretive variation. If no meanings were objectivizable at all, there would be no work for terminologists and no-one would dare to step into a plane.

The TARGET metaphor on the other hand describes a process from a source along a path to a goal. It does not assume an unchanged, reified message. It implies that the translator can participate in constructing the meaning of the message and thus highlights notions of intentionality and rationality. Skopos theory stresses the expertise and responsibility of the translator to select what needs to be translated and to translate it in the most appropriate manner. But this metaphor also prompts questions. Suppose a given process or action does not have a single goal but multiple ones, perhaps regarding heterogeneous receivers? And where actually is a goal located? Strictly speaking, the goal is not in the text but in the mind of the initiating agent, for whom the translation is merely a means to achieve a goal or goals. Further: where in the theory is there any space for an assessment of the goals themselves? Is it really enough to say that any end justifies the means? – We will take up the ethical dimension of this argument below.

4. Ontological status of the theory

Perhaps the most debated problem of skopos theory has been its unclear ontological status. Does it aim to be a descriptive theory (of what *is*) or a prescriptive one (of what *should be*)? Does it describe a real world or an ideal, optimal one?

This ambiguous status is already apparent in its axioms: axioms four and five are openly prescriptive, but the others are not. Reiß and Vermeeer say that there is no such thing as "the best" translation for a given source text. "Es gibt nur das Streben nach Optimierung unter den jeweils gegebenen aktuellen Bedingungen" (1984: 113). – This is an interesting formulation. The "es gibt" looks like an existential, descriptive claim: it is a fact that translators strive, that they do their best. Well, how valid is this fact? We could reply that good translators do indeed do their best, most of the time, but surely there must also be many translators who merely do the minimum, at least sometimes. Professionals must often satisfice, after all. And there are many bad translators, of course (if a translator is anyone who does a translation, as a general theory should surely assume).

It seems to me to be clear that skopos theory is essentially prescriptive, although it has some descriptive assumptions. It aims to describe how *good* translators, expert professionals, work; what good translations are like. It describes an ideal world (see also Chesterman 1998b). Vermeer has acknowledged this (Chesterman 2001a), saying that the theory seeks to describe optimal cases. Elsewhere, however, he also seems to suggest that functional theories in general are both descriptive and prescriptive:

> Skopos theory is meant to be a functional theoretical general theory covering process, product and, as the name says, function both of production and reception. As a functional theory it does not strictly distinguish between descriptive and (didactic) prescription (Vermeer 1996: 26n).

Although the term "functional" remains problematic, I find this claim curious. Consider for instance the analysis of the reception of translations in a given culture in a given period. This would be an analysis of how the translations "functioned" in the target culture (data might include all kinds of responses, critical reviews, library loans, size and number of editions published, allusions to the translations in other writings, use of the translations as source texts for further translations, or as literary influences; sales of commercial products advertised by the translations; changes in the social, political, religious or ideological conditions; and so on). The analysis would not need to be prescriptive in any way. Even if the analysis compared the reception with the inferred intentions of different clients, this would not imply a prescriptive approach.

On the other hand, there is one obvious way in which prescriptive claims can be viewed descriptively, and that is by formulating them as predictive hypotheses, as argued in Chesterman (1999a[*]). Vermeer actually does precisely this at one point (1996: 31): "if you translate in such and such a way then y will happen". Such predictions can then be tested in the normal way, and the results can be generalized in the form of guidelines which, if followed, are reliably assumed to lead to translations which do not give rise to negative feedback ("Protest" in skopos-theoretical terms). This, of course, is precisely what translator training courses teach. It is also what skopos theory aims to do. If you keep the skopos in mind, and translate accordingly, the result will be better than if you neglect the skopos.

5. Empirical status of the theory

As presented, skopos theory is not founded on a search for empirical regularities. This point has been made by many critics (e.g. Koller 1995: 215). We can nevertheless consider how its various assumptions and claims might be tested

---

[*] Paper 5 in this volume.

empirically. It is striking that very little such testing has actually been done. What kind of evidence would falsify or weaken its claims? I will first consider the theory's descriptive adequacy, then comment on its explanatory adequacy and possible testable consequences.

5.1   Descriptive adequacy

Axioms two and three in the original list above are descriptive. Axiom two, on translation as an offer of information, is definitional. It is an interpretive hypothesis, which can be glossed something like this: 'in this theory, we claim that a translation is usefully interpreted as …'. As such, the claim is not falsifiable, but is testable pragmatically, i.e. in use (see further Chesterman 2008a). Has this interpretation been widely adopted and led to further hypotheses? Not notably, it seems. On the contrary, it has aroused some criticism, as it seems to allow the concept of translation to expand too far (e.g. Kelletat 1986).

Axiom three states that translations are not reversible. This claim can certainly be tested empirically, via back-translation. In my view, the claim is too extreme. It would surely be more accurate to say that the smaller the unit of translation, the more reversible it is; that in cases of standardized translations – e.g. in multilingual glossaries of special fields or in the names of institutions, or in many idioms and proverbs, in numbers, etc. – reversibility may well be the norm. In other words, the claim needs to be restricted, made subject to other conditional factors such as size of translation unit, text type, skopos, and so on.

There have been a few empirical studies recently which question some of the other basic assumptions of skopos theory. Koskinen (2008) examines the working conditions of EU translators. One of her findings is that in many cases, EU translations that are not intended for the general public are not directed at a target culture at all, but are oriented by the needs of the source institution (99–100). This goes against the skopos theory assumption that a translation should have optimal functionality for target culture addressees. However, this type of EU case is not evidence against the idea that a translation is primarily determined by its skopos. Here, the skopos is simply not a target-oriented one. Interestingly, Koskinen points out that the special requirements of this kind of translation are experienced as particularly problematic by translators who have been trained in a functional approach: their translation brief seems to conflict with the target-oriented way in which they have been trained to think.

Furthermore, many professional translators do not work as autonomous individuals but as members of a team of experts, including terminologists, subject specialists, revisers, copyeditors and so on. Such conditions do not always support the skopos theory assumption that it is the translator who ultimately decides how to translate, as the expert. ("Er entscheidet letzten Endes, ob, was, wie übersetzt/ gedolmetscht wird." Reiß and Vermeer 1984: 87.) One recent study illustrates this well: Nordman (2009) examines the complex process of Finnish-Swedish translation in the bilingual Finnish Parliament, and highlights interesting disagreements between the translator's preferences and those of revisers or legal experts, and how these are resolved. The translators and revisers she studied seem to have different norm priorities. It is not always the translator's views that prevail.

Even in some literary translation the priority of the translator's expertise has been questioned. In a questionnaire study dealing with poetry translation, Flynn (2004) queries the status of some of the factors which skopos theory assumes, including that of the dominance of the translator's own expertise. Flynn found that the situational factors affecting the final form of the translation are more like sites of confrontation between the various agents involved, including publishers and proof-readers as well as translators. The translator does not necessarily always have the final say. Flynn's results admittedly concern a particular type of translation only, in a particular (Irish) context; but again, we can point out that a general theory should be able to cope with all types.

As another example of evidence against the assumption that it is the expert translator who makes the final decisions I cite an ongoing PhD project by Julia Lambertini Andreotti at Tarragona[*]. She is a qualified court interpreter working with Spanish and English in California. The ethical code there requires that interpreters make no alteration to the register of the legal jargon as they translate. But since many of the clients are not well educated, they simply do not understand the legal terminology, and so do not understand what they are asked. As communication experts, the interpreters naturally wish to adapt the register so that the clients can understand, but this is not allowed. The interpreters are simply not permitted to act as skopos theory assumes.

One might argue that all such examples are cases where a translator is forced to act under duress, against the council of his own expertise, and thus in non-optimal conditions. They would thus fall outside the scope of skopos theory. Reiß and Vermeer explicitly exclude instances of "Translation unter Zwang" (1984: 101). – But there are multiple kinds and grades of duress, including unrealistic deadlines, legal constraints etc., which characterize much real-world translation and interpreting. Indeed, if there are in fact more non-optimal cases than optimal ones, skopos theory itself would deal only with special cases – surely not the intention of the skopos theorists. A general theory should be general enough to encompass all cases.

---

[*] Now completed (2016). See References.

From another point of view, note should be taken of studies on how translators perform under time pressure (e.g. Hansen 2002). These studies suggest that when professional experts work under unusual time pressure, they tend not to waste time pondering about the skopos or the target audience but simply stay on the surface of the text, translating fairly literally, without reformulations or other major shifts which might actually be appropriate for the readership. Here again we have professionals working in a non-optimal situation, without sufficient time for normal working procedures. Under these conditions, the skopos assumptions seem not to represent what actually happens.

Research such as these studies underlines the way in which skopos theory relates more to an ideal, optimal world than to the real and often suboptimal world of everyday translation. In this sense, some of the general descriptive claims and assumptions of the theory can easily be falsified, or forced into more conditioned formulations – if they are supposed indeed to apply to all translation, not just optimal translation done in optimal working conditions. And what about the undeniable existence of a great many really bad translations? These are nonetheless also translations, of a kind; but they are completely excluded from skopos theory. From the point of view of descriptive adequacy, then, the theory is inadequate. But if it is taken as a prescriptive theory, of course, this is not a valid criticism.

5.2   Explanatory adequacy

The first axiom (in the German list above) is a causal one. From the point of view of the production of a translation, it states that the skopos is the most important conditioning factor. This has obvious prescriptive relevance. But retrospectively, as an answer to the question "why is this translation like this?", the axiom formulates a causal explanation. The most important reason why a translation (or, modified: an optimal translation) is as it is, is its skopos. This claim gives rise to several points.

Implied in the axiom is the assumption that every translation *has* a skopos in the first place. Is this assumption testable? Could we in principle refute the claim by finding a translation that does not have a skopos? Perhaps not. Skopos theorists would say that the skopos is always already there, even if not well defined or even definable. Some scholars (e.g. Kohlmayer 1988) have argued that literary translations do not have a skopos; it is certainly not easy to be precise about the skopoi of literary texts.

The theory does not assume that the skopos is the only cause, merely that it is the dominant one. How might this dominance be measured? What other causes might be relevant? One might counter-argue that under some conditions the skopos dominates, under other conditions some other cause (perhaps these other conditions would be non-optimal ones?). Kelletat (1986) points out that Reiß and Vermeer fail to show how different translation traditions, as well as different skopoi, are themselves affected by historical conditions.

Recall Aristotle's four causes: the skopos cause corresponds to his "final", teleological one. It has been argued (e.g. by Pym 1998: 148f) that skopos theory overvalues this teleological cause at the expense of the others. The skopos does take account also of Aristotle's formal cause (the target-culture norms), but what about the efficient cause (the mind and body of the translator plus computer etc.) or the material cause (the source text, perhaps also the constraints of the target language itself)? Pym argues that by imputing purpose to a text, skopos theory neglects the socially determined individuals who are actually doing the translation. Skopos theory also avoids the problem situation in which client and translator differ about the skopos, or where there might be a conflict of loyalty. True, Nord's version of skopos theory (Nord 1988, 1991a and later versions) gives more weight to the material cause by focusing strongly on the analysis of the source text. But Vermeer does not agree with Nord's introduction of the notion of loyalty (see further below).

It is often pointed out in textbooks that skopos theory helped to dethrone the source text as the dominating causal factor determining the form of a translation. It has now placed the skopos on the vacant throne. But perhaps we would achieve greater explanatory adequacy, more nuanced explanations, if we recognized a range of explanatory variables including norms, personal preferences, special situational constraints and so on, all of which impinge on the translator's decisions (see e.g. Brownlie 2003). The relative strength of the different variables in a given case would then depend on the circumstances. This would also allow for non-optimal working conditions, and indeed non-optimal translators. Any generalization about the overall dominance of one independent variable or another could only be based on a wide range of comparative empirical studies.

5.3 Testable consequences

A deductive theory such as skopos theory, if it claims to be empirical, should also generate hypotheses that can be tested and potentially falsified. The theoretical claims should have testable consequences. Curiously, the theory does not seem to have been very productive in this respect. One reason may be the difficulty of operationalizing its central concepts and claims.

One predictive hypothesis that does arise very naturally from the theory's premises is that if the skopos is different, the translation will be different. This can easily be tested: a given source text is translated twice, each time with a different skopos. Norberg (2003) studied precisely this situation, but focused on differences between professionals and non-professionals rather than skopos-determined differences.

Other hypotheses can be proposed, which (as far as I am aware) have not been explicitly tested.

- If a translation is deemed bad, the main reason (*a* reason?) will be that it does not meet the skopos. (Also obvious, surely.)
- The more the translator pays attention to the skopos, the better the translation will be. (Another obvious one.)
- Skopos-type correlates more closely than source-text type with equivalence-type. This one would be more interesting. It would test the relative causal force of skopos vs. source text-type on the source-target relation. But there is a problem here. We have typologies of text types, and typologies of equivalence, but, surprisingly, no generally accepted typology of skopoi. Reiß and Vermeer give random examples, but no systematic typology. Would such a typology necessarily be culture-bound and thus not part of a general theory? Surely not, at least no more than other typologies used in translation research. Prunč (1997a) proposes seven prototype classes, but these are in fact classes of translations, not skopos types. They range from non-translation via pseudotranslation to homologous, analogous, dialogic (involving more interpretation) and triadic (intervening, e.g. feminist) to diascopic translation (gist translation, commentary). Nord (1997) proposes two basic "translation functions", documentary and instrumental; but here too we are dealing with types of translation rather than skopoi.

In a different article, Prunč (1997b) makes a useful distinction between implicit and explicit skopos. The implicit skopos is defined as the lowest common denominator, the default skopos compatible with the current translation norms and the prevailing translation tradition. The explicit skopos then states, where necessary, any divergence from the implicit skopos. But no typology of explicit skopoi is offered here.

Wagner (in Chesterman and Wagner 2002: 45) does offer one specific skopos typology, for use in the EU. These types are:

For information, not for publication
For publication [a very broad category]
For advertising and marketing
For use as a legal document
For text scanning and abstracting

The big gap is the lack of research on how a given skopos or skopos type might actually correlate with given translation strategies or techniques. Even within given language pairs, this would be interesting and useful. Reiß and Vermeer (1984: 85) say that a "complete" translation theory would give "rules" for the analysis of the target recipient situation and how this then conditions the translation strategy. But skopos-based research has not developed much in this direction. One wonders why. (For a recent attempt to operationalize the skopos concept, see Sunwoo 2007.) We look in vain for testable hypotheses of the form: if the skopos is (type) X, professional translators tend to choose general strategies ABC. Or: in the case of translations from language S to language T (under conditions PQR), translators tend to realize skopos-determined strategy A as techniques / translation solutions DEF.

6. The ethical dimension

Partly in order to counter criticisms that skopos theory is too target-oriented and underestimates the value of the source text, Nord (e.g. 1997: 123f) introduced the concept of loyalty, which is defined as meaning loyalty to all the people concerned on both side of the communication exchange, including the source author and sender. Vermeer does not like this development, as he thinks it brings in an unwanted ethical dimension. A scientific theory is value-free, he argues.

> It has been argued that translation involves an ethical aspect. However, I am of the opinion that ethics must not be mixed up with general theoretical considerations about other subjects. Science should be value-free (*wertfrei*).
> (Vermeer 1996: 107)

Toury apparently agrees (1995: 25).

However, I think this position is untenable. In a classic article, Rudner (1953) showed that science can never be value-free. Value judgements are made all the time: in selecting "interesting" research problems (i.e. those that have value…), evaluating the evidence and counter-evidence for hypotheses, prioritizing research goals, and so on. Skopos theory highlights the expertise of the translating agent, who makes decisions. It seems to me that any such theory must include an ethical dimension, at least insofar as ethical issues influence the agent's decisions. (See also Martín de León 2008.) Furthermore, one could argue that a functional theory of translation should also cover the possible general ends which translations serve, their ultimate functions, as it were: some translations are surely more worth doing than others, for instance, not in terms of pay but in terms of the ethical value of the end product (cf. some voluntary, activist translation, for example). It is all very well to say that if we want X we should do A (rather than B, for instance); and we can of course test this hypothesis, checking to see whether A or B is a better means to attain X. The only criterion here seems to be that of effectiveness. But suppose we ask *who* wants X? And for what reasons? For what further end is X itself a means? And who does *not* want X?

The lack of this dimension in skopos theory, where any end is apparently as good as any other, has led to the theory being associated with a kind of robotic, unthinking translation process, which dehumanizes the translator. Baker (in Chesterman and Baker 2008: 21–22) puts this view as follows:

> We soon configure something like skopos theory as a narrative in our minds: the theory evokes (for me at any rate) an industrialized, affluent society populated by clients and highly professional translators who belong to the same 'world' as their clients, who are focused on professionalism and making a good living, and who are highly trained, confident young men and women. These professional translators and interpreters go about their work in a conflict-free environment and live happily ever after. They do not get thrown into Guantánamo or shot at in Iraq, and they do not end up on the border of Kosovo and Albania in the middle of a nasty war, where they would have to decide whether or not to fulfil their commission at the expense of treating potential victims with compassion and respect.

Prunč (1997b) seeks to counter this criticism that the skopos view of translation risks being interpreted as totalitarian. He stresses how skopos theory can account for cooperation between agents, and expands the loyalty concept to include the translator's loyalty to him/herself.

Perhaps Vermeer is equating value-freedom with rationality? Rudner concluded that value-freedom is often confused with objectivity. He argued:

> What is being proposed here is that objectivity for science lies at least in becoming precise about what value judgments are being and have been made in a given inquiry – and even, to put it in its most challenging form, what value decisions ought to be made; in short that a science of ethics is a necessary requirement if science's progress towards objectivity is to be continuous. ([1953] 1998: 497)

7. The competition?

In assessing a theory (or indeed a hypothesis) one also compares it to competing theories. The closest competitor to skopos theory is Justa Holz-Mänttäri's theory of translational action (1984). Indeed, this is so close, albeit with a different terminology, that they are often considered to be variants of the same framework (Vermeer 1996: 61f). Some of the criticism of skopos theory has also been directed at Holz-Mänttäri's work (e.g. Koller 1990).

A more interesting comparison might be made with relevance theory, in its application to translation (starting with Gutt 1991). A detailed analysis would take up more space than is available here, so a few comments must suffice.

In their discussion of the notion of the offer of information, Reiß and Vermeer (1984: 76, 103) write that this "offer" is assumed by the sender to be "interesting" to the receiver. I.e. the sender thinks that the information contains something that is "new" to the receiver, something that will have some effect, which will somehow change the existing state of affairs in the receiver's world. – This formulation suggests the central concept of relevance, as understood in relevance theory. It would seem that skopos theory sees itself as being much broader than relevance theory, including relevance-theoretical insights and much more (Vermeer 1996: 65–68).

Relevance theory clearly aims to be descriptive and indeed explanatory, not prescriptive. But there does seem to be a conceptual overlap, perhaps more than Vermeer seems to accept (see Vermeer 1996: 47f, and his comments in Chesterman 2001a). Both theories assume that human action is rational, and both give importance to the receiver's side. The two theories differ in the extension of their object of study: relevance theory excludes very free translations, and so-called multilingual descriptions, which skopos theory would include (Vermeer 1996: 63). Skopos theory also allows a deliberate change of skopos from that of the source text, which would seem to be excluded by Gutt's application of relevance theory.

8. Concluding remarks

Skopos theory has proved itself to be pedagogically invaluable, as a prescriptive theory; I cannot imagine training translators without using the idea of the skopos. But as an empirical theory seeking to describe and explain translation phenomena in the real world, it is weak, precisely because it relies on an optimal set of working conditions with optimally competent translators. One of the most serious problems in the real translation world, however, is the prevalence of poor translations, coupled with poor working conditions and low pay. These issues are not addressed by skopos theory.

In terms of its productivity, the theory has been somewhat disappointing. It has not generated a substantial body of research proposing and testing new hypotheses derived from the theory, nor significantly developed its conceptual apparatus. True, it has been expounded in numerous textbooks, and applied in numerous training programmes and notably in translation criticism (e.g. Amman 1990). It has succeeded in giving some theoretical weight to an intuitively sensible idea – that translators should consider the purpose of their translations – and certainly helped to shift the focus of theoretical thinking away from equivalence towards other relevant factors and agents which affect the translation process. It has thus helped, perhaps paradoxically, to make translation theory more realistic. And it has prompted some of us to ponder more deeply what we mean by a theory.

PAPER 7

Catford revisited*

The article casts a critical retrospective glance over Catford's influential contribution to Translation Studies. Some of the strengths and weaknesses of tying a translation theory to a linguistic theory are discussed, together with the problems of building a deductive theory relying mainly on invented examples. Catford's evident interest in machine translation is noted, and also his incorporation of pragmatic aspects such as relevance. The distinction drawn between equivalence and correspondence is theoretically important, and his analysis of translation shifts has been highly influential on later work. His definition of translation as textual replacement rather than meaning transfer, and his language-bound concept of meaning itself, have been much debated.

Keywords: Catford, Halliday, linguistics, grammar, shift, equivalence, meaning, data

Catford's classic *A Linguistic Theory of Translation* was published about half a century ago (1965). Its sub-heading is "An Essay in Applied Linguistics", and it was based on a series of lectures at the Edinburgh University School of Applied Linguistics. Translation was only one of Catford's interests: he was also a phonetician and a general linguist. In standard introductions or surveys of Translation Studies, the book is indeed classified as a *linguistic* theory, and the implication is usually that it somehow belongs to ancient history, long before such major developments as Skopos Theory or the Cultural Turn. In a survey of linguistic approaches to translation, Fawcett (1997: 56) dismisses Catford's contribution as "disappointing". Munday (2001) outlines Catford's classification of shifts, but does not seem too impressed. Snell-Hornby, in her own history of Translation Studies (2006), gives Catford no more than a single sentence, which surprisingly appears to take him as a representative of generative grammar. A *Meta* review nearly twenty years

---

* First published in 2012 in Diana Santos, Krister Lindén and Wanjiku Ng'ang'a (eds), *Shall we play the Festschrift game? Essays on the occasion of Lauri Carlson's 60th birthday.* Heidelberg: Springer, 25–33. Reprinted by kind permission of Springer Publishing. This text has been lightly edited for the present volume. Its original publication was prompted by a remark once made to me by Lauri Carlson: he thought Catford had been unduly neglected by contemporary translation scholars. The keywords have been added.

after the book's publication is also disappointed in the book's lack of relevance to the normal practice of translation, and regards it as being of "historical academic interest only" (Henry 1984: 57).

Are these dismissive reactions justified? Perhaps we can now see more in Catford than meets the eye? What kind of conversation might one have with him today, in the light of how translation theory has developed over the past decades?

1. The nature of the theory

Catford establishes his theory of translation within a specific general theory of linguistics: an early version of Halliday's systemic grammar (set out e.g. in Halliday 1961), itself much influenced by Firth. Halliday's framework is taken mostly as given, with only a few minor modifications. The advantage of this is that Catford's translation theory is firmly anchored in a more general theoretical context, and is largely consistent.

Catford assumes that a theory of translation has to do with a kind of relation between *languages*, and is consequently a branch of Comparative Linguistics. This warns us that much of his theory may turn out to be more relevant to Contrastive Analysis than to translation in the normal sense of the word. Relations between languages, however, are said to be not always symmetrical (20): this is of course true of translation, but would not apply to non-directional (e.g. semantically based) Contrastive Analysis. We should recall, too, the linguistic context of the 1960s, and the attempts at that time to be more "objective" about language and meaning.

Logically enough, the presentation starts with a definition of translation, and then outlines a typology. Catford's definition, which has become famous, is: "Translation [is] the replacement of textual material in one language (SL) [Source Language] by equivalent textual material in another language (TL) [Target Language]" (20). At this point, he picks out two of this definition's central terms for comment: 'textual material' and 'equivalent'. (Curiously, he does not take up the term 'replacement' here, which will be crucial to him.) Defending his use of 'textual material' (rather than 'text'), he says that this term "underlines the fact that in normal terms it is not the entirety of a SL text which is translated, that is, replaced by TL *equivalents*" (20, emphasis original). This is because normally there is no replacement of SL graphology by equivalent TL graphology.

This argument, which surfaces at several points, raises a problem. It is only because the underlying linguistic theory sets up graphological (and phonological) levels alongside those of grammar and lexis, that Catford has to say that normally "it is not the entirety of a SL text which is translated". This claim is not justified by reasons internal to translation practice, and thus seems to introduce unecessary distance between the theory and its object. Catford's point here also illustrates his top-down method of arguing, deductive rather than inductive. This is shown most strikingly in his initial typology of translation, which immediately follows his definition.

On the one hand, one would like to applaud Catford for setting up a typology that is explicitly justified by the underlying theory with its categories of levels and ranks. On the other hand his proposed typology seem curiously artificial when set against translation practice, as critics have pointed out. His main categories are: full vs. partial, and total vs. restricted. The first distinction relates to the extent of the translation: for Catford a 'text' can be anything from a morpheme to a complete library, apparently (21); so you can either translate all or some of a text, perhaps leaving some items untranslated. The second distinction relates to the linguistic levels involved. 'Total' translation means replacing all the levels (grammar, lexis, phonology, graphology); but replacements of these latter two levels are not "equivalent". Restricted translation then relates to only one level, for example phonological translation. Further distinctions concern translation at different ranks (clause, group etc.).

As far as I know, the concepts and terms of this typology have not been adopted in later work in the field of Translation Studies. They have not been seen to be pragmatically useful, and in this respect Catford's theory has failed to "catch on". Scholars may also have been less than convinced by Catford's assumption that there is an important distinction to be made between (a) replacing SL textual material with *equivalent* TL material, and (b) replacing it with *non-equivalent* material. The first is the definition of translation itself, and the second is part of the definition of "total" translation (since the replacing graphology and phonology are not normally "equivalent"). It appears from this typology that Catford's translation theory sets out to be so general that the normal everyday world of actual translation is only represented in one small corner of the object to be described. "Total translation" is "what is most usually meant by 'translation'" (22), but it is given rather less space in Catford's presentation than his other types and subtypes. "Lexical" and "grammatical translation" would nowadays be treated as kinds of code-switching.

2. Equivalence and correspondence

In distinguishing between empirically observed textual equivalence and formal correspondence, Catford makes an important point that has been reflected in a good deal of later work. A textual equivalent, he says (27), is "any TL text or portion of text which is observed on a particular occasion [...] to be the equivalent of a given SL text or portion of text". This formulation may remind later scholars of Toury's argument that a translation is any TL text that is accepted as conforming to TL norms about what a translation is supposed to be (e.g. 1995). Toury's argument has been criticized as circular, but his point was that any definition of translation is culture-bound. For Catford, what is or is not equivalent is bound to the view of an observer. This observer is a "competent bilingual or translator" (27). So a text is equivalent if a competent translator says it is: this is precisely the argument proposed by Pym several decades later (e.g. 2004). Equivalence is *produced* by translators, and then implicitly claimed by them, a claim that is (or is not) then accepted by the client and later readers. Catford appears to regard this claim as being dependent on the subjective opinion of a competent translator, rather than on the shared opinion of a community, or on norms; and this ultimately makes his approach more subjective than he may have realized. A single translator appears to be enough. Commutation can also be used to establish what is equivalent: change something in the source, and see what changes in the translation as a result. (Recall Toury's "replacing" and "replaced" segments!) But these changes are also made by the competent bilingual translators, of course (among whom the scholar may include himself, as Catford implicitly does with the examples he cites).

There are, of course, problems here. One is Catford's apparent assumption that these competent translators will agree on what is or is not equivalent, together with the implied assumption that there is, in a given context, just one equivalent. As we know, such agreement is a matter of degree; this means that judgements about equivalence must also be matters of degree, depending on who is judging, on the context, the purpose of the assessment, and so on. Catford appears here to be relying on something like Chomsky's infamous community of homogeneous native speakers. An associated problem is how to decide who is, or is not, a competent bilingual or translator in the first place, as if this were a clear-cut category. – All in all, it seems that Catford is pitching his argument more at an abstract, philosophical level than an empirical one here.

Statements about specific textual equivalents can be formulated in terms of unconditioned, and then conditioned, equivalence probabilities, which in turn lead to the possibility of translation rules or "algorithms" (31). In this way, Catford looks explicitly in the direction of machine translation.

The importance given to formal correspondence underlines the relevance of Catford's theory for Contrastive Analysis. Formal correspondence can only be relative, to be sure. However, it also relies on textual equivalence, since otherwise there would appear to be no motivation to want to state a formal correspondence between two text segments in the first place (32), unless the research context is one of language typology. There thus remains a tension in Catford's theory between a translational view (based on equivalence) and a contrastive view. The contrastive view is reinforced by the focus on relations between *languages* (or *systems*, such as those of prepositions or articles). Catford is indeed concerned with *langue* rather than *parole*, but this tension is also visible in the way he occasionally frames his analysis in terms of utterances (e.g. 37, 39) and even speech acts (e.g. 52). (Austin's *How to Do Things with Words* had appeared a few years earlier, in 1962.)

In hindsight, one can see that Catford's formal correspondence, when applied to texts rather than languages, lives on in Translation Studies as a version of Nida's formal equivalence. It also provides a theoretical justification for what is perhaps the most frequently cited part of Catford's approach, his analysis of translation shifts, defined as "departures from formal correspondence" (73). But there is very little in Catford that would match the notion of dynamic equivalence. There is a chapter on language varieties in translation, which makes use of early Hallidayan categories of register etc. However, explicit mentions of the notion of function are rare, although context, situation and culture are recognized to be important.

3. Assumptions about meaning

Catford's assumption that meaning is language-specific, and thus cannot be "transferred" from one language to another, derives from his adoption of Firth's anti-mentalist theory of language and meaning (see e.g. Firth 1957). Meaning is understood as "the total network of relations entered into by any linguistic form" (35), a view that is simply taken for granted, not argued for. No account is taken of any alternative view, for instance of the notion that meanings are universal and objectively "there", or that meanings are not language-specific but speaker- and/or hearer-specific, or situation-specific. Or that some meanings might be more language-specific than others (although this is perhaps implied by some of the points made later about translatability).

This assumption means that Catford must disregard not only the widespread folk understanding that translators "transfer meaning", but also the very etymology of the word "translation" itself, and that of its many cognates in other languages. However, it is easy for him to show that perfectly acceptable translations do not necessarily have absolutely the *same* meaning. (An alternative approach would have been to argue that meaning is transferred, but not entirely – that translation is largely a matter of metonymy, not metaphor, as argued later e.g. by Tymoczko 1999: 54–55, 279.) But Catford is tied to his parent theory, chooses not to challenge it and accepts the consequences. One consequence is that a new concept and term – transference – must be introduced to account for cases that we might now call the strategy of translating by using a loanword (as when an English translation of a Finnish text contains the word 'sauna'). True, the English item probably does not carry quite the same contextual meaning as the Finnish, so Catford can maintain his claim that meaning is not transferred. But against this one could argue, from the viewpoint of a different theory of meaning, that *some* meaning has been transferred. Meaning, for Catford, often seems to be a black-and-white affair.

In translation, says Catford, conditions of translation equivalence are met if the target text expresses the *relevant* features of "situational substance" that are expressed by the source. This condition of relevance comes as a vital additional requirement to his first statement, which only stipulates that the two texts must share "(at least some of) the same features of [situational] substance" (50). This inclusion of the relevance requirement is the closest Catford gets to bringing in any pragmatic dimension into his theory. "Sameness of situation" is of course problematic, and is accordingly relativized (52).

At this point we see again a disadvantage of being chained to a cover-theory. Catford proceeds to argue that, because of the status of different "substances" (phonic, graphic, situational) in the theory, and because of the way he has defined translation equivalence, there can therefore be no "translation" for instance between the phonic and the graphic, because they are different substances. So he is forced to say that when an oral utterance is replaced by a written one, say in a subtitle, it is not the case that a phonological item has been "translated" by a graphological one. The "translation" comes about only because both items are exponents of a grammatical category that in turn has a contextual meaning that relates to a shared feature of situation-substance. The conclusion follows from the premises, but is so counter-intuitive that one wonders why the premises are not questioned. One could surely do with Occam's Razor here.

In defence of Catford's reliance on a general theory of grammar, it could be argued that he is aiming more to increase the coverage of this theory itself, by showing its relevance to translation, than to develop a specific theory of translation. But I think this argument would still be susceptible to the problems touched on above, which raise doubts about the applicability of the general theory to empirical human translation.

The final chapter on the limits of translatability returns to the notion of relevance. Translatability is, of course, a cline, and the position of a given translation task on this cline will depend primarily on the extent to which linguistically relevant features of the source text are bound to the source language itself, and to which extent these features are functionally relevant, as in the case of puns. This is linguistic untranslatability. Cultural translatability, on the other hand (e.g. the strange notion of a sauna in English), is less "absolute". If one tried to translate 'sauna' into English e.g. as 'bathroom', this would give rise to curious collocations of bathrooms and birch twigs etc., which leads Catford to conclude that perhaps cultural untranslatabilites are ultimately reducible to collocational ones, and collocations are part of linguistics, so all can be covered by a grand linguistic theory. And this in turn would be good news for machine translation…

4. Use of examples

In hindsight, one of the strangest aspects of Catford's book is his use of examples. They are taken from a wide range of languages, but almost every example is invented and given outside any context. So we have for instance "The/A woman came out of the house" in English and Russian, to show different ways of expressing definiteness – Russian uses word order (28); terms for different sibling relations in English and Burushaski (40); or an Anglo-Yiddish joke (for which he thanks his wife) to illustrate the importance of the Yiddish rise-fall tone ^, which I cite in full (54).

Judge:	Did you steal a horse?
Interpreter:	Hot ir gestolen a pferd?
Accused:	Ikh hob gestolen a ^pferd?
Judge:	What did he say?
Interpreter:	He said 'I stole a horse'.

There are two exceptions. On pages 30 and 33 mention is made of a French short story and its translation, which are used as a source of data on the frequencies of different translations of French *dans* and other prepositions. This is a literary text, about 12,000 words long. No source is given. And on page 102 we are surprised to find mention of a "genuine" translation from French, one sentence long, and again from a literary work. Literary works might be assumed to have an obvious, albeit vague skopos (purpose); but none of the other examples in the book are contextualized in any way. In a book purporting to be a theory of translation, this is curious. The only translator assumed to be responsible for the other examples is Catford himself, as a linguist with a good knowledge of at least French, and evidently a scholar's familiarity with aspects of some less-known languages.

I mention this not in criticism of the theoretical ideas themselves (some of which can be criticized on other grounds, as I have indicated), but because of how this use of empirical data relates to Catford's own assumptions about what a theory is. In the Preface, he writes: "The present volume [is primarily concerned] with the analysis of what translation *is*. It proposes general categories to which we can assign our observations of particular instances of translation, and it shows how these categories relate to one another" (vii, emphasis original). That is, the aim is a descriptive theory, consisting of general categories that are related in ways that are motivated by the theory. The categories are thus theory-driven, they are ready boxes into which our various empirical observations can be placed; but they do not derive initially from the empirical observations themselves. Re-reading the book, the categories occasionally remind me of a Procrustean bed, to the dimensions of which all data must be persuaded to fit. If one then mostly invents one's own data, this task is easier. The examples selected become illustrations of the possibility of a given category, but no more than that. They do not substantiate claims that a given category is well-motivated, or prototypical, or notably more significant than some other category.

5. What do we conclude?

One of the striking features of Catford's theory is its degree of consistency, despite the occasional tension between translational and contrastive approaches. Given a particular underlying linguistic theory, the translation theory is logically derived from it, step by step. I was reminded of the similarly top-down approach taken by Skopos Theory (e.g. in Reiß and Vermeer 1984), starting with a series of axioms and deriving more detailed statements from them, although Skopos Theory wavers between descriptive and prescriptive attitudes. Catford is more consistent, keeping to a descriptive line throughout. He has a liking for taxonomies, and is prepared to follow the logic of his categorizations even if they lead him some distance from the primary contours of the actual object of research. Catford is indeed outlining a general theory of translation, one that will cover all types of translation; but throughout the book there is an emphasis on subtypes such as graphological and phonological translations and transliterations which are certainly not central to ordinary practice, and have been virtually neglected by subsequent work in the field.

There is no attempt to be prescriptive. But there is no attempt at explanation, either, which makes the theory somewhat superficial. No extra-theoretical motivation of categories is given, for instance. No testable generalizations are proposed, no hypotheses generated.

The reliance on a particular linguistic theory, and moreover on a particular (early) stage of that theory, is problematic. As the linguistic theory develops, the translation theory becomes dated. In Halliday's later versions of systemic grammar, for instance, the lexical and grammatical levels merge into lexicogrammar (see e.g. Halliday 1985 and later works), but this is obviously not reflected in changes in Catford's translation theory. Other ways of analysing language varieties are similarly left out of consideration, as are later developments that give more weight to pragmatic considerations (such as communicative functions). In this latter respect too, Catford's theory is a child of the 1960s. More generally, we see the risk of setting up any translation theory that is not independent and autonomous, based on its own concepts and terms. (There are of course valid reasons for seeking to embed a theory of translation in a more general theory of language, or of communication, as suggested also by Gutt (1990). But that would be a separate topic of discussion.)

In hindsight, again, it seems clear that Catford had one eye on developments in machine translation and the future of computers. His "conditioned translation rules" have the general form "X is translated as Y, under conditions ABC, with probability P" (my summary of Catford's argument on pp. 30–31). Early machine translation programs operated on just such rules. Translation scholars today may also be reminded of the form of Toury's (1995) "laws" of translation (not concerning the translation of given source-text items, but aiming to capture more general characteristics of the translation process). Toury's laws of interference and increased standardization are similarly conditioned, and similarly probabilistic.

Catford's final comment on cultural untranslatability – that if this can ultimately be described in terms of *linguistic* untranslatability, this would give translation theory more power and also broaden the horizon of machine translation – might even be seen as one of the seeds of the contemporary attempts to set up a semantic web.

His legacy surely includes other seeds too, and not only the shifts idea. Despite his 1960s linguistic framework, he does see the importance of relevance, situation and context; the distinction between formal correspondence and textual equivalence is fundamental (although not exclusive to him), as is the contextualizing of the notion of equivalence itself. While his non-use of empirical translation data leaves him open to criticism, the theory he presents has a high degree of internal consistency, which is both a strength and a limitation. We are reminded how difficult it is to build a theory that is not only internally consistent but also open to refinement (or indeed rejection) as it is tested against evidence; one that allows the generation of new ideas and hypotheses; and one that seeks not just to describe but also to explain.

In my view, then, Catford is still an important source of ideas and insights, and well worth re-reading, albeit with a critical eye. I certainly count him among those who have influenced my own thinking about translation.

PAPER 8

The descriptive paradox, or how theory can affect practice[*]

The paper discusses and illustrates the potential tension between theory and the practice that it describes, beginning with the claim by Jean Boase-Beier that theory can affect translation practice. By way of introduction, a comparison is made with the way artists are influenced by theories e.g. of perspective and colour, following Gombrich. With respect to translation practice, three possible channels are proposed whereby theory might affect practice: prescriptive teaching, tacit theory, and descriptive theory. Each of these channels raises problems. Prescriptive theory is mentioned only briefly; most translators nowadays are untrained. More attention is given to tacit, implicit theory, and its role in the practice of (trained or untrained) translators. But the main focus is on the descriptive paradox itself, as manifested in Descriptive Translation Studies. This paradox arises when the act of describing affects the phenomenon described, so that the description itself no longer fits. The author then draws on his own experience of how his explicit knowledge of translation theory may have influenced his translation of a Finnish novel (*Canal Grande*, by Hannu Raittila; not yet published in English). He is not entirely convinced, however, that he can actually prove the influence of theory in this case.

Keywords: descriptive theory, practice, norms, universals, Finnish

1. Introduction

In her recent book on literary translation (*A Critical Introduction to Translation Studies*), Jean Boase-Beier claims that theory affects, or at least can affect, translation practice (2011: 82, 160). I found myself wondering how this claim could be tested. A universal generalization that theory *always* affects practice would be easy to falsify, if we could produce one instance of translation that had not been affected by any kind of theory. This is a path I will not pursue here. Rather, let us

---

[*] First published in 2013 in *Tijdschrift voor Skandinavistiek*, 33, 1, 29–40. Permission to reprint is gratefully acknowledged. The text has been slightly edited for this volume, and a couple of examples have been dropped from Section 3.

consider the weaker, and presumably more realistic claim, that theory *can* affect practice. Boase-Beier argues that theory can sensitize translators as readers, raise key issues and problems to be solved, and orient translators towards finding appropriate solutions.

In a nutshell, I argue below that if theory can have an effect on practice, there must be channels through which it can work, and I suggest three. But there are problems with all three, and one of the problems is the descriptive paradox. I then test the claim on examples from my own (albeit limited) experience as a literary translator. I end up feeling rather more sceptical than when I started.

Consider first a similar idea from the history of art, an idea that is explored in E. H. Gombrich's *Art and Illusion*, first published in 1960. This book is subtitled "A study in the psychology of pictorial representation". Reading and re-reading this classic, I have long been struck by the relevance of Gombrich's argument to translation, although he does not mention this topic. After all, translations too seek to represent something, they are concerned with mimesis. Where art has often aimed at fidelity to nature, translations aim at some kind of equivalence to a source. But just as "no artist can copy what he sees" (Gombrich, [1960] 1977: xi), no translator can produce a perfect copy of the original. What the artist and the translator do is create an illusion of their source, then (hence the title of the book).

In so doing, however, artists (and translators) do not work in a vacuum. We do not see with innocent eyes, but in the way we have *learned* to see. What we actually see is largely inferred from what we know. And what we know depends largely on cultural conventions. For instance, in art, the discovery of the laws of perspective radically changed the ways in which artists represented relative distance in their pictures. Similarly, the changing styles in the use of colour in art can be seen to have been influenced by the increasing knowledge of how colour is perceived in different contexts. – Look for instance at John Constable's *Wivenhoe Park*, painted in 1816; it is the first colour plate in Gombrich's book. (It can be viewed online e.g. at https://en.wikipedia.org/wiki/Wivenhoe_Park_(painting)#/media/File:John_Constable_-_Wivenhoe_Park,_Essex_-_Google_Art_Project.jpg.) Note the small size of the house in the distance: Constable was certainly familiar with the theory of perspective. Note also the gradation to darker greens in the foreground, and how greens are made to look yellow in the sunlight.

So representations are always interpretations based on what we know, and only metonymic interpretations at that. Knowledge increases, too: hence the ever-present possibility of other possible interpretations, for instance in other styles. For Gombrich, styles are conventional answers to a given skill problem (such as how to represent relative distance), a particular answer that is preferred over alternative answers. The range of alternative answers is restricted by the artist's awareness and knowledge of what previous artists have done, and also by his medium: for instance, the range of possible colours available at the time. In other words, the artist is constrained by the available repertoire of possibilities and norms, although "constrained" here obviously does not mean "totally imprisoned": norms can be broken.

Gombrich suggests further that pictures are artists' experiments with representation; that true representations are those that do not convey false information (compare the notion of equivalence in translation); that form follows from function (cf. Skopos Theory, which argues that the form of translations is determined primarily by their purpose or skopos: see e.g. Reiß and Vermeer 1984); and that artists are pulled by existing schemata (standardized forms, normative solutions), which they may nevertheless seek to adjust or resist and hence develop. Towards the end of the book there is a discussion of equivalence that seems to speak directly to translation scholars. Gombrich emphasizes, for instance, how an artist aims to persuade a viewer to accept a picture as representing something, as if by presenting a hypothesis, but that a viewer may reject this hypothesis; compare claims about possible equivalence, which may or may not be accepted by readers (cf. Pym 1995). In 1843 Joseph Turner painted a work he called *Light and Colour (Goethe's theory) – The Morning after the Deluge – Moses Writing the Book of Genesis* (see e.g. <http://www.tate.org.uk/art/artworks/turner-light-and-colour-goethes-theory-the-morning-after-the-deluge-moses-writing-the-book-n00532>). But it is not easy to see the connection between Moses writing Genesis and the abstract swirl of colour before our eyes. This picture actually shows the direct influence of Goethe's colour theory, which fascinated Turner. Note for instance the use of the colour yellow, which for Goethe symbolized "plus" values such as energy and the sun; yellow was believed to be the first colour derived from light. All colours, thought Goethe, came from the play of light and darkness. Goethe also theorized about the perception of colour: note how Turner represents the image of an eyeball, where the yellow colour darkens towards the edges as the point of view moves away from the centre.

2. How translation theory might influence translators

So is translation like this, with translators being affected by theories? If this is, or at least can be, the case, there must be channels through which this influence can flow. I will now suggest three such channels: prescriptive training; the formation of tacit theory; and the descriptive paradox of explicit descriptive theory.

2.1 Prescriptive training

I suppose the most obvious channel is translator training. This is how theory can be applied prescriptively. In the days before descriptivism came to dominate Translation Studies, the aim of theory was usually taken to be the provision of guidelines to be taught to students, about how best to solve various kinds of translation problems (see e.g. Newmark 1981). Indeed, as discussed in the book Emma Wagner and I wrote on the relation between theory and practice (Chesterman and Wagner 2002), this prescriptive view of theory is what many professional translators still apparently expect of Translation Studies, and they are disappointed to find so little of it there these days. This is because in our current descriptive age, the overtly prescriptive approach has been relegated to the status of an *application* of theory. When we train translators professionally, we make use of theoretical concepts like "skopos" (purpose) or "pragmatic equivalence" (equivalent effect), and hope that these will have a beneficial effect on the quality of the work eventually produced by our students, together of course with masses of practice and feedback. And no doubt this is usually the case, but a number of reservations need to be made.

In the first place, an increasing number of translations done today are not done by trained professionals, but by amateurs who have presumably had very little, if any, prescriptive exposure to translation theory. In these cases, there can have been no direct channel for prescriptive theory to affect their practice via training. I guess that even literary translators have not always been trained as translators; and even if they were, the training may not have included much theory.

In the second place, among translators whose training has exposed them to theoretical work, the effect of the theory may not be beneficial at all, but negative, producing frustration and the need to unlearn what has been learned. An example of this is documented in Kaisa Koskinen's study of EU translation (2008: 98f), which shows that trained EU translators find that their working environment in Brussels and Luxembourg is, in some circumstances, such that all their prescriptive training in target-oriented translation theories must be jettisoned. During focus group interviews with translators on this topic, the responses Koskinen notes ranged from expressions of frustration to outright laughter, as translators recalled their experiences of trying to apply what they had been taught to translation tasks that simply didn't meet the assumptions of their training. As an EU translator, she claims, sometimes one evidently has to forget about the importance of considering the skopos, of the translator being a communication expert, of audience design, of expecting a careful brief, and so on. The reality of EU translation includes the fact that some texts are translated merely because, for legal reasons, they just have to *exist* in all the official languages, not because they are actually going to be *read* by anyone: they are not really going to be instances of communication at all. The EU translators Koskinen interviewed thus experienced a gap between the professional ideal they had learned, justified by a prescriptive functional theory, and some aspects of the reality of working in this particular institution. One wonders how many trained translators working in other environments have also experienced such a gap between the theory they have been taught and their real-life work. If this feeling is widespread, perhaps something is wrong with the theory, or with the way it is taught (or with prevailing expectations of quality?).

There has been little research, as far as I know, on how the explicit prescriptive teaching of different translation theories affects the translation practice of different groups of students. Do courses based on functional theories eventually lead to more successful translation practices (on some measure) than courses based on contrastive analysis or on theories of equivalence? Or, in interpreting: do graduates of the Paris School based on the notion of deverbalization (the idea that good interpreters immediately detach meaning from form; see e.g. Seleskovitch and Lederer 1984) tend to get better jobs than graduates of schools with a syllabus based more on an empirical science approach (such as the Trieste School; see e.g. Gran and Dodds 1989)?

2.2 Tacit theory

A second channel of potential influence from theory to practice centres on the notion of what we could call tacit or implicit theory (compare the concept of tacit knowledge, i.e. knowledge that is difficult to put explicitly into words). Whether we are translators or not, we are all exposed to translations, everyone has some notion of what a translation is. In this sense, everyone has a view of translation – i.e. some kind of implicit theory. Whether trained or not, translators inevitably have some tacit translation theory of their own, such as a set of personal principles, or a favourite metaphor of translation (seeing translation *as* something), and some notion of what an acceptable translation is, as well as personal stylistic preferences. (In this sense at least, I agree that all translation must be influenced by *some* theory!) A translator's tacit theory might also include personal attitudes to norms, based on the experience of other translations and perhaps also an awareness of the feedback given to one's own or to other translations, e.g. in reviews or, in the case of crowdsourced translation (done usually online by a large group of people such as a community of fans, often voluntarily), by way of alternative translations proposed by other translators.

Here too there are problems. Mere exposure to translations will presumably not contribute to the formation of a tacit theory if the translations are not read as translations, and this is surely often the case. Reading your daily newspaper, do you normally take note of how much of the content is translated? Such a situation might of course lead to the tacit assumption that all acceptable translation is invisible. Perhaps people who themselves translate are more aware of the translations they read? I do not know of any research on this.

On the other hand, many of the translations we see are all too visible, in the sense that they are unnatural target language, or plainly inaccurate (if one compares them with the source texts). Since these highly visible translations continue to exist, indeed to multiply, maybe they become the new norm. In Finland, for instance, more and more subtitling is currently done by amateurs, unfortunately, as fees are cut and professionals boycott certain major employers. But what will be the effect of poor translations on the tacit theory of translation that is spreading through the next generation? We are often told these days that the reading matter of many young people is primarily subtitles – i.e. translations.

What kinds of personal principles and preferences might a tacit theory contain? Consider some examples from a pioneering study of the causal effects of (literary) translators' attitudes by Siobhan Brownlie (2003). Among the personal preferences she analyses are issues like the following, where opinions varied: whether or not to opt for literal translation; whether or not to respect sentence boundaries in the case of long source-text sentences; and whether a translation should be clearer and/or smoother than the original. Brownlie also discusses the possible discrepancy between what translators say their principles are and how they actually translate, under given conditions. She noted, for instance, that although the translators she studied disapproved of major semantic shifts, these were nevertheless found in her data. And although there was agreement that unusual expressions should be reproduced, this was not always what happened. Opinions were divided as to whether the target text should be clearer than the source, but it very often was. There was also simplification in all the texts studied, although translators had different views on whether this was acceptable. Unnatural expressions were not favoured, but nevertheless found in the data.

Tacit theory, then, is formed by exposure to translations, and by popular ideas about translation. Sometimes even a particular metaphor of translation can affect practice. Recall the influence of the theoretical notion that literary translation can be seen as cannibalism, and how this has influenced translators especially in Brazil, far beyond any specific training programme; it has been widely seen as a way of encouraging translators to treat source texts with more creative freedom (see e.g. Vieira 1994). Translation-as-cannibalism has been an idea that seems to have spread by osmosis, notably from the translations and writings of the brothers Haroldo and Augusto de Campos outwards, via imitations and discussions of many kinds. A theoretical idea like this can become part of the tacit knowledge of a whole professional community – or indeed a non-professional one too.

Tacit theory is also formed by the public discourse on translation (such as is manifested in book reviews, letters to the editor, statements of language or translation policy, interviews with translators, etc.). There may also be input from explicit descriptive theory, which is also part of the discourse of translation, but a rather special part, to which we now turn.

2.3 The descriptive paradox

In the history of Translation Studies, it is a commonplace observation that a major shift took place during the 1960s and 1970s, from a prescriptive approach to a descriptive one, as mentioned above. Descriptive Translation Studies became the new paradigm, aiming to study translations as they are, not as they should be. I will not expand here on the huge explosion of research that this paradigm has given rise to, but focus briefly on one problem, which will then be illustrated by my own experience. This is the problem of what I call the descriptive paradox: the idea that descriptive theory can affect practice. This has the curious consequence that when it does affect practice, the practice being described will no longer remain exactly what it was before the descriptive theory was applied to it. Compare the observer effect in physics, or the observer paradox in sociology, where the very act of observing or measuring something changes the state of the thing that is being observed.

In translation theory, one manifestation of this paradox derives from descriptive research on so-called translation universals, i.e. very general tendencies that appear in translations regardless of the language pair, culture, genre or historical period. (For a survey, see the papers in Mauranen and Kujamäki 2004.) What might happen if one teaches students about some of these very general tendencies? I do not mean prescriptive teaching, but simply exposure to some of the findings of descriptive empirical research. Would students' awareness of these features actually have the effect of changing their frequency of occurrence in subsequent translations done by these same students? Such a hypothesis was tested in Riitta Jääskeläinen's experiment (2004) on sensitizing students to the idea that translators tend to avoid repetition. She found that informing her students of this potential universal did have the effect that the students were less likely to follow it later: in other words, this descriptive information changed their practice. This is an example of the descriptive paradox. It suggests that merely teaching *about* potential universals might have the eventual effect of refuting the hypotheses concerning the very universals that are discussed! This also implies that teaching the theory may end up changing not only the practice but eventually the theory itself, if theory seeks to describe practice.

I suppose that Jean Boase-Beier, whose argument originally set me thinking, assumes or hopes that her own theoretical book will affect the translation practice of those who read it; indeed, perhaps it will improve their practice, by making them more sensitive to close readings, translation possibilities, and so on. So she is evidently hoping that her descriptive research will have a prescriptive effect: and this is the paradox.

3. A personal experience

I will now get personal. It has also been my own recent translation experience that has alerted me to the problem of the descriptive paradox. I have never been trained as a translator (apart from very basic courses in a BA degree in modern languages), and I have never been a professional translator. I have translated a couple of academic books, and a number of smaller assignments, but never translated for a living. However, I have spent a large part of my academic life teaching and studying translation and translation theory. When I recently came to translate a literary work, from Finnish to English, I found myself wondering how my knowledge of translation theory would affect how I translated. When I started the project, I obviously had my own tacit theory, but it was not particularly unusual. I wanted to produce a translation that read well, in natural English. The translation did not need to sound Finnish, or foreignized. I aimed to respect sentence boundaries as far as possible, and also respect the various registers and voices of the original as much as I could. But how might my knowledge of descriptive theory affect how I translated? – The novel in question is Hannu Raittila's *Canal Grande* (2001). A German translation by Stefan Moster was published in 2005, but there are no other translations available, as far as I know. Mine is not yet published.

Let us look first at some of those so-called translation universals. As a TS scholar, I am aware that one of the most studied universals concerns the general tendency for translators to explicitate, even when this is unnecessary (see e.g. Pápai 2004). Consider the following examples from the novel and my translation. In (1) and (2) the parts in bold are added, as necessary explicitations.

(1) Miehet olivat ilmaantuneet viraston ovelle sumusta kuten hakkapeliitat Reinille…
 > They had appeared out of the fog at the door of the office like the Finnish cavalry on the bank of the Rhine **during the Thirty Years' War**…

(2) Heikkilän mielestä italialaiset hiihtivät väärin. En uskonut, että suomalaisilla on vähään aikaan mitään sanomista kenenkään hiihtelyistä. (226)
 > He thought the Italians skied in the wrong way. **In the light of recent events on the winter sports front back home** I didn't think Finns had anything much to say about anyone's skiing efforts at the moment.

In cases like these, I thought some extra information must be given to explain the reference, and so I went along willingly with the attested tendency to explicitate. Regarding (2): shortly before the novel was published there had been a huge doping scandal concerning the Finnish skiing team.

Research on explicitation has indicated that there tends to be rather less of the opposite strategy: implicitation. The result can be that the translation ends up saying too much, underestimating the reader's ability to construct meaning. I aimed to explicitate when necessary, but also to implicitate sometimes when possible, as in (3), where the bold part has been omitted (represented by italics in the translation).

(3) Vene kiikahteli taas ja kuului lorinaa. Nyt kai puolestaan amerikkalainen kusi laidan yli **laguunin veteen**. (173)
> The boat rocked again, and there was another trickling sound. This time I guessed it was the American having a pee over the side *[into the water of the lagoon]*.

Another general tendency is the way translations typically over-represent or under-represent items, in comparison with their distribution in non-translated texts in the same language. A study by Maeve Olohan and Mona Baker (2000), for instance, showed that reporting *that* was over-represented in English translations. So I went through my whole text: I was horrified to see how many unnecessary *that*'s I had, and cut most of them out. In Finnish, the corresponding item *että* is compulsory, which of course helps to explain their overabundance in my first draft.

(4) Ylikomissario väitti, **että** häntäkin on pari kertaa ammuttu sorsana. (303)
> He said Ø he too had been shot at a couple of times by hunters taking him for a duck.

Sonja Tirkkonen-Condit (e.g. 2004) has suggested that translations tend to under-represent target items that are unique to the target language. By "unique items" she means target-language items for which there is nothing in the source language that is formally similar enough to trigger them as a direct equivalent. Translations into Finnish, for instance, tend to under-represent typical Finnish particles like *-kin*, *-hAn* and *-pA*[*], because most of the source languages studied lack corresponding items. When the target language is English, I am aware that one of the "unique" forms that is often under-represented is the *-ing* form of the verb. So I added some.

---

[*] It is conventional, when writing about Finnish, to use a capital *A* to denote 'either *a* or *ä*': the variation is due to vowel harmony, i.e. depending on whether other vowels in the word are front or back. On unique items, see Paper 21 below.

(5) Ma rupesin olemaan aika hysteerinen. Mä nauroin ja itkin. (328)
> I was getting pretty hysterical, laughing and crying. *[Rather than: I laughed and cried.]*

In one of the first large-scale empirical studies on possible universal tendencies, Sara Laviosa (Laviosa-Braithwaite 1996; see also her subsequent publications) found evidence of simplification, i.e. lower lexical density and variety, and more use of the most common words of the target language. I deliberately tried to compensate for this tendency by occasionally using rarer words than the source.

(6) Nyt pyhkii jonkun laivan valonheittäjä samaa avoveden pakkasilmaan nostamaa huurteista **utuverhoa**. (263)
> Now a ship's searchlight sweeps through the same frosty **shroud** *[instead of 'curtain']* of mist raised into the freezing air by the open water.

(7) Saraspää **peiteltiin** takapenkin nurkkaan. (229)
> He sat **huddled** *[instead of 'he was covered']* under a blanket in the corner of the back seat.

Not all potential universals are tendencies that I felt I wanted to counter. The tendency to reduce repetition, for instance, I willingly followed at some points.

(8) Lehtijutussa selitettiin, että se oli ollut "kosmopoliitti, kirjailija ja lehtimies, **arvostettu tyylintuntija**, [...]." Just. "Saraspää oli sukupolvensa johtava hahmo ja **arvostettu tyylintuntija**, Suomessa harvinainen jos kohta snobistinenkin intellektuellityyppi." (320)
> The article said he had been "a cosmopolitan, writer and journalist, an **esteemed connoisseur of style**, [...]." Yeah, right. "Saraspää was a leading figure of his generation and a **recognized aesthete** *[rather than 'an esteemed connoisseur of style' again]*, an intellectual type that is rare in Finland, albeit verging on the snobbish."

As to any personal principles I had: I felt free to add commas, but I also added many semi-colons, partly because the source text had practically none (semi-colons are rare in Finnish, but not so rare in English), but partly also because I am personally fond of them; so I allowed a personal preference to have some influence here. It would be *my* text, after all.

(9) Levitin veronalaisesta kirjakaupasta hankkimiani karttoja hotellihuoneen lattialle. (216)
> I spread out the maps on the floor; I had bought them at a bookshop in Verona. *[Instead of: I spread out the maps, which I had bought from a Verona bookshop, on the floor of the hotel room.]*

I have of course been aware of the increasing interest in translator agency in recent years (the ability of translators to act as social agents in their own right; see e.g. Kinnunen and Koskinen 2010), and the debates about translation ethics. This awareness may have encouraged me to make corrections to the source text occasionally: for example, there are many instances of brief phrases in French or Italian, but some of them contain orthographic or grammatical slips, which I corrected. I was ethical enough, however, to check with the writer that I could do this. He even agreed to let me omit a non-existing Latin phrase completely, because I felt it did not fit with the cultured and educated image of the character in question:

(10) [...] laguunin laivaliikenne on kokouksen aiheena ehdottomasti *causa contradictio antagonis*, sovittamattoman riidan aihe. (168)
 > as far as the agenda is concerned, the ship traffic in the lagoon is an absolutely classic case of antagonistic contradiction, i.e. unresolvable dispute.

One theoretical idea I have long been interested in is the equivalence hierarchy: sometimes semantic equivalence takes priority over formal, or stylistic, or pragmatic equivalence, for instance, whereas sometimes some other kind of equivalence is given priority. For instance, at one point, I decided that a particular lexical solution was so good that formal equivalence should be sacrificed: in (11) I rearranged the adjectives in order to fit in *bucking bronco*.

(11) Se heristi vihkoaan ja hihkaisi innostuneena kuin cowboy, joka ratsastaa rodeonäytöksessä villillä hevosella tai pukkiloikkia hyppivällä härällä. (235)
 > Brandishing his notebook, he was yelling with enthusiasm like a cowboy riding a **bucking bronco** or rodeo bull. *[Instead of: ... like a cowboy who rides in a rodeo show on a wild horse or a bucking bull.]*

Finally, a comment on the relevance of empathy. In much of my own published work, I have defended a general empirical methodology and not been so attracted to the hermeneutic approach to translation, which I have often found conceptually confusing and unhelpful. Now, however, I found myself leaning on hermeneutic notions like empathy, as a way of getting myself inside the voices of the characters. The novel is written in three voices: one narrator is a super-rational engineer, one is a decadent but cultured hedonist, and one is a street-wise young woman. Perhaps unsurprisingly, I found that I could identify both with the engineer and the hedonist, but much less so with the young woman. Her voice was much more difficult to articulate.

I grew particularly fond of the old hedonist, looking forward to his next section, and enjoying the expression of his voice. I even managed to slip in some Latin in one of his sections, to compensate for the earlier omission:

(12) Ilman Tuulin kielitaitoa emme olisi ikinä selvinneet sokkeloisten käytävien ja salien läpi määränpäähän, jonne ihme kyllä saavuimme käymättä lainkaan ulkoilmassa. (75)
> Without Tuuli's language skills we would never have found our way through the labyrinthine corridors and chambers to our destination, where we eventually arrived, **mirabile dictu**, without taking a single step outside. *[The Latin translates ihme kyllä, literally 'a wonder indeed'.]*

So in this personal case, I can find some evidence suggesting that my theoretical knowledge at least *may* have influenced my translation practice.

4. Concluding remarks

Marx famously wrote that although philosophers have sought to understand the world, the point is to change it. But in his essay "Imaginary Homelands", in the collection of that name, Salman Rushdie suggests that the distance between understanding and changing may not be so great. He notes that "description is a political act" (1992: 13). One always describes from a particular point of view, and often with a background ideology that colours the description and "spins" it in a certain direction, and the effect of this spin may be to change something, e.g. an attitude. Rushdie is writing about the descriptions of India by emigrant Indian writers, but the same point seems to apply to our descriptive paradox in Translation Studies, in the sense that descriptions have (or at least can have) effects. Indeed, Rushdie goes on to say that "the first step toward changing the world is describing it" (1992: 13). So if descriptive translation theory does really influence translators, we have the descriptive paradox.

But does descriptive theory have this effect, really? Maybe my own overt knowledge of theory had much less effect on me than I have suggested. I cannot prove such a causal relation in this particular case: I might have translated in the same way just on the basis of the tacit theory I have absorbed, or simply on instinct, or common sense. (Indeed, perhaps instinct is in fact an initial tacit theory.) How could one *prove* that an artist has been influenced directly by a theory? The challenge recalls the difficulties of finding empirical evidence for norms. In art, maybe we find some explicit evidence in a picture title, like the Turner example responding to Goethe's theory of colour. Or maybe there is biographical evidence, as we have in Constable's case. Or a picture may overtly illustrate the (playful) *rejection* of a theory, as in William Hogarth's *Satire on False Perspective*, for instance, designed to accompany a pamphlet on perspective, in 1754 (available e.g. at <http://www.wikipaintings.org/en/william-hogarth/the-importance-of-knowing-perspective-absurd-perspectives>).

With regard to translation, we can look for evidence in translators' prefaces and in their other paratextual reflections on their work, and in their biographies and social contexts. But evidence from these sources may not always be conclusive: I am not even sure how to interpret my own experience!

SECTION III

Causality and explanation

The papers in this section pick up several threads, concerning ways of analysing different kinds of causes and explanations, and also the notion of progress in TS (cf. Paper 3, above). Ideas about hypotheses are taken up in more detail in a later section (VI) in this volume.

An early philosophical influence on my thinking about explanatory hypotheses was certainly Karl Popper, but I have also been influenced by the philosophical work of the Finn Georg von Wright and the Norwegian Dagfinn Føllesdal, both of whom are interested in the kinds of explanations and hypotheses that are used in the humanities. I first saw Translation Studies as an empirical discipline, and argued for the centrality of causal explanations and falsifiable hypotheses. In retrospect, this position seems more restricted than my current view, which is more open to the significance of other kinds of explanation and other kinds of hypothesis (see also Paper 18).

Gideon Toury's influence is evident in the papers in this section. He sees norms as explanatory hypotheses, and his "laws" of translation have both explanatory and predictive significance, as can be seen from their general form: *given conditions ABC, translators will tend to do X / translations will tend to have such-and-such features.* Such hypotheses can be tested empirically in experimental settings, and are falsifiable if "tend" is defined explicitly (a problem I will return to in the section on universals, below). They can also be tested non-experimentally, against data that already exist but have not yet been analysed for the purpose of testing the hypothesis or hypotheses in question. For instance, the generality of a hypothesis supported by data from one language pair, or one genre, can be tested against similar data from other languages or genres.

Michael Carl (in several personal communications) has drawn my attention to the importance of generating and testing predictive hypotheses even when we do not have convincing explanations available. Such research is particularly relevant to the development of better CAT tools. Predictive hypotheses that are supported of course stimulate the search for explanations, just as explanations can be tested by seeing whether predictions based on them are realised. Paper 5 above also argued that prescriptive pronouncements are actually predictive hypotheses.

Some of the topics discussed in Paper 9 are further developed in the chronologically later Papers 4 and 5 above, concerning translation effects and prescriptivism, and in Paper 10 below. Paper 9 is not revised here, but re-reading it now I do have some reservations. In the discussion of translation typology, my comment about a possible "default prototype concept of translation" now looks rather naïve, given the enormous variation of culture-bound and period-bound concepts of translation that have now become increasingly visible in TS research. This "default" view is obviously also culture-bound… In hindsight, I note that I have too readily assumed that our typical translator is a single agent, and overlooked the possible contributions of other agents such as editors. And the term "quasi-falsifiability" now seems to me to be of dubious usefulness. The point could be more effectively made in terms of the importance of testing *generalizations* (as opposed to predictions in the strict sense).

Paper 10 is a slightly later essay on causality, based on a paper read at a memorable conference in Manchester; it covers some of the same ground as Paper 9. Interpretive hypotheses are discussed in more detail in Paper 18. With respect to the examples here concerning the retranslation hypothesis, note that these are for conceptual illustration only. It has been clear for some time that this particular hypothesis is not tenable in its general form, because so much counter-evidence has been uncovered. (See e.g. Paloposki and Koskinen 2004, and (in Finnish) Koskinen and Paloposki 2015.)

Paper 11 is an attempt to explore a semiotic approach to causality and explanation, with special reference to Greimas. It has occurred to me since this paper was published that Greimas' modalities could also be usefully applied to the analysis of agency, which has recently become a popular research focus in sociologically-oriented studies of translation. (See e.g. Kinnunen and Koskinen 2010, Paloposki 2009.) A modality analysis of this kind would offer a broader conceptualization of agency than one that focuses only on its manifestations, for it would include motivation to act (*vouloir*, perhaps also *être*), ability to act (*pouvoir, savoir*), and also the contextual constraints on action (*devoir*, also *pouvoir*). (For a study of agency that aims to cover similarly broad ground but does not use these modalities, see Haddadian-Moghaddam 2014.)

Paper 12, on explanation, is a synthesis of my thinking on this topic. The key Hempel quote is repeated in other papers in this volume.

PAPER 9

Causes, translations, effects[*]

Conceptual analysis has a role to play in translation studies, but it is a means, not an end. An empirical paradigm gives central importance to testable hypotheses. Empirical research on translation profiles should result in a translation typology: one such typology is discussed. Translations have multiple causes, and we can already propose some possible causal laws. Three laws of translation effect are also proposed, and various parameters of effect are discussed, together with the associated problems of sampling and prescriptivism. I argue that prescriptive statements are hypotheses about translation effects; as such, they should be tested like any other hypothesis.

L'analyse conceptuelle joue bien sûr un certain rôle dans la traductologie empirique, mais en tant que moyen, non pas en tant que fin. L'empirisme assigne la priorité plutôt aux hypothèses testables. La recherche empirique sur des profils traductionnels devrait avoir pour résultat une typologie traductologique, dont nous fournissons un exemple. Les causes d'une traduction sont d'une multiplicité hétérogène, mais on a déjà proposé des lois de causalité traductologique. Nous proposons ici trois lois d'effet, en considérant aussi quelques paramètres d'effets possibles et deux problèmes particuliers: celui de l'échantillon et celui du normativisme. Nous soutenons que les déclarations normatives ne sont que des hypothèses d'effet traductionnel, de sorte qu'elles devraient être soumises, elles aussi, aux tests empiriques.

Keywords: causality, translation typology, translation profile, laws of translation effect, prescriptive statement

A number of trends can be distinguished in translation studies over the past decade or so. One is a broadening of interest from *translational* studies (focusing on translations themselves) to *translatorial* studies (focusing on translators and their decisions). Another is a move from prescriptive towards descriptive approaches. However, I think the most important trend has been the shift from philosophical conceptual analysis towards empirical research. This article outlines a general

---

[*] This paper was first published in 1998, in *Target* 10, 2: 201–230. Reprinted with kind permission from John Benjamins Publishing Company, Amsterdam/Philadelphia (www.benjamins.com). A few references are updated here. The keywords have been added.

empirical paradigm which incorporates both translational and translatorial approaches, but also accommodates prescriptive claims. The centre of focus is on translations as phenomena that have both causes and effects. After a discussion of translation types and causes I propose some preliminary laws of effect, and raise some of the problems involved in the analysis of translation effects. Prescriptive statements turn out to be none other than particular kinds of hypotheses about translation effects.

1. Conceptual analysis

Conceptual analysis has played a major role in the history of translation theory. We have spent much ink and paper arguing that translation is or is not possible, pondering on different scholarly definitions of translation or equivalence, exploring different metaphors of translation and translating, investigating the ways in which postmodernism gives us new insights into the translator's role and status, and so on. We have spent much time and energy honing our conceptual tools with more and more delicacy, but we have spent rather less time actually *doing* anything with these tools.

What, after all, can you do with a definition or a metaphor? Yes, of course you can think with them. Yes, conceptual analysis can lead to greater understanding or new philosophical arguments: a fresh or redefined concept can enable us to see something in a different way. And yes, of course we need *some* kind of preliminary definition of our central concepts, and we usually look at the research object through *some* kind of metaphorical lens. But it often seems that we take such theoretical considerations to be the ultimate goal of our research. This point of view has two disadvantages.

First, we make it harder for translation theory to appear relevant to professional translators, to translation practice (see e.g. Berglund 1990). For instance, professional translators would find it more useful to know about *clients'* conceptions and expectations of what a translation is, and about the *general public's* attitudes to translation, rather than the opinions and arguments of scholars. – If we knew more about such general attitudes and about how they are formed, we might even be in a better position to start changing them.

The second and more important disadvantage is that if conceptual analysis becomes an end rather than a means, it makes it harder for translation theory to adopt something like a standard empirical methodology, one in which hypotheses can be proposed and tested, and then corroborated or falsified. Falsification can be a tricky enough matter in empirical practice, but how can you even try to falsify a definition or a metaphor? Definitions are matters of agreement and convention:

let us agree to call this thing or this concept X; if someone wants to call it Y, or if someone wants to use X to refer to something else, there might be some confusion; but there is no empirical claim here that can be tested against evidence. True, metaphors and definitions can become worn and outdated, and are in this sense "tested" by time; so are empirical theories tested in one sense – but I do not mean this sense here.

For instance, some scholars use the term "adequacy" to refer to the target-source relation ("equivalence"), others to refer to the relation between the translation and its function ("acceptability"): this makes for confusion, but on what ground can we claim that one or the other usage is wrong? The probable outcome is either that one or the other usage will prevail, or that the term will sink out of sight altogether as scholars get frustrated with having to explain which sense they mean. The co-existence of conflicting definitions is thus tested in the scholarly community and probably found wanting, but the definitions or usages themselves are not either right or wrong.

An empirical paradigm gives less emphasis to the fine-tuning of definitions and the play of metaphors. Instead, it explores hypotheses that can be set up on the basis of perhaps rough-and-ready definitions, trying to test claims and predictions against evidence. Better definitions may then emerge as one result of such testing; so might new metaphors that could suggest further hypotheses. Only in this way, I think, can translation theory claim to make any real progress.

2. Translation typology

2.1 Background

At the centre of an empirical paradigm are translations themselves. With Toury (1995) and many others, I take this to be the natural starting-place (rather than source texts). Also with Toury and others, we can take the initial empirical aim of translation theory to be the description of translations: both at the most general level, and at levels pertaining to a specific culture and/or time and/or text-type and/or translator etc. We do not need an ultimate definition of "translation" before we start; we can begin by looking at the things people seem to call translations, with a preliminary, working definition, and continue from there. The demarcation problem ("what is the boundary between a translation and a text that is not a translation?") may solve itself, as we learn more about what we are looking at: it does not necessarily have to be solved in advance. We may even find that the kinds of things some people call *translations* sometimes differ somewhat from the kinds of things that other people call *Übersetzungen* etc.

Research in translation description can take several directions: (a) describing the *intralinguistic profiles* of translations as compared to the profiles of non-translated texts of the same text-type etc. in the target culture (parallel texts); (b) describing the *interlinguistic profiles* of translations in terms of the relations between translations (of a given type) and their source texts, i.e. what kinds of equivalence relations seem to exist; and (c) describing the *extralinguistic relations* between translations and the circumstances under which they are produced and the socio-cultural context in which they become embedded. All these methods are well established, and many studies of these kinds can be found in the descriptive literature (add your favourite references here!).

One result of such research into translation profiles should be a basic theory of translation types (as distinct from text-types such as "literary" or "technical"). Such a taxonomy would be of relevance to both theory and practice. There have been some proposals along these lines, but we do not yet seem to have a generally accepted, systematic typology that would be more sophisticated than simple binary systems such as literal vs. free, semantic vs. communicative, overt vs. covert, documentary vs. instrumental; and more interrelated than lists of isolated special types such as dubbing or subtitling or gist translation, which foreground one particular feature. Over 60 terms for translation types are mentioned in Shuttleworth and Cowie (1997); many of these are near-synonyms, or overlap with others. Various criteria for a translation typology have been discussed e.g. by Gouadec (1990), Ibrahim (1994), Sager (1994: 179–184; 1997) and Nord (1997: 50f); the following proposal has borrowed from all these. It is an exercise in conceptual analysis, with the aim of developing preliminary conceptual tools that can be used in subsequent empirical research. Subsequent research might of course also show that these conceptual tools are inappropriate, too complex, or incomplete… in which case we can try to adapt the model, or simply abandon it and try again in a different way.

A typology of translations, i.e. of translation products, can be set up as a configuration of a limited number of variables. Each variable may have any of several different values. We can start by distinguishing four sets of variables:

A. Equivalence variables (source-target-text relations)
B. Target-language variables
C. Translator variables
D. Special situational variables

Let us now expand each set in turn. More delicacy could obviously be added, but even with the following set of 16 variables we arrive at a fairly complex typology.

2.2 Equivalence variables

A1. *Function*: same or different? – Is the main function of the target text intended to be "the same" as that of the source text, or not? If not, what? (Different function leads to an adaptation of some kind.)

A2. *Content*: all, selected, reduced or added, or some combination of these? – Does the translation represent all the source content, or select particular parts of it (keyword translation) or reduce the content overall (summary translation, gist translation; subtitling), or add some elements such as explanations (exegetic translation)?

A3. *Form*: what are the formal equivalence priorities, what formal elements of the source text are preserved? – The main ones are text-type ("same" or different? Different genre, e.g. verse to prose, sonnet to lyric?); text structure; sentence divisions (full-stops preserved: a common interpretation of what is meant by literal translation); word/morpheme structure (gloss translation, linguistic translation); other (e.g. sounds – phonemic translation, transliteration, transcription; or lip-movements – dubbing).

A4. *Style*: evidently intended to be "same" or different? – If different, in what way (another sense of adaptation)?

A5. *Source-text revision* for error correction: evident or not (implicit or explicit)? Minimal or major? – Has the translator "edited" the source text during translation, corrected factual errors, improved awkward style and communication quality, or is the source reproduced without corrections or improvements? This is the "cleaning-up transediting" mentioned by Stetting (1989). (For cultural transediting, see under B2.)

A6. *Status*: is the status of the target text, with respect to the status of the source text, autonomous, equal, parallel or derived? (Sager 1994: 180.) – This status is *autonomous* if the source text had only provisional status, such as a draft letter or notes; *equal* if both texts are functionally and legally equal, such as legislation in bilingual countries, official EU texts; *parallel* if the translation appears alongside the source text and is functionally parallel to it, e.g. in multilingual product descriptions (incidental translation); *derived* in other cases. To these status categories we might add one that we could call *subordinate*, referring to cases where the source text is co-present, as in gloss or interlinear translation, but the target text is not functionally parallel. Yet another aspect of status, occurring together with any of the above-mentioned ones, is whether the source text actually used in the translation is the original text (direct translation) or some intermediary version in a third language (indirect translation); in the latter case, the status of the target text might be said to be *once-removed* (or even twice-removed, etc.).

2.3 Target-language variables

B1. *Acceptability.* – A small number of subtypes can be distinguished here.
  i. Good native style: fluent and readable, may involve editing (communicative translation).
  ii. 100% native style: no signs of translationese, conforms to target text-type norms (covert translation).
  iii. Deliberately marked, resistant to target stylistic norms (foreignized translation).
  iv. Grammatical: grammatically faultless but clearly a translation, features of translationese (overt translation, whether by intention or not).
  v. Intelligible: comprehensible, but with grammatical and stylistic weaknesses. Usually not publishable without native revision.
  vi. Machine translation (with or without postediting).
  vii. Unintelligible.
  (Some of these subtypes thus require a competent native speaker of the target language.)

B2. *Localized* or not? – Is the translation adapted to local cultural norms (localized translation, yet another sense of adaptation)? Stylistic norms such as British or American English also come in here.

B3. *Matched* or not? – Is the translation matched with a defined set of previous texts, e.g. those produced by the client's company, to conform to client-specific norms (e.g. via the use of a translation memory system)? (EU "hybrid translations", for instance, or translations that have to be standardized to a particular format.) An extreme form of literary translation might even seek to match the style of a particular individual writer (parody translation).

2.4 Translator variables

C1. *Visibility.* – Is the translator visible, e.g. in footnotes, a commentary or preface, via inserted terms from the source text in brackets, via evidence of the translator's own particular ideology (learned translation, philological translation, commentary translation, thick translation; feminist translation, polemical translation)?

C2. *Individual* or team? – Are there indications suggesting that the text was translated by more than one translator?

C3. *Native speaker* of target or source language, or neither (– inverse translation if the translator is a native speaker of the source language)?

C4. *Professional* or amateur? This is obviously a complex continuum, not a simple binary difference. At the professional end we expect to find, for instance, evidence of adequate world and domain knowledge, adequate background documentation, adequate technical equipment, adequate knowledge of intended readership, etc. Are there indications of non-professional translatorial behaviour, such as carelessness?

2.5 Special situational variables

The number of situational variables is virtually infinite, and many (such as client helpfulness, actual availability of documentation…) may leave no visible traces in the translation. Here are three main ones:

D1. *Space*: constraints of layout, screen space, speech bubbles, total pages…
D2. *Medium*: same (written or spoken) as source text, or not? (E.g. sight translation, from written to oral.) Also: use or presence of other semiotic systems, other media, diagrams… (screen translation, dubbing, Gouadec's diagrammatic translation…).
D3. *Time*: are there indications suggesting that the translation had to be done in an unusual hurry? A careless translation might (rightly or wrongly) give such an impression, for instance.

2.6 Default values

Mathematically, the total number of possible combinations of these variables is enormous. Fortunately, by no means all of them are equally likely to occur, and not all the configurations are even logically possible. We might start reducing the number of possible and reasonably likely types to a more manageable size, first, by specifying default values for each of the variables, for example as follows (where "same" is of course understood to have quotes around it):

A1: Same function
A2: All content
A3: Same text-type and structure
A4: Same style
A5: Minimal implicit source-text revision
A6: Derived status, direct translation
B1: Good native
B2: Not localized

B3:   Not matched
C1:   Invisible translator
C2:   Individual translator
C3:   Target language native
C4:   Professional
D1:   No special space constraints
D2:   Same, written, medium
D3:   Adequate time…

This set of default values would thus correspond to what we might call the *default prototype* concept of a translation, in the minds of most clients or readers of translations. It purports to represent the "folk view" of what a typical translation is. (Note: the view of professional translators, on the other hand, might well be rather different with respect to some of these variables… Such possible differences would in themselves be worth researching.) Strictly speaking, of course, these default values actually represent no more than my hypothesis about what such a folk view might be, and as such is open to testing and possible refutation or refinement.

Other fairly frequently occurring combinations of values might also be specified, such as the following, which highlight one particular value or group of values.[1]

Localized: values as default (unless otherwise specified), except for B2.
Source-edited: values as default (unless otherwise specified or determined by A5), except for major source-text revision.
Localized and source-edited: both the above combined.
Absolute translation (Gouadec's term): values as default, except for A5 (there is absolutely no editing, no alteration to content or quality of communication, all mistakes in the original retained, perhaps marked with [sic]); perhaps also except for C3 (not relevant?). The value for B1 may also be affected.
Summary translation: default values for A1, A6, B, C and D; A2 reduced content, and A3–5 as affected by this value for A2.
Matched or *standardized translation*: default values except for B3, allowing for the effects of this B3 value on other variables as required.

2.7   Applications

What might be the use of such typological analysis? There are two main areas of application, one upstream and the other downstream of the translating act. An ideal translation brief, for instance, might be defined as one that specified all the relevant values for all these variables, or at least for those that were considered most relevant, or those for which the values were not default ones. The values would then represent task requirements. Clients might be given a form to fill in, in which they are asked to tick relevant boxes etc. for a particular translation task. For such purposes, a translation agency can develop its own set of frequently used types, such as those suggested above, alongside the default prototype. Clients who have been informed what is meant by "default" have to indicate "Default or not?" If not, "Some other frequent type? – Please indicate" If not, "Please specify values required". In some circumstances, particular choices of values may lead to different costs: requirements at A5, B, C4 or D, for instance. At B1, would level (iv), (v) or (vi) be adequate for the client's needs? You get what you pay for. Such a procedure may help to convince clients that translating is a more complex business than might appear, and encourage them to clarify their own expectations and attitudes. In current practice, it is more likely that the translator will have to *infer* the relevant values on the basis of what he or she can find out or intelligently guess.

The second application is purely descriptive and empirical, downstream. Here, the values are not specified in advance but discovered after analysis; they are characteristics of the translation profile, not the translation brief. In this sense, they are conceptual research tools. (This is the sense in which the values have been formulated, above.)

For example: I have just bought a Post-it Memoboard, one of those notice-boards with a self-stick surface. The instructions for use come in several languages, but since it is marked "Made in USA" I assume the English version is the original. Here is the English, followed by the French translation.

- Lay the Bulletin Board on to a flat surface with its cork pattern facing down. Peal the backing from one side on each of the pieces of foam tape and apply to the back of the board as shown [there are pictures alongside, in the original].
- Next, peal the backing from the exposed sides of the foam tape.
- Your Bulletin Board can now be mounted on a wall. (Be sure the surface is clean and dry). Visually position it before applying. Then press it against the wall at the areas corresponding with the mounting tape.
- The clear, protective film must now be removed from the cork pattern surface. Use your fingernail to scratch up a corner and slowly peal it back at 180°. Wait 5 minutes before using.
- Posez le panneau d'adhésif repositionnable Post-it^{TM} 558 sur sa face liège, et répartissez les pastilles de mousse au dos comme indiqué.
- Retirer le papier protecteur des pastilles de mousse.
- Appliquez votre panneau sur une surface propre, sèche, et de préférence lisse.
- Retirez le film protecteur transparent, lentement et selon un angle de 180°. Attendre 5 minutes environ avant la première utilisation.

Of what type is this translation? There does not seem to be a single label available that would be adequate, but we could characterize it as follows:

A1: same function
A2: mostly all content, but some reduction and some addition
A3: text-type and overall text structure
A4: intended to be "same"
A5: no source-revision
A6: parallel, presumably direct
B1: grammatical, at least
B2: presumably localized (use of brand name)
B3: presumably not matched (I have not checked this)
C1: not visible
C2: no evidence
C3: seems native French
C4: perhaps amateur? (cf. the odd variation between imperative and infinitive)
D1: space constraint of layout
D2: same medium; presence of diagrams alongside
D3: perhaps some evidence of time pressure?

This characterization can then be compared to that of the other translations accompanying this particular product. Do the others seem to be done by native or non-native speakers of the target language, for instance? (I could perhaps check this, and some of the other points, by contacting the manufacturer or importer.) How do these translations compare with other product descriptions of a similar type? Can I offer the above characterization as applying generally to translations of instructions for use accompanying simple kinds of office equipment? In other words, does it actually represent a common type of translation?

This kind of profile description can obviously be linked to quality assessment: are the values discovered (characteristics) close enough to the values set by the client (requirements), or to those needed or expected by the readers (expectancies)? Some of the characteristics might seem to be intentional, others unintentional (e.g. with respect to B1).

Descriptive studies of translation profiles can thus incorporate a classification of translations, as belonging (prototypically or marginally) to a particular translation type, characterized by certain values of certain variables. Ultimately, these types are no more than generalizations based on frequently recurring profiles.

Toury takes descriptive studies one step further, with his point (1995: 15f) that we can also test the adequacy (in the sense of 'quality') of our descriptions by making predictions, hypotheses. On the basis of our profile analysis, we can predict that, given certain conditions, translations of this kind of source text will tend to look like that, they will tend to have that feature: more generally, they will tend to be translations of a given type. (These are of course probabilistic predictions only, not absolute ones.) This is an important methodological step, because in this way we can test the generality of our descriptions and expose them to the risk of falsification, or at the very least to rigorous criticism. Only in this way can they become robust. Unfortunately, however, it seems that we often take our descriptive results for granted, generalizing from particular case-studies without testing. We are too often content with a *post hoc* description, an analysis of what has happened in this particular instance. Such a description can be a source for important hypotheses, and is a valuable first step in a research project; but, without further testing, the validity of the description itself can extend no further than the case in question.

Compare the common procedure followed in experimental research: I set up certain conditions, select my subjects (e.g. translators) and perform my experiment, and see what happens. I discover that my subjects tend to do such-and-such, that their think-aloud protocols have these features, that the resulting translations look like this. This might lead me to posit various generalizations or hypotheses, which I can then go on and test on other subjects in (I hope) the same conditions. The results of this testing procedure might, or might not, confirm what I had noticed in the first experiment. If so, my hypotheses are corroborated; if not, I must look for an explanation: are the hypotheses wrong, or were the conditions somehow different, or have I overlooked something, or what? – Descriptions of translation profiles are, from the viewpoint of empirical methodology, very similar to such experimental hypotheses.

3. Translatorial causality

3.1 Proximate causes

Chomsky is often given the credit for introducing the concept of explanatory adequacy into linguistics in the 1960s. His claim was that linguistics should seek not only to describe linguistic data / the structure of language, but also to explain why the structure had to be like this, i.e. to relate linguistics to psychology.

In translation theory, the study of relationships (interlinguistic, intralinguistic, extralinguistic) leads first to statements of correlation, of covariance: we might observe that a given socio-cultural feature seems to co-vary with a given translational feature. Statements or hypotheses of correlation might in some cases be the strongest ones we can make with proper justification, but in other cases we might also wish to make even stronger ones, involving causality. One difficulty here, however, is that in translation theory the search for causal explanations includes not only psychology, but much else besides. After all, any event or phenomenon may have multiple causes, and translations certainly do.

If we focus on the question "why?" as we look at our descriptive data, the immediate answer is obvious. Why do we have this feature in the translation, why is the translation of this type, why do our variables seem to manifest these values? In the example above, of the Post-it noticeboard: why did the French translator include the trademark, why the omission of some content in the third and fourth sections? Simply, because the translator made such-and-such a decision. So the first step towards explanatory adequacy takes us from translational matters into translatorial ones. At this point, think-aloud protocols come into their own as one way of getting at the decision-making process: they can offer hypotheses about the immediate or *proximate cause* of translational phenomena, the proximate cause being something in the translator's mind. Here too, we can test our hypotheses by making predictions about the ways translators (of a given type) will behave when faced with certain types of source texts and translation tasks.

One reservation needs to be made here. These proximate mental causes have also been called reasons, as a subtype of cause. By including them within a broad notion of causality we can appeal to forms of explanation in terms of motivation, justification and rationale; but at this point predictability may lose something of its relevance. After all, certain human actions may be very hard to predict, but, once they have taken place, it may be relatively easy to attribute a rational motivation to them, after the fact. (See also Melby 1995: 95.)

The causality chain does not end in the translator's head, of course. We can then ask: why did the translator make this decision? In our example, why decide to vary between French infinitive and imperative (if this was indeed a conscious decision)? This then opens up a whole host of issues; some of these have been treated explicitly in terms of causality (for instance in Gutt's application of relevance theory, 1991), but with respect to others the causality aspect has been only implicit. Let us explore a few of these external causes.

3.2 Aristotelian causes

As part of his general discussion of causation and translation history, Pym (1998) applies Aristotle's four causes to translation approximately as follows. Material cause: the source-language text, a word processor etc. (I would add the target language, from which the target text is sculpted.) Formal cause: translation norms. Efficient cause: the mind, body and personality of the translator (this seems partly to be a proximate, internal cause); we might also add the client, who initiates the translating process. Final cause: the translation skopos. Each of these causes can be explored empirically, in a way that can generate testable hypotheses.

Research in contrastive analysis has to do with the material cause, the linguistic material with which the translator works. We can set up hypotheses of the form:

given this SL item, I predict that translators (of this type, given this kind of translation brief) will select item X from the target language – or even that a machine translation system will do this. I might predict, for instance, that translators who are non-native speakers of the target language will be less familiar with text-type norms, such as the French ones concerning infinitives in instructions.

A central conceptual tool here is that of the translation strategy. By this, I mean a standard, well-tried textual solution to a particular kind of translation problem, either one that is specific to a given source-target language pair, or one that is valid more generally. We observe the results of strategies as features of translation profiles: in our example, we note a variation between infinitives and imperatives, for instance, that seems significantly different from the frequency of occurrence of these forms in comparable parallel texts. Such observations can also be formulated as kinds of relation between source and target texts: there are changes from source imperatives to French target infinitives. In the example, we also note that the French translator has made some use of a strategy according to which sentence breaks can be changed (in the first and third sections). He or she has also made changes in cohesion (nothing corresponding to *Next* in the second section), has made liberal use of the strategies of omission and implicitation in sections three and four. We can perhaps infer from this that the translator implicitly or explicitly knows the existence of these strategies; we might also infer that the translator knows (or, if we are critical of the result, that the translator does not know) the conditions under which they can appropriately be used. The target text has the profile it has *because* the translator has used these strategies. This is a causal explanation at the Aristotelian level: material cause, a particular manipulation of target-language material on the basis of a source-text input. (For more on strategies and their various types, see Chesterman 1997a: Chapter 4.)

But why did the translator do this? Not only because he/she thought it was possible and perhaps appropriate, but also no doubt for other reasons. Because of a wish to conform to a particular translation norm, for instance – a particular belief, on the part of the client or the target public or the professional translator community, about what proper translations should be like (i.e. a formal cause). Norms are also central categories in an empirical translation theory, precisely because they provide explanatory hypotheses. I will not go here into the various classifications of norms that have been proposed, but they all share an implicit causality aspect. In our example, we might refer to a norm of optimum communication or acceptability, believed in by the translator, which underlies the decision to use omission and implicitation strategies: this would make for better readability, for instance. Other norms might have to do with the optimal relation with the source text, or with target text-type conventions, or the like. The translator's awareness of such norms, and the wish to conform to them (or not to conform to them), thus constitute the motivation for the decisions in question. (Alternatively, of course, an amateur translator may have *no* awareness of such norms – which in itself might be one form of explanation.)

Another way to answer "why?" is to appeal to the efficient cause, the translator himself or herself, even including such intangible aspects as cognitive processes and personal values. I translate like this because the human mind works on the relevance principle when communicating, it seeks an optimal balance between effort invested and benefit predicted. Or: I translate like this because it is the best I can do; I know I am not a native speaker of French but I have been asked to do the job and I need the money and I can't afford to get the translation checked by a native and the client doesn't care so much about the final textual quality anyway, as long as it is comprehensible; I'm not a very good translator, I admit, certainly not a professional. Or: I translate using non-sexist language because I have certain ethical convictions, for instance. My personal beliefs and opinions, and to some extent perhaps even my personality, affect the kinds of solutions I tend to prefer, the decisions I make. Translators with different beliefs and personalities might decide differently: here again, we might propose testable hypotheses.

For some scholars, Aristotle's final cause is the most important one, a kind of ultimate cause: I make this decision and use strategy such-and-such because of the skopos of the translation, a skopos that I have defined for myself in accordance with the brief and the client's wishes (or perhaps in spite of the brief). Change the skopos, and we can predict that the translation profile will also change.

3.3 Socio-cultural causes

But beneath these Aristotelian causes we can find still other, underlying causes: social, political, economic, ideological, historical, biological… These are the causes we have to appeal to if we ask "why do translation norms like this exist in this culture?", "why do people have these beliefs and attitudes about translation?", or "why do translators tend to have these personality features?", or "why does this target language prefer nominal structures?". Or even "why on earth is this text being translated at all (into this language)?" Or: "why does the client give the job to someone like me, knowing that I'm not French?" The so-called cultural turn in translation studies has focused largely on this level of causal explanation, looking at the way translation profiles and translatorial decisions are affected by broader socio-cultural and historical factors: in short, it has started to look at translation sociology. An extremely pertinent question, for instance, is that concerning the initiator of the translation: is this someone (or some institution) in the source culture, so that the translation is "imposed" on the target culture, or someone in the target culture who "requisitions" the translation from the source culture, or someone else entirely (Dollerup 1997)? The identity of the initiator from this point of view may be a major cause of particular translatorial decisions.

Here too, we can venture some predictive hypotheses, although few scholars seem to have done so, to test the validity of our explanations. Given certain social and cultural conditions, for instance, will it indeed always be the case that translators will tend to translate according to some kind of fluency ideal (conforming to an acceptability norm) rather than in some other way? To some extent, hypotheses derived from the analysis of one historical situation can be tested on other historical data: claims that are tested in this way I have called "quasi-falsifiable" (Chesterman 1997b), for such hypotheses are not predictive in the strictest chronological sense of the term: they are not tested in not-yet-existing future situations, but in already-existing situations that the scholar in question does not happen to have investigated yet. For instance, Venuti's hypothesis (1995) about the exalted status attributed to dominant-culture source texts when these are translated into smaller, emergent cultures does not seem to be supported by data from Finnish translation history (Paloposki 1996), and is thus (partially) quasi-falsified by such data.

Factors such as those we have been considering are sometimes presented as constraints on translatorial freedom – but such constraints also have causal force. Lefevere (1992a), for example, lists patronage (= mainly the client), target-language poetic conventions, the socially acceptable universe of discourse (subject matter), the source and target languages themselves, and the translator's own ideology as constraints which determine the way in which translators can manipulate texts.

3.4 Causal laws

Eventually, well-corroborated hypotheses might be crystallized into laws: probabilistic laws determining translatorial behaviour under certain conditions. Such laws are of course also open to testing and amendment, even rejection, as circumstances change or as our understanding of translatorial causality changes. They are laws about what translators tend to do: either all translators in general, or perhaps some subset of them, such as accredited professional translators (see Chesterman 1997a: 70f). As a result, they are also laws that incorporate predictions about translation profiles. Toury (1995: 259f) proposes two candidates for such laws: the law of interference and the law of standardization. He also suggests a number of associated and testable hypotheses. The task of empirical research is then to establish the conditions under which such laws seem to hold, with what probability, or under which they do not hold. When, for instance, do translators tend to translate in a transgressive fashion, deliberately exploiting interference? And when do they tend to reject this way of translating and prefer an overall strategy of fluent, standardized target style? What kinds of social, historical and other reasons seem to affect such laws?

Toury presents these two laws in a descriptive framework, as relations between variables (some variables being conditions, others being translatorial actions or the resulting features of translation profiles). Ultimately, however, such laws are causal. In same way as I can reply (e.g. to a child's question "why?") that the glass falls off the corner of my desk *because of* the law of gravity, so too I can say that translators tend to do this (or that translation profiles tend to look like this) because of the law of interference or standardization. Beyond this explanation I can then suggest others, as responses to subsequent "why" questions, as suggested above. At the psychological level: translators tend to do this sort of thing because human nature is like this, human cognition works like this in communication (– the relevance-theory position), the language faculty of a bilingual person seems to favour these sorts of tendencies. Behind this psychological causation we can then see other possible kinds: social, cultural, ideological, economic – all the other factors that impinge upon the translator's mind. It is precisely these underlying factors that need to be specified as part of the conditions under which a given law is hypothesized to hold: then we can start testing.

A third causal law that might also be worth testing further is this:

Law of translatorial divergence: even given identical source texts and translation briefs and identical target languages, different translators will tend to make different decisions at some points, and thus the resulting translations will not have identical profiles.

This is a corollary of Quine's (1960) argument about translation indeterminacy. One underlying reason why this law seems to hold is that there is always a difference at the level of Aristotle's efficient cause: no two people have the same cognitive and emotional make-up. But it would be interesting to investigate the conditions under which such built-in variation tended to be more evident or less evident, where professionals, for instance, tended to agree on the form of an optimal translation (of a given item) and where they tended to disagree; whether professionals tended to agree more or less often than trainees, and so on. (See also the discussion in Melby 1995: 158f.)

The general point I want to stress here is that unless we *test* our hypotheses about causes, they remain speculative guesswork. And we can only test them by using them to make predictions, and then checking out these predictions. Only in this way can we ensure that our causal explanations are adequate (not necessarily true, of course, but at least reasonable approximations). One empirical goal of research on translation profiles, then, is to propose and test causal hypotheses, in the search for robust causal laws.

4. Translation effects

4.1 Laws of effect

So far, we have been considering translations as the results of various causes, both within the translator's mind and outside it. But empirical translation theory is also interested in translations themselves as causes, for translators are also agents of change, not just passive recipients of causal impulses. The decisions that translators make, and hence the translations that they produce, have effects on the people that read them, and also on intercultural relations more widely.

The empirical study of translation effects is currently a messy field, mixed up with beliefs about "sameness of effect", evaluative reactions of various kinds, and prescriptive statements. For a start, the effect of the mere *existence* of a translation needs to be distinguished from the effect of the *way* a given text has been translated. Effect itself is difficult to define, and even more difficult to measure. A preliminary definition, good enough to start us off, might be: an effect is a change of mental state (emotional, cognitive...) in the reader. This would be a *proximate effect*, comparable to the concept of proximate cause mentioned above; neither are directly observable. Some *secondary effects* might then be defined in terms of subsequent actions on the part of the reader or a group of readers, actions that are observable (such as buying a bar of chocolate, starting a washing-machine, converting to Christianity, ordering a meal in a restaurant...). These could be called behavioural effects. Other secondary effects are less easily observed (effects due to an increase of knowledge, an aesthetic experience...). *Tertiary effects* might then be observable in the target culture as a whole, and also in the intercultural relations between the source and target cultures. The target language norms (and the target language itself) might be affected, under the influence of incoming translations. Literary genres might shift. People might start to eat different kinds of food. There might be mass conversions to another religion. War might break out. Historical studies can examine the secondary and tertiary effects of translations as well as their causes.[*] Hypotheses about the effects of particular translation

---

[*] In a later paper (2005), included in this volume as Paper 4, above, I suggested the terms *reaction*, *response* and *repercussion* for these three kinds of effects.

types or methods or strategies can also be tested and perhaps quasi-falsified (see above) on other historical periods or other cultures, as well as experimentally. In this way, we might arrive at a limited number of general laws of effect, parallel to the causal laws I mentioned earlier.

To begin a conceptual analysis of the overall field of translation effect, I suggest three possible laws. I propose these as plausible initial hypotheses or candidates for laws, not as facts; however, I think you will agree that there is no shortage of general corroborating evidence to support them.

Law of heterogeneous effect: translations tend to have different effects on different people.

This law goes hand in hand with the third causal law mentioned above, that of translatorial divergence. People are different, with different cognitive backgrounds and life experiences, different aesthetic values and so on. It is scarcely surprising that we do not all react to a given translation in exactly the same way: we react differently even to texts that are not translations. Not necessarily completely differently, of course; but not identically, anyway. A particularly clear illustration of this is to be found in Puurtinen (1995): Puurtinen asked a group of translation studies students for their reactions to two very different Finnish translations of that American children's classic, [L. Frank Baum's] *The Wizard of Oz*. Opinions turned out to be divided, between those who preferred one translation (more fluent) and those who preferred the other (formally closer to the original). The reasons given showed different expectations about what children's literature should be like, what kind of language it should exploit, its basic function, and so on. It is also reasonable to expect that native speakers and non-native speakers of the target language will react differently, that reactions will depend also on degree of familiarity with the subject matter, on whether or not the reader can also speak the source language, etc. Here again, there is ample scope for research: under what conditions do we tend to find more compatible effects, and under what conditions do we find the biggest differences?

From this law (if indeed it holds good) we can derive the following fallacy of homogeneous effect: the belief that a given translation has the same effect on all readers.

My second law of effect runs as follows:

Law of changing effect: even with respect to a single reader, the effects of a translation change over time.

This also seems to be an obvious point: readers grow older, their socio-cultural environment changes, and so does their language. We therefore observe delayed effects. For example, professional translators can look back on translations they did years before and thought good then, and be surprised or even horrified at what they then submitted to the client... On a larger scale, cultures and languages change over history, and translation effects likewise. At least, this is what we would surely expect. It would be of interest to study cases where this law appeared not to hold (or not to hold so strongly), i.e. where reader reactions tended to remain surprisingly constant over time. An obvious example is the Authorized Version of the Bible in English, and certain translations of literary classics that have become classics in their own right, as translations. These are perhaps exceptions to the law of changing effect. (Research topic: are there correlations between the profiles of such translations and their tendency to trigger more constant reactions? Obviously yes; but what other factors might be involved? Sacred text status? Age at which readers encounter such texts for the first time? Other circumstances of initial encounters?)

The corresponding fallacy is represented by the belief that effects necessarily remain constant over time.

Third law of effect:

Law of multiple effect: even with respect to a single reader at a given time, translations tend to have more than one effect.

Even if we can pinpoint a central effect, there are usually side-effects as well. I might understand the translation telling me how to use my new washing-machine, and learn how to switch it on appropriately, but I might also be amused or puzzled at some aspects of the translation. A translated book about Poland during the war may give me information I did not know, but also move me to tears. A translated advertisement can be informative and persuasive and funny, all at the same time.

The associated fallacy is thus the belief in a single effect.

These three proposed laws have been stated here at the level of the individual reader. However, the laws apply even more obviously at the collective level of groups of readers, or the level of whole cultures. The larger the group, the more heterogeneity we would expect to find, the more historical variation and the greater the multiplicity of effect. Cases where this expected correlation appeared to be weak or non-existent, or even inverse, would be of particular interest.

4.2 Parameters of effect

Effects, however they are defined and at whatever level, can be potentially classified along a number of relevant parameters. In so doing, we usually need to abstract away from the level of the individual reader, and we also need to generalize upwards from detailed differences between effects. Classes of effect type are of necessary very rough and ready, open to further refinement. But we must start somewhere. Let us consider four possible parameters.

An obvious initial distinction is that between *intended* and *unintended effect*. Intended by the translator, that is, and/or intended by the client and/or the original writer. A relevant subdivision is then: (un)intended effect on intended vs. unintended readers: cf. below on sampling, and also Pym (1992b) on excluded, participative and observational receivers. I by-pass the problem of how to get at the intended effect exactly: intentions are notoriously slippery things. However, they are scarcely more slippery than the notion of skopos: indeed, the skopos of a translation might well be paraphrased precisely as its intended effect on its intended readers. This is perhaps the main parameter for the consideration of translation errors: compare the functionalist definition of error proposed by Nord (1997b: 73): "a particular expression or utterance is not inadequate in itself; it only becomes inadequate with regard to the communicative function it was supposed to achieve."

Reader reactions that relate to this distinction may be illustrated by the following list (adapted from Chesterman 1997a: 122).

- You mean this is supposed to be funny?
- You mean this is meant for children??
- Well, I followed these translated instructions, but the machine still didn't work.
- I wonder what on earth the translator was thinking of when he/she wrote that?
- I wonder what this bit means? It doesn't make sense.

A second parameter is the effect of the translation *de re* as opposed to the effect *de dicto*. The *de re* effect is that of the message itself, whereas the *de dicto* effect is that of the form of the message, such as the readability level. A translation critic or an examiner, for instance, usually observes *de dicto* effects in addition to *de re* ones; other kinds of readers tend to neglect the *de dicto* effects unless their attention is specifically drawn to them. Translation scholars unfortunately look at every translated text they meet at this *de dicto* level… Some sample reaction-types for *de dicto* effects:

- X doesn't sound right.
- It sounds old-fashioned.
- There is something about the style that I don't like, but I can't quite put my finger on it.
- What a lot of misprints!
- I wouldn't say it like that.
- This reads just like a translation.
- I kept getting distracted by the language itself, which made it difficult to focus on what was being actually said.

A third parameter ranges from *desirable* to *undesirable effect*. Desirable, after all, may not coincide with intended. And then come the question: desirable to whom? To the same party as the one doing the intending, or a different one? Further subclasses arise: desirable to the translator, the client, to the reader… This is another central parameter for the consideration of translation errors. Examples of typical reactions relating to this parameter (in addition to the above *de dicto* ones):

- I think the client would reject this.
- I am the client, and I do reject this.
- [A thank you from the client, or even from the reader.]
- Comment by the original writer: Your translation is even better than my original!
- Comment by sales manager: Our sales have doubled since that last ad campaign based on your translation!
- The translator has acted unethically here, misrepresenting the source culture.

A fourth parameter is provided by the notion of sameness or *similarity*: effects that are (more) similar to those of the source text on source readers vs. those that are not similar or less similar (either by intention or by oversight…). Here again we meet the question of which source/target readers, intended or unintended, etc. Sample reactions:

- X doesn't mean the same as that source-text item.
- The style seems quite different from the original.
- The original was funny, but this isn't.
- The play was a great success in America, but its Finnish version got a poor response in Helsinki.[2]

Some of these reactions are evaluative, but some are purely descriptive. A full analysis of effect would have to account for all these parameters, and no doubt more as well. Additionally, a quantitative aspect might be added: degree or intensity of effect, along each of the various parameters. How to measure this intensity, however, remains problematic. One possible approach might be provided by relevance theory, and its notion of mental processing effort on the part of the receiver of a communication (Sperber and D. Wilson 1986, Gutt 1991). In most cases, the more the effort needed to process the message, the more benefit should accrue when the message is finally interpreted. Relevance is thus understood as a relation between processing cost and contextual benefit (where "contextual" means roughly 'concerning the receiver's state of knowledge'). This processing cost can be partly measured in terms of time taken, but other methods need to be developed as well: I guess that processing time alone will not necessarily correlate with degree of intensity along all the various parameters mentioned above, although it is obviously one factor (additional *de dicto* reactions presumably take more time, for instance). Moreover, processing effort in relevance theory primarily has to do with the effort invested to interpret a given message, not with possible reactions to the message after it has been interpreted. We need additional methodological tools here, and more differentiated notions of effort. Allusions, for instance, seem to produce more reader satisfaction if *no* effort is required to interpret them, as Ritva Leppihalme (1997: 32–3) has suggested: readers then feel flattered, addressed as members of an in-group that recognizes such allusions, together with the author.

4.3   The sampling problem

We cannot investigate what effects a given translation has on every reader, not even on every intended reader. We therefore have to use samples, and this raises a serious problem. How do we know that the people manifesting the reactions we want to study are typical (and intended) readers? If they are not typical, how can we generalize from our observations about them? This may sound an all-too-obvious point, but consider the cases where translation effects are most commonly assessed: a translation examiner or instructor assessing the work of trainees, a reviser checking the work of a junior translator, a literary critic reviewing a new translation of a novel, a translation scholar evaluating the translation of some political texts, a professional translator justifying his/her own strategies and principles. On what grounds can we take the reactions of these kinds of people to be typical? Do they even think of themselves as typical readers?

They are in fact highly *un*typical in several respects. They have an in-built focus that includes *de dicto* factors, unlike most naive typical readers, as mentioned above. They usually have some proficiency in the source language as well as the target language, unlike the typical reader. They usually have the source text available, as a source of comparison, unlike the typical reader. Their very purpose in reading a translation is in order to criticize or analyse or monitor it, not simply to receive and understand the message conveyed.

It would be good to see research on how close the reactions of this professional subset are to the reactions of the wider set of which they form an untypical part. Do the general public who read EU documents intended for a wide readership actually appreciate the use of an EU style which the client institution and many of its professional translators seem to prefer, or would the man in the street actually prefer something different (desirability parameter)? It would also be good to see more research directly studying the reactions of this wider readership.

A recent paper by Cumps (1996) provides a suggestive example. He studied the reactions of law students to texts that were written (not translated) in legalese vs. other versions written in plain English. Law students, note, not the general public; but certainly the subset of the public that would constitute the intended readership of such texts. The background to Cumps' study was earlier findings that English-speaking judges and lawyers showed a strong preference for plain English versions rather than legalese versions. Cumps hypothesized that law students would manifest different attitudes, because legalese would correspond more closely to the style they would *expect* legal documents to be in. The results were about 50–50, a roughly equal preference for each style. When required subsequently to translate the two versions into Dutch, students performed much better on the plain English one, as might be expected.

It would be interesting to see such studies replicated for other languages, with a variety of text types, and on a wider scale.

4.4 The prescriptive problem[3]

In order to check hypotheses about translation effects, we can test them out. We make predictions, of the form "translations with these features will tend to have such-and-such effects", and then check to see whether our predictions come true. Or do we? Mostly, it seems, we do not, but rely on our experience and imagination… As translators, we imagine what the effects of particular translational features will be, perhaps on particular readers, and then decide to incorporate or not to incorporate such features accordingly. I tend to avoid ungrammatical sentences because I guess my readers will not like them; at least in the past, at university, my teacher always put a red line through ungrammaticalities… As scholars, on the other hand, we should perhaps be testing our predictions and hypotheses rather more than we do.

I suggest that this point applies in particular to prescriptive statements.[*] After all, a prescriptive statement is simply a form of hypothesis, usually concerning the desirability parameter. To say, prescriptively, that "translators should do X" is simply to predict that if they do *not* do X the resulting effect will be undesirable in some way (usually unspecified). Effect on whom? In the first place, presumably the effect on the person making the prescriptive statement. But is this person necessarily a typical reader? – This is the sampling problem again…

---

[*] See above, Paper 5 in this volume, for a fuller discussion of this point.

We can appeal here to ethical principles, taking a utilitarian view of ethics: if an ethically good translation is defined as one that has ethically good effects (i.e. effects that are deemed desirable according to some agreed ethical principle or value), then ethical translators should seek to produce such translations, with such effects. This ethical appeal would require that we do indeed *know* that such translations have such effects, because we have tested and corroborated this hypothesis by examining past translations of a comparable kind and identifying their resulting effects on readers and cultures, or because we have convincing experimental evidence.

Many traditional prescriptive statements are of course the result of years of experience, of a wide knowledge of translation norms and practices, so that these hypotheses have been *implicitly* tested many times over. I do not need to test the law of gravity every day by pushing a glass off the edge of the table. However, all too often such testing and corroboration is neglected, and we seem faced with general prescriptions that translators "should" translate literary works in a transgressive or abusive way, or that they "should" follow EU official style in all text-types, or that creative metaphors "should" be translated in such-and-such a way, or that translators "should" use footnotes in such-and-such cases, or that they "should always" or "should never" improve the original style. My willingness to accept such statements would be much enhanced if they were backed by evidence that they had been properly tested and corroborated. Here again, I would make a plea for much more application of reader response theory, for more psychological studies of comprehension and readability with respect to various kinds of translations, for sociological questionnaire surveys of reader preferences, and so on.

In the recent history of translation theory (perhaps since James Holmes), the urge to reject prescriptive statements has been understandable, because so often they have seemed devoid of any empirical justification, mere teachers' or scholars' prejudices. But I would argue that this rejection has been mistaken, insofar as it has made it difficult for translation studies to develop an empirical theory of translation effects. Rather than reject prescriptivism, we should incorporate it into our empirical theory, testing its hypotheses just as we would test any others. Such testing needs to be aware of the sampling problem mentioned above, the various types of possible readers. We might also profit by broadening the focus of our testing to encompass other effect parameters apart from that of desirability. And we should be realistic enough to accept that, just as a knowledge of causes cannot permit us to predict exactly what a given translation profile will look like (law of translatorial divergence), so too we will never be able to predict exactly what effects a given translation profile will have (cf. all my three laws of effect).

5. Conclusion

I have argued that empirical translation theory has three main aims (cf. also Chesterman 1997a: 48): (a) to describe what translators do, what strategies they use, under what conditions; (b) to explain why they do this, and to propose testable causal laws; and (c) to assess the effects of translatorial actions on readers and cultures, and to propose testable laws of effect. So much for purely theoretical research. What we then *do* with the resulting knowledge is another matter entirely, although eventual applications may of course serve to motivate such theoretical work. We might apply it in translator training, in developing methods of evaluation, in refining codes of translator ethics, in writing dictionaries, in programming computers, in attempts to change translation norms, in intercultural social engineering – whatever.

Notes

1. This section has been inspired by Emma Wagner's call for a theory of the translation product, and by her own suggestion for a translation typology (private communication) for use in the translation of EU texts. [See, subsequently, Chesterman and Wagner 2002: *Can Theory Help Translators?* Manchester: St. Jerome Publishing.]

2. Precisely this observation has been made by Ritva Leppihalme, with respect to Mamet's play *Oleanna*, in a paper ("*Oleanna* in Finnish – what went wrong?") read at: David Mamet at 50: A Birthday Celebration and a Conference. Oct. 30–Nov. 1, 1997, Las Vegas, Nevada. [See now Leppihalme 2000a.] Leppihalme also contributed a number of other observations on a first draft of this article, for which I am grateful. Many thanks also to Outi Paloposki for her comments, and to Daniel Gile for his. Final responsibility for the text remains my own, of course.

3. The germ of the argument developed here first came to me during a seminar paper given by Lauri Carlson, at the University of Helsinki; Carlson argued that the whole prescriptive vs. descriptive distinction was a red herring.

PAPER 10

A causal model for Translation Studies[*]

Three basic models of translation are used in translation research. The first is a comparative model, which aligns translations either with their source texts or with parallel (untranslated) texts and examines correlations between the two. This model is evident in contrastive studies. The second model is a process model, which maps different phases of the translation process over time. This model is represented by communication approaches, and also by some protocol approaches. The third model is a causal one, in which translations are explicitly seen both as caused by antecedent conditions and as causing effects on readers and cultures.

The four standard kinds of hypotheses (interpretive, descriptive, explanatory and predictive) are outlined and illustrated with reference to the phenomenon of retranslation. Only the causal modal can accommodate all four types, and it is hence the most fruitful model for future development in Translation Studies. Descriptive hypotheses (such as statements about universals or laws) can have explanatory force, but almost all causal influences are filtered through the individual translator's mind, through particular decisions made by the translator at a given time.

Keywords: causality, model, effect, hypothesis, universal

1. Models

'Theory' and 'model' are slippery concepts. The recent *Dictionary of Translation Studies* (Shuttleworth and Cowie 1997) refers only to the following as theories: Skopos Theory, Polysystem Theory, and the Interpretive Theory of Translation. The only entries containing the word 'model' are on the Ethnolinguistic Model of Translation (Nida) and the Operational Model (Bathgate). This is interesting:

---

[*] First published in 2000 in Maeve Olohan (ed,), *Intercultural Faultlines. Research Models in Translation Studies I. Textual and Cognitive Aspects.* Manchester: St. Jerome Publishing, 15–27. Reprinted by kind permission of the current copyright holders, Taylor and Francis Group. [http://www.tandfonline.com/]. One reference has been added, and a few small revisions have been made to reduce overlap with other papers in this volume. The keywords have been added.

some approaches are designated as theories and others not (there is a Manipulation School); some models but not others seem to have attained proper-name status. There is obviously much conceptual work still to be done in Translation Studies on clarifying what we mean by a theory or a model.

I shall not go further into this theme here, but I do need to explain how I see the relation between the terms 'theory' and 'model'. I use the term 'theory' in a wide and rather loose sense that derives from the etymology of the word: I take a theory to be a set of concepts and statements (claims, hypotheses) that provides a systematic perspective on something, a perspective that allows us to understand it in some way, and hence perhaps to explain it. The notion of a model often overlaps with this sense of theory, but models are usually less abstract; they are often understood as being intermediate constructions, between theory and data. A model typically illustrates a theory, or a part of a theory. For instance, Nord's "looping model" (1991a: 32–35) provides a visual representation of certain aspects of skopos theory.

This intermediary status of models is also exemplified in the expression 'research model'. Here, the assumption seems to be that there are several possible research models available, i.e. different ways of testing or developing a theory or producing or exploring new data to stimulate new theories or test existing ones. Good examples of research models, in this sense, would be think-aloud protocol studies, or corpus studies, or deconstructionist studies. The first two would share a more general research paradigm: that of empirical or descriptive studies. The last would belong to a different paradigm, with different assumptions about research goals and means.

In this paper, I shall use 'model' in a sense that combines its theoretical aspect and its methodological aspect. I shall refer to 'models of translation', by which I mean preliminary, pretheoretical ways of representing the object of research; I shall then claim that any model of translation has specific methodological consequences: translation models constrain research models, and hence the construction of translation theories.

1.1 The comparative model

In the history of Translation Studies we can distinguish three basic models of translation: comparative, process and causal [but see the comment on nexus models, in the introduction to Papers 1–4]. Each of these has several associated theories and approaches. I will outline these three models (or types of model) in turn, and eventually suggest that the causal one is the most fruitful.

The earliest theoretical model of translation seems to have been a static, product-oriented one, centred on some kind of relation of equivalence. I will call this a comparative model. At its simplest, the comparative model looks like this:

$X = Y$

That is, a relation is posed between two entities. In this case, the relation is one of equality or identity – this was one of the earliest ways of conceptualizing the notion of equivalence, of course. Applied to Translation Studies, we get

Source text (ST) = Target text (TT)

However, it has long been clear that this is an inaccurate representation of translation, so the relation between the two texts is better represented as being more approximate, one of similarity, or indeed difference:

$ST \approx TT$ or $ST \neq TT$

This way of looking at translation underlies the contrastive approaches taken by scholars such as Catford and Vinay & Darbelnet. The problem of translation is primarily seen as one of alignment: the task is to select the element of the target language which will align most closely (under contextual constraints) with a given element of the source language. This is an approach that obviously has close links with contrastive linguistics, but there the traditional variant of the model has placed languages systems (langues) rather than texts (instances of parole) on either side of the relation:

Source language (SL) $\approx$ Target language (TL)

The comparative model is useful for charting clear equivalences, for instance in terminology work. It is also useful for discovering cases of complex equivalence or lacunae, as illustrated thus:

$$\text{SL item X} \approx \begin{cases} \text{TL item A (under conditions ...)} \\ \text{TL item B (under conditions ...)} \\ \text{TL item C (under conditions ...)} \end{cases}$$

SL item X = TL item Ø (i.e. no equivalent)

For a classic example of complex equivalence, see the section on conditioned probabilities in Catford (1965: 29–31).

A more recent variant of the comparative model is used in corpus studies which compare translations with non-translated, parallel texts. Here too we have the same basic picture, centred on a relation between two entities:

Translated texts ≈ Parallel texts

The research task here is to discover the nature of the similarity relation, with respect to a given linguistic feature. In what respects do translations tend to differ from parallel texts? If there is a difference (for instance in the distribution or frequency of a given feature), is this difference indeed significant?

The goal of research based on a comparative model is therefore to discover correlations between the two sides of the relation. These may be correlations between features of language systems (including stylistic features), or texts, or sets of texts. The compared texts may be in different languages or in the same language. Comparative models allow statements about language-pair translation rules (Catford), about language-system contrasts, or about translation product universals.

1.2   The process model

The second model represents translation as a process, not a product. It introduces the dimension of time and is thus a dynamic model. At its simplest, it represents a change of state (from state A to state B) over a time interval (between time 1 and time 2), like this:

A (t1) → B (t2)

Several variants have been proposed to represent the translation process. Some are based on the familiar communication model. Here are some examples:

Sender → Message → Receiver
S1 → M1 → R1/S2 → M2 → R2
ST → Translation process → TT
Specification → Preparation → Translation → Evaluation
Input → Black box → Output
Problem 1 → Tentative Theory → Error Elimination → Problem 2

I represent these variants in a linear form here, but most of them acknowledge that in reality the process they describe is more complex, with feedback loops etc. Process models are well illustrated by Nida's river-crossing metaphor (Nida 1969), Sager's industrial process model (1994), Nord's looping model (1991a), García-Landa's semiotic model (e.g. 1990), Schiavi's narratological model (1996), some

Think-aloud protocol models, and my own Popperian model (Chesterman 1997a). [Some of these are illustrated above.]

Process models are useful if one is interested in sequential relations between different phases of the translation process. They allow us to make statements about typical translation behaviour, such as the micro-level use of time (e.g. the Translog project, see Hansen 1999), or the temporal distribution of different translation tasks (Mossop 2000), or decision-making in a sequence of choices that we can represent as a flow diagram (following Krings 1986). They thus enable us to say something about possible process universals.

1.3 The causal model

Neither of the model-types considered so far are explicitly causal. True, they may well be open to a causal interpretation. For instance, a comparative model could be said to be implicitly causal to the extent that the relation can be read as a cause-effect sequence:

> If X (in the source text), then Y will follow (in the target text)

Similarly, process models are also open to a causal reading, as soon as you say, for instance, that an output is caused by an input, or that what a translator does during a given phase is determined by what was done in a preceding phase, or indeed by the skopos. (For that matter, one could also argue that Vinay & Darbelnet's model (1958) is implicitly dynamic, insofar as they seek to follow the mind of the bilingual as it moves from one language to another.) However, in the above two types of model causality is not overt, not central, and not explicit. Comparative and process models help us to describe the translation product and its relation with the source text, but they do not help us to explain why the translation looks the way it does, or what effects it causes. The questions asked are "what?" and "when?" or "what next?", rather than "why?"

Causality (cause and effect) has already entered translation studies implicitly, in several ways. Nida's dynamic equivalence includes the idea of achieving the same effect. Skopos theory foregrounds one kind of cause, i.e. the final cause (intention), and skopos itself could be defined as intended effect. The polysystem approach and scholars of the "cultural turn" use causal concepts such as norms, in both source and target cultures, to explain translation causes and effects; they also build in other causal constraints such as patronage and ideology. Gutt's application of relevance theory makes explicit appeal to cognitive effects, and posits optimum relevance (in the technical sense of the term) as an explanatory factor to account for communicative choices in general (Gutt 1991). Toury's (1995) proposed laws of interference and standardization seek to take us beyond description into explanation. Some protocol studies look for the proximate (cognitive etc.) causes of a translator's decisions.

Further, the long tradition of translation criticism and assessment can be seen in terms of translation effects. A translation criticism is the reflection of an effect that a given translation has, in the mind of the reviewer / teacher / client. Prescriptive statements about what translators should or should not do are implicit hypotheses of effect: they predict good / bad effects of particular translatorial choices. Reception studies also look at translation effects.

All these aspects of translation studies can be logically linked if we adopt a causal model of translation (see e.g. Chesterman 1998a*). At its simplest, any causal model can be represented like this, where I use the symbol '⇒' to signify 'causes' or 'produces':

Cause ⇒ Effect

Applied to Translation Studies, we get

Causes ⇒ Translation(s) ⇒ Effects

Causality itself is a complex phenomenon. There are many kinds of causes, Aristotelian and otherwise. Some causes are deterministic (gravity causes things to fall), others are more like vague influences (social pressures, literary influences). Different types of causes are linked to different kinds of explanations. (For a thorough discussion of this, see von Wright 1971; for applications to Translation Studies, see Chesterman 1998a, 2000c†; Pym 1997: 83f.) In an attempt to reflect this range of causality we can refer more loosely to causal conditions (CC) rather than simply causes. So we can write:

CC ⇒ TT ⇒ EF

where TT = target texts and EF = effects, broadly understood.

There are obviously many levels of causation that we must consider: at least cognitive (the translation act), situational (the translation event) and socio-cultural. There are also corresponding levels of effect. So our model can be expanded as follows (Figure 1):

---

*   Paper 9 in this volume.

†   Paper 3 in this volume.

Socio-cultural conditions   (norms, history, ideologies, languages...)
⇓
Translation event   (skopos, source text, computers, deadline, pay...)
⇓
Translation act   (state of knowledge, mood, self-image...)
⇓
Translation profile   (linguistic features)
⇓
Cognitive effects   (change of cognitive or emotional state...)
⇓
Behavioural effects   (individual actions; criticism...)
⇓
Socio-cultural effects   (on target language, consumer behaviour, discourse of translation, status of translators...)

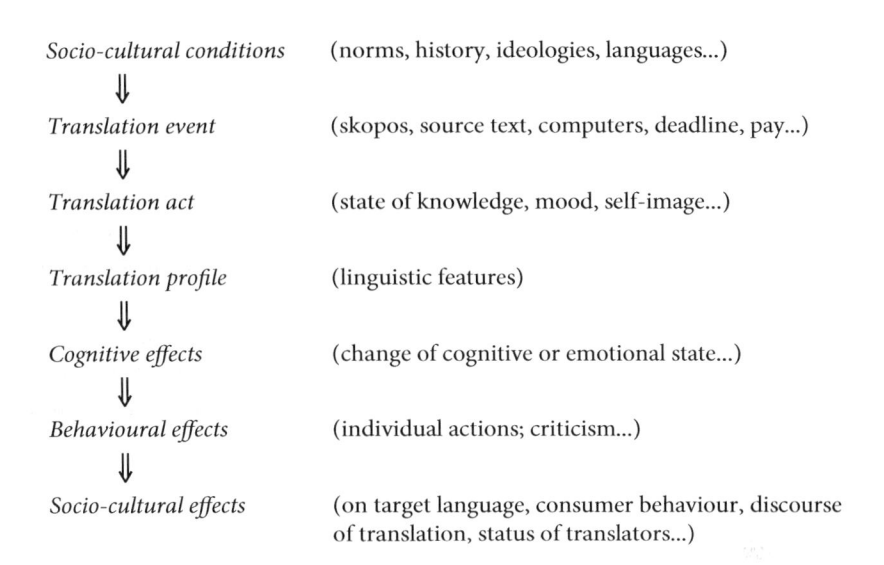

Figure 1. The causal model[*]

This looks like a causal chain here, but in reality the situation is of course more complex, and with no clear first cause or last effect.

A causal model like this allows us therefore to make statements and hypotheses about causes and effects, in response to questions such as the following:

– Why is this translation like it is?
– Why do people react like this to that translation?
– Why did this translator write that?
– Why did translators at that time in that culture translate like that?
– How do translations affect cultures?
– What causal conditions give rise to translations that people like / do not like? (What people...?)
– Why do people think this is a translation?
– What will happen if I translate like this?

And of course it is always possible to continue asking "why?"

A causal model is the richest and most powerful of the three I have been discussing, because it also contains the other two. The source text and source language are present in the model as part of the causal conditions of the translation.

---

[*] In the chronologically later Paper 4, above, I suggested the terms *reaction*, *response* and *repercussion* for cognitive, behavioural and socio-cultural effects.

And the dynamic time element is automatically present in any cause-effect relation. However, the most important reason for the primacy of a causal model is a methodological one: it encourages us to make specific explanatory and predictive hypotheses.

2. Hypotheses

Any rigorous academic discipline progresses by way of hypotheses: first discovering and proposing them, then testing them, then refining them. Otherwise we are condemned simply to go round and round in circles and to reinvent the wheel for ever. There is no difference here in principle between hard or soft sciences, nor even between empirical and hermeneutic approaches. Where methodological differences arise it is in the kinds of hypotheses that are used and in the ways they are tested. Four kinds of hypotheses are commonly distinguished in the philosophy of science. I will outline these, with some examples concerning the phenomenon of retranslation, and then show how our three models seem to allow (or at least encourage) the formation of different kinds of hypotheses.*

2.1 Interpretive hypotheses

An interpretive hypothesis is based on the concept *as*. If we want to understand something new or complicated, a good way to start is to consider what it seems to be like, what we might compare it to. Hence the usefulness of metaphors in science. To cite a classical example: if we want to understand the significance of the witches in *Macbeth*, we can propose an interpretive hypothesis to the effect that we should see them as representing Macbeth's subconscious. We thus "interpret" the witches, we interpret what they "mean" in the play, in a way that seems to be revealing or useful, a way that makes sense in relation to other aspects of the play, etc. This constitutes a hypothesis, because what we are really saying is: *if* we see the witches in this way, *then* we gain some good insight. [Cf. especially Føllesdal 1979.] More specifically, we can state the typical forms of interpretive hypotheses as follows:

– that something can be usefully defined as, or seen as, or interpreted as, X
– that X is a useful concept for describing or understanding something
– that something means X

---

*   See further Papers 18 and 19 below.

Interpretive hypotheses are fundamental to any scientific endeavour, because they provide the concepts, definitions, classifications, etc. that we can use. They are tested against evidence of course, and also in use: do they or do they not turn out to be useful, offering good insights, leading to other hypotheses, etc.? Translation Studies is full of them. Indeed, sometimes it seems that we have been spending more time thinking about what concepts to use and refining our conceptual tools than actually doing anything with these concepts.

Let's look at some examples from the study of retranslation, that is, situations where there is more than one translation, in the same target language, of a given source text. (For some background on retranslation, see Gambier 1994; and the special issue of *Palimpsestes* 1990 (4).) Here are some interpretive hypotheses:

a. Retranslation can be distinguished from revision as follows: revision focuses on a previous translation, retranslation on the original.
b. Goethe's three phases can be reduced to a dual opposition between "freer earlier" and "closer later".
c. The distance between ST and TT can be validly measured in terms of...
   - frequency of strategies ABC
   - analyses of formal/semantic/stylistic equivalence
   - Leuven-Zwart's (1989/1990) model of transeme analysis...
d. Only retranslations can become great translations. (A. Berman 1990)

Hypothesis (a) concerns a conceptual distinction, based on the belief that it is useful to make such a distinction, in this way. Hypothesis (b) proposes a conceptual move from a tripartite distinction to a simpler one, presumably in the belief that this will be useful, or easier to test. The hypotheses grouped under (c) propose various ways of operationalizing the concept of distance, i.e. they propose that 'distance' be understood *as* this or that. Hypothesis (d) plays with the definition of a 'great translation'; it proposes a definitional constraint on the class of 'great translations', in that they must be retranslations. In other words, this hypothesis implicitly claims that it would be somehow beneficial for us to classify great translations in this way. Empirically, we could test this last claim for instance by listing lots of translations that are considered (by whom?) great, and seeing whether they are in fact all retranslations. Conceptually, we could argue about the interpretation of 'great', and perhaps propose competing definitions of great translations, i.e. competing interpretive hypotheses.

A frequent problem in translation research is that interpretive hypotheses are not presented explicitly as such, to be tested like any other hypothesis.

2.2 Descriptive hypotheses

A descriptive hypothesis makes a claim about the generality of a condition. That is, it claims

- that all instances of a phenomenon X have feature Y

It thus makes a descriptive claim, to the effect that feature Y is a valid element of the description of all instances of X. It is important to note that the condition or feature must be empirically observable: the claim is an empirical one, not a conceptual one. For example, I might claim that all deciduous trees lose their leaves in winter. If a tree does not lose its leaves in winter, it therefore does not belong to the class of deciduous trees. In many fields, including Translation Studies, descriptive hypotheses are probabilistic rather than universal. So they take the form: instances of X tend to have the feature Y; or, most instances of X have feature Y. This is obviously a weaker claim, and is therefore harder to falsify.

In translation research descriptive hypotheses concern translation universals or laws. At a lower level of generality, we also find descriptive hypotheses pertaining to translation types (not all translations) or translator types (not all translators), or text types. With respect to retranslation, the so-called retranslation hypothesis is a descriptive hypothesis that can be formulated as follows:

- Later translations (same ST, same TL) tend to be closer to the original than earlier ones. (See e.g. *Palimpsestes* 4, 1990)

The jury is still out on this one: there seems to be evidence both for and against. Much depends on how "closeness" is to be measured, of course.

Descriptive hypotheses are thus attempts to answer "what?" questions. What are translations like? What special features do they exhibit? What are translations of this kind like? How do they differ from source texts / from parallel texts / from other kinds of translations / from earlier translations?

2.3 Explanatory and predictive hypotheses

An explanatory hypothesis proposes an explanation for a given phenomenon, and a predictive one claims that under given conditions, this phenomenon will occur. Predictive hypotheses are often used to test explanatory ones; but it does not always follow that if you think you know the cause of something you can therefore predict exactly when it will occur, or even that it will occur every time the conditions seem right. Knowing the causes, being able to explain something, may simply lessen your surprise when it does in fact occur. (Examples: volcanoes; children being sick after too many sweets; the consequences of revolutions and election promises.) The general form of these hypotheses is as follows:

Explanatory hypothesis:

- that the cause of / reason for explanandum E is X
- that E is (probably) caused by / influenced by conditions ABC

Predictive hypothesis:

- that factor X will cause event or state Y
- that in conditions ABC, event or state Y will (tend to) occur

In our general causal model of translation, there are two places where explanatory hypotheses fit in, and similarly two for predictive ones. Explanatory hypotheses refer (i) to the relation between the target text and the causal conditions: the translation, we propose, has this particular feature or features because of such-and-such a cause; and (ii) to the relation between effects and translation: a given effect was caused by such-and-such a feature of the translation. Similarly, we can make predictions either from causal conditions to target texts, or from target texts to effects. [...]

More complex explanatory and predictive hypotheses can also be proposed, e.g. that these conditions will give rise to this kind of translation, which will in turn have those effects.

Let us return to the retranslation example. If indeed our descriptive hypothesis holds water, why should this be true? Explanatory hypotheses include the following. Retranslations tend to be closer to their original texts because

- later translators take a critical stance to the earlier translation, seek to improve on it
- the existence of the earlier translation in the target culture affects the potential reception of the new one, and the translator knows this
- the target language has developed and allows the translator more freedom of movement
- TC [Target Culture] translation norms have become more relaxed, allowing a closer link to the source text.

It is not yet clear which of these (or other) explanations carries most weight, or even if any such general explanation could be valid for all the cases where the descriptive hypothesis seems to be corroborated.

As for predictive hypotheses, we could formulate one as follows:

- Later translations of a given text will be found to be closer than earlier ones [where "later" means either 'not yet studied' or 'not yet existing'].

Much testing obviously remains to be done.

2.4 Hypotheses and models

I would now like to propose a relation between the three models of translation and the four kinds of hypotheses. My point is that only a causal model allows us to make all four kinds of hypotheses, and that this model is therefore one that we should explicitly seek to develop in translation research.

All three models obviously make use of, and rely on, interpretive hypotheses. All three models also allow the formulation of descriptive hypotheses. The comparative model does not allow predictive or explanatory hypotheses; not, at least, unless causality is covertly introduced. The process model allows predictions to some extent – I can claim that phase B will follow phase A (although there may be an implicit causality relation embedded here) – but not explanations. Only the causal model explicitly makes it possible to posit explanatory predictions. Since the primary goal of any science is to understand and (somehow) to explain the phenomena it investigates, a causal model seems essential also in Translation Studies. The explicit use of such a model would also encourage the formulation of explicit hypotheses.

3. Conclusion: universals and laws

A causal model thus offers a comprehensive empirical research programme for Translation Studies, a basis on which to construct a translation theory or theories. From the extensive research already done, we need to distil specific explanatory and predictive hypotheses that we can test. We need to develop better conceptual and empirical tools for defining and systematically analysing translation effects. We need to create new hypotheses that link causal conditions, translation profile features and translation effects. And then we might be able to develop corroborated hypotheses into probabilistic laws, as envisaged by Toury.

It is worth noting in conclusion that the above discussion of hypotheses also bears on the issue of the status of translation laws and universals. [Claims about] product universals – like "Translations tend to have a simpler style than parallel texts" or "Translations are always marked by interference" – are in fact descriptive hypotheses. [Claims about] process universals – like "Translators tend to reduce the amount of repetition" or "Translators tend to explicitate" – are also descriptive hypotheses. However, such hypotheses (especially if they seem to be well corroborated) can also be used as explanatory hypotheses. If I discover that a translation manifests less repetition than its original, or has a lower index of lexical variety than comparable parallel texts, I can argue that this is (partly) because, indeed, all translations (of this kind) tend to be like this. I can thus offer a subsumptive explanation, whereby a feature of a particular instance (this translation) is explained by reference to a general law which states a regularity pertaining to all such instances. Descriptive hypotheses can thus have explanatory force.*

With respect to the causal model, a crucial role is played by cognitive causes, in the mind of the translator. We could also call these proximate causes, because these are the ones that are most immediately responsible for the appearance of a given feature in a translation profile. Why this additional phrase in this translation, why this reduction of repetition? First answer: because the translator decided to translate in this way. We can then go on and ask why the translator made this decision; but insofar as explanatory hypotheses appeal to situational factors such as the skopos or socio-cultural factors such as translation norms, it must be borne in mind that these only actually affect the translation *via* the translator's own mind. This realization places the translators themselves at the centre of a causal model. If we exclude alterations made to a translation after it has been submitted to the client, there are no causes which can bypass the translators themselves. They themselves have the final say. It is their attitudes to norms, skopos, source text, translation theory, etc. that ultimately count, rather than these external factors *per se*. All statements about laws and universals, if they are given causal force, must thus accept that all causal influences are filtered through the translator's own mind, through subjective decisions taken at a given moment. In this sense, such statements are relative ones, contingent on individual translation decisions.

So far I have stressed the theoretical importance of developing a causal model. One useful practical consequence of research based on a causal model would be its applicability in translator training and quality assurance. If we can demonstrate specific links between causal conditions, translation profile features, and observed effects, this should lead to a greater understanding of how to produce translations that have more desired effects and fewer unwanted ones. And this in turn might highlight the importance of the circumstances under which translators have to work. If we want high quality, let us establish empirically (and make publicly known!) what the appropriate conditions are.

---

* See further Paper 12.

PAPER 11

Semiotic modalities in translation causality*

A common feature of much modern translation research is the notion of causality. This is true not only of empirical descriptive research and applied studies, but also of hermeneutic studies, since concepts influence action. Different approaches focus on different kinds and levels of cause and effect. Some focus on the broad socio-cultural context, some on the situational level (translation event), some on the cognitive level (translation act) and some on the linguistic level of the translation product itself (translation profile). Aristotle's classification of kinds of cause has already been applied in translation studies. This paper proposes an analysis of translation causality, based on Greimas' modalities of *faire, être, devoir, savoir, pouvoir* and *vouloir*. It is argued that the study of causality does not imply a deterministic standpoint; that translation causality must include the translator's subjectivity; and that the search for regularities in cause-effect relations does not imply a neglect of what is unique about every translation. A causal reading of the modalities of *être, devoir, savoir, pouvoir* and *vouloir* as factors influencing the translator's action (*faire*) allows us to relate different kinds of causes at different levels, including the individual translator.

Keywords: translation, causality, modality, Greimas, subjectivity

1. Causality in Translation Studies [...]

2. Criticisms

[The] general causal paradigm [outlined in Section 1, omitted here] naturally has its critics. Before we proceed, let me present a collective picture of this criticism. Here I am drawing on the work of several scholars, especially Rosemary Arrojo (e.g. 1998), Douglas Robinson (1991, 1999), Lawrence Venuti (1995), Theo Hermans (1999), and Maria Tymoczko (1998). The arguments include the following points:

---

* First published in 2002 in *Across Languages and Cultures* 3, 2: 145–158. Permission from Akadémiai Kiadó to reprint it here is gratefully acknowledged. This version omits the first section of the original, which outlines different views of TS as a discipline and introduces the causal model: the material of this section is covered by Papers 3, 9 and 10 in this volume.

a. Focusing on norms and putative laws puts the translator in a subjugated position, as someone virtually deprived of free will, someone who simply does what he/she is told to do. In other words, this focus seems to presuppose the acceptance of some kind of determinism.
b. Focusing on external causal factors underestimates the translator's subjectivity as a human being.
c. Focusing on general laws means that we overlook the particular, contingent nature of every translation, as it appears in its own unique socio-historical context. We look at similarities but overlook differences.
d. Focusing on the universal means that we are blind to the way all theories are discourse-bound; all discourse is culture-specific and therefore non-universal. There can be, for instance, no universal definition of 'translation'. Even prototypes are culture-bound.
e. Focusing on causes is ultimately fruitless, because we can never arrive at ultimate causes (diachronically), nor even at a complete list of possible causes (synchronically).

In their extreme forms, I think all these arguments are straw men.

Ad (a): In the general causal paradigm I outlined above, we are not talking about determinism, about "absolute" causes, but about a whole array of causal conditions and influences that affect what translators do and what translations look like. Some of these causes or influences are obviously stronger than others. So we are using the term 'cause' in a very loose sense. A translator is neither completely free nor completely determined: some individual textual choices are more determined than others. (I personally like semi-colons and often use them liberally in my translations…) We are only at the beginning of an endeavour to understand a translator's subjective decision-making in this way, in the middle ground between determinism and freedom/creativity. In this respect, translational action is no different from any other kind of human action: we are all free to do what we like up to a point, but not absolutely.

Ad (b): The causal paradigm does not focus exclusively on external causes, but also covers the affects of internal, subjective factors on translatorial choices. These can include very subjective factors like attitude, emotional state, personality, gender, even sexual orientation. Furthermore, all external causes at the socio-cultural and situational levels only affect the translation itself via the cognition of the translator. The translator's subjective self thus acts as a filter. Whatever the prevalent ideologies may be, whatever the client says, whatever the language or translation norms may state, it is the translator who in the last instance decides what to do, how to translate, what word to write. It is the translator's attitude to the norms that counts as part of the efficient cause, not the norms themselves. A translator may decide to resist socio-cultural causal pressures, or to adapt to them. This is a central point in Gutt's application of relevance theory to translation theory. Claiming that all the various cultural and situational factors that have been noted by translation studies in recent years are implicitly covered by relevance theory, he writes (2000: 21): "no external factor has an influence on either the production or interpretation of a translation unless it has entered the mental life of either the translator or his audience. Its mere existence 'out there' is not enough to influence the translation." Thus, a translation can only have effects on the wider situation or culture via the individual people that read it, via individual cognitive, emotional or aesthetic reactions.

Ad (c): Suppose I am studying trees. I might spend years studying a single oak tree, a particular specimen. I might also be interested in its relation to other oaks, or to other deciduous trees, or to trees or flora in general, or to other things I find in this bit of the forest. My oak tree will have particular characteristics, but it will also share features with wider sets of phenomena. Translations are no different. Each is particular, in some sense unique; and I can acknowledge this. But no translation is totally unique, unlike any other translation in any way at all. I can always look for similarities and try to make generalizations that go beyond my particular oak tree. Indeed, this is the fundamental goal of any science: to look for regularities, generalities, patterns. It is only against a background of generalities that the particularities of a given individual become visible. We need to see both the wood (similarities) and the trees (differences).

Ad (d): This post-structuralist argument is sometimes taken to the extreme of denying the possibility of agreeing about anything at all: how do I know that my concept (my "theory") of an oak tree is *exactly* the same as yours, that we are talking about *exactly* the same thing? The answer is that I do not know, and do not need to know. It is enough if I have reason to believe that there is sufficient overlap between my mental picture and yours – sufficient for whatever purpose is at hand. It is realistic to assume that sometimes more overlap is required (e.g. in technological communication) than at others (e.g. in aesthetics). Some forms of discourse, in other words, are more culture-bound than others. Translation scholars can try to be aware of the extent to which their definitions and theoretical concepts are culture-bound; they can try to be as explicit as possible. They might want to aim for maximum overlap; or indeed to show that the overlap is less than was assumed.

Ad (e): It is obvious that we can never list all the causes nor all the effects of a translation, since even a simple linear chain extends theoretically ad infinitum in both directions: causes are caused by other causes, and effects have further effects. It is also obvious that we can never list the total range of factors that exert some causal influence at a given moment. It does not follow that we should give up trying to discover at least the main ones.

3. Modalities

I now propose to introduce a conceptual framework for understanding different kinds of causality in translation, a framework that seems highly relevant to the arguments about determinism and subjectivity. This is Greimas' semiotic analysis of *modality* (Greimas 1983; Schleifer 1987).

Greimas' theory was originally developed to describe the relations between the elements of a sentence, such as the roles of subject and object. Greimas saw these roles in a kind of anthropomorphic light, so that the subject really "did" something to the object in a transitive clause. He then applied his concepts to discourse structure, and to narrative structure, synthesizing the ideas of Propp.

What he called "modalities" were the various kinds of relations that could exist between different actants, whether in a sentence or in a narrative. He classified these relations into those concerning causality, those concerning teleology, and those concerning power. By causality he meant external causes; by teleology he meant internal reasons, desires. He ended up with four basic modalities, which I list here under the French names by which they are normally referred to:

- *devoir*: to be obliged
- *vouloir*: to want, desire
- *pouvoir*: to be able
- *savoir*: to know

Greimas acknowledged that these were provisional modalities, not necessarily universal, because they were only based on Indo-European languages. In addition to this basic group, he also needed the modalities of being (*être*) and doing (*faire*). One way of classifying the whole set is into external and internal modalities, thus:

exotactic:	*devoir*	*pouvoir*	*faire*
endotactic:	*vouloir*	*savoir*	*être*

Modalities can be combined in different ways. Greimas refers to various phases of modalisation of the acting subject. So we have "virtualities", formulated as *vouloir-faire* or *devoir-faire*; "actualizations" formulated as *pouvoir-faire* or *savoir-faire*; and "realizations" formulated as *faire-être* (Schleifer 1987: 99).

If we now reorganize the structure in such a way as to focus on *faire*, representing translatorial action, we can see five kinds of causality which either constrain or enable / liberate the translator's action. Each modality of course also has a negative counterpart.

$$\left.\begin{array}{l} devoir \\ pouvoir \\ vouloir \\ savoir \\ être \end{array}\right\} \Rightarrow faire$$

In other words, what the translator actually does (decides) is influenced / caused / constrained / made possible by:

devoir: what must be done / must not be done, where there is no choice: deadlines, basic rules of grammar, norms;

pouvoir: what is possible / impossible: what is within the ability of the translator, and what the target language permits…;

vouloir: what the translator personally prefers, wants to do; creative licence; ethical beliefs; attitudes to norms;

savoir: what the translator knows: knowledge of source language, target language, cultures, available strategies and norms, etc., translation theory;

être: what the translator actually is: state of mind and emotion, attitudes, personal history…

The modalities of *vouloir*, *savoir* and *être* thus represent "reasons" (internal to the actor); *devoir* represents a "cause proper" or at least a strong pressure – necessary, allowing no option; *pouvoir* represents the constraint of the possible: you cannot do what is not possible, or not possible for you (but there may be things that are possible that you are not aware of – *savoir*). This gives us an overall picture of the translator acting in a field that one might imagine as being magnetic in a complex way, criss-crossed by pressures and forces. These come partly from within (cognitive level), and partly from outside (socio-cultural and situational levels).

The five modalities *vouloir*, *savoir*, *devoir*, *pouvoir* and *être* are all factors affecting a translator's freedom of action (*faire*): some factors act as constraints on this freedom in the sense that they exclude certain options, for instance because they are impossible – ruled out e.g. by the grammar of the target language or by the required relation with the source text. Such constraints are "negative causes", they prevent or prohibit certain actions. Other factors act more as positive enablers or encouragers, exerting a pressure on the translator to select a given option.

142 Reflections on Translation Theory

(Compare the [pull and push] mechanisms that are used as explanatory concepts in the study of language change.)

Consider a simple example. In the building where I work in Helsinki there is a copying machine which will allow you to copy overhead-projector transparencies as well as ordinary sheets of paper. In the past we have had problems, though, because if you put the wrong kind of transparencies in, something goes wrong and the machine jams. So we now have the following notice by the machine, in Finnish:

Vain kopiointiin soveltuvia kalvoja, kiitos.
'only for-copying suitable transparencies, thank-you'
(i.e. 'only for transparencies that are suitable for copying')

How could this be translated into English? The modalities work as follows:

Devoir: This modality constrains the relations with the source text and with the target language. Obviously, the translation must give the same basic message. Something like "do not sit on this machine" would not be a permissible translation. Nor would the gloss I have given above, because it would break the norms governing the acceptable form of instructions or warnings in English. Nor should the translation be ungrammatical or difficult to understand. The translator cannot do just anything: the freedom to act is constrained by what is necessary.

Pouvoir: The translation can nevertheless exploit a wide range of possibilities. There are various words in English for describing the objects concerned: transparencies, slides, films, visuals, overheads, sheets… And various grammatical structures could be used, with or without imperatives or negatives, for instance. ("Use only… / Do not use any… except… / This machine is only for…") The possibilities offered by the target language (English) for expressing the intended message differ to some extent from the possibilities offered by the source language, from which the original writer has chosen a particular formulation. Finnish norms for the use of *kiitos* are not the same as those for English *thank you*; Finnish can express things in case endings that English expresses in prepositions; there are different rules for word order; etc.

Savoir: Of the range of possibilities that are theoretically available, the translator can only choose from the subset comprising the ones he/she is aware of. So the modality of *savoir* immediately narrows down one's freedom of action. If I do not know that *visuals* is sometimes used in the sense intended, I will not choose this word – I cannot, as it is not available to me in this context. The translator's choice is also constrained by what he/she knows of the intended function of the text, where it will be placed, who will read the notice, and so on. (In fact, it will also be read and needed by people who are not native speakers of English, yet do not read Finnish.) The translator also has knowledge of the world, maybe including some knowledge of how such instructions are phrased in English or American universities. Or maybe he/she knows how to find this information. The translator may even have some knowledge of translation theory, of the way in which such translation problems can be analysed. All these forms of knowledge affect the eventual decision.

Vouloir: Within those options that are possible and known, the translator can exert some personal choice. Personally, I do not like the term *visuals*; personally, I often use the word *skins*, like several of my colleagues here, because of interference from the Finnish word that also has this sense, although I know it is not a standard English term for this concept; personally, I find *transparencies* too long and formal, and *slides* reminds me of the other sense, in photography – maybe this word would also confuse some other readers. Personal preferences such as these would influence my final choice, if I was translating the sentence.

Être: My mood of the day might also influence my decisions; my feelings about overhead projectors and copying machines; my native dialect (British or American English); my natural tendency towards more or less formality; and so on.

All these modalities have somehow impinged on the translator of the notice, who actually ended up writing:

Copy-specific projector films only, please.

The last part of this paper will now offer a brief survey of the current field in translation studies, showing how different approaches tend to focus on different aspects of causality and different modalities.

4. Applications of the modalities

Since the so-called cultural turn in the 1980s, many scholars have become interested in the cultural and ideological causes and effects of translations (e.g. Bassnett, Lefevere, Hermans, Venuti, Tymoczko). There is an emphasis here on the modalities of *devoir* and *vouloir*. Topics have included the ways in which translations can help to construct a national identity or express an ideology (feminist scholars), or indeed suppress one (e.g. Cheyfitz [1991]). Some scholars are particularly interested in the long-term ethical effects of a translator's decisions (e.g. Venuti, Pym): that is, the effects on the target culture's perception of the source culture, and on the intercultural relations between the two. These scholars, like some feminist scholars, take an overtly prescriptive attitude, arguing that translators should translate in such-and-such a way because this will give rise to desirable ethical effects. Other scholars stick to a descriptive approach. Those working with polysystem theory investigate for instance the translation norms that guide the translator's decisions, which in turn manifest themselves in linguistic features of the translation itself, and at the way translations affect the existing literary norms of the target culture (Toury, Even-Zohar [1990]). The cultural turn in general looks at formal causes (norms) and final causes (intentions).

Functional schools of translation studies, in turn, have tended to focus on the situational level of causation. The skopos school and those who have applied action theory and communication theory to translation studies have been interested in the ways in which the client's formulation of the aim of the translation, as understood by the translator, affects the translator's decisions (Holz-Mänttäri, Vermeer, Reiß, Nord). They have taken the translator to be an expert in communication, one member of a chain of partners who need to cooperate across cultural boundaries. The concept of the skopos can be interpreted as the intended effect of the translation upon the recipients. The translator's job is then to analyse the intended effect, and make the appropriate decisions in order to achieve it. These scholars tend to downplay the causal influence of the source text, giving priority to the skopos, as Aristotle's final cause. They also tend not to emphasize the purely linguistic aspects of translation, preferring instead to contextualize the process as one of communication in a more general sense. Another point stressed by these scholars is the need for the reader to understand the translation – hence the importance of readability and fluency (Nida). Misunderstanding, or no understanding, will lead to unwanted effects. The most important modality here is *devoir*: one must meet the skopos.

Teachers are primary readers of the translations of their students, and the feedback they give is usually immediate. By setting themselves up as *typical* readers (fair?), teachers can also seek to represent the wider socio-cultural effects of a translation. So can critics, whose published reviews are in fact manifestations of the initial behavioural effects of a translation, subsequent to the cognitive effects aroused by the translation in the critic's head. Both teachers and critics thus operate mainly at the situational level, and both are concerned with the modality of *devoir*. Teachers, of course, are also concerned with *savoir*, in that their task is to build the trainees' expertise (*savoir-faire*).

Work at the cognitive level is the major domain of think-aloud-protocol (TAP) research, which looks for the immediate cognitive causes of a translator's decisions

(Aristotle's efficient causes). The main modalities here are perhaps *être* and *vouloir*, but the others come in as well. One framework for cognitive research on translation causes and effects is offered by relevance theory, first adapted from pragmatics to translation studies by Gutt. This theory seeks explicitly to be explanatory, aiming to explain "how it is possible for a human communicator to convey to an audience in language B what someone expressed in a different language A, what chain of causality in the human mind makes that possible, what factors contribute to its success or failure, and how" (Gutt 2000: 235). Gutt's stress here on explaining *how* rather than *why* reveals an interest in material and efficient causes rather than formal or final ones. The theory's central concepts are defined in terms of contextual effects, but "contextual effect" has here a specific cognitive sense that could be glossed "change of cognitive state". A speaker seeks to formulate utterances in an optimally relevant way, i.e. in such a way as to obtain the maximum contextual effect in the hearer's mind at the least cost, i.e. the least expenditure of the hearer's effort. The speaker must therefore have some image of how the hearer will react to various alternative formulations of a given idea, various alternative utterances, in order then to select the one that is most relevant in this sense. For translators, this means again that their own subjectivity (*être*) plays a major role: the translator's imagination, empathy with the implied or intended reader, provides the information necessary to make the appropriate, optimally relevant selection. Translators thus need to project themselves into the minds of their prospective readers in order to anticipate possible contextual effects (*savoir*).

At the centre of this general causal model is the linguistic description of the translation itself, the translation profile: its relation (a) to the source text and (b) to the target language. At this level we can attempt to formulate universals of translation – either with respect to source texts or with respect to target languages. E.g. that translations tend to show evidence of interference, or reduce repetition; or that they tend to be more explicit or more standardized than comparable target texts. If these hypothesized universals turn out to be well corroborated (they are still being tested), they will then have explanatory force: it will become possible to say that such-and-such a translation has such-and-such a feature *because* this is what all translators tend to do (with this kind of text, under these translation conditions, with these source and target languages, or universally). To the extent that these potential universals are bound to particular language pairs, the research results of contrastive analysis are highly relevant here – revealing possibilities and formal constraints on translatorial action. This is the domain of the *pouvoir* modality.

5. Conclusion

What you do, then, depends on what is possible, what you know, what is necessary, what you want, and what you are. What translators do (*faire*) depends on their knowledge (*savoir*) of how to exploit what is possible (*pouvoir*) in order to meet the demands of what is required (*devoir*), in a way that they desire (*vouloir*) and that is in accordance with their own subjectivity (*être*).

The study of translation causality, looking for general patterns of cause and effect, does not mean a reduction or elimination of the translator's humanity, nor an acceptance of determinism. The complex causality of translation – translation as effect and also as cause – is a rich mine for research.

PAPER 12

On explanation[*]

As Descriptive Translation Studies expands its goals to include explanatory hypotheses in addition to descriptive ones, it has made use of different notions of explanation, all of which are relevant to Gideon Toury's work. This essay analyses these different notions in the light of some work in the philosophy of science, beginning with the apparent contrast between explanation and understanding. It then focuses on explanation in terms of generalization, causality, and unification. The crucial concept underlying all these is that of a relation. This point of view also allows a characterization of what is meant by explanatory power, and shows how explanation can emerge from description.

Keywords: explanation, generalization, causality, unification

> Conducting research on a 'wish-to-understand' basis
> Gideon Toury (2006: 55)

1. Introduction

My key word in the title of Gideon Toury's book *Descriptive Translation Studies and beyond* (1995) is the last one, *beyond* – beyond description, i.e., towards explanation of some kind. This does not mean that we no longer need descriptive work, of course: without this, we would not really have anything specific to ask "why?" about. But Toury's title does serve to remind us that description is not usually the end-point of a scientific endeavour. We also want to be able to explain things.

What kinds of things need an explanation? A singular surprising event, perhaps; or a surprising generalization or pattern in a set of data; or a problem that needs a solution. We look for an explanation when something puzzles us, or when something unexpected occurs, or when we are faced with an unknown

---

[*] First published in 2008, in Anthony Pym, Miriam Shlesinger and Daniel Simeoni (eds), *Beyond Descriptive Studies. Investigations in homage to Gideon Toury*. Amsterdam and Philadelphia: Benjamins, 363–379. Reprinted with kind permission from John Benjamins Publishing Company (www.benjamins.com). One reference has been added.

phenomenon that we want to explore. An explanation "fills a gap" of some kind in our understanding. It answers an "explanation-seeking" question (Sintonen 1984: 7) in a way that seems relevant to the questioner. In other words, "explaining" is a communicative act. Proposed explanations may not necessarily be complete, or adequate, or even true; but to the extent that they satisfy the questioner, in a given context – to the extent that they are adequate to the questioner's needs – they contribute in the first instance to the questioner's understanding.

I take "understanding" here to be a state of mind rather than an act. An explanation is thus initially an explanation *for someone*, i.e., its adequacy and acceptance *as* an explanation depends partly on the questioner's cognitive context, their experience of a gap or puzzle that needs explaining. To the extent that an explanation is indeed true, it also contributes to knowledge. The overlap between "understanding" and "knowledge" is evident. In the present context, I will just note that understanding seems the more subjective notion, residing primarily in Karl Popper's World 2 [Popper 1972: 106f]. Knowledge resides in World 2 as well (as subjective knowledge), but also in World 3 in a publicly available form. To put it simply, we could thus say that explanations contribute both to understanding and to knowledge.

But there is also a further conceptual problem here. Traditionally, the two concepts of "explanation" and "understanding" have been associated with different conceptions of science. This was the theme of Georg von Wright's seminal book *Explanation and Understanding* (1971), and the relation between the two concepts has been widely discussed since then (see, e.g., Salmon 1998). The broadest distinction runs between the natural sciences (which are said to seek explanations) and the human sciences (which are said to seek understanding). Alongside and underlying this distinction there are arguments about different notions of causality, of determinism, of explanation itself, and of epistemology in general. Several of these philosophical distinctions and arguments have left their mark on Translation Studies. (See in particular the series of contributions to the Forum section of *Target*, beginning with the initial article by Chesterman and Arrojo in 2000[*] and ending with volume 14.1, in 2002.)

As outlined above, I take the view that all kinds of explanation may lead to greater understanding (and greater knowledge), particularly when the object of research is one that is as complex and multidisciplinary as translation. No discipline, no social science, nor indeed any other field of science, can manage without some kind of preliminary assumptions (which are also a form of understanding), without the interpretation of both concepts and data, and hence without hermeneutic

---

[*] Paper 2 in this volume.

explanation of some kind. Some research problems are, in addition, amenable to other kinds of explanation. My attitude to the opposition "explanation *vs.* understanding" is therefore that this is a false opposition. Not "*vs.*" but "and" (cf. von Wright 1971:135). We need both concepts, and neither is a simple one.

2. What counts as an explanation?

The past decades have seen growing interest in ideas and ways of explanation in Translation Studies. Explanations have taken several different forms, most of which appear somewhere in Toury's work. Attempts to explain translational phenomena have been based on different initial assumptions about what actually might constitute an explanation. This paper explores the main kinds of explanation that have been proposed recently in Translation Studies, and seeks to show the relations between them.

Explanation is not a unitary notion (see e.g. Sintonen 1984: 12–13). In everyday English, we use the verb *explain* in several different ways (discussed e.g. in Salmon 1998). We can explain, for instance,

a. what something is
b. what something means, what its significance is
c. how something is possible
d. how something has evolved, developed
e. how something works
f. how to do something
g. why a particular fact is true
h. why an event took place
i. why a general regularity exists
j. what something is for
k. to what end something occurs.

These uses can be grouped into some obvious categories. Types (a-b) above could be called descriptive or interpretive or hermeneutic, in the sense that they have to do with definition and interpretation. Types (c-f) are explanations concerning how something can be or comes to be possible, or can be made possible, and thus focus on *necessary* conditions. Types (g-i) have to do with why something is necessarily the case, i.e., with causality, and focus on *sufficient* conditions. Types (j-k) concern purposes, functions and goals.

Let us illustrate these main types briefly, before going into more detail. Interpretive explanations often take the form of metaphors or comparisons. We can make some sense of an unfamiliar or complex phenomenon by comparing it to another phenomenon that we know better; in other words, we try to see the unfamiliar *as* the familiar. We compare light to waves, or to particles. We compare translation to crossing a river, or to cannibalism. All such metaphorical comparisons serve as explanations in the sense that they relate the *explanandum* ("that which is to be explained") to a more familiar *explanans* ("that which explains"), in a way that sheds light on the phenomenon in question, making it a bit less mysterious. Such explanations are only explanations "to some extent", yes; but most, if not all, explanations are also only "to some extent", ultimately.

Explanations "how" have to do with processes or instructions. In Translation Studies, research using Think-Aloud Protocols and keystroke data (e.g., using Translog), and also sociological research observing working procedures, can offer explanations of this kind. By examining the details of the translation process, that is, we come to understand more about the conditions that made the final product possible. The same is true of historical research on the background social conditions of a given translation. In this case, the timescale of the process concerned is different, but the general structure of explanation is the same: these were (some of) the historical / political / social conditions that made this translation what it is.

Causal explanations have been proposed at many levels in Translation Studies, and we shall return to consider them in more detail below. A very simple causal explanation might suggest, for instance, that a given lexical error in a given translation was caused by the poor bilingual dictionary that the translator consulted. Some interpretations of causality overlap to some extent with the "how"-type explanations mentioned above, as we shall see.

Teleological explanations have been most evidently implied in Translation Studies by skopos theory: a given translation is as it is because of its purpose. I say "implied" because this theory is fundamentally a prescriptive one, aiming to highlight the importance of the goal or intended function of a translation as a guiding principle for translators' decisions and in translator training. Implicitly, however, the theory can also be interpreted as assuming a *post hoc* explanation of why a given translation is as it is; and this implied explanation is a teleological one. (For further comments on different interpretations of skopos theory, see Chesterman 1998b.) Teleological explanations are also implied by relevance theory: a given translation solution is chosen because of the relevance principle guiding all human communication.

Any proposed explanation may of course turn out to be a wrong one, or an inadequate one, which needs to be replaced by a better one. An explanation of any kind thus starts life as a hypothesis (or, if you like, as a theory). Some causal explanations may allow corresponding predictions to be made, either absolute or probabilistic ones; and these predictions can then be tested, to test the proposed explanation itself. But not all kinds of explanations entail corresponding predictions, and other ways of testing them are needed. Explanations about how something became possible allow what von Wright calls *retrodictions*: "[f]rom the fact that a phenomenon is known to have occurred, we can infer back in time that its antecedent necessary conditions must also have occurred in the past. And by 'looking into the past' we may find traces of them (in the present)" (1971: 57–8) and thus test the explanations to some extent (cf. the "backward predictions" mentioned in Toury 2004b: 23–24).

In Translation Studies, there are many kinds of *explananda*. Translations are not only effects (i.e., they have causes of various kinds – see below); they themselves are also causes (i.e., they have effects). On one hand, we might want to know why this translation has such-and-such a feature or textual profile; why the translator made a given decision; why the client decided to employ this translator; why the task conditions are as they are (deadline, fees, etc.); why the prevailing translation norms are as they are. On the other hand, we might wonder why the client, or readers, react to a translation in a given way (e.g., why it is judged to be of a publishable standard or not); why a given translation had such a significant effect in the target culture; and so on (see Delabastita 2005 for a wonderful list of such questions). In fact, we often get interested in causes because our attention has first been drawn to effects – desirable, undesirable, or otherwise interesting ones. It follows that we may need many kinds of explanation, to account for all these *explananda*.

To sum up so far: an explanation is an attempt to make sense of something. The purpose of an explanation, we could say, is better understanding and better knowledge.

3. Generalization

The final chapter of Toury's book introduces two potential "laws" of translation: the law of interference and the law of growing standardization. "Laws" are understood as "theoretical formulations purporting to state the relations between all variables which have been found relevant to a particular domain" (1995: 259). Toury distinguishes this scientific sense of laws from non-lawlike generalizations such as lists of possibilities or directives. However, it is not clear to me whether Toury's proposed laws are genuinely "nomic", i.e., whether they capture *necessary* relations between variables or whether they are simply generalizations that happen to be the case, i.e., contingent generalizations (see von Wright 1971: 178, note 62; and Chalmers 1999: Chapter 14). There is more to a nomic law than a mere statement of regularity; and probabilistic laws are not nomic.

Formulating a law is nevertheless one way of formulating generalizations about features of translations that seem very widespread, perhaps even universal, regardless of the languages, text-types, or cultures concerned. Other scholars have preferred the term "translation universal" or "pattern" or indeed just "regularity". In later articles, Toury (2004a: 24; 2004b: 29) leaves open the terminological question of whether it would be more appropriate to speak of "high-level regularities" or "universals" or "laws". The point is that "'hunting for regularities' is the name of the game" (Toury 2004b: 28). Interesting regularities may also be sought at less general levels: some may be genre-specific, media-specific, or language-pair-specific, for instance.

Observations about regularly occurring features of translations are of course much older than the 1990s, when the advent of corpus translation studies made research on translation universals a hot topic, but the earlier proposals tended to be presented in a purely pejorative spirit, as "typical weaknesses" or "deformations" of translations (Chesterman 2004a[*]).

But in what sense is a generalization about a potentially widespread feature an *explanation* of this feature? Surely a generalization is a way of describing something, perhaps part of the conclusion of a description; not part of an explanation? Yes and no. Sandra Halverson (2003) has drawn the attention of translation scholars to an important insight discussed by William Croft ([1990] 2003), who argues, I think convincingly, that between description and explanation there is not really a clear dividing line. Following on from my own point above, we could say that any (good) description, too, can increase understanding. Explaining "what something is" (type (a) on my list above) is surely equivalent to describing it in some way. Croft argues as follows:

> Instead of using the dichotomy of description vs. explanation, one can describe grammatical analysis – or any other sort of scientific analysis, for that matter – with a scalar concept of degrees of generalization. The basic concept is that a more general linguistic statement can be said to explain a more specific one, though it may itself be explained by a yet more general statement. Thus, any given statement is an explanation for a lower-level generalization, but a description in comparison to a higher-level generalization. (Croft 1990: 246 / 2003: 284)

Croft argues (2003: 285) that "[a] successful generalization shifts the kinds of questions that are asked to a higher plane". The lower-level questions are no longer asked; they are no longer interesting. Applying Croft's various levels of generalization to translation research, we can illustrate as follows:

---

[*] Paper 20 in this volume.

Level i.: Observation: description of basic facts.
[We note, for instance, that there are some shifts in a particular translation.]

Level ii.: Internal generalization about these facts.
[We note that similar shifts occur elsewhere, with the same language pair.]

Level iii.: Higher internal generalization.
[We generalize to other language pairs; further, we hypothesize that these shifts manifest a universal tendency: in translation, shifts always occur.]

Level iv.: External generalization.
[We hypothesize that this tendency can be accounted for in terms of constraints of human psychology / biology / sociology, etc., and/or in general differences of language structures, etc.]

Consider now how the explanatory power of the generalizations increases as we go up the scale. At level (ii) our surprise at the existence of a given set of shifts – concerning, say, explicitation – is somewhat reduced because we see that they are not particular to the translation in question, but also occur elsewhere: so the ones we noted at level (i) are not so special, not so surprising. At level (iii), after examining quite a few other translations, we find so much evidence of these shifts that we would be surprised if a translation (longer than just a few words) turned up with *no* such shifts. They are in fact to be expected. So we propose that the occurrence of these shifts is universal. Toury uses the example of shifts in general to illustrate a potential universal (i.e., "translation involves shifts") that has a rather trivial status, both because it is pretty obvious anyway and because, as thus formulated, it does not make any more specific claim, e.g., about types of shifts or relative frequencies of different types (such as explicitations vs. implicitations) (see e.g. Toury 2004b). However, as counter-evidence to the notion of equivalence-as-identity, the universality of shifts in general is surely significant. From the point of view of explanation, moreover, if it is indeed the case that shifts are universal, this fact does present an obvious way of offering some kind of explanation of the occurrence of the observed shifts we started off with. They occurred *because* all translations contain shifts, *because* all translators introduce shifts. Thus formulated, such an explanation is not a genuinely causal one, of course, since the mere existence of a universal tendency does not itself constitute or imply a nomic principle (like, say, the law of gravity). Some might argue that it is not a real explanation at all (see e.g. Malmkjær 2005; and, in historical linguistics, Lass 1980), but that depends on what you accept as an explanation in the first place. We do not claim (at this level of explanation) that we know *why* the proposed universal tendency exists; it just does (or may do). We shall return to some of the complexities of causality below.

At level (iv) the proposed explanation becomes stronger, because a causal link is claimed beyond the field of translation itself. Translation shifts make sense if we look at the ways in which the translation process is constrained by human cognition, task conditions, etc. This is the level at which Halverson (2003) proposes an explanation for translations, in terms of cognitive constraints on human information processing. Current attempts to move to this level of generalization remain, however, largely speculative. Notwithstanding, the more we find we can generalize at the lower levels – the more evidence there is for the universality of a given kind of shift, for instance – the more there is a need to explain such generalizations at this higher level (iv): there is more that needs explaining.

At each of these levels (ii-iv) the explanation proceeds by positing relations between the data in question (these shifts here) and other data: other translations, "all" translations, other kinds of data. The more relations we can see, the more powerful the explanation seems to feel.

Toury's formulations of possible laws are all probabilistic and in their full form they are all conditional, of the general form: "if X, then the greater/the lesser the likelihood that Y" (1995: 265). Some formulations are correlational: "the more X, the more Y" (e.g., 271). What matters is discovering the relations between the variables, the scholar's "fervent search for interdependencies" (237). Toury seems to avoid using the explicit verb "cause". He speaks indirectly of "conditioning factors" (e.g., 277), or how variation in a social variable may "lead to" differences on the textual level (e.g., 278). But these hints of causality are rather tentative (see further below).

Laws can of course be correlational, not causal. Behind any correlation, however, we may naturally suspect some kind of causal influence one way or another and perhaps try to test for it. One obvious way of testing would be by means of comparative studies in which two or more cases are selected which differ in respect of one particular variable but are similar with respect to other ones; in this way, the influence of the variable concerned can be checked (cf. Susam-Sarajeva 2001; for a powerful example of the comparative method applied to matters even more complex than translation, see Diamond 2005).

This is a good point to recall Hempel's classic statement about the goals of empirical science, which Toury also cites at the beginning of his book.

> Empirical science has two major objectives: to describe particular phenomena in the world of our experience and to establish general principles by means of which they can be explained and predicted. The explanatory and predictive principles of a scientific discipline are stated in its hypothetical generalizations and its theories; they characterize general patterns or regularities to which the individual phenomena conform and by virtue of which their occurrence can be systematically anticipated. (Hempel 1952: 1; cited in Toury 1995: 9)

As I have argued elsewhere (2001b), I think Hempel's key concepts can also be interpreted in such a way as to apply to more hermeneutic approaches. There too, many scholars seek generalizations, general principles, patterns; they seek to describe and explain; and many scholars work – even if only implicitly – with hypotheses (for instance interpretive ones). A hermeneutic understanding may also allow probabilistic anticipation (if not precise prediction), and hence reduce surprise.

Formulating a generalization, then, is one way of at least beginning to explain.

4. Causality

I now turn to one of the most complex aspects of explanation: causality. This is a more prominent notion in empirical research than in hermeneutics, and it has a long history of conceptual debate behind it, which I am not competent to summarize. But I would like to make some general points that may be of interest to translation scholars. We have already noted that explanations come in many forms; there are also several types of causality, which have been variously interpreted.

There is, perhaps surprisingly, no entry for "causality" in the subject index of Toury (1995), although there are many references throughout the book to explanation and explanatory hypotheses. He prefers to speak of explanation more generally, or of the "justification" of translator decisions. His "justification procedure" (*ibid*: 36–39) outlines the way in which a researcher can "speculate" about the background or conditioning factors (such as norms) that may have influenced or constrained a set of translation decisions. The results of these decisions are seen in the target text, which provides the primary evidence (together with data from interim drafts, where available). Toury's evident reluctance to talk explicitly about "causes" may indeed be well justified (see below). Norms, for Toury, are above all sources of explanatory hypotheses (e.g., p. 59). These hypotheses concern not only the concept of translation (and thus of equivalence) underlying a given translation or set of translations; they also concern aspects of the translation decision process (e.g., pp. 93–4) and the workings of the black box (p. 180f).

A major *locus classicus* on causality in Western philosophy is Aristotle, who proposed four types of causes. These have been applied to Translation Studies by Anthony Pym (e.g. 1998: 148f; see also Chesterman 1998a[*]). They can also be considered as four basic patterns of explanation.

---

[*] Paper 9, above.

Material cause
The *explanandum* is as it is because of its material conditions of occurrence. Translations are made of the abstract "material" of language, in the broadest sense of the term, including different media. More specifically, they are constructed in the target language. So one general explanation for the question "why is this translation like this?" is "because of the nature of language, and particularly of the target language itself, and also because of the relation between the target language and the source language". This kind of causal explanation is implied by equivalence-based theories of translation. It works at the textual level of translation theory, and underlies much corpus-based work.

Final cause
The *explanandum* is as it is because of the goal of the agent(s) producing it. This is a teleological explanation. Its most obvious application in Translation Studies is in skopos theory. This is curious in a way, because skopos theory has generally been interpreted as being prescriptive and pedagogically valuable, showing that good translations are guided by their purpose (see e.g. Vermeer 1996: 15, and 67, footnote 24). But seen as proposing an important explanatory factor to account for translation, skopos theory comes across in a different light. With respect to relevance theory (Gutt 2000), to the extent that the agent (the speaker/translator) intends to communicate in an optimally relevant way, this approach also employs a notion of final cause. This kind of causal explanation works at the social level of translation theory, where we are concerned with the objectives of the client and the translator and the function of the translation itself.

Formal cause
The *explanandum* is as it is because of the formal requirements of what is expected. In other words, because of the norms. In the case of translation, these norms are primarily in the target culture, but also in the relevant translation tradition more generally. This kind of causal explanation is offered, e.g., by polysystem theory, and by norm-based research in general. It is widely represented in the cultural turn in translation research.

Efficient cause
The *explanandum* is as it is because of the physical and mental/emotional nature of the agent(s) involved. For us, this means primarily the body and mind of the translator. These kinds of causes are investigated by cognitive research in Translation Studies, such as TAP research (for a survey, see e.g. Jääskeläinen 2002). In translation, the efficient cause is the proximate one: that is, the one nearest to

the *explanandum*. All other causes (material, final, formal) are filtered, as it were, through the translator's mind, either consciously or by unconscious routine.

Other philosophers have been interested in defining the line(s) between causal and non-causal explanation, rather more precisely than I did above. Von Wright (1971: 85) proposed a four-fold taxonomy of explanations, as follows.

Causal explanations proper
These must be based on a nomic (i.e., lawlike and necessary, not just universal) connection between a given causal condition and its effect. They are also known as "covering law" or "subsumptive" explanations, because they can be expressed in terms of a general law (like the law of gravity). They are (or have been) typical of the natural sciences. Such explanations are also known as deductive-nomological explanations, because they are based on deductive argument. Some philosophers have argued that causal-proper explanations may also be statistical (e.g., Salmon 1998), accounting for the *explanandum* in terms of the relative probabilities of relevant conditional factors.

Quasi-causal explanations
These have to do with (non-nomic) reasons, justifications, rather than causes proper. Such explanations are typical of the behavioural and social sciences (von Wright 1971: 135f). One example discussed by von Wright is the causes of the First World War (*ibid.*: 139f). He analyses these as a network of different events, including the assassination of the Austrian archduke, which all played some contributory role. What connects the nexus of events "is not a set of general laws, but a set of singular statements" (p. 142). These statements function as premises to practical inferences or syllogisms (to which we return in a moment), which von Wright sees as central to teleological explanation. One could also appeal here to the notion of contributory conditions; these are less strongly causal than sufficient or necessary ones, but in combination with other conditions they may make a given event more likely, and hence more understandable. Toury (e.g. 2004a: 22) describes such conditions as "enhancing" the causal effects of other conditions. Moreover, some conditions may be more relevant than others, a point highlighted by Salmon (1998).

Teleological explanations
As their name suggests, these have to do with human intentions; they are not nomic. These kinds of explanations are central to the human sciences, and von Wright argues that they can be explicated in terms of what he calls a practical inference or syllogism (p. 26f, 96f; the term itself is not new, and the idea is found in Aristotle):

A intends to bring about *p*.
A considers that he cannot bring about *p* unless he does *x*.
Therefore *A* sets himself to do *x*.

Von Wright claims that "the practical syllogism provides the sciences of man with something long missing from their methodology: an explanation model in its own right which is a definite alternative to the subsumption-theoretic covering law model" (*ibid.*: 27). The syllogism reminds us of the underlying rationale of skopos theory, and the role of the translator as decision-maker.

Quasi-teleological explanations
These are the functional explanations found, e.g., in biology (why does a frog have long back legs?). They do not involve intentions, and they depend on nomic connections between phenomena.

Von Wright's types of cause do not overlap exactly with Aristotle's, but we can see some relationships between them. Aristotle's classification has to do with the potential sources of causal explanation, whereas von Wright focuses on the internal logical structure of different kinds of causal or explanatory claims: different patterns of explanation. Aristotle's final cause looks like von Wright's teleological cause. Aristotle's material cause would presumably have to do with von Wright's "causal-proper" explanation, in that the material concerned would be subject to the causal-proper laws affecting it. But language, from which translations are constructed, is not a natural material of the kind studied by physics or chemistry. Causal-proper explanation may only apply to translation insofar as we try to account for our *explanandum* in terms of the physical constraints of the human body or mind, or of the medium in question. Quasi-causal explanations, on the other hand, look highly relevant to our field; they seem to cover partly the same ground as Aristotle's formal causes. In this context, von Wright discusses the notions of norms and normative pressure at some length (p. 147f), and their relation with teleological explanation (e.g., a person's wish to avoid sanctions that might follow the breaking of a norm). Quasi-teleological explanations do not seem relevant in their literal (biological, organic) sense, but we can and do say that texts, translations, or institutions "have functions", and these can usually be distinguished from the intentions of the various agents involved (cf. von Wright 1971: 153f).

In terms of this analysis, it may seem unreasonable to speak about causes at all in Translation Studies (causes proper, that is), except in a very limited way. On the other hand, we could argue that we nevertheless find it useful to use the term "cause", albeit sometimes in a loose sense, in order to refer to a wide range of factors that seem to impinge in some way on translations and people's reactions to them. Sometimes it does seem possible to isolate specific causes of specific decisions or shifts, e.g. by interviewing translators or via contrastive study of the source and target texts. But we should be wary of slipping into a stricter interpretation of "causality" than can be justified, given the nature of the evidence we are examining. And not all explanations are causal anyway – a point to be explored in the following section.

5. Unification

Explanations why something is the case, or how something is possible, may also be based on unification. This form of explanation is highlighted in Wesley Salmon's work (1998: e.g., 69f). He sets it alongside causal explanation as one of the main categories of explanation. This kind of explanation works by showing how the *explanandum* fits into a wider context, how it relates to "broad structural features of the world" (*ibid.*: 359), and thus reduces the number of assumptions that have to be made in order to understand it. In so doing, such an explanation also "colligates facts under a new concept", to use a classical phrase (see von Wright 1971: 200, note 2). In its widest sense, unification provides a way of relating a phenomenon to an overall conception of the world, a *Weltanschauung* (Salmon 1998: 360). Salmon argues that the notion of explanation by unification has developed from the traditional view of explanation in terms of covering laws (*ibid.*: 362). A good example is Darwin's theory of natural selection (*ibid.*: 360), which could be called a functional explanation. Darwin was not aware of the causal mechanisms provided by genes, but he did create a coherent picture which brought together a number of different facts and ideas: the existence of variation and chance mutations, the ideas of the competitive struggle for survival and adapting to the environment, and so on. Darwin's unification "made sense" of the evolution of life-forms, and has since given rise to a wealth of more detailed hypotheses.

Salmon's discussion mainly concerns the natural sciences, but he also refers to the relevance of this view for some behavioural and human sciences, such as archaeology. It seems to me that in the human sciences, examples of unification explanations are also given by explanatory narratives (and in the prescientific age by myths). These make sense of complex phenomena by linking them together into "stories", such as are used in psychotherapy, history, politics, and sociology. (For a recent example illustrating the relevance of explanatory narratives to Translation Studies, see Baker 2006.) I suggest that further illustrations of unification are the general principles that have been proposed as bases for functional explanations in linguistics, such as economy (in grammar, accounting, e.g., for certain syntactic and morphological features) and relevance (in pragmatics, accounting for some of the characteristics of human communication). Against this view, with special reference to historical linguistics, Roger Lass (1980) has argued that functional explanations of language change are not really explanations at all; one reason is that they are non-causal, and another is that they appear to be non-falsifiable (p. 71f). His interpretation of what constitutes an explanation is thus stricter than the one I am exploring here. He agrees that generalization and unification, and also, e.g., the creation of useful taxonomies, are valuable contributions to knowledge, but he does not wish to call them "explanations". Nevertheless, by offering a coherent "vision" of some kind, they all contribute to the creation of conceptual order; they bring intelligibility (*ibid.*: Chapter 5, especially 156f).

Salmon argues that unification is "top-down" explanation; it complements "bottom-up" explanations, which are framed in terms of explicit causal mechanisms. Both types of explanation are needed, they complement each other. In the human sciences, Salmon suggests that unification may involve reduction too. For instance, psychology may offer ways of understanding *explananda* in fields as different as sociology, economics and political science (1998: 358).

Salmon's explanation-by-unification seems partly similar to von Wright's quasi-causal explanation. Salmon also implies a link with causality in a general sense. He writes: "[t]o give scientific explanations is to show how events and statistical regularities fit into the causal network of the world" (*ibid.*: 104).

Fitting something into a network: this reminds us of Toury's insistence on the importance of contextualization, which he sees as vital for both description and explanation (1995: 29, and Part Three, "Translation-in-Context"). This form of explanation has been much used by polysystem scholars, and increasingly by scholars working in the sociology of translation (see e.g., the special issue of *The Translator*, 11, 2, 2005), but notions of what the most relevant context actually is tend to vary. As Pym points out (2006), a given observation can be contextualized in any number of ways, depending on the researcher's point of view; but priority should presumably be given to the contextualizations that seem to bring the most new understanding and has the most explanatory power (see below), depending on the particular research design in question.

Ultimately, attempts to explain via unification are motivated by the old dream of consilience, the unity of all knowledge.

6. Multiple explanations

What is known as the underdetermination thesis claims that any body of evidence can admit of more than one explanation (or theory or interpretation). In other words, the choice of explanation is underdetermined by the evidence: there always seem to be alternative explanations available. One consequence of this is the value – and necessity – of entertaining multiple explanations at the same time (like the theory that light is composed of particles, simultaneously with the theory that it is composed of waves). True, the possibility of multiple explanations may appear confusing at first.

Pym (1998: 158 and preceding sections) points out that one of the major weaknesses of the various theories proposed in Translation Studies is that they tend to focus only on one kind of causal explanation. We have theories of equivalence, of skopos, of polysystems, but no theory (as opposed to individual studies) that uses a broader range of explanations. This is a good point. We have no reason to suppose that only one kind of explanation would suffice to account for all the complexities of translation. The perceived inadequacy of these too restricted theories is one good reason to seek alternative and additional explanations.

A simple way to combine different causes (or sets of conditioning factors) would be to model them as a linear chain: factor A affects factor B, which affects factor C, and so on. So one could argue that sociocultural norms, for instance, affect the task conditions of a given translation (including source text and skopos), and that these, together with the knowledge and skills of the translator, then affect a translator's decisions and strategies, which in turn affect the profile of the translation itself (cf. Chesterman 1998a). But this is to oversimplify. It would be more realistic to model multiple causality as a cluster of factors that may all influence each other, at the same time or at different times. Several scholars have made proposals along these lines, including Toury (e.g., 2004a: 22). Siobhan Brownlie (2003), for instance, uses four sources of explanation for observed characteristics in different English translations of some French philosophical texts: the individual situation, including context of production and translator attitudes; textuality; norms; and the influence exerted by intersecting fields such as publishing and academia.

Pym (2006) observes that potentially conditioning factors (we might also think of these as possible contributory conditions) may influence each other to different degrees, and that the dependent variable itself (i.e., the *explanandum* in a given research design) may also causally affect some of these factors. Such interaction may manifest what Pym calls "asymmetric causation", in that factor A may affect factor B more than B affects A. Examples are readily found in sociocultural research on translation, discussed by Pym. Sometimes, for instance, it seems that cultural factors have more effect on social factors than these do on cultural factors, and sometimes the opposite appears to be the case.

But we can go further than merely stressing the potential of multiple causal explanations. Understanding may be increased by a combination of different kinds of explanation, not just the causal type. As Salmon puts it:

> When discussing scientific explanation, it is important to avoid thinking and talking about *the* unique correct explanation of any given phenomenon. There may, in general, be several different *correct* explanations of any such phenomenon. There will normally be many different sets of explanatory facts from which to construct *a* correct explanation. […] [A] given fact may have correct explanations of different types, in particular, correct causal explanations *and* correct unifying explanations.
> (Salmon 1998: 360; emphases original. Note especially this last point!)

7. Conclusion: relations

This brief conceptual exploration suggests a number of conclusions. We have outlined several forms of explanation. One feature which they share is the fact that they all take their explanatory power from the establishing of *relations* of different kinds, between the *explanandum* and various other phenomena or variables. These relations fall into three broad groups: relations of similarity, cause, and context.

Many explanatory relations have to do with *similarity* in one way or another. We could distinguish three aspects of similarity here: similarities expressed via metaphors or similes, via generalizations, and via correlations. What we could call "metaphorical" relations (where X is seen *as* Y) can be perceived between phenomena of a different kind but nevertheless with some salient similar features. We say that translating is like changing clothes, for instance; or translations carry memes like organisms carry genes; or chemical transformations can be conceptualized as translations. Relations of generalization, on the other hand, capture similarities between phenomena of the same kind. A given translation can be shown to be like a great many other translations, in certain respects: i.e., we can propose a generalization covering a whole set of translations, perhaps even all translations (a universal feature?). A generalization can also create a more general category that was not evident before: if we show, for instance, that translations are like non-native texts in some respects, we thereby posit a more general category of texts comprising both translations and non-native texts, about which some interesting claims can be made. Finally, a third kind of similarity is a correlation. Correlations show related variation across different variables: e.g., the hypothesis that the more experienced the translator is, the less interference there is (cf. Toury 1995: 277).

Not all relations have to do with similarity, however. Some relations are *causal*, in a strict or loose sense. In addition to covering laws, we can speak of conditioning factors, constraints, background influences, etc., as discussed at more length above.

And some relations are what we could call *contextual*, showing how the *explanandum* fits into a broader network of phenomena: this is the unification pattern of explanation. Contextual relations show relevant connections with surrounding networks of phenomena and thus contribute to the formation of a holistic view of the *explanandum*, which increases our understanding of it.

Explanatory power increases if predictions become more accurate, or if they have a higher probability of occurrence. Explanations are also more powerful if they are more general, so that they are relevant to a greater range of phenomena. We can make our explanations more general by increasing the number of relations encompassed by our hypothesis; by increasing the range of different types of factors with which a relation is posited; or by relating the *explanandum* to larger networks or systems of factors (cf. Pym 2006). All these expanding relations lead ideally to general theoretical concepts and principles of one kind or another: in the final analysis, it is these that do the explaining. The theory itself is ultimately the *explanans*.

This observation brings us back to the fuzzy borderline between description and explanation. For is it not true that description, too, is a matter of establishing internal and external relations? After all, we describe a translation by showing its relation with the source text, with the target language, with other translations, perhaps also the social and cultural context, and so on (recall the classic descriptive model offered by Lambert and van Gorp 1985). So what then is the difference between describing and explaining? I think part of the answer is the point I just made about explanatory power. The more relations involved, the more we can generalize away from the particular observed case, the more types of factors are covered, and the wider the systems, then the further we shift along the continuum from the descriptive end towards the explanatory end. As we saw with Croft's argument about generalization, a generalizing description is already a kind of preliminary explanation. The other part of the answer is that description becomes increasingly explanatory when it becomes more closely related to some general theoretical principle, such as might be offered by a unificatory explanation. Explanation is thus a matter of degree.

There is still one factor that I have scarcely mentioned: chance. Not even our physical world is ultimately deterministic, let alone the social one. Toury's insistence on the probabilistic nature of what he calls translation laws shows that he is only too aware of the existence of chance. The Nobel laureate physicist Max Born wrote:

> I think chance is a more fundamental conception than causality; for whether, in a concrete case, a cause-effect relation holds or not can only be judged by applying the laws of chance to the observation. (Cited in Kaplan and Kaplan 2006: 277)

The same reservation actually holds for all our concepts and definitions, including those concerning explanation, causality and relations. As Kaplan and Kaplan put it in their recent book on probability (2006: 289), "'[m]eaning', 'sense', 'interest', are the statistical signatures of a few rare, low-entropy states in the universe's background murmur of information."

From this point of view, it is good to be reminded that "[u]nderstanding is always a journey, never a destination" (Fortey 2004: 25). But the journey does have a starting point: our current state of puzzlement. We might, of course, also wish (like Marx) not only to understand the world, but to change it; but that is another story.[1]

Note

1. Warm thanks to Kaisa Koskinen, Ritva Leppihalme, Daniel Gile, Anthony Pym, Seppo Kittilä and Fred Karlsson for helpful comments on earlier drafts of this text. Any remaining defects are of course my own responsibility.

SECTION IV

Norms

As introduced to TS in Toury's work, norms are explanatory hypotheses, but of course they only represent one way of explaining why a given translation is the way it is, or why a particular translation decision was taken. Other possible explanatory factors include e.g. personal preference, the translator's habitus and attitudes to norms, deadline constraints, resources available, the distribution of power among relevant agents, and cognitive constraints (perhaps manifested in "universal" translation tendencies – see later in this volume). Translation is not *only* norm-governed behaviour. Crisafulli (2003) shows that Cary's decisions translating Dante can be explained not only by norms and general translation tendencies but also by his personal preferences concerning style and indeed ideology. For further discussion on the tension between explaining by norms and explaining by universals, see Malmkjær (2007). We obviously need multiple explanations. And it remains to be seen which explanations might lead to the best predictions.

The study of norms has its problems. One is terminological: what exactly do we understand by a norm? What is the relation between a norm and a tendency, or a norm and a value? Another is methodological: when do we know that we have found a norm? How can we test a hypothesis about a norm?

The first paper in this section discusses an old philosophical debate about the difference between factual statements and value statements. It formed the background to the more detailed presentation of norms in my *Memes of Translation* (1997, 2016). I have later discovered other work in philosophy that deals with the same debate, and I draw interested readers' attention in particular to Putnam (2002). In hindsight, it seems to me that a concept such as "professional translator" is what Putnam calls a "thick ethical concept" (2002: 35), in which a descriptive and an evaluative sense are entangled together, like "cruel". If Jane *is* a professional translator, it follows that she *ought* to be capable of producing reasonably good translations (under appropriate conditions); if one of her translations turns out to be poor, the client can reasonably be surprised and disappointed – more so than if she did not have the status of being a "professional".

Paper 14 is a response to a conference discussion which seemed to indicate that some conceptual analysis could usefully clarify a number of apparently widespread misconceptions about norms and how they can be investigated. The weakly explanatory "tendency" sense of norms was discussed in more depth in Paper 12 above, on explanation. The notion of a tendency is further discussed in the introduction to the section on "Universals", below.

PAPER 13

From 'is' to 'ought'
Laws, norms and strategies in Translation Studies[*]

Translation studies need to cater for both description and evaluation. This can be achieved via the study of translation norms. The norms governing translation are: (a) professional norms concerning the translation process (= norms of accountability, communication and target-source relation); and (b) expectancy norms concerning the form of the translation product, based on the expectations of the prospective readership. While general translation laws account for the behaviour of translators in general, normative laws describe the translation behaviour of a subset of translators, namely, competent professionals, who establish the norms. Normative laws originate in rational, norm-directed strategies which are observed to be used by professionals. These laws are empirical, spatio-temporally falsifiable, probabilistic, predictive and explanatory.

La traductologie doit prendre en charge la description et l'évaluation, par la voie d'une étude des normes qui gouvernent la traduction: (a) des normes professionnelles, qui concernent le processus de la traduction (normes de responsabilité, de communication, de relation cible-source); (b) des normes de l'attente inspirées par les lecteurs potentiels relativement à la forme du texte traduit. Tandis que les lois générales de la traduction décrivent le comportement de traducteurs en général, les lois normatives décrivent celui d'un sous-groupe, les traducteurs professionnels compétents, qui établissent les normes. Les lois normatives trouvent leur origine dans des stratégies rationnelles adaptées aux normes, et utilisées par des professionnels. Ces lois sont empiriques, falsifiables sur le plan spatio-temporel, probabilistes, prévisionnelles et explicatives.

Keywords: norm theory, law, strategy, professional, Jodl, ethics, explanation

---

[*] Originally published in 1993 in *Target* 5, 1: 1–20. Reprinted with kind permission from John Benjamins Publishing Company, Amsterdam/Philadelphia. [www.benjamins.com] One reference has been updated. The keywords have been added.

1. Descriptive plus evaluative

Translation is increasingly seen as a process, a form of human behaviour. A theory of translation, therefore, should seek to establish the laws of this behaviour, as e.g. Toury has argued recently [in a 1991 conference paper, eventually published in 1996]. "Law" in this sense may be glossed simply as 'observable regularity'. Such laws would be purely descriptive, giving an empirical account of actual translation behaviour. They would take the general form: Under conditions ABC, translators (tend to) do (or refrain from doing) X. I will refer to such laws as "general descriptive laws". This stress on a descriptive approach is no doubt partly due to the long tradition of confusion in translation studies, between descriptive and prescriptive aims

General descriptive laws of translation behaviour could be set up (i.e. behavioural regularities could be stated) for any and every type of translator, however competent, and for any kind of translation – on one condition: that the kind of behaviour studied is such that it can (appropriately) be called translating, i.e. that the resulting product is accepted as "a translation". This descriptive view, by definition, would consider both the degree of proficiency of the translator and indeed the quality of the translation irrelevant. What one studies is the behaviour of (people who call themselves or are called) translators, together with the end-results of their behaviour, which they call translations and which are accepted as such.

This latter point is worth stressing. Who has the right to designate a given text "a translation"? First, the translator: it is a translation if I, the producer of the text, say so. The translator may be the only person with access to both source and target texts, and thus the only person in a position to establish the translation status of the target text. Second, a text is a translation if its receivers indeed accept it as a translation; they normally do so, of course, in accordance with the translation status of the text as claimed by the translator, i.e. they accept his or her word. In cases of conflict between the writer's claim and the readers' judgement, the translation status of the text is in dispute. Macpherson might have thought "they think my Ossian poems are translations, but actually they aren't"; and we can also imagine a situation in which readers would deny that a given text was a translation, despite the writer's claim (or hope) – for instance if the text were unacceptably distant from the purported source text. But if the readers accept the writer's (honest) claim that a text is a translation, this is normally enough.

It is thus by no means the case that some mythical "perfect equivalence' (or even "adequate equivalence") has to exist before a text can be appropriately called a translation. Some translations are appalling, but they are nevertheless appalling *translations*. Other texts are claimed and accepted to be translations even though the relation between target text and source text is tenuous. Recall, for instance, the experimental symbolist translations of phonetic form alone, as in Jandl's (1966) German translation of Wordsworth's *My heart leaps up when I behold / A rainbow in the sky* as "Mai hart lieb zapfen eibe hold / er renn bohr in sees kai" (quoted at greater length by Toury (1980: 44)). This is undeniably a translation, of a sort (apart from being a *Lautgedicht* in its own right).

In fact it seems that the only necessary and sufficient condition for a text to be appropriately called "a translation" is that there must be *some* perceived relation between target text and source text.[*] This condition is met if (a) the translator claims that such a relation exists, and (b) the receivers of the text (intersubjectively) accept that such a relation exists (cf. also Toury 1985). The claim of translation status is obviously the stronger, the larger the proportion of receivers who agree. If receivers disagree, all we can say is that the translation status of the text in question is in doubt, as it would be if the (majority of the) receivers disagreed with the translator's claim.

Descriptive translation studies will therefore set out to describe and explain any behaviour which leads to something that can be appropriately called a translation. Obvious forms of descriptive research are thus the study of individual translation products, and also the study of the translation process using for instance the protocol method.

In this respect, the study of translation behaviour, and the general descriptive laws (statements of regularities) that emerge from this study, are similar to those pertaining to any other form of human behaviour. Such laws would be probabilistic, of course, and not universal. They would describe what people (at various levels of translation competence) tend to do, under certain given circumstances.

But now a problem arises. A purely descriptive approach will not incorporate any evaluative elements, so that a study of the translation behaviour of a beginner is, *qua* translation-theoretical study, just as valid as the study of the behaviour of a competent professional. As argued above, good translations and bad translations are nevertheless both *translations*. Unfortunately, of course, such an approach necessarily overlooks much of the motivation for studying translation behaviour in the first place and inevitably leads to a rather one-legged theory. What we need to know, not instead of but in addition to these general descriptive laws, is what makes a *good* translation. On what criteria do we want to say that translation behaviour A is better than translation behaviour B? Constitutive laws of behaviour-that-can-be-defined-as-translation-behaviour must surely be supplemented by regulatory laws of *good* translation behaviour.

---

[*] In retrospect, I would now say: a relation of *relevant similarity*. And also with respect to the relation norm, below. For Toury, there are "shared features" which are transferred from source to target text and form the basis of this relation.

Translation theory, if it is to take the form of a theory of translation behaviour, must include both a descriptive and an evaluative element. One way of doing this is via norm theory. Indeed, the concept of norms has played a part in the development of translation theory since the 1970's. Delabastita (1991) has recently argued that it is precisely via the study of translation norms that historical studies can be linked to purely theoretical research.

2. Laws and norms

Toury (1980: 51) sees translation norms as falling between "objective, relatively absolute rules" and "fully subjective idiosyncrasies". Norms govern behavioural tendencies, or rather a continuum of more or less mandatory behavioural tendencies. Further, a distinction is made between norms and "universals" of translation behaviour: universals are actual tendencies that may or may not be desirable – such as the translators' well-known habit of tending to make explicit in the target text what was implicit in the source text, or Toury's own example of textemes tending to be translated as repertoremes (Toury 1991, and especially 1996). "Universals" therefore do not have prescriptive force; norms do.

Toury returns to this distinction in a later paper (1991). Speaking now of "laws" rather than "universals", but (I assume) with the same intended sense, he stresses again that the laws of translation behaviour are not prescriptive, not directives. "They are designed to facilitate the *prediction* of 'real world' phenomena and/or their *explanation*" (p. 187, emphasis original); however, "in themselves they do not oblige anybody, *unless they are accepted as binding norms* within a (recipient) culture" (*ibid.*, emphasis added). Some laws thus become norms: in other words, certain behavioural regularities are accepted (in a given community) as being models or standards of desired behaviour.

We may therefore analyse norms descriptively as objects of study. But, insofar as they are indeed accepted by a given community as norms, they by definition have prescriptive force within that community. Bartsch (1987: 4) defines norms as the "social reality" of "correctness notions". With respect to language norms, people in a given society have, intersubjectively, certain notions of what constitutes correct or appropriate linguistic behaviour (in given situations) in that society; these notions reside in the social consciousness as norms. "Residing in the social consciousness" entails that norms be consciously known (or at least, that they be potentially accessible to conscious knowledge) by individuals in a society: to put it bluntly, "norms not known to exist do not exist" (Itkonen 1983: 73).

Norms function by virtue of their social existence plus their internalization by individual members of a given society. The function of norms is to regulate behaviour, to establish "acceptable margins of deviation" (Bartsch 1987: 70); they also create and maintain social order, and they save time and effort. Norms "reduce the complexity of perceiving and evaluating states of affairs and behaviour and thus make effective action possible" (Bartsch 1987: 173). Norms function basically as expectations:

> Successful ways of perceiving and acting become persistent and thus 'frozen patterns' of orientation. They are more than social habits as they acquire a normative force in the population. As norm kernels [i.e. the actual contents of norms], the regularities in these patterns provide the individuals in [a population] P with an orientation towards reality (facts, possible states of affairs) and action; this orientation is coordinated for the members of P. It consists basically of expectations about socially relevant things and events, of expectations about the behaviour and intentions of others, and of expectations about others' expectations about one's own behaviour and intentions. (Bartsch 1987: 173)

Norms that relate to language and the use of language are primarily a subclass of technical norms (other relevant norms are social and ethical norms) (Bartsch 1987: 170f). Technical norms comprise (a) production norms, having to do with methods and processes; and (b) product norms, having to do with the form of the end-results of processes.

3. Validation of norms

How are norms validated? Some norms are validated by a norm authority: the imperative theory of norms takes these as central (cf. Bartsch 1987: 76f). The practice theory of norms, on the other hand, acknowledges that some norms are validated by their very existence alone (see also von Wright 1968). According to this view (cf. Raz 1975: 53, cited in Bartsch 1987: 76), a valid norm (or "rule" in Raz's terminology: this is an unfortunate confusion of terms, but I am taking Raz's "rule" as a synonym for "norm" here, as does Bartsch) exists to the effect that x ought to do H under condition C in society S if and only if the following conditions hold:

1. Most members of S regularly do H under C.
2. If somebody does not comply with the rule [i.e. norm], he or she will be criticized by other members of S and such criticism will be looked on as justified by others members of S, such that this criticism is not criticized by them.
3. Members of S refer to the rule [norm] by expressions like 'An x should do H when C', or 'It is a rule [norm] that x ought to do H when C' in order to justify their actions, or demands made of others, or criticism of behaviour.

Note the way in which members of a society can thus appeal to norms to justify their actions, criticism etc. This shows the difference between norms and customs or conventions: breaching a convention gives no cause for sanction if no norm is involved.

This difference between norms and conventions is not always maintained. Following David Lewis (1969), Nord (1991b) stresses that conventions are arbitrary regularities of behaviour, arbitrary in the sense that they are not necessarily motivated. As Nord points out, norms are binding, and their violation usually arouses disapproval of some kind among the community concerned. But conventions are not binding, they embody only preferences. Nord (1991b: 100) also distinguishes between "regulative" translation conventions (which "refer to the generally accepted forms of handling certain translation problems") and "constitutive" conventions (which "determine what a particular culture accepts as a *translation*" (emphasis original)).

Now, it seems to me that Nord's conventions are actually norms, not conventions. They are norms precisely because their violation gives rise to some critical comment – her own. In Nord's own words, the conventional concept of translation, consisting of the sum total of constitutive conventions, *determines* the regulative conventions the translator may have to observe…" (1991: 100, emphasis added). These conventions look pretty binding. Bartsch (1987: 110) adds a further clarifying comment: norms of language may be conventions from a phylogenetic point of view, with respect to their origins, but "from the ontogenetic point of view, i.e. relative to the individual who has been born into a speech community, they are norms" – that is, they are experienced as binding by every new generation and every newcomer.

A good example of norms which are validated by their very existence, being generally considered rational and desirable behaviour but not laid down by any authority, are the norms governing queue behaviour in many societies. One observes the norm of recognizing one's own and other people's place in the queue, perhaps also the norm of "keeping a place" for someone else; and deviations from the norm are usually met with criticism in the form of sardonic or irritated comments.

On the other hand, accepted classroom behaviour at school (as distinct from actual "school rules", which are regulations rather than norms) concerning hand-raising, movement, talking etc. is guided by norms of another kind, given by an authority, the teacher.

Some norms are validated both by authority and by accepted usage: there are notices (by authorities) on the Helsinki underground asking people waiting for trains to let passengers disembark first before they themselves enter the train. This "official" norm of course does no more than make explicit what most people do anyway: in this case the norm already exists before the authority validates it.

4. Translation norms

Ullmann-Margalit (1977: 9; cited in Bartsch 1987: 104) points out that some norms are "solutions to problems posed by certain interaction situations". They have a problem-solving function, in fact. Translation norms would appear to be precisely of this type. They exist in order for communication to take place in a situation where it would otherwise be impossible. (See also Hermans (1991), who similarly discusses the applicability of norm theory to translation studies.)

On what basis does a society establish norms for translation behaviour? In the first place, a subset of individuals who translate can be isolated, a subset whose translation behaviour is accepted to be standard-setting; this is the subset of "competent professional translators". (I beg the question here of how to define "competent" and "professional" precisely: this is an important issue, but not central to the present argument.) In the second place we can isolate a subset of (translated) texts which are similarly accepted to represent a "model" of the desired quality: they are precisely those that have been, or (in the opinion of their readers) could have been, translated by competent professional translators. Both subsets are, I think, best defined *de facto*: an individual or a text will count as belonging to the relevant subset if there is a consensus of opinion in the relevant sections of society (i.e. sections that society accepts as being relevant) that such is the case: quite simply, such is the case if it is ("generally") *accepted* to be the case. These two subsets – one behavioural and one textlinguistic – are the sources of translation norms. I shall call the two kinds of resulting norms *professional norms* and *expectancy norms*. Both are factual, not ideal, norms. (Compare again Nord's (1991b) regulative and constitutive conventions.)

4.1 Professional norms

Professional norms are the norms constituted by competent professional behaviour. They are, in effect, kinds of production norms, governing the accepted methods and strategies of the translation process. Some professional norms control detailed aspects of translational behaviour such as source text analysis, needs analysis of the prospective readership, professional use of reference materials and so on. However, I claim that all professional norms can be subsumed under three higher-order norms which can be formulated as follows.

i. *The accountability norm*: a translator should act in such a way that the demands of loyalty are met with regard to the original writer, the commissioner, and the prospective readership. This is thus an ethical norm requiring professional standards of integrity and thoroughness. By his or her action the translator shows that he or she accepts responsibility for the translation. (Cf. the concept of loyalty in Nord 1991b, and the "true interpreter" norm in Harris 1990.)

ii. *The communication norm*: a translator should act in such a way as to optimize communication between the original writer and/or commissioner and the prospective readership. This is a social norm specifying the translator's social role as a communication expert. The communication norm can he derived, according to Bartsch (1987: 194), "by applying the principle of rationality to the overall goal of communication, understanding". It requires that we should communicate in such a way that others recognize and interpret the means of communication in the way we intend them to, in the same way as we do ourselves. I return to the principle of rationality below.

iii. *The relation norm*: a translator should act in such a way that an appropriate relation is established and maintained between target text and source text. The nature of this relation – the type and degree of equivalence, in other words – is determined by the translator, on the basis of his or her understanding of the intentions of the original writer and/or commissioner, the type and skopos of the text, and the nature of the prospective readership. (Recall the discussion of what counts as a translation, Section 1, above.) Being thus defined inter-textually, the norm is a linguistic one.

Consider now how these professional translation norms are validated. Some translation behaviour is indeed regulated by norms set up by an authority – by professionals of one sort or another. Translation teachers, examiners, translation critics, even professionals who check the drafts of other professionals – all are implicit norm-authorities, who are accepted as having norm-giving competence. Professional norms, then, are at least in part validated by norm authorities. But they also constitute the actual practice of competent professional translators: they are accepted as existing, as being the guidelines that such translators tend to follow.

4.2 Expectancy norms

Yet this norm-constituting behaviour is itself governed by higher-order norms: the expectancy norms. These are established by the receivers of the translation, by their expectations of what a translation (of a given type) should be like, and what a native text (of a given type) in the target language should be like. For instance, if a translation is expected to be covert (House 1981), it should match non-translated parallel texts in the target culture. For covert translations, then, the expectancy norms will be essentially the same as those that hold for native texts of the same type. If a translation is expected to be overt, on the other hand, the expectancy norms will be different. Whether a translation is expected to be overt or covert, and how this expectation then affects the translation itself, will he determined partly by the translation tradition in the target culture (see e.g. Hermans 1991).

Expectancy norms are in effect kinds of product norms. They are not validated by any actual norm-authority (unless the total set of receivers is so designated), but are valid by virtue of their existence in the target language community and in the specific communicative situation. A professional translator, in other words, seeks to design a target text in such a way that it will meet the expectancy norms pertaining to it. Thus, a translation enters the "translational subsystem" (Hermans 1991: 159) and *de facto* becomes part of that system, which itself is part of the target culture communication system as a whole. As Hermans puts it,

> the "correct" translation... is the one that fits the correctness notions prevailing in a particular system, i.e. that adopts the solutions regarded as correct for a given communicative situation, as a result of which it is accepted as correct. In other words: when translators do what is expected of them, they will be seen to have done well.   (1991: 166)

We can thus set up subclasses of syntactic, semantic and pragmatic expectancy norms, for a given target language culture at a given time.

It is worth noting that the key issue here is not, for instance, grammaticality *per se*, but rather a degree of grammaticality that meets the expectations of the readership. There might well be texts where syntactic incorrectness is appropriate – e.g. in representations of a foreigner's speech, in innovative advertising and the like. Pragmatic appropriateness is what counts.

It is in thus seeking to meet the *expectancy* norms as adequately as possible that the translator *de facto* conforms to the *professional* norms.

One qualification needs to be made at this point. I have stressed the importance of expectancy norms, the expectations of (among others) the target language readership. Unfortunately, it may well be that such expectations are not very high, given the daunting quantity of badly written texts that translators themselves are the first to complain about. In other words, by no means do all native texts necessarily conform to general ideals of order, clarity etc. This is a truism. But it does have the theoretical consequence that we should probably define these expectancy norms more stringently than we have so far done. That is, we should define them – at least in part – in terms of readers' expectations pertaining to *good* native texts, not just any native texts or even most native texts. Good native texts are a subset of all native texts. And the only reasonable operational definition of this subset is "texts that are accepted (with probability p by n% of native speakers) as being good". "Goodness of a text" is thus also a norm of sorts, of a higher order than the expectancy norms defined so far, but validated in the same way: by being generally accepted as such. (A further specification might define a subset of native speakers who were accepted as being particularly competent to judge the quality of a text, but I shall not go into this here.)

5. A normative science

At a general level, then, translation studies can be seen as a science of norms; in other words, as a normative science. Unfortunately, "normative" is an ambiguous term. It has two basic senses: (a) prescriptive, as in normative grammar; (b) descriptive, either of norms themselves or of products, processes or behaviour that are taken to constitute or represent norms. In their insistence on an empirical, descriptive approach, recent translation scholars have tended to shun the use of the word because they take it exclusively in its prescriptive sense. Hermans (1991: 166), for instance, actually seems to equate "normative" and "prescriptive". I am using the term in its legitimate descriptive sense, however: to describe the behaviour of a subset of individuals who are taken to represent a desired professional standard, and to describe a subset of texts that are similarly taken by their readers to represent a desired standard.

Is this fair? Can I thus place normative statements, albeit in the descriptive sense (b) above, on a par with other descriptive statements? Am I not thereby falling into the naturalistic fallacy, with the assumption that *ought* can he derived from *is*?

The gap between *ought* and *is* has dogged moral philosophy ever since Hume, and especially since Moore. There is indeed a respectable tradition of argument that value-statements cannot be logically derived from descriptive statements; that value-statements (non-natural) are different in kind from statements of fact (natural). However, it must also be pointed out that this tradition is one of argument only: a consensus has not been reached, and there is moreover an equally respectable opposing tradition which argues (in several different ways) precisely the opposite. (Several of the central papers are reprinted in Foot 1967.) Searle (1964), for instance, arguing from speech act theory, sees nothing illogical in deriving *ought* from *is,* at least in some cases; and Austin (1962: 148) casts doubt on the whole normative vs. factual distinction.

Within ethics, furthermore, there are theories that appear to be strikingly similar in structure to the view of translation theory which I am defending here. Friedrich Jodl (1918) set up a detailed theory of ethics as an empirical discipline based on the study of what a society holds to be ethical norms. In other words, his ethics describes what people have thought about ethical norms, what criteria people have used for evaluating ethical phenomena. These norms and criteria are not given once and for all, *a priori*, but vary through history and between societies: in Jodl's view they become increasingly refined, evolving into higher and higher norms, and one task of the moral philosopher is indeed to contribute to this process of refinement. All ethical imperatives thus have a social source, based on social approval or disapproval: norms correspond to average tendencies of approval/disapproval in a given society at a given time. They are not static, not absolute; there may therefore occur conflicts of norms, between historical periods or different societies. Historically, norms originate in customs which gradually become accepted as prescriptive behavioural laws. Throughout the historical development of norms, their regulating ideal does not lie in some intuitively apprehended absolute perfection, but simply in whatever seems to be desirable and attainable in given circumstances, in whatever appears to be conducive to the good of the society in question.

In Jodl's theory, then, there is a sense in which the *ought* is not non-existent, non-*is*. Rather, the *ought* is a subset of the *is*: certain existing behavioural phenomena are found (by a given society at a given time) to be desirable, and are therefore taken as embodying models to be aimed at. In other words, these phenomena establish norms. What genuinely exists in the (relatively) shared social consciousness is an awareness of what these norms are; we are not claiming that some perfect *realization* of, say, loving behaviour (or of the ideal of love that would motivate such behaviour) would necessarily exist there. The situation is, I claim, precisely parallel with respect to translation norms. Here too, we have an *ought* that already *is*: there already *is* a subgroup of individuals and of texts which we are taking as embodying norms and from which we can thus derive *oughts* for other individuals and other texts. Furthermore, here too we are not taking these individuals or texts to be perfect realizations of some ideal, but as instances which conform to agreed criteria, to an extent which justifies our taking them as norms. They are accepted to be the best we have, so far. But we acknowledge that some of these norms may conflict with others, that they may vary between societies, and that they may change over time. Indeed, it may even happen that a norm is overtly broken and replaced by something else, which is deemed to have a higher priority and thus becomes a new norm.

It is in precisely this sense that translation studies should be normative, norm-describing and indeed norm-refining; and I have suggested there are two broad types of norms which are relevant to it: professional and expectancy norms. How are these norms actually achieved?

6. Strategies and normative laws

To answer this question, we need to assume that human translators are rational beings, and that their translation behaviour is governed by rational decisions. The rationality of translation behaviour is descriptive (or procedural) rather than prescriptive (or substantive), in the terms discussed by Itkonen (1983: 87–90). That is, the translator typically chooses *an* adequate option, heuristically, the best he or she can think of at the time; not (usually) the single possible (predetermined) option. (Cf. the minimax strategy, Levý 1967.) Furthermore, the set of options in translating is not (necessarily) fixed in advance in any mathematically precise sense: "procedural rationality, when confronted with problem situations, combines past experience with selective heuristics for reaching a satisfactory choice" (Itkonen 1983: 88).

We thus posit the existence of a Rationality Principle. Itkonen (1983: 66) first gives such a principle the following form: "if the context is C and the goal is G, the rational thing to do is A". However, in light of the heuristic nature of the translator's rationality, it would seem more appropriate for our purposes to formulate the principle as: if the context is C and the goal is G, *a* rational thing to do is A (cf. Itkonen 1983: 100). Rational behaviour is thus determined by the context of the behaviour and the goal of the behaviour, plus the prerequisite of rationality.

With respect to translation behaviour, a rational act A (as defined above) is what is often referred to as a translation strategy (or sometimes a tactic). I will follow Lörscher (1991: 76) here and define a strategy thus: "a translation strategy is a potentially conscious procedure for the solution of a problem which an individual is faced with when translating a text segment from one language into another". In Itkonen's terms, the context C of such a strategy is constituted by the source text, the circumstances of the commission, the target text situation/readership, the possibilities of the target language, etc. The goal G of the strategy is, at the most general level, to conform to the relevant professional and expectancy norms. A strategy may start out as a hypothesis, a rational attempt to reach a given goal. If a strategy turns out to used regularly, it will *de facto* take on the status of a probabilistic law of translation behaviour: most translators will be observed to use it (in given circumstances). And if a given strategy turns out to be regularly used by competent professional translators, it will *de facto* take on the status of what I would like to call a *normative law*. (Cf. Zalán 1990.)

A normative law in this sense is a descriptive statement concerning an observed regularity in the behaviour of competent professionals who are accepted as embodying translation norms. Normative laws of translation are a subset of the general descriptive laws of translation; normative laws describe not just any translation behaviour, but only such behaviour that is recognized as being maximally compatible with professional and expectancy norms. It would in principle be possible to incorporate the differences between professional (normative) and non-professional translation behaviour in terms of differing conditions under which descriptive translation laws apply. However, unlike general descriptive laws, normative laws have prescriptive force for members of a given translating community; they are prescriptive from the ontogenetic point of view. But as statements about the behaviour of a subset of translators they are descriptive, in the same sense as statements about the behaviour of any translators, i.e. in the sense of general descriptive laws of translation.

The three key concepts of *law*, *norm* and *strategy* can thus be precisely related as follows: a normative translation law is a norm-directed strategy which is observed to be used (with a given, high, probability) by (a given, large, proportion of) competent professional translators.

A brief example may be helpful here. Let us assume that there is a kind of professional translation norm, derived from the communication norm, to the effect that: *in certain text types, source-language culture-bound terms should be expanded or explained in translation*. This professional norm is governed by the expectancy norm which states that readers do not expect unknown concepts in a text of this type. There might then be a general descriptive law of translation behaviour to the effect that, say, 70% of translators tend to explain culture-bound terms in such texts and 30% tend not to. Obviously, the 70% that do are following the norm; consequently they are better translators in terms of this parameter. But general descriptive laws cannot neglect the existence of less good translators who do not follow this norm, perhaps because they are not aware of it. A normative translation law would state that, say, 99.9% of competent professional translators do follow this norm; and indeed this is why we know it *is* a norm, this is how it is validated. Those translators that do adhere to this norm would be using a strategy that might be formulated as: if the source text contains culture-bound terms that would be incomprehensible to the prospective target language readers, explain these terms; the strategy would then go on to mention[*] methods by which this explaining might be done – footnotes, explanation in the text together with original term, explanation alone without the original term, replacement by a related target-culture term, and so on – and further specify the conditions under which each method would be the most appropriate one, or the priorities governing the different methods.

---

[*] Well, ideally; or "in theory"...

7. Empirical status

In the preamble to her book, Bartsch (1987: 3) talks about the desirability of integrating linguistic theory into the general theory of action. This would give linguistics a firm empirical basis. A normative theory of translation behaviour would be clearly empirical, in that its (probabilistic) laws would indeed be spatio-temporally falsifiable. Norms function as standards or models of a certain kind of behaviour and of a certain kind of behavioural product (i.e. a text). Normative translation laws both predict and explain, in a standard empirical sense (as do general translation laws).

7.1 Prediction

The predictions will be probabilistic like any other predictions concerning human behaviour. They can be tested, and confirmed or disconfirmed.

Predictions start out as hypothetical strategies. For instance, we might hypothesize that, for a given sample of professional translators (or in a given sample of translated texts), strategy A will tend to be selected under given circumstances. If this indeed turns out to be the case, to an accepted degree of probability, we can proceed to test the hypothesis more widely, and if there is no disconfirming evidence the strategy can eventually be formulated explicitly as an empirical law. A normative translation law is thus strictly speaking a hypothesis that has not yet been disconfirmed. If, notwithstanding, it subsequently turns out to be the case that (a significant proportion of) professional translators do not, after all, behave in this way – for instance if it turns out at some later point that translation behaviour has changed over time – then the law is thereby falsified and must be modified, e.g. by bringing in (more) conditioning factors.

It is worth stressing that the scientific status of translation laws is no different from that of sociological laws, or indeed laws of linguistic behaviour of any kind. We might say that translation laws are simply a subclass of the set of general "texting" laws of language behaviour: translating is "texting" under specifically restricted conditions.

7.2 Explanation

Like any theory, a translation theory sets out to explain as well as describe; it asks not only "what?" but also "why?" Why do competent professional translators behave as they do? Why do they make the decisions that they do? Why do they use certain strategies rather than others'? At the most general level the answer is simply: "because these translators seek to conform to the norms of translation behaviour". (Similarly, less-than-professional translators make the decisions they do because they are not conforming to the norms.) But it is also useful to look for answers at a more specific level, to establish basic types of answer. In different ways, these answers therefore constitute explanations of translation behaviour. The answers are not mutually exclusive, of course: a given act may have several simultaneous explanations. Some of these are causal, others teleological: both types are relevant to translation theory.

Potential sources of explanation can be classified with relation to the major kinds of translation norms outlined above (compare also the types of interpretation norms suggested by Shlesinger 1989, Harris 1990), as follows.

1. *The source text.* A translator performs act A because the source text contained item/feature X. (Cf. the relation norm.)

    This answer gives a causal explanation for A: the occurrence of X is temporally prior to the act A, and determines this act. The strategy (of using act A) is specific to given source and target languages, and will be based on the translator's knowledge of the conditioned probabilities of equivalence between a given source item and a given target item. Compare machine translation and the kind of translation laws it requires.

2. *Target language norms.* A translator performs act A because of the expectancy norms of the target language community regarding grammaticality, acceptability, appropriateness, style, textuality, preferred conventions of form or discourse and the like.

    This kind of explanation is partly causal, in that the target norms already exist, are known to the translator and thus determine his behaviour; but it is also teleological, in that (as argued above) if the translator is aspiring to the professional norms the intention will be precisely to conform to these expectancy norms, by definition, and this intention also determines the translation behaviour. Traditionally, it is true, it would be said that we are talking about reasons rather than causes here, since the translator's goals and knowledge are agent-internal. Yet to know the reason for an act is also to understand that act; a reason is also an explanation. I am therefore taking the concept of cause in a wide enough sense to include reason.

3. *Normative translation laws.* A translator performs act A because this act conforms to given normative translation laws. (Cf. professional norms in general.)

    That is, the act A is motivated by the translator's knowledge of existing translation laws which have already been shown to be generally valid in professional

translation behaviour regardless of specific source or target languages, e.g. concerning standard ways of translating metaphors, allusions, priorities among kinds of equivalence, and so on. In the sense mentioned above, this explanation is also both causal and teleological.
4. *General communication maxims.* (Cf. the communication norm.) A translator performs act A because this act conforms to overall communicative or co-operative maxims, principles which are accepted as valid for any kind of communication, not just translation. One formulation of these maxims is the familiar Gricean one of quantity, quality, relevance and manner (Grice 1975). Again, this explanation is both causal (if such maxims form part of the already existing general or professional knowledge of the translator) and teleological.
5. *Ethical values.* (Cf. the accountability norm.) A translator performs act A because this act conforms to ethical principles. For example, a translator may take the trouble to check a name or date which he suspects may be wrong in the source text.

8. Applications

We expect of a scientific theory not only that it should serve to describe and explain certain phenomena, and that it should be able to predict their occurrence reliably, but also that it should be useful. A theory is also a tool.

A theory of translation norms has both practical and theoretical applications. On the practical level, such a theory has evident pedagogical relevance. If the professional and expectancy norms are formulated in a learnable way, they can be explicitly taught to trainees: they can become part of the trainees' knowledge base and thence help to determine appropriate translational action. Bartsch, too, points out that "an important property of norms is that they have to be learned" (1987: 178). They are learned either by overt prescription, as authority-given norms, or else by the observation of model behaviour, as existence-validated norms. Trainees can he taught, for instance, to think consciously about alternative strategies, to observe and evaluate the results of different strategies, and so on.

This approach also has implications for the assessment of translation quality. Translation behaviour, the process, can only be assessed in terms of the translation product. (Unorthodox processes which nevertheless arrive at appropriate products – in compatible time etc. – are not in themselves open to criticism.) In the first place, translations can be assessed with respect to professional norms, and this includes the attainment of an appropriate relationship between target text and source text. But ultimately translations must be assessed with respect to expectancy norms: the relation with target-language parallel and background texts from which the readers derive their expectations.

On the theoretical level, this kind of approach would provide an organizing structure which would give coherence to the enormous range of disparate information we already have about translation norms. Ethical codes of a professional translator's accountability can be supplemented by accounts of how these norm-giving translators actually do behave. Expectancy norms need a systematic hierarchical taxonomy, covering both language-specific and language-independent norms, particularly pragmatic norms. Translation quality assessment needs an explicit statement of the relevant norms against which quality is judged.

Research is also needed on the translation laws themselves, on formulating and testing them and then reformulating them. The theory is thus open-ended, ever seeking to improve the probability of its predictions. It is also optimistic in Jodl's sense, ever seeking to refine the norms of translation itself.

PAPER 14

A note on norms and evidence*

There are two senses of the concept "norm": one is descriptive and weakly explanatory, and the other is causal or prescriptive and more strongly explanatory. Studying norms in the causal sense means looking for plausible links between observed regularities and evidence of normative force: this may be found in belief statements, in criticism of norm-breaking, or in norm statements. Norms are explanatory hypotheses, and can be tested in various ways.

Keywords: norm, normative force, regularity, explanation, hypothesis, testing

1. Introduction

Norms have become a key concept in Translation Studies, at least since Toury (1980). But there is still disagreement about how best to define them, and also how to study them. One stage in the conceptual debate was summarized in the contributions to Schäffner (1999), a collection of papers which debated several important issues concerning the interpretation of norms within Descriptive Translation Studies (DTS), such as the relation between norms and conventions, and between norms and expectations.

The starting-point for the present paper was a conference organized in 2004 by the School of Languages and Area Studies at the University of Portsmouth, on the topic: "Translation norms. What is 'normal' in the translation profession" (see Kemble 2005 for the Proceedings). As the conference title indicates, the perspective here was not exclusively that broadly taken by scholars working within DTS; the scope of the term "norms" was taken in a wider sense, to include "what is 'normal'". However, this wider scope was the cause of some conceptual confusion, which was evident not only at the conference itself but also in the written proceedings (as pointed out e.g. by myself in the same Proceedings). This leads not only to

---

* First published in 2006 in Jorma Tommola and Yves Gambier (eds), *Translation and interpreting – training and research*. Turku, University of Turku, Department of English Translation Studies, 13–19. The keywords have been added.

misunderstanding but also to methodological difficulties: different interpretations of the norm concept imply different methodological decisions.

If we can clarify the concept of norms more sharply, and agree more explicitly about what would count as evidence for norms, it might be easier to answer some of the problematic questions that arise when we consider appropriate methodologies for studying norms.

2. The two senses

Let us start by stating the two interpretations as explicitly as possible.

Under interpretation (a), a norm is defined as a tendency; it denotes an instance of typical behaviour. In this sense, a norm is a descriptive notion, and is close to the concept of a convention and to the idea of what is "normal". In this sense, I could claim that payment norms for subtitlers seem to be gradually falling, as more and more work is done by less qualified translators for lower rates, and clients appear to be satisfied with poorer quality: this is becoming "normal". This claim does not imply anything about what *should* be the case.

Under interpretation (b), on the other hand, a norm is understood as something rather more complex. According to Bartsch (1987: xiv), norms in this sense are interpreted as "the social reality of correctness notions". This definition can be further specified as implying the following three elements (paraphrased from Bartsch 1987: 76):

X manifests / is caused by a norm *if*
i. most people (in a given society or group at a given time, under given conditions) regularly do X; and
ii. they think they should indeed do X; and
iii. they can justifiably be criticized if they do not do X.

This is the general sense in which norms have been understood in most DTS. Unlike interpretation (a), interpretation (b) is a causal one, not just a descriptive one. It implies that people behave in a given way *because of* certain norms. Norms in this sense carry a normative (or prescriptive) force: they thus affect behaviour.

Both interpretations are social, but in different ways. Interpretation (a) is social in the sense that it describes a general tendency covering more than a single instance distributed across time and/or place. The discovery of only one badly paid subtitler would not justify a description of this practice as being "normal". Interpretation (b) is social by definition, in opposition to purely personal principles which may also motivate behaviour. I can claim that I always brush my teeth after breakfast "because I think I ought to", but this "ought" is not normative in our sense (b), unless it can be shown that it is shared by a significant number of other people who also brush their teeth after breakfast (e.g. rather than before). Norms are not personal (although attitudes to them may be personal).

3. Descriptive and explanatory

Before we proceed to some methodological implications, a reservation is in order. The distinction I have just suggested between the descriptive sense (a) and the explanatory sense (b) is not an absolute one. If we know that translators have a tendency, for instance, to reduce repetition, and we are wondering why a given translator has reduced some source-text repetition in a particular translation, we can offer this explanation: she did it *because* that is what translators typically do. We have explained this translator's behaviour by relating it to a general tendency. True, this explanation is a rather weak one, in that it does not show that we know anything about *why* translators in general tend to reduce repetition. Nor does it show that a given translator did this because she was *aware* that this is what translators often/generally do. But our realization that this translator is behaving just like many other translators certainly lessens any surprise we may feel at her reductions: they are, in this sense, quite normal, quite expected. (For further discussion of generalization as a first step towards explanation, see also Halverson 2003.)

It is in this sense that Toury's proposal for translation "laws" relates to the title of his book: *Descriptive Translation Studies and Beyond* (Toury 1995). The "beyond" refers partly to the explanatory power of the proposed laws (of interference and growing standardization). If these general tendencies do indeed exist, they do serve to explain some aspects of translatorial behaviour in some way. The same is true of the increasing body of reseach on translation universals (see e.g. Mauranen and Kujamäki 2004).

But Toury's book also offers explanatory concepts of a stronger kind: norms, in our sense (b). Norms in this sense can of course be described (i.e. not prescribed, not laid down by the researcher), and so we can take a descriptive approach to them, just as we can take a descriptive approach to ethical values for instance, or the language of instructions. Having identified and described norms, we can then appeal to them in order to formulate explanatory hypotheses e.g. about the occurrence or distribution of certain translational features. A translator may, for instance, naturalize source-text "miles" to target-text "kilometres" because she is following a domestication norm to this effect, or perhaps because she is deliberately resisting an opposite norm according to which she should keep the foreignizing "miles". However, it is relevant to underline that this formulation of a causal link is strictly speaking imprecise: norms do not affect behaviour directly, because their influence must be filtered through the translator's mind as decisions are made during the translation act. Translators adopt attitudes to norms, if they are aware of them: to follow them or not, as the case may be. A translator follows a norm because she chooses to, for whatever reason; or, she does not follow it because she does not choose to (or of course because she does not know about it).

Norms, especially in sense (b), are thus abstract, intangible. How can we study them? What counts as evidence for the existence of a norm? These questions lead to the methodological implications of the two interpretations.

4. Regularities

If data analysis shows up regularities, repeated patterns, tendencies, this of course constitutes evidence for norms in our interpretation (a). Indeed, to say that a regularity reveals a norm, in this sense, is no more than a pleonasm.

But an observed regularity does not constitute sufficient evidence for a norm in our interpretation (b), the DTS sense. This sense is a causal one, as mentioned above. The cause of an observed regularity *may* be the existence of a norm, but it does not have to be. Other possible causes include cognitive constraints, time and task constraints, or factors concerning the translator's background knowledge and proficiency – and of course chance. If amateur translators regularly produce poor-quality translations, for instance, we do not assume that they are following a norm to this effect. Interference, too, is a regular tendency, but it is not often likely to be directly influenced by norms (although norms may of course affect people's reactions to interference).

On the other hand, we cannot argue that something is a norm *without* some evidence of a regularity which would manifest this norm (or, as mentioned above, which would manifest the translator's attitude to this norm). (Cf. condition (i) in Bartsch's definition, above.) An isolated case, without the support of other similar cases, cannot be adequate evidence of a norm; nor can non-systematic instances which do not suggest a tendency of any kind. Observed regularities are thus *necessary* conditions for norms in our sense (b), but not sufficient ones.

The challenge of research into norms is in fact to show plausible links between observed regularities on the one hand and evidence of normative force on the other.

5. Evidence of normative force

Evidence of normative force comes, I suggest, in three forms.

Belief statements
These are statements which people use to justify an action. They have the general form: "I think people should (not) do X (under conditions ABC)". (Compare condition (ii) in Bartsch's definition.) Translation research can find this kind of evidence e.g. in interviews with translators, in translator notes and prefaces (translator's statements), in essays or letters written by translators about their work, in texts by critics or clients or consumers of translations. If such evidence is not found in the form of explicit belief statements, a researcher may be able to argue that there is at least implicit or circumstantial evidence of this kind: there may be evidence that people *seem* to believe that they should (not) do X. However, the mere existence of belief statements is not a sufficient condition for postulating a norm, because of the gap between what people say they believe and what they actually do believe and/or what they actually do. If people do not in fact follow a given norm N, although they say they believe they should do so, we do not have strong evidence for the existence of the norm. Maybe there is another norm, a competing norm M, which people actually follow.

Explicit criticism
Criticism against behaviour that does not conform to a given norm can be evidence of the existence of the norm. (Recall condition (iii) in the defintion above.) Bartsch points out (1987: 76) that such criticism is considered to be justified by other members of the society concerned, in that the criticism itself is not criticised. Criticism of norm-breaking in Translation Studies can be found in teachers' comments and feedback, in translation reviews, and also in clients' and consumers' reactions, perhaps also in the reactions of other translators. However, criticism may also have other causes. A critical reaction may also be due to a personal preference or opinion, bad temper, rivalry, or some other reason.

Norm statements
A norm statement (or norm codification: Bartsch 1987: 177) is an official statement by a norm authority of the content of a norm. They have the implicit form: "we hereby declare that (under conditions ABC) people should (not) do X". A norm authority is a person or institution authorized by a given society to issue and maintain norms. In the field of translation, norm authorities may be trainers, publishers, patrons, literary critics, clients, cultural institutions, governments, and so on. A publisher or a large company, or an international body such as the EU, for instance, may issue style norms which translators have to follow.

There may also be explicit norm statements about changes permitted or forbidden, such as the EU norm about not changing sentence breaks in translations of legal documents. In this category we can also include official statements about what may or may not be translated: translation censorship. (See e.g. the special issue of *TTR*: 2, 2002.)

Norm statements by norm authorities can make a norm valid. But not all norms have associated norm statements: a norm may become valid simply by being followed. I have never seen a notice in a lift forbidding eye-contact with strangers, but there does seem to be a norm to this effect: people simply avoid prolonged eye-contact in these circumstances, because it feels uncomfortable. There is a shared feeling that one ought not to do it; it would be rude. Anyone breaking this norm may provoke irritation or embarrassment.

On the other hand, if (most of) the relevant people do not actually conform to a given norm statement, it is hard to argue that the norm in question actually exists. A norm that is not followed is not really a norm at all, because it has no social existence. So norm statements in the absence of evidence that a norm is being followed (regularities, tendencies) do not make for persuasive evidence.

A researcher who wishes to propose that a given norm N exists therefore needs to produce as much evidence of normative force as possible, and to link this plausibly with evidence of observed regularities. Both kinds of evidence are necessary; neither suffices on its own.

But norms are slippery, abstract things. If they exist at all, they are somewhere in the social consciousness, in Popper's World 3 (see e.g. Popper 1972: 106f). Norms themselves lie hidden behind regularities and beliefs and norm statements. In other words, norms themselves are best considered as explanatory hypotheses rather than observable facts.

6. Testing hypotheses about norms

The main point of Sections 4 and 5 above can be summarized by saying that this is how hypotheses about norms (in the DTS sense) can be generated. One can either start with observed regularities and look for related signs of normative force, or one can start with some evidence for normative force and check for corresponding regularities; or even work both ways at the same time. In translation research, both textual (e.g. regularities, norm or belief statements, written criticism) and extratextual sources are relevant (observation of translator work procedures, interviews etc.). But like all hypotheses, these claims then need to be tested. How? Here are some suggestions.

Triangulate the evidence. Triangulation (in research) means using different methodologies or data to explore the same research question, and then looking for connections or correlations between the results, in the hope that the results gained by one method can corroborate the results gained by another method. If research can show, for instance, that different kinds of evidence of normative force can be found concerning the same regularities, the norm hypothesis in question becomes more convincing. A good example of this is some research by Brownlie (2003), in which she correlated data from questionnaires sent to translators with data from their translations themselves. She asked the translators about their attitudes towards literal translation, cutting up long sentences in the source text, foreignizing, clarifying the source text, the treatment of technical terms, and so on. These data are then related both to publishers' instructions and to textual features. Brownlie also discusses several of the issues raised in the present paper.

Norm-breaking. A researcher might deliberately break a hypothesized norm, and see what happens. Does this provoke criticism? Sanctions? (Try eye-contact with strangers in a lift and see what happens.) This means in fact formulating a predictive hypothesis.

Counter-evidence. Alternatively, one can look for counter-evidence (always a good idea) and honestly report what one finds. By this I mean looking not only for evidence of norm-breaking which is *not* followed by criticism, but also evidence of competing norms that may be being followed under the same conditions.

Norm-conforming. Test for the results of conforming to a given norm. How do people in a foreign culture react if you try to follow their norms? (I.e. try another predictive hypothesis.) I read recently of a western journalist attending a Hindu religious rite in India, in a small boat on a river. All the other westerner observers had cameras and filmed everything excitedly, but she behaved quite differently, sitting quite still and respectfully, with no camera, like the local believers taking part in the rite. Her boat was the only western one allowed to float undisturbed to the centre of the area where the rite was taking place: she had conformed to the behaviour norm.

Elicit a belief statement. Ask a member of the society concerned whether it is true that (under conditions ABC) people should do X. Or ask openly whether a given observed regularity is a norm.

Elicit a norm statement. Ask a norm authority the same questions.

Expand the data-base. If we see regularities in one text, or set of texts, which we suspect to be norm-governed, we can check for the same regularity in other texts which might be assumed to be within the scope of the same norm. Translation scholars may also be able to check paratexts and extratextual sources.

None of these tests might be conclusive, of course. But they might well strengthen or weaken a norm hypothesis.

SECTION V

Similarities and differences

The research literature on shifts and strategies has multiplied over the past few years, with debates and disagreements about concepts, terminology, and typologies. I have commented elsewhere (Chesterman 2007a) that TS has traditionally been more interested in differences between source and target texts than similarities between them. We have a few classifications of different kinds of equivalence but we have many more suggestions about how best to analyse differences. Classifications of "shifts" have been proposed by some scholars, while typologies of "strategies", "procedures" or "solution types" have been suggested by others (see e.g. Schreiber 1998). For a more recent critical survey of these terminological and conceptual issues, see Gambier (2008). The latest contribution to this topic that I am aware of is Pym (2016), which offers a wide-reaching historical survey of previous proposals as well as Pym's own proposal of seven basic "solution types".

To prepare the ground for some discussion of kinds of difference, Paper 15 is an essay on the concept of similarity, inspired by some work in philosophy, psychology and pragmatics. The main distinction drawn there, between two kinds of similarity, has also been applied to translation equivalence by Pym (2007a, 2010).

Paper 16 aimed for clarity, but may only add to the conceptual confusion around this topic (compare Gambier 2008). Despite my criticisms of the term "strategy", I have tended to stay with it, for the admittedly not-too-persuasive reason that I have simply got used to it.

Paper 17 partly concerns translation and partly contrastive analysis (Finnish and English). Some of the contrastive data from newspapers may of course also include translated material. The topic discussed – a possible "salience threshold", with different "heights" in different languages – may also relate to general translation tendencies such as standardization (see the section on "Universals" below). Data relevant to this suggestion could now be interestingly analysed via Appraisal Theory, particularly the concepts of Gradation, Force and Focus there. (See e.g. Martin and White 2005.)

PAPER 15

On similarity[*]

This short paper outlines some research in logic and pragmatics that sheds interesting light on the concept of similarity. A recent proposal (Sovran 1992) suggests that there are two basic kinds of similarity: divergent and convergent. These seem to be directly relevant to how we conceptualize equivalence in Translation Studies and in Contrastive Analysis, respectively.

Keywords: similarity, equivalence, Contrastive Analysis, Tversky, Sovran

It is widely agreed these days that translation equivalence, whatever it is, is better conceived of as a kind of similarity rather then as a sameness. Yet little note seems to have been taken so far of philosophical and psychological research into the concept of sameness, and how people make judgements of similarity. (True, Wittgenstein's notion of family resemblances has been taken up by several translation scholars.) A recent article on the concept of similarity (Sovran 1992) raises a number of points that seem of direct relevance to translation theory.

Similarity is a well-known problem concept in philosophy and logic. Similarity is not necessarily symmetrical (*This copy of the Mona Lisa is incredibly like the original* but ??*The Mona Lisa is incredibly like this copy of it*). It is often non-reversible (*Richard fought like a lion* but ??*[The] lion fought like Richard*). It is not necessarily transitive: if John is like Mary in that they both have a weakness for chocolate biscuits, and Mary is like Kate in that they both hate getting up early, it need not be the case that John is judged similar to Kate in any relevant way.

One reason for such problems is that similarity is partly a matter of cognition: it seems to be a subjective or intersubjective concept, not an exclusively objective one. Two entities "are" similar if they are *judged to be* similar – judged by someone. Furthermore, no two people necessarily perceive the same similarities, or even judge the same two entities to be similar at all. On the other hand, it might be claimed that *any* two entities can be perceived as similar in *some* respect, provided that we are imaginative enough to find this shared feature. Judgements of

---

[*] Originally published in 1996 in *Target* 8, 1: 159–164. Reprinted with kind permission from John Benjamins Publishing Company, Amsterdam/Philadelphia [www.benjamins.com]. I have updated a reference. The abstract and keywords have been added.

similarity must of course be made on some grounds, not arbitrarily: there must therefore be some objective evidence for such judgements. The problem arises, however, when we try to generalize, for it seems that practically anything can be taken as evidence of similarity of some kind. It all depends… – which is precisely the point.

Another problem is the measurement of degree of similarity, its quantification: how do we judge two entities to be "more similar" than two other entities? The standard approach to this is represented by Tversky (e.g. 1977), who defined degree of similarity in terms of the number of shared features two entities are perceived to have. A feature is any property that can be perceived or deduced from our knowledge of the world. Similarity judgement is thus a matter of feature matching. "Shared features", however, seem to entail "sameness": a feature is judged to be shared by two entities if both entities are perceived to manifest this "same" feature. "Similarity" is this reduced to "sameness" at one level down.

A modification of this view is offered by prototype theory, which appears to downplay the "sameness" issue by assuming that features themselves may be manifest in different degrees, not absolutely present or absent, and therefore shared not discretely but fuzzily. Furthermore, some features are more prominent than others, and thus more relevant to judgements of similarity. In a classic essay, Goodman (1972) argues that all similarity judgements boil down to judgements about the relative importance of different features, and because "importance" is a volatile concept, similarity itself is a constantly shifting, culture-bound and theory-bound concept, philosophically "insidious". In an obvious way, similarity judgements are also influenced by the context in which the judgements are made: "big" in one context may be "small" in another.

Tversky (1977) reports various empirical experiments that illustrate this context-dependence. For instance, asked to estimate the relative degree of similarity between Austria and certain other countries, subjects responded quite differently when the context was "Austria, Sweden, Poland and Hungary" as opposed to "Austria, Sweden, Norway and Hungary": in the first context, Austria was judged similar to Sweden; in the second, it was felt to be more similar to Hungary.

Others have made the same point by appealing to notions of salience or relevance, which function as constraints on feature-counting or feature-matching. "Circumstances alter similarities", as Goodman puts it (1972: 445). The perceived degree of similarity also correlates with the range of entities being assessed: the more entities, the less the pertinent degree of similarity. Compare an assessment which classifies all Romantic poets as similar (i.e., which justifies a shared label), and an assessment which sees Wordsworth as being more similar to Keats than to, say, Coleridge.

Judgements of similarity are (inter)subjective, yes, but they are not arbitrary; they are nevertheless based on objective evidence. Triangles all have three sides, and this objective fact makes it particularly easy to perceive a similarity between them – precisely the similarity that enables us to categorize such shapes as triangles. But not all similarity judgements are so straightforward. Think of the why-is-an-X-like-a-Y? sort of riddles. These riddles precisely challenge the hearer to find a similarity, however far-fetched this might be. Tversky ends up with the view – as argued above – that similarity is partly objective (defined by intrinsic properties of the entities themselves) and partly (inter)subjective (defined by people's perceptions of these properties). Features of entities have degrees of intensity (objective – at least in principle, like the number of sides of a geometrical figure) and degrees of diagnosticity (salience for a given subjective judgement).*

Judgements of equivalence in translation studies and in contrastive studies are obviously instances of similarity judgements. So are attempts to set up *tertia comparationis*. It is therefore worth stressing the intrinsic subjectivity and relativity of such concepts.

Sovran's paper (1992) offers the interesting proposal that similarity itself is not a unitary concept at all, but binary. One brand of similarity starts from the concept of oneness. We could call this divergent similarity, and illustrate it thus:

$A \rightarrow A^i, A^{ii}, A^{iii}...$

This is the kind of similarity that results from a process going from one to more-than-one, like a copying or reproduction process; cases of mistaken identity (where A^i is mistakenly taken as A) also come under this heading. Assessments of divergent similarity are expressed by such utterances as: *This is a forgery of the original painting, The rebuilt church is strikingly similar to the original building that was destroyed in the war, This computer is an IBM clone.*

The second kind of similarity starts from separateness. Let us call this convergent similarity. It can be symbolized thus:

$A \leftrightarrow B$

Here, we start with two entities that are distinct, and we then perceive a similarity between them, as when we perceive an analogy or a surprising resemblance not noticed before. Examples of such convergent similarity assessments are: *They look*

---

* Medin and Goldstone (1995: 106) argue that similarity is, logically speaking, a "multi-placed predicate", such that expressions of similarity can be explicated thus: "*A* is similar to *B* in respects *C* according to comparison process *D*, relative to some standard *E* mapped onto judgments by some function *F* for some purpose *G*".

very much the same, There is certainly some analogy between the two countries' policies, The music reminded me of a song I heard once in Macedonia.

Sovran goes on to examine the type-token relationship (divergent if seen top-down from type to token, and convergent if seen bottom-up from token to type), and the overlap between lexical items expressing sameness and similarity in English. (Sameness is no more than a special case of similarity: *the same dress* can mean the same token or the same type.) She also stresses the role played by the imagination in perceiving and judging similarity. In Hebrew, she points out, the word *dimyon* means both 'resemblance' and 'imagination'. Seeing a similarity is thus seeing something "as" something else, which is an imaginative act; and this ability to see something as something else is central to human cognition. It is also central to hermeneutics, particularly the Gadamerian kind.

Sovran's proposal sheds interesting light on the relation between translation studies and contrastive analysis, and also on our understanding of the translation process. In terms of her two kinds of similarity, the translation process is clearly based on divergent similarity: a source, entity A, gives rise to other entities, A^i, A^{ii} etc., and these entities are desired to be, and/or perceived as, similar in some relevant way to the source entity. Contrastive analysis, on the other hand, is based on convergent similarity. We take two distinct entities, and seek the similarity or similarities which they manifest (and the differences, of course). On the basis of these similarities, thought of as *tertia comparationis*, we then carry out a comparison.

In this respect, the target-oriented approach in translation studies (cf. most recently Toury 1995) seems more like contrastive analysis. Toury's discovery procedure starts from a target text (A^i), establishes the source text (A), and then seeks to define, via a comparative investigation, the nature of the similarity between them (in his terms, the nature of the equivalence norm evidently adhered to by the translator). The approach starts with separateness, and seeks to discover the linking similarity.

One additional point. What we might call the equative view of translation equivalence has traditionally argued that the translation situation is what we could represent as follows (omitting the time difference between the existences of the two entities):

$A = A^i$

That is: two separate entities are related, in fact made equal, by "equivalence", understood as some kind of sameness. Recall early views about Biblical translation, where the *significatio* had to remain constant (see e.g. L. Kelly 1979). There is an underlying metaphor of movement, in that A "becomes" A^i: a message is carried across to a new readership, etc.; but the state of affairs after translation has taken place is presented as an equative one. The analogy is of course with mathematics, formulas like 2(a + b) = 2a + 2b.

An alternative view can now be offered based on the formula for divergent similarity, with one addition. The addition is necessary, because the source entity itself stereotypically remains in existence somewhere; it propagates rather than moves.* Translation is thus not equative but additive: it goes from a situation where one entity exists to a situation where more than one entity exists. The only true sameness that is preserved intact through the translation process is the source text itself (when it is not destroyed). With this addition, what we have is the divergent similarity relation:

$A \rightarrow A + A^i + A^{ii} + ...$

This also illustrates, incidentally, how an original entity may give rise to more than one additional similar entity. It underlines the fact that translation is open-ended – any number of translations may be offered for a given source text, all characterized by different kinds of similarity. Translation is also additive in that it brings added value, as enhanced status for the original entity A and as additional readers. And like the similarity relation in general, translation is usually non-reversible: back-translations from A^i do not usually arrive at the original A, but at another source-language version, itself divergently similar to A^i.

Both divergent and convergent similarity thus seem relevant concepts to translation theory. They are explored further in Chesterman [1998c].

---

* Note that the view presented here also conflicts with the traditional transfer metaphor of translation.

PAPER 16

Problems with strategies*

The term "translation strategy" has been used by various translation scholars to describe different kinds of textual procedures used by translators. Other terms that have been proposed for these or related concepts include techniques, procedures, shifts, operations, transfers, changes, methods, trajections and transformations. There actually seem to be more terms than concepts. This paper offers a critical analysis of some of the conceptual and terminological problems in this area of translation studies. Distinctions are made between concepts pertaining to result and to process; linguistic vs. cognitive levels; problem-solving vs. routine procedures; and global vs. local strategies. Different systems of strategy classification are briefly compared, and the problem of their operationalization and application is raised, particularly with respect to their use as pedagogical tools. Finally, a terminological and conceptual solution is proposed which takes into account the main distinctions discussed and also shows links between this conceptual field and two other areas of translation studies: translation typology and equivalence typology.

Keywords: strategy, technique, shift, method, similarity, equivalence

At the textlinguistic centre of translation studies there lies the problem of how best to describe what happens when a translator turns a source text into a target text. The final relationship between the two texts is something we have traditionally referred to as "equivalence", either in some ideal sense or more realistically as some kind of relevant similarity. But how is this relationship created? By what kinds of textual manipulation does the translator proceed?

Adherents of the deverbalization idea (i.e. that translators and interpreters deal directly with meaning or "sense") would argue that this question is badly formulated: translators (or interpreters) do not manipulate texts, they process meanings, messages, intentions. That is true, of course, in some sense. But translators do also have to deal with texts. For many scholars, translation itself is defined in terms of

---

* First published in 2005 in Krisztina Károly and Ágota Fóris (eds), *New Trends in Translation Studies. In Honour of Kinga Klaudy*. Budapest: Akadémiai Kiadó, 17–28. Reprinted here by kind permission of the publisher. This text is slightly edited.

texts. Thus Neubert and Shreve (1992: 25) offer a text-based definition according to which translations are "text-induced text productions".

What terms and concepts are available to us, to describe textual procedures? Here are some: operation, procedure, technique, strategy, change, solution type, shift, method. Are these all synonyms? What concepts do we actually need? What would be the best terms to use? How can we classify instances of whatever these things are? – Most of what follows is a raising of questions and a diagnosing of problems. I do end up with a proposed solution to some of the problems, but, as it will become clear, there is a lot of thinking that still needs to be done.

1. The terminological problem

The basic terminological problem is that different scholars use different terms for what seems to be more or less the same thing. This variation is perhaps a sign of the relatively young age of our discipline, but it is also an obstacle in the path towards true professionalization. If we had an agreed term, or set of terms, which professional translators could use as well as scholars, life would be easier. We shall only have space here for a consideration of possible generic terms, but the problem is of course multiplied many times over when we move down the conceptual hierarchy and try to name and classify various types of … whatever they are.

Several recent contributions have attempted to make sense of the terminological confusion in this area of translation studies. Kinga Klaudy (2003) introduces the main parts of her book on *Languages in Translation* with a brief historical discussion. She points out (153) that early terms (such as "transfer" or "operation") tended to be used in a metaphorical way rather than a precise, technical one. She mentions Vinay and Darbelnet's (1958) now classical set of "procedures"; Nida's (1964) "techniques of adjustment"; Retsker's (1974) "transformations"; Newmark's (1982, 1988) use of "techniques" and "procedures"; Catford's (1965) "shifts". The term she prefers herself is "transfer operation".

In an article on precisely this terminological problem, Molina and Hurtado Albir (2002) cover similar ground. They include "strategy", but do not mention shifts, which is curious omission. They show how a given term (such as "procedure") is often used in very different ways. They also point out that one of the causes of the variation in terms is the different origins of the terms: some come from the comparative stylistics tradition; others come from Bible translation; some derive from pedagogical applications (such as Delisle 1993), so that some are given prescriptive force (see e.g. Leppihalme 1997: 26–28). For instance, Delisle et al. (1999) take "omission" and "addition" as kinds of translation error, not standard translation procedures. Molina and Hurtado Albir argue for the term "techniques", which is also the term used by Fawcett (1997: Chapter 4).

Of these writers, only Fawcett mentions the proposal by Malone (1988), which is "trajections". Malone actually coins quite a number of new terms, very few of which seem to be current nowadays in mainstream translation studies (zigzagging, recrescence, repackaging...). My own preference has so far been "strategy" (used e.g. in Chesterman 1997a); but I will return to this below.

So we have about a dozen terms – in English – for these phenomena. This state of affairs raises a number of awkward questions. Do we really have a dozen different concepts, all needing a separate label? Why do we have these terminological disagreements? Do they matter? Is there anything we should / could do about it? How can we best analyse the differences between source and target texts, and discuss stages in decision-making? What conceptual tools are most useful? What kinds of arguments can we use to defend our terminological decisions? Some of these will be offered answers in what follows, but much conceptual spadework still remains to be done.

2. The conceptual problem

The answer to the question about whether we have a dozen concepts that need these dozen terms, must surely be "no". A number of semantic distinctions nevertheless emerge from the various analyses that have been proposed.

a. Result vs. process

Research using think-aloud protocols has used the notion of strategy in a process sense, to denote a cognitive, problem-solving operation of some kind (see e.g. Jääskeläinen 1999). However, text-oriented research has not been so clear about whether the focus is on processes themselves or the results of processes. Many writers have pointed out, for instance, that Vinay and Darbelnet's "procedures" seem to describe various kinds of resulting differences between source and target texts, rather than real procedures taking place through time. And many have preferred to keep the term "shift" as a generic term for these textual differences (notably, and in most detail, Leuven-Zwart 1989/1990).

Sample definitions along these lines are given by Catford and Popovič. For Catford (1965: 73), shifts are "departures from formal correspondence". For Popovič (1970: 79) a shift is "all that appears as new with respect to the original, or fails to appear where it might have been expected". This latter definition has a broader scope than Catford's, and is more subjective, in that the existence of a shift is governed by someone's expectations (whose?). But both agree that shifts are not dynamic procedures but characteristics of the textual relationship between source and target texts. Zabalbeascoa (2000), on the other hand, argues for "solution-type", because "shifts" highlight notions of change; many solution-types, on the other hand, highlight some kind of equivalence. A solution-type is "the shared characteristic of a number of different solutions" (2000: 122) – a definition that opens up any number of subsequent classifications.

However, Molina and Hurtado Albir (2002) seem to give this sense to their term "technique":

> Techniques describe the result obtained and can be used to classify different types of translation solutions. Strategies are related to the mechanisms used by translators throughout the whole translation process to find a solution to the problems they find. The *technical procedures* (the name itself is ambiguous) affect the results and not the process, so they should be distinguished from strategies. We propose they should be called translation techniques. (507)

There seems to be some confusion here between procedures and results of procedures. The authors then say that "some mechanisms may function both as strategies and as techniques" (508). Paraphrasing, for instance, can be a reformulation *strategy* or an amplification *technique*. And then: "we define techniques as procedures to analyse and classify how translation equivalence works" (509).

Nida (1964) also used "techniques" ("techniques of adjustment"), and these too seem to denote procedures (addition, omission, alteration).

At the root of this confusion may lie the fact that many of the terms used to describe these different kinds of textual procedures are, in English at least, nominalizations of verbs, like "compression, omission, compensation". The nominalization form itself is often ambiguous between a process reading and a result reading. On the other hand, some terms favour only one of these senses: "operation" highlights the process aspect; a calque, on the other hand, is a result.

b. Linguistic vs. cognitive

Klaudy (2003: 156) refers to her "transfer operations" as "mental transformations", or, on the next page, as manifestations of complex mental transformations, "taking place whenever the road from the mind to the linguistic form is not direct but leads through another language". Klaudy thus seems to take the middle ground: these operations are both linguistic (as "manifestations") and cognitive, in that they are the results of "conscious decision-making activity" (156). In other words, they seem to be psycholinguistic. As she points out, however, we cannot observe these mental operations directly; all we can do is to compare the source and target texts.

As results of mental transformations, these phenomena are obviously textual, linguistic. It might therefore be more fruitful to begin by looking at these textlinguistic results of whatever mental transformations may have taken place. If we notice that a noun in the source text corresponds semantically to a verb in the target text, we can classify this at the linguistic level as an instance of transposition. But no added value seems to be gained if we also say that this is the result of a "transposition operation".

c. Problem-solving vs. routine

Some scholars prefer to keep "strategies" for cases where the translator has a problem to solve. The underlying idea here seems to be that many "solutions" are routine, but that sometimes a feature or unit in the source text poses a problem which halts the smooth flow of the translator's work. (This is indeed the picture of the translation procedure that we get from TAP studies. For an annotated bibliography, see Jääskeläinen 2002.) Where there are problem spots, then, the translator resorts to a strategy. This is the interpretation offered by Lörscher (1991: 76): "a translation strategy is a potentially conscious procedure for the solution of a problem which an individual is faced with when translating a text segment from one language into another". This definition is clearly placed on the cognitive level, not the textual one. Similarly, Molina and Hurtado Albir (2002: 508) see strategies as "the procedures (conscious or unconscious, verbal or non-verbal) used by the translator to solve problems that emerge when carrying out the translation process with a particular object in mind". In this sense, though, strategies cover a wider area than just the kinds of textlinguistic phenomena we are considering. They have to do with problem-solving more generally, and include analytical strategies, search strategies, reformulation strategies, and so on. Both these definitions see strategies as procedures; however, we can also see them statically, as plans of action that are only potentially dynamic, stored in the translator's memory or toolbox of competences.

Muñoz Martín (2000), after surveying of some of the issues I have been discussing above, ends up with a proposal that we use "strategies" to refer to sets of similar solutions to a given problem type (such as: how to translate culture-bound terms). His main reason is a pedagogical one: empirical analysis of different solutions can be exploited to show students the range of possible strategies available. A very similar approach was taken by Leppihalme (1997), ending with a decision-tree of strategies for translating allusions.

Defining strategies in terms of problem-solving means that we need to be clear about what we understand by a translation problem (see Nord 1991a: 158f, Toury 2002[*]). This is not always obvious. A problem for translator X may not be a

---

[*] See also the updated version in Toury 2012: Chapter 2.

problem for translator Y, translating the same text; but both translators may arrive at the same solution. And strategies may become automatized with time. Should we then say that (inexperienced) X has used a "strategy" but (experienced) Y has not? If what we are aiming at is a description of the resulting relationship between source and target texts, this possible difference in procedure seems irrelevant.

d. Global vs. local

Jääskeläinen (1993) uses "strategy" in a sense that is more general than the ones mentioned above. She includes as "strategies" very general principles such as "texts need not be translated word-for-word". These principles are not restricted to problem-spots in the source text. Hönig and Kußmaul (1982) had a similar usage, using the term "strategic decisions" to refer to aspects of the skopos such as reader-orientation. One way of clarifying this point is to distinguish between global and local strategies, as done e.g. by Jääskeläinen (1993), following Séguinot (1989). Global strategies are those that affect decisions about translating the text as a whole, having to do with style, initial norms etc. Local strategies are those that have to do with particular points or units in the text: local problems. "Local strategies" is thus one term that has been used for the phenomena we are considering. I used it myself originally (Chesterman 1997a), but I now think it was not a good term, mainly because of the ambiguity between the procedural (behavioural or cognitive, problem-solving) and the textual senses.

Before I offer my own current hypothesis about how best to conceptualize these distinctions, let us look at the next set of problems.

3. The classification problem

Whatever we decide to call these phenomena, how can we list and then classify them? How many might there be? Lists offered by the different authors vary from four to several dozen. This variation is of course explained by the different levels of delicacy (detail) adopted, the level of generalization. You might argue that there are three or four "big" classes, as Nida does: change, add, omit. Or compare Catford's few shift types. But there is no end to the amount of detail one might go into if desired. Leuven-Zwart had three main types, but a great many subtypes. Vinay and Darbelnet have seven main procedures. Malone has many more. Molina and Hurtado Albir end with a list of 18 techniques. – I have no space here to do more than point to the need for further careful conceptual analysis which would aim to establish major types and subtypes and systematize the possible connections between the classifications that have been proposed.

This work might start by considering the classificatory criteria themselves, and how the alternatives might best be structured. For instance, Vinay and Darbelnet work partly with a criterion of relative distance, such that their procedures are arranged in order of distance from formal equivalence. Molina and Hurtado Albir use an alphabetical order, and do not group their techniques in any way, although e.g. some highlight the preservation of similarity and others highlight different kinds of changes. Chesterman (1997a) grouped strategies into syntactic, semantic and pragmatic types. The pragmatic types I listed are a rather miscellaneous bunch, some applying more generally (to the text as a whole), and others more locally. Catford used purely formal criteria to distinguish types of shifts. Klaudy's main division is between lexical and grammatical operations, with many subtypes in each group. The main division is said to be according to the scope of the operation (what kinds of textual segments it affects); the subtypes are then classified according to the kind of operation involved (omitting, adding, contracting, generalizing, and so on).

A special difficulty is how to deal with compensation. For some (e.g. Klaudy) this is also an operation; for others (e.g. Chesterman) is is seen as a possible motivation for a strategy, not a strategy itself.

One distinction that is frequently made – but not by all the sources referred to in this article – is between obligatory and optional changes. Obligatory changes are determined by the constraints of the target language grammar, etc.; these are the domain of contrastive linguistics, and would rarely involve strategic, problem-solving thinking. Optional changes, on the other hand, occur in places where the translator has a choice: there are alternatives available, which would also be grammatically OK. These are the domain of translation studies. After all, the translator's competence includes the ability to see a range of possible alternatives and then select the most appropriate one (cf. Pym 1992a: 175f).

Although this distinction seems unproblematic, there is nevertheless a grey area between the two classes. A given change might be made because of relatively strong rhetorical constraints which one would not quite call "grammatical". Or there might be strong stylistic pressures and genre-related features that do not quite count as "rules" but as "preferences" in a given target language. For instance, we know from contrastive analysis that French typically makes more use of rhetorical questions than English. If a translator then chooses to translate an English statement as a French question, to what extent can we say that she has a choice? True, she could have kept the structure as a statement, but there are stylistic preferences at play which presumably influence her decision. We must surely conclude that the translator sometimes has more freedom of choice, sometimes less. The distinction between optional and obligatory is thus not an absolute one, but it nevertheless seems to be useful and necessary.

4. The application problem

When it comes to applying the concepts to empirical research, we are faced with more problems. How can they best be operationalized? How can we reliably recognize an instance of one or another type? It is clear for a start that they are not all mutually exclusive. In my own terms, pragmatic strategies imply simultaneously the use of semantic ones, and both usually involve the use of syntactic ones as well. In other words, in terms of the resulting textual changes, a given change may be evidence of several strategies all operating at the same time.

Here is an example. One episode of the comic strip Calvin and Hobbes starts with Calvin talking to himself as he plays with a toy car on the sofa, like this:

> ST   Here is successful Mr. Jones. He lives in a 5-acre home in a wealthy suburb. Here is his new Mercedes in the driveway.

In the French translation of the strip, this becomes:

> TT   M. Jones a bien réussi. Il vit dans une maison immense, dans un quartier riche. Et voilà sa nouvelle Mercedes dans son allée.

The first clause shows evidence of structural and thematic changes, with a transposition inside them (adjective to verb), plus a semantic/pragmatic shift (addition of *bien*). The second sentence shows what we could call an adaptation of some kind, involving a semantic generalization (*5-acre > immense*), and a lexical shift (*suburb > quartier*). The third sentence changes the cohesion (*> et*) and changes the structure of a noun phrase (article + noun > possessive pronoun + noun). Does the cohesion shift "contain" the latter one, because cohesion applies here at the sentence level, above the phrase level? Throughout the text, the retention of the name *Jones* could be taken as evidence of a foreignization strategy; however, at later points there is also evidence of domestication, e.g. when miles are converted to kilometres.

The second frame continues:

> ST   It's anyone's guess as to how much longer Mr. Jones can meet his monthly finance charges.
> TT   Qui peut dire combien de temps M. Jones pourra payer son crédit mensuel ?

At sentence level, we have a rhetorical shift from statement to question. Within this, we have several semantic and syntactic changes (*guess > dire, how much longer > combien de temps, can > pourra, finance charges > crédit*).

This problem of overlapping is related to the difficulty of defining the actual units in question. As we have seen, some of the proposed strategies seem to apply to higher-level units such as whole texts; others apply to more local units. But even at this local level it is not always evident what the unit is. For instance, Eriksson (2004), in a detailed study of the notion of transposition, argues that it applies not to word classes, as originally proposed by Vinay and Darbelnet, but to phrases and clauses.

Consider another example: "compression" or "condensation". These procedures seem to be applicable to a range of syntactic units, from phrases to sentences, even to paragraphs. What counts as one instance of "compression" and what as two successive ones? The answer is not obvious. Foreignization and domestication are sometimes taken as general, text-level strategies, but as the example above shows, they can also have more local manifestations. So far, studies have needed to make largely ad hoc decisions about how the units concerned should be operationalized.

Note in this context that we do not even have agreement on what a "unit of translation" is: a whole text, a chunk of source text, a chunk of meaning, a chunk of bitext in the translator's mind, a chunk of keyboard activity between two pauses of a given length – or what?

5. The pedagogical problem

Whatever we decide to call them, some of these phenomena may be useful conceptual tools in translation training. We can teach trainees to recognize and then to use these textual tricks of the trade. But in order for this to be possible the problems sketched above must be solved. The concepts must be made so explicit and so simple that they can be taught: in a word, they must be made "portable". The pedagogical challenge is to sort out the conceptual mess into some usable structure. Some scholars have responded to this challenge by creating their own systems (e.g. Malone 1988), perhaps in despair. Others have tried to adapt and adjust existing definitions and classifications, but this has tended to lead to even more confusion, as identical terms become used by different scholars in very different senses. For instance, for Molina and Hurtado Albir (2002) "substitution" is the technique of changing linguistic elements into paralinguistic elements such as gestures, or vice versa. Malone gives the term a much wider sense, covering translation solutions of many kinds that lack identity with the source: the opposite of what he calls "equation". This takes us back to the terminological problems mentioned earlier.

Some suggestions for simple exercises based on what I then called strategies are given in Chesterman (1997a, Chapter 6). These start with definitions and recognition exercises, and then proceed to practice using specified strategies at given points in a text, evaluative analysis of the uses of strategies in published translations, and the exploratory use of alternative strategies. However, these suggestions by-pass most of the terminological and conceptual problems we have been discussing here. Pedagogically they have appeared to be useful (for me at least), but they do not yet rest on a reliable conceptual foundation.

6. Proposal for a solution

We have been discussing various kinds of terminological and conceptual problems arising within one particular area of translation research. I can obviously not offer definitive solutions – progress is seldom like that – but I will conclude with a proposal that has helped me clarify this section of the translation field for myself, at least. One aim of this proposal is to make explicit links between different parts of our field. Another aim is to reduce the overall number of terms used. (And: what do we need them for?)

First of all, I am happy to follow those who reserve the term **method** to denote a general way of translating, not a local solution. I suggest that we correlate method with the notion of a translation **type**: a given translation method leads to a translation of a certain type, such as free, literal, semantic, communicative, gist, philological, etc. Method thus designates an overall kind of translation process.

Following many writers, I propose that we restrict the term **strategy** to its basic problem-solving sense, as a plan that is implemented in a given context. The implementation is procedural, although the plan itself, as a cognitive schema, is not. Strategies are formulated and implemented for many kinds of problems, at different phases in the translation process, but are not relevant to routine, problem-free, automatized processing. They thus relate e.g. to the attention units indicated in TAP research. Examples of strategies might include the initial choice of source or target orientation, decisions about foreignizing or domesticating, search strategies, revision strategies. (This usage of the term is thus narrower than the one I have used in my own earlier work.) As plans, strategies are cognitive, not linguistic.

This will then free the term **technique** to refer to routine, micro-level, textual procedures, as proposed by Molina and Hurtado Albir, for instance changing a noun to a verb (transposition) or adding more explicit cohesion. Techniques are thus linguistic procedures; they are ways of manipulating textual phenomena.

However, unlike Molina and Hurtado Albir, I propose that the term **shift** be kept to refer to the result of a procedure. Shifts are observable as kinds of difference between target and source. Many of the traditional names for shifts overlap with names given to techniques – recall the point above about the ambiguity of nominalizations – but the two should be kept conceptually separate. From the pedagogical point of view, what we can teach are textual techniques and problem-solving strategies, and indeed translation methods. We do not teach shifts, although we can of course study them in different corpora and learn from them about techniques and strategies. A shift may represent the solution to a problem (i.e. the result of a strategy), the result of a routine technique, or indeed the consequence of a misunderstanding, an unsuccessful strategy or a badly chosen technique. Some shifts are therefore justifiable (in a given task context), others are less so. As we know, all translations manifest shifts.

But all translations also manifest similarities with their source texts. It thus seems that **shifts** and **similarities** are parallel concepts. Shifts indicate textual differences, dissimilarities; similarities indicate textual equivalences. Both are "solution types" (cf. Zabalbeascoa 2000). It is curious that Translation Studies has developed complex typologies of differences (shifts), but much less complex typologies of similarity.

Perhaps we should try to develop both sides of the picture together, as illustrated by the concluding table below, which indicates parallels between some classic types of equivalence and some types of shifts. Both *similarities* and *shifts* here refer to features of the relation between the translation product and the source text. In this sense, they are both *textual* terms.

Table 1. Types of similarity and difference

Types of equivalence – similarities	Types of difference – shifts
formal	*syntactic*
	transposition
	unit shift (e.g. clause > phrase)
	…
semantic	*semantic*
	modulation
	generalization
	…
stylistic	*stylistic*
	variation (e.g. of dialect)
	foreignization
	…
pragmatic	*pragmatic*
	addition
	omission
	explicitation
	reduction
	…

PAPER 17

The unbearable lightness of English words[*]

The paper postulates a "rhetorical salience threshold" which may have different heights in different languages. This threshold marks the point at which a given item of information or component of meaning is judged to be salient enough to be worth expressing. In translation, if source and target languages have different salience thresholds, rhetorical adjustments may need to be made which have the effect of "toning down" or "toning up" the salience. If there is no such rhetorical compensation, the translation may sound either "too pompous" or "a bit pathetic". Evidence is offered which suggests that Finnish and English have different salience thresholds: the English threshold seems lower than the Finnish one.

Keywords: salience, silence, Finnish, shifts, Contrastive Analysis

1. The initial question

An English TV ad for a shampoo says that if you use it your hair will be *Fuller, thicker, fresher, cleaner – better than ever*. When this same ad appears on Finnish TV something happens to the adjectives: three of them lose their comparative status, thus: *Raikkaat, puhtaat, terveet hiukset – kauniimmat kuin koskaan* ('Fresh, clean, healthy hair – more beautiful than ever'). (One adjective – thicker – is dropped, but the Finnish retains the four-word rhythm by adding the noun.)

A Finnish text in a translation exam into English mentions a research fund that has succeeded in accumulating a sizeable sum of money from scratch *lyhyessä ajassa* (literally, 'in a short time'). Of 25 examinees, 14 indeed do translate the passage as something like "... the contribution of the fund is significant in that the University has been able to raise the sum from zero to the present level in a short time"; the examiner feels there is something stylistically odd about the end of the sentence. Eleven examinees feel the need to add something to the phrase: *in such a short time* or *in a very short time*; the published translation also adds *very*. Why?

---

[*] Originally published in 2007 in Riitta Jääskeläinen, Tiina Puurtinen and Hilkka Stotesbury (eds), *Text, Processes, and Corpora: Research Inspired by Sonja Tirkkonen-Condit*. Joensuu: Joensuun yliopistopaino, 231–241. I have made some minor editorial revisions. The keywords have been added.

2. Thresholds of silence and salience

Research on silence has looked at different forms and functions of silence, and examined the different roles which silence can play in different cultures (see e.g. Tannen and Saville-Troike 1985, Laaksovaara and Farell 1992, Kukkonen 1993, Jaworski 1993). One well-established result in work by Finnish scholars is that Finns' tolerance of silence is notably higher than that of, say, Americans. In other words, Finns tend to have a higher **silence threshold** than, for instance, speakers whose native language is English. This threshold is the point above which speakers feel it necessary to say something.

The approach taken by much of this research is semiotic: silence is seen as a sign like any other sign, with its own range of *signifiés*. Silence is not "just" silence, the absence of meaning; silence means something. And this "something" is determined by the whole cultural semiosphere in which a silence exists, for different semiospheres will create different contexts for silence, different frames of reference within which silence can have a meaning. The Finnish semiosphere is particularly interesting in this respect. Tarasti (1988) has argued that it is less profuse, more sparse than the semiosphere of some other cultures, especially when compared to the Anglo-American one. Some may see this as a weakness, a mark of semiotic poverty. But this is not necessarily so: in a sparse semiosphere, individual signs can be stronger, they can carry more weight.

Parallel to the culture-bound silence threshold I suggest there is also a culture-bound **rhetorical salience threshold**, defined as follows:

> *The rhetorical salience threshold marks the point above which something is felt to be significant enough to be worth saying.*

Note the difference from the silence threshold: whereas that marks the lower edge of the felt need to say anything at all, the salience threshold marks the point at which a given *signifié* is felt to be worth uttering. The higher the **silence** threshold, the smaller the need to speak; the higher the **salience** threshold, the more meaningful something must be in order to become rhetorically salient enough to be uttered. Information below the salience threshold is deemed "insignificant", not worth uttering. Admittedly, some information may remain unexpressed because it is deemed too important to utter: see e.g. Leppihalme 2000b: 98–90.

Recall the examples given above. In both cases, we seem to see evidence of an adjustment of the salience threshold. A "closer" Finnish translation of the first one would give: *Raikkaammat, puhtaammat, terveemmät hiukset* ('fresher, cleaner, healthier hair'). But for a native Finn, this perhaps sounds "too strong", "over-written". And a literal translation of the second example would seem, as I suggested above, somehow not strong enough, as if it were "written too quietly". "Writing too quietly" may mean no more than "uninteresting subject matter" (for a given reader); but a text may also fall beneath the salience threshold for rhetorical reasons. Specifically, however, I am interested not in why texts might fall beneath this threshold, but in what writers do (in different languages: here, Finnish and English) to ensure that their texts do **not** fall below it, or that they do not rise too far above it.

I suggest that the salience threshold is lower in English than in Finnish. Evidence may be found in situations where a given *signifié* is shared (or assumed to be shared) between two texts, one Finnish and one English: we can then examine differences at the level of the *signifiant*. An obvious source of such data is translations, and another is newspaper reports in different languages dealing with the same incident.

The structure of my argument is as follows. I assume (a) that all language use must rise above the salience threshold, and (b) that languages may vary in the degree of salience that must be manifest in a *signifiant* in order for it to be worth uttering. I then argue that some *signifiants* in English may seem too "light" (i.e. not salient enough) to justify expression above the salience threshold unless they are supplemented in some way that compensates for this "lightness". In Finnish, the use of *signifiants* for the same *signifiés* does not seem to require such supplementary compensation. I infer that (in these cases) Finnish *signifiants* are therefore intrinsically "heavier", more salient.

The converse argument is also possible: i.e. that if certain Finnish *signifiants* are supplemented in the same way as corresponding English ones, the result will be a Finnish text that is felt to be "over-written" or cluttered, sensationalist or the like. This opens up possibilities of empirical reader-response testing that I have not yet explored.

But first, some caveats. Considerations of word length and word frequency are excluded here, although one might certainly argue that low-frequency items are less predictable, hence more informative, and hence given "supplementary weight" in some sense. And I also exclude differences which are solely determined by grammatical constraints, where the writer has no other stylistic choice available. In the present context I also omit discussion of the way the overall hypothesis might relate to different politeness conventions in the two cultures.

Furthermore, differences of situation and context must also be eliminated: it is obvious that in some contexts X might be worth saying and in other contexts not. Hence the usefulness of newspaper texts, from which I shall present some evidence: we can assume a large degree of similarity between newspaper-reading situations in Finnish and English, and the newspapers selected can be approximately matched on the quality-popular scale.

3. Some preliminary evidence

Some evidence for my general argument that Finnish words are "heavier" than English ones comes from a comparison of newspaper texts. When I first started investigating the the salience threshold some years ago, I took one issue of the national daily *Helsingin Sanomat*, of December 8, 1992, and the issue of *The Independent* of the same day. Both these newspapers are quality papers; neither is linked to any particular political party.

I then selected pairs of articles from the international news pages that dealt with the same events, each article being by a different writer. These were: rioting between Muslims and Hindus in India, the clash in the Russian Parliament between the supporters and opponents of Yeltsin, corruption scandals in Japan, and the final match of the Davis Cup (tennis).

I looked for specific *signifiés* (i.e. sememes) that occurred in both newspapers. The focus of analysis is on the differences in the ways these *signifiés* were expressed. These differences are assumed to indicate various ways of compensating for possible differences of salience. Let us look at some data first.

The article on unrest in India dealt with the destruction of a Muslim mosque. I will take one aspect of the journalistic treatment of this event in the two newspapers, by way of illustration. Since I am interested in qualitative differences rather than quantitative ones, and the data are very limited, frequency figures are not given. Both articles naturally make repeated reference to the process in which the mosque was the object, in the semantic role of Patient. The English text uses the following verbs or verb phrases or nominalizations to denote this process: *demolish, destruction, overrun, attack, demolition, destroy, smash with sledgehammers, storm*. Compare this list with the equivalent expressions used in the Finnish article: *tuhoaminen* ('destroying, destruction'), *tuho* ('destruction'), *purkaminen* ('taking to pieces, dismantling, demolishing'), *hyökätä* ('attack'). No other verbs or nominalizations are used to express the process in question, in either text. It seems that the Finnish items are, on the whole, somewhat less emotional, less marked. In particular, the neutral sense of 'taking to pieces' (which actually occurs twice in the Finnish) is noticeably absent from the English article, which seems to make more of a point of selecting stronger terms. The English also gives more physical detail (*sledgehammers*). The headlines of the two articles are also revealing: the English was: *Sectarian rioting kills 200 in India*. This focuses on a transitive verb, in the present tense, and selects *rioting* as the agent. The Finnish had: *Satoja ihmisiä kuollut Intian levottomuuksissa* ('Hundreds of people dead in riots in India'). This has an intransitive verb and refers to the riots literally as "incidents of unrest". One might say that *riot* is a hyponym of "unrest", a specific type of it, marked e.g. for high conflictual content.

The pair of articles on Japanese corruption scandals exhibited a similar tendency. Consider, for instance, the terms used to describe the group of criminals allegedly involved. The English refers to these as: *gangsters, gangster syndicates, a yakuza gangster syndicate*. It also uses the term *gangster row* in the headline. In referring to these same groups, the Finnish text uses *järjestäytynyt rikollisuus* ('organized crime'), *jakuzat* ('yakuzas') and *rikollisuusympyrät* ('criminal circles'). It does not use the term *syndikaatti* ('syndicate'), a possible but low-frequency item, and prefers a more neutral mode of expression; it also avoids any close equivalent for *gangster*. The Finnish headline does mention *rötösjutut*, which can be literally translated as 'criminal matters' but has culture-specific connotations of corruption; but note that whereas this Finnish term refers only to events the equivalent in the English headline includes a premodification referring to human Agents: *gangster row*.

The articles on the Russian Congress debates offer rich material for analysis along the same lines. I will pick out two examples. The first is the modes of reference to the various groups of Congress representatives involved. Here are the terms used in the English text: *hardline Communists, belligerent nationalists, conservatives, rival camps, stodgy veterans, rival forces, centrist deputies, opponents*. Note how many are preceded by emotive attributes. The Finnish text (slightly shorter) used a more limited set of terms to denote the same participants: *vanhoilliset* ('conservatives'), *enemmistö* ('the majority'), *vanhoillinen enemmistö*, ('the conservative majority') *erittäin suuri enemmistö* ('an extremely large majority'). It is interesting that the English text at no point uses "the majority" to refer to the representatives themselves: the term is only used in its technical sense, *a two-thirds majority*.

The second example from this incident has to do with the expressions used to describe the emotional atmosphere of these debates. The English article had: *an all-or-nothing showdown, dramatic sabre-rattling, unruly and unpredictable Congress, head-on confrontation, within a hair's breadth of a humiliating defeat, loathed by many stodgy veterans, political deadlock, political paralysis, back-room haggling, political pyrotechnics*. The Finnish text had: *tunteita kuumentava kysymys* ('a question which [raised] heated feelings'), *sekoileva kongressi* ('a congress that was making a mess of things'), *julkaisi yleisen tuomitsevan lausuman* ('made a general condemnatory statement'), *vastustivat kynsin hampain* ('resisted tooth and nail'), *ehkä varmistaakseen epäjohdonmukaisuutensa* ('perhaps in order to ensure their inconsistency'), *punainen vaate vanhoillisille* ('a red rag to the conservatives'), *tulenhehkuvan riidan syy* ('the cause of a fiery conflict'). Some of these Finnish expressions are strongly emotive, it is true, but the general effect overall is clearly less marked than the English.

The tone of both articles is set by their headlines. Whereas the English has *Unruly Russian MPs sheath their sabres*, Finnish settles for a matter-of-fact *Jeltsinin vastainen rintama supistui kongressissa* ('The front opposing Yeltsin diminished in Congress'). Again, Finnish shows a preference here for a verb that is syntactically intransitive and a neutral tone.

My final text was a sporting one, and this turned out to be the most revealing of all. Not only did both newspapers treat a distinct series of events differently, but the Finnish even contained a translation of a quotation used verbatim in the English. The articles are reports of the Davis Cup tennis final, in which the USA defeated Switzerland.

The headline of the English article stresses competition and a positively regal supremacy: *Courier predicts a long reign*. The Finnish report stresses co-operation, with the headline: *Courier on joukkuepelaaja* ('Courier is a team player'). The first paragraph of each report places the event in the context of the US defeat the previous year. But notice the different ways in which this is done. The English text talks of the present victory *eclipsing the painful memory of their unexpected defeat by France in Lyons last year*. In other words, this focuses on a personal emotional memory, and on the previous defeat being unexpected. The Finnish simply has: *USA:n tennismaajoukkue paikkasi vuoden takaisen tappionsa Davis cupin loppuottelussa* ('The US national tennis team patched up their last year's defeat in the Davis Cup final match'). Here, in contrast, the focus is non-personal, non-emotive, and the previous defeat is not given any epithet.

Elsewhere in the texts, both writers make use of the image of setting a seal on something. The Finnish says that Courier *sinetöi* ('set the seal on') the championship by winning his match, but the English use of the image is intensified to *Courier ... put the final seal on a successful if sometimes erratic year ...* Here the seal had to be *final*.

The difference between the two styles also comes out in references to previous defeats suffered by Sampras, another American player in the team. The Finnish text simply states bluntly that last year *Sampras hävisi molemmat kaksinpelinsä* ('Sampras lost both his singles matches'). Compare the English version: *His Davis Cup debut in last year's final was a personal nightmare as he lost both of his singles matches*.

The Finnish continues: *Tällä kertaa hän esiintyi nelinpelissä John McEnroen kanssa* ('This time he appeared in the doubles with John McEnroe'). But the English adds a figurative image: *...in tandem with John McEnroe*. The Finnish description of this match goes: *Sveitsin pari ... voitti kaksi ensimmäistä erää ... mutta kolme viimeistä menivät kotijoukkueelle* ('The Swiss pair ... won the first two sets ... but the last three went to the home team'); note the simple verbs. Compare the English: *[Sampras and McEnroe] fought back to win the doubles after trailing by two sets to love ...*; note the emphasis on verbs of conflict.

The American Courier is quoted at the end of the article as having *the utmost respect* for the Swiss players; the Finnish translates the same quote as *Arvostan ... hyvin korkealle* ('I respect [them] very highly'). "Very highly" is certainly high, but surely less high than *utmost*: here again, the Finnish is content with a slightly lesser degree of persuasion – and even this seems perhaps too strong.

4. Salience adjustment

Examples such as these suggest various ways in which writers can adjust the level of rhetorical salience to the relevant cultural norms. In the preliminary list of syntactic, semantic and stylistic/pragmatic variables below, "shift up" means "do this in order to increase salience", and "shift down" means "do this in order to decrease salience".

- Positive vs. comparative vs. superlative
  Shift up: move towards the right of this scale
  Shift down: move leftwards
  Example: the shampoo ad
- Presence or absence of adjective
  Shift up: add adjective
  Shift down: omit adjective
  Example: *unexpected defeat* vs. *tappio* ('defeat')
- Presence or absence of intensifier
  Shift up: add intensifier
  Shift down: omit intensifier
  Example: *lyhyessä ajassa* → *in a very short time*
- Transitive vs. intransitive verb
  Shift up: choose strong semantic role, e.g. Agent
  Shift down: choose weaker semantic role, e.g. Dative
  Example: *kills* vs. *on kuollut* ('has/have died')
- Presence or absence of emotive feature
  Shift up: add emotive feature
  Shift down: remove emotive feature
  Example: *stodgy veterans* vs. *vanhoilliset* ('conservatives')
- Figurative vs. literal
  Shift up: choose figurative expression
  Shift down: omit figurative expression
  Example: *sheath their sabres* vs. *supistui* ('diminished')

- Hyponym vs. superordinate term
  Shift up: choose lower-level, more specific, more informative term
  Shift down: choose superordinate term
  Example: *smash (with sledgehammers)* vs. *tuhota* ('destroy')
- Trope preference
  Not examined in any detail yet, but salience might be increased by conflict metaphors; compare emotiveness.
  Example: *fought back to win* vs. *menivät* ('went')
- Use of register
  Shift up: choose a down-to-earth, colloquial register
  Shift down: choose a neutral register
  Example: *stodgy* vs. *vanhoillinen* 'conservative'

5. Conclusion

The tentative hypothesis outlined above – the concept of the salience threshold, and its explanatory power in accounting for some translation shifts – may be linked to the results of some other research. Séguinot (1982), for instance, studied the kinds of editing changes made to journalistic texts by translators working from French to English. She found that, after changes made to improve readability, the second most frequent category was composed of changes that included the reduction of emotive and figurative language. This seems to suggest that the salience threshold is lower for English than for French, as the French originals needed to be "toned down" to meet the acceptability norms of English. Vehmas-Lehto (1989) notes the necessity of a similar toning down in translation from Russian to Finnish.

Jantunen (2001) studied synonymity and lexical simplification, using part of the Savonlinna Corpus of Translated Finnish (see Mauranen 2000 for details). He analysed a subcorpus consisting of 1.2 million tokens of original Finnish and 1.2 million tokens of Finnish translations from English. One of his results was that there is a difference in the use of boosters (words like *erittäin* 'extremely', *hyvin* 'very', *todella* 'really') in translated and non-translated texts, particularly in narrative prose. His Table 1 shows that in translated Finnish, boosters occur about twice as frequently as in original Finnish. He does not speculate on possible reasons, and does not give examples, but I find his result a striking one. I suggest that what his data show is an effect of interference: perhaps the equivalent boosters existed already in the English source texts (not present in the corpus), and were simply transferred as such into Finnish, without any adjustment to the salience threshold.

All the evidence I have discussed is only circumstantial, at best. Some of the differences noted in the journalistic texts may be specific to particular journalistic conventions, and this is obviously something that should be checked against other material. Yet the notion of the salience threshold, and the hypothesis that in English this tends to be lower than in Finnish, both seem interesting enough to warrant further study.

SECTION VI

Hypotheses

Although most of my thinking about translation has concerned conceptual analysis in various ways, I have also been interested in research methodology, particularly in the role played by different kinds of hypotheses, and the development from descriptive to explanatory hypotheses. When hypotheses began to form part of the discourse of science in the 19th century, knowledge could be seen as fallible, not certain: a major development. Hence the importance of doubt as a fundamental research principle. Hence too the need to test claims and ideas, and to state, if possible, the kind of evidence that would show that a given hypothesis was wrong. Charles Darwin, for instance, was careful to mention possible counter-evidence at many points in his *Origin of Species* (1859): if such-and-such is discovered to be the case, the idea of natural selection must be mistaken...

I agree with Popper that an important characteristic of *empirical* hypotheses is that they should, in principle, be falsifiable; however, I accept that falsification is not a straightforward issue, since for instance a negative test result may indicate a flaw in the test itself rather than the hypothesis being tested. (Hence the dubiousness of claiming that a given test has "proved" or "verified" a hypothesis, rather than more modestly "supporting" it.) And I accept too that even after negative results scholars may cling to a hypothesis in the hope that more evidence in support of it may emerge later, perhaps because its background theory seems so persuasive. These issues were of course discussed by Kuhn; the debate between Popper and Kuhn is the subject of Fuller (2003).

As mentioned at several points earlier in this collection, *interpretive* hypotheses, unlike empirical ones, cannot be falsified. But they are of prime importance in all research: Paper 18 offers a more detailed discussion of various kinds of interpretive hypothesis. I am aware that some scholars might not want to call these hypotheses at all, seeing them e.g. as models or assumptions. For me, however, the similarities they share with empirical hypotheses are more significant than the differences, so that they can usefully be defined as a subclass of the "hypothesis" category. – This interpretation is itself an interpretive hypothesis, of course.

Paper 19 is an assessment of the literal translation hypothesis. The conceptual issues discussed at the beginning of the paper have to do with competing interpretive hypotheses, although this term is not used there.

The ground covered by these two papers is explored further in Chesterman (2012).

The concept of a hypothesis can also be most useful simply as an expository strategy, as it can crystallize a claim in an explicit way, thus sharpening the discussion. An excellent example of this rhetorical use is Kranach (2014).

PAPER 18

The status of interpretive hypotheses[*]

In the natural sciences the task of the researcher is usually seen as the generation and testing of hypotheses. These hypotheses are taken to be possible answers to questions concerning the description, prediction, and explanation of natural phenomena. But there is also another kind of hypothesis, an interpretive hypothesis. The status of interpretive hypotheses is not as clear as that of descriptive, predictive or explanatory ones. This paper aims to clarify this status, showing the respects in which interpretive hypotheses are like other kinds, and the respects in which they are different. Hermeneutic research methods based on the generation and testing of interpretive hypotheses do not seem fundamentally different from those of traditional empirical sciences. Interpretive hypotheses simply apply to different kinds of data. They can be particularly relevant to the research goal of explanation.

Keywords: meaning, hypothesis, hermeneutics, method

1. Interpreting obscure meaning

Daniel Gile (2005a) has suggested that research in Translation Studies uses two main paradigms, one taken from the liberal arts tradition and the other from empirical science. I would like here to explore one sense in which these two paradigms may not be so different after all.

In the natural sciences, and in the philosophy of natural science, the task of the researcher is usually seen as the generation and testing of hypotheses. In Popper's terms, science proceeds by a process of conjectures and refutations, i.e. by developing hypotheses and then testing them, trying to falsify them (e.g. Popper 1963). These hypotheses are taken to be possible answers to questions concerning the description, prediction, and explanation of natural phenomena. But there is also another, conceptual kind of hypothesis, an interpretive hypothesis.

---

[*] First published in 2008 in Gyde Hansen, Andrew Chesterman and Heidrun Gerzymisch-Arbogast (eds), *Efforts and Models in Interpreting and Translation Research. A tribute to Daniel Gile*. Amsterdam/Philadelphia: Benjamins, 49–61. Reprinted with kind permission from John Benjamins Publishing Company [www.benjamins.com]. One endnote has been updated.

Interpretive hypotheses are conjectures about what something means. Their general relevance to translators and interpreters is neatly illustrated in Gile's Sequential Model of Translation (e.g. Gile 2005b: 102), which shows how a translator seeks a meaning hypothesis for segments of the source text, and then checks it for plausibility. As a first formulation, we can state the basic form of these hypotheses as follows: *the interpretation of X is hypothesized to be Y,* or simply *X is interpreted as Y*. We shall revise this formulation in due course.

Such hypotheses have their roots in hermeneutics. The term "hermeneutics", of course, takes us back to Hermes, the messenger god, who was also the god of translators. After all, translation involves interpretation. Many phenomena need interpreting: not just ancient or complex, difficult texts, as was often the case with the original use of the term "hermeneutics", but any semiotic object or message, from works of art to dreams. However, I will use the term in a somewhat narrower sense here, drawing largely on Niiniluoto (1983: 165f). It is particularly in cases where conventional linguistic, community-based meanings do not suffice for understanding, but we nevertheless suspect some hidden significance, that we need a hermeneutic approach in this narrower sense. As Gadamer put it (Misgeld and Nicholson 1992: 69–70), "it [hermeneutics] is entrusted with all that is unfamiliar and strikes us as significant."

It is customary to distinguish various types of obscure meaning as objects of hermeneutic research. The *historical (intended) meaning* of X is its original meaning, in the place and time that X was created. For instance, we might wish to know how the notion of translation was understood in Ancient India, and how that interpretation then changed (see e.g. Trivedi 2006). And any translator trying to understand a source text may be searching for its historical meaning, i.e. what it meant to its original readers, particularly if the skopos involves pragmatic equivalence.

The *hidden meaning* of X is the meaning of which the agent (here, the creator of X) may be unaware, such as the unconscious meaning of a dream. A curious example of hypotheses about hidden meaning in Translation Studies is Venuti's article (2002) on the potential psychoanalytic significance of errors. Venuti argues that certain symptomatic errors (such as his own slip, translating Italian *superstite* as "superstitious" instead of "surviving") reveal something about the translator's unconscious attitude, e.g. towards the source text, or, in the case of another translation discussed by Venuti, towards a father-figure. The hidden meaning in the text is thus taken to point to something outside the text. Another example is a recent article by the psychoanalyst Adam Phillips (2007) on the new Penguin translations of Freud's work. The publisher of the English "standard edition" of Freud (translated by Strachey) insisted that the new translation should not draw on existing translations, and clearly did not like the idea of the retranslation project. Phillips interprets this attitude in the light of Freud's analysis of Moses and the rise of monotheism, resisting the challenge of other gods: the scholar here finds a kind of hidden significance via this comparison. Phillips then analyses translation in general as involving a kind of psychoanalytical transference. In psychoanalysis, transference works to bring about change. Retranslations can also bring about change, by introducing new voices (interpretations) into the conversation, providing more food for thought and scope for further understanding of the original; retranslations add to a text's history of influence. Here too the argument is about a phenomenon's hidden meaning.

The *internal meaning* of X is the meaning that X (e.g. a work of art) has quite apart from its context of creation. These are the meanings of objects in Popper's World 3, objective products of human minds. Such meanings may differ from those intended by their creators.

And finally, the *scholar's meaning* is the meaning of X to the researcher, the analyst, or the contemporary world: for instance the significance of X to some application of it. This is the kind of meaning that is involved when we wonder what lessons we might draw from history, or what the modern relevance of an ancient text or law might be. Under what circumstances are the prescriptive statements offered by the classical translators of the past still relevant today?

This last kind of meaning leads to an important point concerning the relation between interpretive hypotheses and other kinds of hypothesis. It is widely assumed that the "hermeneutic method" as such is a method that is particularly, even exclusively, appropriate for certain of the human sciences, such as history, anthropology, literary theory, aesthetics, semiotics. However, interpretive hypotheses are also relevant to the natural sciences. In other words, it is not the case that interpretive hypotheses are somehow outside the methodology of the hard sciences. Consider for instance how traces of collisions between particles in the experiments at CERN may one day be interpreted as evidence of the existence of the mysterious Higgs boson particle.[*] The traces in the collision chamber are read as obscure texts, which contain or suggest a meaning. In other words, the meaning of the observed traces is first of all the scholar's / scientist's meaning: what do these traces mean to us (in this example: physicists)? Scientific observations are always "interpreted" in the light of a theory.

---

[*] The Higgs particle has now (apparently) been discovered, in 2012.

2. Varieties of hermeneutic *AS*

The fundamental methodological similarity between empirical and hermeneutic methods has been explored in particular by the Norwegian philosopher Dagfinn Føllesdal. He argues (1979) that the hermeneutic method is simply an application of the basic hypothetico-deductive method to a different kind of data – data that are meaningful, that have to do with meaning. He defines the hypothetico-deductive method as follows ([1979] 1994: 234; emphasis original):

> As the name indicates, it is an application of two operations: the formation of *hypotheses* and the *deduction* of consequences from them in order to arrive at beliefs which – though they are hypothetical – are well supported, through the way their deductive consequences fit with our experiences and with our other well-supported beliefs.

As an example, he discusses the meaning of the mysterious Passenger in Ibsen's *Peer Gynt*, who makes a surprising appearance in Act V, first on the boat with the hero and again later. This figure has been interpreted by scholars in various ways: as representing fear, death, the devil, Ibsen himself, or Byron's ghost. The research debate then concerns the assessment of these competing hypotheses. (I return to the crucial issue of hypothesis testing below.) Føllesdal points out that it may not be possible to arrive at a final conclusion, because the data in such a case are not exhaustive. So several interpretations are left hanging in the air together – perhaps as Ibsen intended. (See also Føllesdal et al. 1984, where other examples are also discussed, e.g. from historical research.)

Note the formulation I just used: the strange Passenger is interpreted *as* something, or *as* representing something. The central notion of this "*AS*" in hermeneutics captures something of how we often conceptualize our ability to understand: we understand something unfamiliar *as* something more familiar, i.e. in terms of something that already exists in our conceptual repertoire. The actual term "the hermeneutic *as*" comes from Heidegger (see e.g. 1962: 186f), but the idea is much older. – Note further that the relevant verb before *as* need not be "interpret" or "understand". We can also see / regard / consider / take / view / accept / … X *as* (or e.g.: in terms of) Y. These can all be variant expressions of different kinds of interpretive hypotheses. To make matters more complex, the hermeneutic *as* may not be explicitly expressed at all, and remain implicit. The formulation "in this paper, the term X refers to Y" can be explicated as "in this paper, I choose to interpret the term X as denoting Y".

I will now distinguish five kinds of hermeneutic *as*, corresponding to different forms of interpretive hypotheses. These do not correspond directly to the types of meaning outlined above, although some meaning types may be more frequently involved with some kinds of *as* than others. I will present the five kinds as separate categories, but I suspect that water-tight borderlines are hard to draw here, and my types are not all mutually exclusive. One reason for this is that different kinds of hypotheses, and different alternatives of the same kind of hypothesis, may be used in different contexts. My list is an attempt to conceptualize some of the rich variety of interpretive hypotheses, and at the same time shed light on what an interpretive hypothesis is.

I will start with the type of example discussed by Føllesdal, which is perhaps the prototypical type of interpretive hypothesis. I will call this the *representing as*, or the *symbolic as*. As in the Ibsen example, this *as* has to do with the interpretation of works of art, including texts, signs of all kinds, from ancient hieroglyphs to contemporary emoticons. The meanings thus represented may be hidden, as in the Venuti and Freud examples above. But they may also be internal as well. Consider for instance Christine Brooke-Rose's experimental novel *Between* (1968). The heroine of this novel is an interpreter, who is forever moving between conferences, countries, languages and cultures, and seems to have lost her identity. This is symbolized in the fact that the novel contains not a single instance of the verb "to be", in any form. This absence is also a sign, which we can easily interpret as representing the loss of identity: a hidden meaning, perhaps, but also an internal one, part of the artistic structure of the novel, intended and created by the novelist.

The other types I will suggest are not discussed by Føllesdal, but they seem to me to represent entirely plausible extensions of his basic insight. My second type of hermeneutic *as* is the *metaphorical* or *analogical as*. It signifies that X is being interpreted as being like something else, as being like Y. This similarity gives X some of its meaning, it helps us to understand X. The kinds of meaning involved in such comparisons seem to be partly scholar's meaning, and partly perhaps also hidden meaning. For instance, translation itself has been seen in terms of a great many metaphors: a traditional one is that of the bridge across a cultural and linguistic border. (See Round 2005 for a recent survey.) Other examples can be taken from two recent proposals concerning our interpretation of the translator's role. Michael Cronin (2000) suggests that translators can be seen as nomads, metaphorically (or even concretely) travelling from place to place, perhaps rootless. This *analogical as* implicitly links translation studies to travel theory (see e.g. Polezzi 2006). Carol Maier (2006), on the other hand, suggests that the translator can also be seen as a "*theoros*", someone who in Classical Greece travelled, looking with wonder, in search of wisdom. This metaphor, Maier argues, can shed light on our reading of the role of translators as characters in fiction.

Thirdly, there is a *classificatory as*. Here, X is interpreted as a kind of Y. In other words, this *as* postulates a hypernym under which X can be classified, and thus suggests a particular perspective, revealing some facets of X and hiding others. This kind of *as* abounds in translation research. A well-known example is André Lefevere's claim (1992a) that translation can be seen as a form of rewriting. Rewriting is the cover-term, beneath which translation sits beside anthologizing, paraphrasing, summarizing, and so on. More recently, translation has been seen as a form of intervention (Munday 2007), a perspective which puts a rather different light on translation, implicitly aligning it e.g. with political debate or activism, or perhaps medical treatment. Compare the earlier view of translation as a kind of manipulation, illustrated e.g. in Hermans (1985a). Such analogies seem to reveal aspects of scholar's meaning.

Then there is a *compositional as*, which offers a way of conceptualizing a complex concept in terms of its possible subtypes (as I am doing now, with the concept "interpretive hypothesis"). This type is the converse of the *classificatory as*. If I define equivalence as consisting of two types, or five types, I am positing "equivalence" as a hypernym and the various types as its hyponyms. I am in effect proposing an interpretation about the composition of this hypernym. In such cases, the hermeneutic *as* is often only implicit. Formulations such as "there are four types of X" can thus often be explicated as "X can be interpreted as consisting of four types".

And finally there is a *definitional as*, which is used in many forms of definition. Consider, for instance, the many ways in which scholars have defined the meaning of equivalence: as identity, as similarity, as interpretive resemblance, as a mapping or matching, and so on. Or the competing definitions of translation itself. All definitions are ultimately interpretations. And like interpretations, they can vary; they can develop into more accurate or more comprehensive definitions. Consider the various definitions of the metre, for instance. Since 1983 this length has been defined as *the length of the path travelled by light in vacuum during a time interval of 1/299,792,458 of a second*, but it was originally interpreted as being one ten-millionth part of the quadrant of the Earth, and there have been several quite different definitions in between.[1] The definitions have become increasingly precise. But extra precision tends to reduce the extension of a term: witness the sad fate of the ex-planet Pluto, now no longer deemed to fall within the definition of a planet. On the other hand, in our own field, Toury's norm-based definition of translation (1995) created a wider extension of the term.

I claimed above that interpretive hypotheses are also relevant to the natural sciences. Analogies may be used in the preliminary conceptualization of the research problem or field, as when we see light as waves or as particles. Definitions and category classifications are used in data analysis. Test results need to be interpreted. In these respects, interpretive hypotheses are unavoidable, especially insofar as scientific research relies on natural language. We might compare some of these hypotheses to the core assumptions of a theory, which are not necessarily tested in a given research project. Interpretive hypotheses are thus essential conceptual tools, with their own functions in any research project.

This section has aimed to extend the interpretation of what an interpretive hypothesis is, partly by offering a compositional *as*. The implication of this is that the definition of the notion can be wider than the one that seems to be implicitly assumed by Føllesdal. But what kind of empirical basis can be found for these interpretive hypotheses?

3. Assessing interpretive hypotheses

Empirical hypotheses are testable. They are tested against evidence, against criteria of parsimony, logic and descriptive or explanatory power, and against alternative hypotheses. Popperians would add a further requirement: empirical scientific hypotheses should be falsifiable. What is the situation with interpretive hypotheses? Are they only tested "conceptually" (cf. Gile 2004a, Chesterman 2004b)?

Conceptual testing – perhaps a better term would be assessment – takes place by argument, practical reason. One can argue about the logic and parsimony of an interpretive hypothesis; but one can also check how well it fits the evidence and how fruitful it turns out to be. In practice, this means that if a given definition or analogy etc. proves to lead to good research questions or analyses or empirical hypotheses, this counts as added value. Weaker alternatives gradually fade from use in the scholarly community. I agree with Gile that this process is partly Kuhnian (Kuhn 1970), in that it is influenced by social and convenience factors; but I think it is also Popperian, in that even conceptual testing can weed out weak hypotheses. If this is "Popper-inspired" assessment, rather than strictly Popperian testing (Gile 2004b: 125), so be it. Interpretive hypotheses are not falsifiable, then – they are not right or wrong: they are "revisable agreements" (Misgeld 1991: 177), better or worse than alternatives. Some may be very weak indeed, of course, and be rapidly overwhelmed by counter-evidence and/or argument.

With this in mind, we can refine the basic form of an interpretive hypothesis in terms of an underlying abductive inference, thus: it is hypothesized that *if X is interpreted as Y, added value will ensue* (the added value being that we will understand X better, be able to examine it fruitfully, derive further interesting research questions, solve a problem, improve a situation, and so on). This formulation is implicitly comparative. It implies that the hypothesized interpretation of X *as Y* is better (in some sense) than (a) no interpretation at all, and (b) alternative interpretations. The formulation is also predictive: if no added value ensues, we can dump the hypothesis…

That said, it must be acknowledged that scholars often tend to be more concerned with inventing and propagating new interpretive hypotheses than in assessing or revising existing ones. In the studies referred to above, Cronin and Maier focus on the new insights that their hypotheses can shed on the role and status of translators, on the benefits of adopting this particular perspective; they thus seek to show its added value. The authors' use of evidence is illustrative, to support the hypothesis under consideration, to justify the possibility of this particular interpretation. But it would be good to see more work which compares such hypotheses with others, or tests them against data which might cause difficulties for them. One example of this kind of testing is Pym's (2007b) assessment of some alternative definitions of translation.

The tendency towards the generation and illustration of hypotheses rather than their testing is not inevitable. Let us return to Føllesdal's original example, the strange Passenger. In his analysis of the way the competing interpretations have been defended, Føllesdal suggests a number of empirical factors that need to be considered. The most obvious one is the relation between the proposed hypothesis and the actual data that prompted it: this particular scene in the play (and later scenes in which the Passenger appears). How well does the interpretation fit this evidence? At least well enough for the evidence to act as an illustration of the hypothesis: a minimum requirement, for the interpretation must at least be possible. Second, there is the relation between the hypothesis and other evidence in the play: other scenes, where the Passenger does not appear. How well is the hypothesis supported by this additional evidence? Does a hypothesis concerning only a part of the play lead to a coherent and comprehensive understanding of the play as a whole, or fit with our preliminary understanding of this whole? Or is there counter-evidence elsewhere in the play? Third: what about quite different evidence, such as biographical evidence, data from Ibsen's letters, interviews, his other work, and so on? (This looks exactly like the triangulation method used in some empirical research projects.) Does this external evidence also support the hypothesis? Again, what about counter-evidence? Fourth: how well does the hypothesis fare in competition with other hypotheses? Are other possibilities taken into account, and shown to be less adequate? And finally, what consequences does the hypothesis imply? In particular, what *testable* consequences?

Føllesdal points out that these criteria are, in principle, largely the same as those used in testing empirical hypotheses in the natural sciences. Indeed, as I have said, Føllesdal's basic argument is that there is no fundamental methodological difference between natural sciences and humanities using a hermeneutic method. A hypothesis is tested against primary evidence, against additional evidence, against alternative hypotheses and possible counter-evidence. The fact that scholars in the humanities do not always follow such a rigorous testing procedure in practice is another matter. Føllesdal shows that if this kind of testing is carried out, some of the proposed interpretations of the meaning of the Passenger look distinctly better than others. He also points out, however, as mentioned above, that it may be impossible to arrive at a conclusive solution because there is simply not enough evidence. This is not unusual when we are dealing with meaningful data.

A strict falsificationist position is thus inappropriate in research on meaningful data. An analogy, for instance, is not falsifiable. But strict falsificationism may not be a realistic position for hard scientists either, as argued by Lakatos (1970), since falsification can seldom be absolute: after all, testing methods and decisions about operationalization rely on auxiliary hypotheses that are also fallible. Nevertheless, we can at least underline the importance of checking interpretive hypotheses against potential counter-examples and additional evidence, and against alternative interpretive hypotheses. Counter-evidence will not actually falsify an interpretive hypothesis, but it can provide a good reason for preferring some other alternative instead, when different hypotheses are weighed against each other. The assessment of interpretive hypotheses is thus relative, not absolute. To what extent do we find a given hypothesis convincing? (This is often the case for empirical hypotheses in the hard sciences as well, of course, e.g. when one assesses the relative probabilities of a given hypothesis vs. the null hypothesis.)

Nevertheless, in a Popperian spirit, we can try to specify the kind of evidence that would indeed count against or weaken a given interpretive hypothesis. In his discussion of the Passenger in *Peer Gynt*, Føllesdal notes ([1979] 1994: 238) that in assessing competing hypotheses, one criterion is the degree of specificity of the evidence called upon: the more specific the evidence, the stronger the claim can be. If a hypothesis is based primarily on very general evidence and there is specific evidence that runs counter to the hypothesis, or if not all parts of the phenomenon are taken into consideration, then the hypothesis is much less convincing. And we can also note the importance of deriving testable consequences from interpretive hypotheses. If, for example, we were to propose that students will become better translators if they are taught to see their professional role as that of a *theoros* (this is not Maier's claim, just an invented example), we could in principle test the claim with a comparative study based on two teaching methods with matched groups of students, one highlighting the *theoros* metaphor and the other, say, the translator's role as bridge-building mediator.

With data of the kind we are discussing here, meaningful data in a broad sense, one contribution of interpretive hypotheses can be their cumulative effect. Given that the assessment of these hypotheses will seldom be conclusive, a new interpretive hypothesis at least offers a new way of seeing, in addition to existing ones. This characteristic is particularly relevant for our understanding of works of art, of course, which may benefit from being amenable to a multiplicity of interpretations, offering a rich mixture of meanings. Take the metaphorical or analogical *as*, or the classificatory *as,* for instance: in theory, anything can be seen as similar in some respect to practically anything else, and can be classified in any number of ways, depending on the purpose, perspective, context etc. Every analogy and every classification highlights some aspects and obscures others. From this point of view, the cumulative effect of interpretive hypotheses can enrich understanding. The added value of an interpretive hypothesis may indeed be literally "additional" depth of understanding or range of significance, rather than the defeat of an alternative hypothesis. And there may be no end to possible interpretations.

4. Interpretive hypotheses and explanations

I would finally like to compare interpretive hypotheses with the standard empirical types: predictive, descriptive, explanatory. Interpretive hypotheses are predictive in the implicit abductive sense mentioned above (if X is interpreted as Y, added value will ensue); but unlike empirical predictive hypotheses they are not falsifiable. Interpretive hypotheses are more closely related to descriptive ones, since descriptive hypotheses, with the basic logical form *all X (of type T) have feature F*, implicitly involve definitions and interpretations of X (and T) and F. But the closest similarity is with explanatory hypotheses. After all, an interpretation is already an explanation of a kind, since it is a way in which someone "makes sense" of the phenomenon in question.

This aspect of interpretive hypotheses is especially evident in qualitative research, such as that carried out within a framework such as Grounded Theory (Glaser and Strauss 1967). In such a framework, data analysis proceeds by a series of interpretive hypotheses which are subjected to continuous testing against further data, until one arrives at an explanatory interpretation that best accounts for the totality of the dataset. With respect to our example of *Peer Gynt*, for instance, one could argue that the play as a whole is better explained / interpreted as being about sin, love, identity and/or death than about Byron.

This kind of interpretive explanation is largely a form of unification (see Salmon 1998). Explanation-by-unification works by relating the *explanandum* to its wider context, making explicit its relations with a wider network, so that it is no longer an isolated phenomenon. If a strange event, for instance, is interpreted as being analogous to some other, more familiar event, or as being a hyponym of a more familiar type of event, the strange event itself seems less obscure. It is this sense of the strange event *no longer being isolated* that gives us the feeling that we understand it, to some extent at least. (For further analysis of varieties of explanation, with particular reference to Translation Studies, see Chesterman 2008b*.)

In this context, it is interesting to see a similarity between the role of hermeneutic empathy and the role of inference by analogy (Niiniluoto 1983: 176). Classical arguments by analogy are based on the idea that if certain phenomena share a number of given features, we can infer that they may also share some other features. We can thus infer something about interpreting by studying translation (and vice versa), because the two modes share many features. The role of empathy in hermeneutic research, as a source of understanding e.g. a literary work, is similar, in that it is based on the analogy between the scholar and the writer as human beings, with emotions, needs, imagination, etc. Both empathy and analogy can thus serve as aids in generating explanatory hypotheses: the inferences made can then be tested in the ways outlined above.

5. Conclusion

My conclusion concurs with that of Føllesdal: interpretive hypotheses are what we use when we try to understand meaningful yet obscure phenomena. The method of generating and testing such hypotheses does not significantly differ in principle from the standard hypothetico-deductive method used in the natural sciences, except for the point that interpretive hypotheses are not falsifiable (although they can certainly be unconvincing).

To return to a hermeneutic perspective: one's interpretive hypotheses help to constitute one's horizon, in Gadamer's terms. To the extent that this horizon is shared with other people, e.g. within a given research paradigm, it provides an initial framework for understanding (Gadamer's *Vorverstehen*). To the extent that this horizon exists and is shared via discourse, interpretive hypotheses may appear to be more or less convincing partly according to the effectiveness of this discourse rhetoric itself, which may thus play a more influential role here than is the case with empirical hypotheses: another point of difference.

Like all hypotheses, interpretive ones too are tools to be made use of in our quest for understanding. If a hypothesis turns out not to be so useful after all, or rather less useful than an alternative, we can refine it or drop it. On the other hand, if it leads to interesting new questions and new empirical hypotheses, let's run with it as far as it takes us![2]

---

* Paper 12 in this volume.

Notes

1. See physics.nist.gov/cuu/Units/meter.html
2. Warm thanks to members of the MonAKO research seminar, and to Anthony Pym, for helpful comments on an early version of this paper.

PAPER 19

Reflections on the literal translation hypothesis*

This paper examines the well-known literal translation hypothesis and discusses its significance for translation theory. The hypothesis claims that as translators process a given text chunk, they tend to start from a literal version of the target text, and then work towards a freer version. The idea has been implied or explicitly studied by many scholars, and does not seem to have a single source.

After some preliminary conceptual analysis an optimal formulation of the hypothesis is proposed. The paper then assesses the hypothesis in terms of the kinds of wider significance any hypothesis can have. The criteria discussed are testability, relations with other hypotheses, applicability, surprise value and explanatory power. Some of Englund Dimitrova's research (2005) on the hypothesis is discussed. A rather different study, by Lieselott Nordman (2009), is argued to have implications for the broader contextualization of the hypothesis.

Keywords: literal translation, hypothesis, revision, research methodology

1. Introduction

Research projects in Translation Studies often either start with a hypothesis which they set out to test, or aim to generate one based on argument and/or data analysis. Some of these hypotheses attract wider attention, and they are then subject to further testing, either in replication studies with similar data or in other kinds of conditions. These hypotheses are usually dignified by an easily citable name, with the definite article in English: "the X hypothesis". Insofar as such hypotheses are widely corroborated, and probably refined and conditioned as well, they may eventually become part of the fundamental structure of a general theory of translation.

---

* First published in 2011 in Cecilia Alvstad, Adelina Hild and Elisabet Tiselius (eds), *Methods and Strategies of Process Research. Integrative approaches in Translation Studies*. Amsterdam/Philadelphia: Benjamins, 23–35. Reprinted with kind permission from John Benjamins Publishing Company [www.benjamins.com].

In the past two or three decades many interesting hypotheses have been proposed and tested in connection with the search for translation universals. Examples are the explicitation hypothesis, the simplification hypothesis, and the unique items hypothesis (see e.g. the articles collected in Mauranen and Kujamäki 2004). These hypotheses make claims about very general features of translations as textual products, and obviously have implications concerning underlying cognitive process(es). But there are also a few hypotheses that make direct claims about the translation process itself, such as the literal translation hypothesis to be examined here.

I will first explore some of the conceptual background underlying this hypothesis, and propose an explicit formulation of it. I then proceed to examine the significance of the hypothesis in terms of a number of basic criteria. The argument will be that on most of these criteria, the literal translation hypothesis is indeed rather important. After this general assessment two recent studies are briefly reviewed, in order to show possible new lines of research.

2. Conceptual background

Like many other terms in Translation Studies, "literal translation" has meant different things to different people (see Shuttleworth and Cowie 1997: s.v.). There is its vague general sense, in opposition to "free" translation. One interpretation more or less equates a literal translation with a word-for-word one that is minimally adjusted to meet the demands of grammaticality (e.g. Catford 1965: 25). For some, a literal translation is ungrammatical; for others, it is grammatical, although it may still sound odd: cf. Vinay and Darbelnet (1958), where literal translation is given as one procedure implementing a "direct" translation strategy, alongside the use of a loan or calque. Like Vinay and Darbelnet, many scholars list literal translation as a possible technique or procedure which a translator can use when the conditions are appropriate, either in general or at some specific point in a text. Indeed, for some (e.g. Newmark 1988: 68–69), literal translation is seen as a default solution, from which a translator deviates only when, for some reason or other, a literal translation is not appropriate. I will start by taking a literal translation as one that is formally close to its source but nevertheless grammatical.

The brief list of varying views above illustrates one point where agreement is easy. Applied to a translation solution, the term "literal translation" may refer either to a complete text, or to a translated fragment of a text. Similarly, applied to the translator's decision-making, literal translation may be a global or a local strategy. A given translation may thus be generally free, but contain elements that are literal; and a generally literal translation may contain elements that are not literal. (Cf. Englund Dimitrova 2005: 51–52.)

Literal translation is also closely related to some other terms that are used both in translation research and in contrastive analysis: equivalence, correspondence, congruence. Catford (1965: 32) distinguishes between (textual, or situational) equivalence and formal correspondence: this latter is defined as holding between source-language and target-language "categories" if they "occupy, as nearly as possible, the 'same' place in the economy" of the two languages. (For Catford, following Halliday, the categories are those of unit, structure, class and system.) This concept is thus a relative one, in the sense that the sameness is not absolute.

Catford's conceptualization of formal correspondence is not without its problems. There are different ways of measuring the degree of formal closeness, for instance, and it is not clear whether one should have priority over another. And it should be noted that his concept is defined in terms of languages, i.e. language systems, not texts. We can nevertheless infer that the notion of formal correspondence could form the basis of a possible definition of literal translation, as follows: a literal translation is one that shows the maximum of formal correspondence (within the constraints of the target language grammar). For any given source-text sentence or string, there would thus only be one translation in a given target language that would be called "literal": the one with the highest degree of formal correspondence. This restriction, however, is rather a drawback. We would surely like to be able to say that, of a whole range of possible or actual translations of a given source-language string, several are literal, and some are more literal than others, although version X is the *most* literal (with degree of literalness measured in some specified way).

The field of contrastive analysis also makes use of notions of equivalence and correspondence, and sometimes also of congruence. Various kinds of equivalence are recognized (see e.g. Krzeszowski 1990: 23f), including translation equivalence. "Congruence" is a term used by some contrastivists, particularly those working within a generative framework, to refer to a relation between grammatical sentences in two languages which are semantically equivalent and "consist of the same number of lexical words, representing equivalent grammatical categories, arranged in the same linear order" (Krzeszowski 1990: 135). This too is a highly restricted notion. If we imagine a source string and a set of possible target translations, congruence in this sense would not necessarily hold for any of them, although we might still wish to say that some were more literal than others.

Both formal correspondence and congruence define states of affairs towards one end of a continuum of *formal similarity*. Formal correspondence between individual categories seems to indicate an even higher degree of similarity than congruence between strings or sentences, in that a part of a sentence might be formally corresponding although the whole sentence is not congruent. Beyond these cases we can imagine even closer matches, but they would no longer be grammatical.

What about the other end of the continuum, the non-literal end? There are obviously translations that bear no formal similarity at all with the source (although they must surely bear some other kind of relevant similarity if they are to be called translations at all). But there are also many translations that are formally similar only, for instance, to the extent that the target string is, like the source string, a sentence. Such sentence-similar translations, however, may well be non-literal in most other respects. Or, at a higher level, what about translations that bear a formal similarity only at the level of paragraph, or section, or chapter, or even at the level of the complete text? The conclusion I draw is that, in order to be useful, the notion of literal translation must be a comparative one. We can thus say that in given respects, translation A is *more literal* (i.e. is formally more similar to the source, on given criteria) than translation B. True, criteria vary and may conflict, so they need to be defined in each case. However, there seems no obvious borderline between literal and non-literal translations; they are not two distinct sets. This conclusion applies both to the notion as referring to the text as a whole and as referring to a local strategy. Our initial assumption must thus be refined a bit: a literal translation is one that is formally *closer* to its source than some other translation of the same source chunk, on given criteria. (See the example below.)

There is one further conceptual complication, having to do with the relation between different kinds of formal similarity on the one hand and equivalence on the other. For Catford, formal correspondence does not imply (textual) equivalence. For Krzeszowski, however, congruent strings are a subset of (translationally, or semantically) equivalent strings. In translation studies, we have long argued about the notion of equivalence, and I will not repeat the debate here. (For a recent survey, see Pym 2010.) In the present context it will suffice to follow Krzeszowski's general line: translation research looks at the creation of equivalence, the various forms it can take, and what effects these forms may have. "Equivalence" here can be glossed as 'relevant similarity'. On this view, it makes sense to restrict the kind of formal similarity we are interested in to cases that occur within the bounds of this translational equivalence. Data that may show some formal similarity but no evidence of any translational equivalence are not relevant to the present argument (although they might well be relevant to language typologists or contrastivists, of course).

3. The hypothesis and its significance

The *literal translation hypothesis* does not refer synchronically to the final product of the translation process, nor to local instances within that product. It makes a diachronic claim about the translation process. In view of the discussion above I will formulate it as follows: *during the translation process, translators tend to proceed from more literal versions to less literal ones.* The underlying assumption is that the translator's cognitive processes will tend to be influenced, initially, by formal features of the source text. Note that this formulation of the hypothesis states a change in a certain direction. It does not start by postulating "a literal translation" as a starting-point of this change. There are two reasons for this. One is the difficulty of specifying an operational borderline between the range of possible translations that are somehow formally similar, and the range of translations that are not, as discussed above. Without a clear cut-off point, it is simpler to focus on the direction of change rather than the initial point of change. The second reason is that normally we are looking at a single translation, not multiple translations of the same text; and in any case we are not normally taking account of potential "shadow" translations that could have been used but were not. (The term "shadow translation" is from Matthiessen 2001: 83.) This means that in such cases we have no other translation with which to compare translation A. But by formulating the hypothesis in terms of a direction we provide ourselves with a point of comparison: the hypothesis claims that initial (or earlier) draft version A is formally closer to the source than the later version B. – An alternative statement of the hypothesis makes this explicit: in effect, we are talking about a *deliteralization* hypothesis, i.e. a move from more literal to less literal.

Let us consider a simple example, from my local Eniro telephone directory, which gives information in Finnish, Swedish and English. I assume that Finnish is the source language.

(1) Finnish: Kotimaan kaukopuheluita voit soittaa usean eri verkon kautta.
   ['domestic long-distance calls you can call via several different networks']
(2) Swedish: Du kan ringa inrikes fjärrsamtal via flera olika nät.
   ['you can ring domestic long-distance calls via several different networks']
(3) English: Long-distance calls in Finland can be made over several different networks.

A shadow English translation could have been:

(3a) You can make domestic long-distance calls via several different networks.

This structural choice would have been formally more similar to the Swedish version, with the same order of main constituents as the Swedish. The published English version (3) explicates *domestic* to *in Finland*, and introduces a shift from active to passive verb, but preserves the thematic order of the Finnish, starting with the *calls*. If we now compare the two English versions, we can say that (3) is more similar to the Finnish source on the criterion of preserving the thematic order, but (3a) is more similar on the criterion of preserving the voice of the verb phrase. With respect to the shift in (3) to *in Finland*, the literal translation hypothesis would claim that the translator first thought of the unshifted alternative *domestic*, as in (3a), but then adopted the less literal version in (3). Given explicit criteria, judgements of relative similarity are thus not difficult. However, in order to assess whether (3) or (3a) is formally more similar *overall* to the Finnish source, we would need some justified way of prioritizing different criteria. If syntactic structure is held to take precedence over thematic structure, the literal translation hypothesis could claim that (3a) as a whole occurred to the translator's mind first, as being syntactically close to the source, and was then modified in several respects: the shift to *in Finland*, the voice change, and also the change from literal *via* to *over*.

The hypothesis itself is by no means a new idea, of course. Toury (1995: 191) already cites Ivir (1981: 58) on the idea that translators start from target versions that show formal correspondence, and then move on to freer versions when they need to in order to achieve a relevant equivalence. The rejection of the initial literal version is assumed to be made by some kind of cognitive monitor, and several scholars have proposed a "monitor model" to represent this (see e.g. Tirkkonen-Condit 2005).

Before considering some recent empirical evidence I would like to bring up a different question: why might the literal translation hypothesis matter? Why might it be significant? I will suggest several reasons. My intention here is also to indicate in what respects the hypothesis can serve as a good methodological model in translation research.

First, it can be tested empirically. If we operationalize the verb "tend" in the above formulation of the hypothesis (e.g. to: during the translation process, translators in at least x% of cases studied proceed from more literal versions to less literal ones, rather than in the opposite direction), the hypothesis can also be falsified. It is therefore vulnerable, which is a merit. Degrees of formal similarity can be operationalized in terms of the number and type of shifts. The most complex model of shift analysis so far proposed is that by Leuven-Zwart (1989/1990), but simpler measures could also serve the purpose.

Second, it can be tested in several quite different ways. This is also a merit, partly because it makes the hypothesis more vulnerable (and possible multiple corroboration is correspondingly more meaningful, especially if different analyses can be triangulated), and partly because it indicates that the hypothesis may have relevance to different research frameworks and thus perhaps encapsulate a fairly general insight. The various ways in which the hypothesis can be tested include the following (most of them are used or referred to in Englund Dimitrova 2005):

- Think-Aloud Protocols. Do translators' verbalizations show movement away from more literal versions? (See e.g. Englund Dimitrova 2005.)
- Keystroke logging analysis, such as Translog data (e.g. Jakobsen 1999).
- Interim solutions analysis (the study of the revision process across a series of drafts). This was the context of Toury's reference to Ivir, cited above.
- The study of repairs in simultaneous interpreting (cf. work referred to in Tirkkonen-Condit 2005). Interpreters appear to use fewer repairs when there is more syntactic similarity between strings in the two languages, which suggests easier processing.
- The study of the time taken to translate different kinds of idioms, some of which have formally matching versions in the target language (and tend to be translated faster) and some of which do not. (Also discussed in Tirkkonen-Condit 2005).
- The study of interference in general. Interference is of course a sign of some (usually) unwanted similarity that has been carried over from the source text into the target version.
- The study of differences between novice and professional or expert translators. A plausible corollary to the hypothesis would suggest that professionals and experts proceed more quickly, and further, along the path away from an initial literal translation; or that they actually start their processing from a less literal point. (See e.g. Englund Dimitrova 2005.)
- The study of translation performed under conditions of unusual time stress. One might expect that when processing time is strictly limited, more recourse is taken to literal versions, but research on this has so far been rather inconclusive (see e.g. Jansen and Jakobsen 2000).

If such tests are replicated with different language pairs and translation directions, one result might well be that the strength of the literal translation tendency varies under different language conditions, and indeed according to other kinds of conditions as well. (Cf. the survey of interference conditions in Murphy 2003.)

Third, the hypothesis is openly a counter-hypothesis to a competing claim: the deverbalization hypothesis, proposed and indeed assumed (but not empirically tested) by the so-called Paris school of interpreting, a claim implying the separation of form and meaning during processing. True, the deverbalization hypothesis was originally proposed for interpreting, but it has also been taken to apply to translation (see e.g. Seleskovitch and Lederer 1984). Nida's well-known river-crossing model of translation (e.g. 1964), comprising the three stages of analysis, transfer and restructuring, appears explicitly to assume deverbalization, at least insofar as the formal structure of the source text is initially reformulated at what Nida calls a "near-kernel" level of abstraction. In Nida's model, however, the initial deverbalizing move away from the source surface structure is represented as taking place within the source language, not the target language. Evidence in favour of the literal translation hypothesis would thus suggest some initial transfer to the target language *without* analysis, which would go against the model. Yet there might also be evidence of a move towards freer renderings during the restructuring process, which does take place within the target language. That said, it is clear that Nida's model is not based on explicit empirical evidence, and was presumably intended to have pedagogical and prescriptive priorities, as indeed was the deverbalization idea. Nevertheless, the fact that the literal translation hypothesis stands in a dialectic relation with a competing claim gives it a sharp theoretical relevance. It also has the rhetorical advantage of enabling scholars to formulate their discussions about it as a confrontational debate, as Englund Dimitrova does in her explicitation study (2005).

Fourth, the literal hypothesis can also be linked supportively to other current hypotheses in ways which bring it greater explanatory power, because these extend beyond linguistic description towards underlying cognitive processing. Two examples are the unique items hypothesis (Tirkkonen-Condit, e.g. 2004; Chesterman 2007b[*]) and the gravitational pull hypothesis (Halverson, e.g. 2003, 2007). The former is more specific than the literal translation hypothesis, and the latter is more general. Halverson's idea of gravitational pull focuses on how target-language category prototypes and superordinate conceptual schemata tend to influence the translator's choices, leading to the over-representation of certain kinds of items. This cognitive pull, argues Halverson, explains such putative translation universals as simplification, standardization and generalization. But underlying this idea there is obviously the assumption that salient source-text features will also exert a pull (i.e. leading to interference of some kind). In her discussion of the unique items hypothesis, Halverson (e.g. 2003: 223) makes this point explicitly. In the absence of any conceptual overlap between source and target structures, it is only to be expected that target-language-unique forms will be under-represented. In other words, if there is a choice between a target structure that is formally similar (and hence cognitively salient at the moment of target-item selection) and one that is not, the translator will tend to select the formally similar one and thus save processing time and effort. Halverson also makes the important point that similar effects have been observed in studies on second language acquisition. This implies

---

[*] Paper 21 in this volume.

that so-called translation universals may not be specific to translation, but have to do more generally with language use under particular constraints.

Fifth, the hypothesis also has interesting potential applications in the description and explanation of individual translator styles, and perhaps in the optimization of revision procedures (see e.g. Mossop 2000, 2007). There may be more than one tendency at work: some translators (perhaps under certain working conditions, or with certain language pairs or translation directions or text types, or with certain personality types, or whatever...) may tend to process in a *deliteralizing* direction, from more literal towards less literal, while others work in the opposite direction, beginning with a freer version and then pulling it back closer to the source text during processing or revision (i.e. *literalizing*).

In one respect, the literal translation hypothesis does not seem so significant. Because it appears to be highly plausible, it is a rather cautious hypothesis, not a bold one. Research results that went against it would really surprise us. Bolder, and potentially more interesting, sub-hypotheses might eventually emerge when we know more about the specific conditions under which a processing move from more to less literal tends to occur, and when it tends not to occur.

4. One recent study, and one different one

So what kind of empirical evidence has been found for or against the literal translation hypothesis? Englund Dimitrova (2005) has much of relevance to say about our hypothesis in her rich study on explicitation and translator expertise. Her subjects were three small groups of language and translation students and translation professionals, working from Russian into Swedish. The text to be translated was a short one, six paragraphs from an art album on the life and work of a Ukrainian poet and artist; a total of 30 sentences. And note that this was an experimental situation, not an authentic one. Several research methods were used: TAP, videotaped keystroke logging, and revision analysis (interim solutions). This revision analysis covered both revisions made during drafting and those made during the post-writing stage. Englund Dimitrova discusses many of the points mentioned above, and her results certainly support the hypothesis (which is not actually stated as such, in this study), running clearly counter to the deverbalization hypothesis.

Englund Dimitrova's formulation of what she means by literal translation starts from the local sense of the term. For her, a literal translation is "a TT fragment which is structurally and semantically modelled upon the ST fragment while respecting TL grammatical constraints" (2005: 53). This formulation does not imply a single "maximally" close version (i.e. *the* literal one), but allows, for a given fragment, a range of translations that could be said to be "modelled" on the source fragment, to different degrees and in different ways. It thus seems open to the borderline difficulty discussed above, and to the difficulty of a lacking point of comparison. But Englund Dimitrova is mainly interested here in explicitation, and her operationalization of a literal translation is: one that is not explicitated (51). In this way, she implies one clear criterion for measuring the degree of formal similarity: an explicitated translation is less formally similar to the source than a non-explicitated one – and there is the point of comparison. In other words, although she starts by positing an initial literal translation, the operationalization of the decrease in formal similarity is done in terms of the presence or absence of explicitation shifts.

Her definition also includes some notion of semantic similarity (… "structurally and semantically modelled"). One may debate the extent to which semantics is a matter of form, but her sense of "literal" does seem to be slightly wider than mine.

She found that there was "a tendency for syntactic revisions to result in structures that were more distant from the structure of the ST than the first version chosen" (121). This tendency was particularly evident in the revisions made by the group of professionals. The TAP data also showed that the subjects tended to be aware of the need to move away from literal versions. She wonders (146, 232) why professionals bother to write down a literal version at all, since it will probably be changed at a later stage. Perhaps this is a way of economizing on short-term memory. (*Pace* Nida, transfer can thus take place in the absence of any analysis, even in the case of professionals.) She also notes that literal versions are often the ones that are first verbalized, before anything is written down. This supports the idea that the literal version is a default solution. She acknowledges (148) that this conclusion is only based on an analysis of the revision of syntactic structures and does not take into account semantic or pragmatic changes. – However, if literalness is defined strictly as *formal* similarity, this limitation would be less problematic, although there would remain the challenge of sorting out priorities between potentially clashing formal criteria (as mentioned above).

In her conclusions, Englund Dimitrova underlines the importance, for professional translation competence, of knowing how best to exploit literal translation during the translation process. She found three prototypical patterns (234): (i) literal translations are formulated orally, then revised orally before a version is written; (ii) literal translations are initially written, then evaluated and revised during drafting; (iii) literal translations are written as provisional solutions, and revised during post-drafting revision. She concludes that for professionals, the use of literal translation is thus a *processing* strategy. Its frequency no doubt varies according to the typological relation between source and target languages.

A brief aside is worth adding here. Machine translation, when not drawing on a huge translation memory of human translations, can also provide a literal translation, of a kind (cf. pattern (ii) above). Pym (2009) reports an exploratory study on how translator trainees can use a machine translation as a way of arriving at a fast first draft. And here is a professional literary translator describing how he dealt with a translation of a family memoir from Italian to English: "Since Italian is not one of my working languages, I did the translation in two stages, the first of which was to run [the] Italian original through a commercial translation software called Systran" (A. Wilson 2009: 34). The result was a very literal version indeed, "not yet English, but very helpful", and he proceeded to polish it.

How valid are Englund Dimitrova's results? The study only used nine subjects, selected by convenience, and one short translation. As the author notes, it was only an initial, exploratory study. And there were other research questions which were more central to the project than the issue of literal translation. But with respect to the literal translation hypothesis, I find Englund Dimitrova's results rather convincing.

The second study I would like to mention briefly is very different, and does not explicitly test the literal translation hypothesis at all. However, I shall reinterpret one of its results and suggest that it shows how the hypothesis could be placed in a wider context, and also opens up a new perspective on it. The study in question is a PhD thesis on revision by Nordman (2009). Nordman's research examined in general how the revision system works for the Swedish translation of laws in the Finnish Parliament. (Laws are usually first drafted in Finnish and then translated into Swedish, Finland being a bilingual country.)

In Nordman's case, the revision in question is not self-revision but other-revision. The system she studied consists of a number of professional translators, revisers and legal experts, located in different offices (the Government translation unit, the Ministry of Justice Swedish revision unit, and the Swedish Department of the Finnish Parliament). Initial translations are passed up the chain, subject to different revisions at four different stages. So we are dealing with a case of institutional, team translation. The research project involved textual revision analysis, questionnaires and interviews. The texts in question are very different from those in Dimitrova Englund's study, and they have a different skopos. Here, we are dealing with legal texts, the drafts of bills that will become laws; and the revision situation is authentic. It is also relevant to point out that the translators studied were of course aware that their work would be revised, as normal. Despite all these differences between the two studies, I will argue that Nordman's work does suggest a new angle on the literal translation hypothesis.

Nordman analyses her revision data partly in terms of four norms: legal adequacy, correct translation, correct language and readability. Of these, "correct translation" has to do with formal and semantic similarity with the source. An example (op.cit.: 158):

Finnish source: (3) luoda edellytykset radiolaitteiden mahdollisimman vapaalle liikkuvuudelle [...] ['to create conditions for the maximally free mobility of radio sets']
Initial translation: (3) att skapa betingelser för att radioanläggningar ska får röra sig så fritt som möjligt [...] ['... so that radio sets can be moved as freely as possible']
Revised version: (3) att skapa betingelser för att en så fri rörlighet för radioanläggningar som möjligt [...] ['... a mobility ... that is as free as possible']

The other three norms relate to conformity to target language and genre, and to official recommendations for legal Swedish style, such as adding missing commas, or normalizing introductory structures in a list. At the four stages of revision, Nordman found that there was variation in the way corrections and changes could be ascribed to these different norms. At the first stage, the "correct translation" norm accounted for 15% of the revisions made. But – and this is the point I want to pick out – during the three later stages this proportion did not decrease; on the contrary, it rose to about 30% of the revisions made at each of these later stages (Nordman 2009: 219).

This is surprising. One might have expected that adequate equivalence would have been established early in the revision process, with later changes having more to do with target language requirements (along the lines of Nida's restructuring, perhaps). That would have shown a deliteralizing process that continued through the revision phases. But what we seem to have here is evidence of *reliteralization*. Later revisers, in other words, have felt that the similarity relation is not close enough and altered the text accordingly. One reason for this may be the fact that in this context the source text is not entirely constant, being itself subject to some small changes as the text is finalized; but this seems to account for only some of the later equivalence revisions. Another reason may be the structural weakness of the whole revision system itself, spread over four different offices between which cooperation is not always optimal, and there is some duplication and disagreement. In particular, among the agents involved, there is some variation of *attitude* towards the norms mentioned, with different priorities apparently depending at least partly on personal preferences.

5. Concluding comments

I have argued that the literal translation hypothesis is an important one. It has interesting theoretical implications about the cognitive relation between form and meaning; it is testable in multiple ways; it has explanatory power, in that it connects with different kinds of research results and relates to several other claims, some of which run counter to it; and it opens up new research questions. In the wider context of revision in general, one wonders for example whether there might be a pattern: deliteralization in self-translation, and reliteralization when the revision is done by someone else? Or would the different tendencies correlate rather to text type? To what extent might the translator's knowledge of an institution's revision system affect initial textual choices and strategies? Would the knowledge of the coming revision encourage more risk-taking at the initial stage, for instance? Such new questions might lead to interesting new hypotheses.

Suppose the hypothesis turns out to be largely supported by empirical evidence (as now seems), but not always. Then, as I have been suggesting at different points, we could ask:

- Under what conditions (textual, situational, psychological...) do we find in *self*-revision a tendency towards deliteralization, and under what conditions one towards reliteralization?
- Under what conditions do we find in *other*-revision each of these tendencies?
- If the conditions affecting deliteralization or reliteralization in these two forms of revision turn out to be similar, what might this imply about the most likely cause of the tendency? To what extent might (unconscious) cognitive factors be relevant, and to what extent (potentially conscious) attitudinal factors?
- How then could this information be best exploited to optimize translation quality control systems?

There are thus implications here for making further connections between the translation act (cognitive, psychological) and the wider translation event (situational, institutional, sociological).*

---

* The distinction between translation acts and events is discussed in Paper 26, below.

SECTION VII

"Universals"

The search for so-called translation universals has been a major trend in recent research. However, the term itself is unfortunate, since the implied connection with language universals is misleading. In TS, some have preferred to speak of "laws" (e.g. Toury, and also Chesterman), but this is perhaps also not an optimal term. We are simply looking for generalizations, patterns, regularities, tendencies, in the usual sense of these terms in empirical research. To call them "universals" is rather to jump the gun, as we cannot demonstrate that such features are in fact literally universal. Proposals concerning universals are of course descriptive hypotheses, and many studies have shown that a proposed tendency has turned out not to be so universal as was first thought. (See the papers in this section for some examples.)

If we formulate our search as one for general tendencies, a more serious problem arises, one that is often overlooked: in a given research project, what exactly do we mean by a tendency? Whatever working definition we choose will have implications for what we will accept as counter-evidence. If a tendency means "occurs always, under certain conditions", a single non-occurrence under these conditions will falsify the hypothesis. But what about "occurs often", or "occurs sometimes"? What would be accepted as counter-evidence, apart from total non-occurrence? A better definition would be: "occurs more often than not, i.e. in more than 50% of potential cases (under given conditions)"; here at least, counter-evidence can be quantified too. Or: "more often than expected" – if the expected probability is defined and justified. Or, perhaps more usefully: "occurs more often than the opposite tendency". For instance, a hypothesis about the translation tendency towards explicitation could be defined and its support measured in terms of its relation to the opposite tendency of implicitation. Or a tendency could be defined as something that occurs more often, i.e. with a higher probability, under condition X than under condition Y. Whatever the details of the definition used, the ideal is to state a testable probability, but this is rarely done.

Yet another problem has to do with the creation of corpora on which hypotheses about universals can be generated and tested. Do we have a universally accepted definition of translation, in the first place? I think not. Furthermore, opinions differ as to whether the general concept of translation is best considered as a prototype category (e.g. Halverson 1998a) or a cluster category (e.g. Tymoczko 2006).

And what about bad translations? A bad translation is also a translation of a kind, but if the corpus excludes them, we have already built in some kind of quality criterion, which rules out conclusions about *all* translations. (Not to mention the difficulty coming up with a universally accepted definition of quality itself…)

Paper 20 relates the search for translation universals to other kinds of generalization. It developed from several conference presentations, and especially a memorable conference in Savonlinna. There is some overlap between this paper and Paper 23.

Paper 21 also started as a conference paper. It is a conceptual analysis of one particular hypothesis, also discussed at the Savonlinna conference, on the relative frequency of "unique items" in translations.

Paper 22 is rather different, focusing on a special case: Kundera's view of what one might call stylistic universals. I suggest that this view may be related to Kundera's experience of being "a stranger" in France.

Paper 23 concerns the ongoing argument about "universalism" as a general attitude in TS as a whole, which is sometimes seen as Euro-centrism. The paper opened a Forum debate in the journal *Translation Studies* (2014, vol. 7, nos. 1 and 3). Maria Tymoczko (in her Response in the debate's opening issue, 2014, 7 (1): 101) summed up the position I argued for as follows:

> What matters is (1) achieving a deeper understanding of translation; (2) testing ideas to see the limits of their applicability to understanding translation as a general phenomenon and to avoid claims about universality prematurely; and (3) attempting to search for patterns that apply to translation data in general through time and space. To accomplish these goals, we would agree that it is necessary to be receptive to data of all types and to look beyond what we think we already know. In particular, we would agree that data from all areas of the world are helpful because they are more inclusive than data from any particular region (such as Europe) alone.

Some scholars have argued that any search for abstract generalizations or so-called universals is not useful, because this conceals the fact that all translations are unique, and contingent on particular times and places. Hermans (2003), for instance, suggests that a good model for cross-cultural translation studies is "thick translation" (Appiah 1993), with its detailed opening-up of contextually embedded meanings, as a way of resisting the "universalizing urge" of theory. He advocates research that is bottom-up, not top-down. But surely both directions are valid. Looking for generalities is a fundamental characteristic of human intellectual endeavour. Some people are predisposed to focus on similarities, and others on distinctions. We do not need to rule out either one or the other approach, but rather seek to relate the two.

PAPER 20

Beyond the particular[*]

Translation scholars have proposed and sought generalizations about translation from various perspectives. This paper discusses three main ways of getting "beyond the particular": traditional prescriptive statements, traditional critical statements, and the contemporary search for universals in corpus studies. There are a number of problems with each of the approaches.

Keywords: regularity, tendency, generalization, fallacy, universals

1. Introduction

Any science seeks generalities. The aim is to transcend knowledge of particular cases by discovering general regularities or laws, or by proposing general descriptive hypotheses that cover more than a single case. Only by looking for similarities between single cases, and then generalizing from these, can a science progress to the ability to make predictions concerning future or unstudied cases. Only in this way can any discipline progress towards an understanding of the general explanatory laws that are relevant in its field. And only in this way can a discipline create links with neighbouring disciplines. An interdiscipline like Translation Studies will be doomed to stagnation if this striving towards the general is neglected.

Seeking generalities means looking for similarities, regularities, patterns, that are shared between particular cases or groups of cases. Such a search does not deny the existence or importance of that which is unique in each particular case; nor does it deny the existence or importance of differences between cases. At its best, such research allows us to see both similarities and differences in a perspective that increases our understanding of the whole picture, and also of how this picture relates to other pictures.

Translation Studies has sought to escape the bounds of the particular in three ways. All three routes have meant looking at (and for) linguistic features which

---

[*] First published in 2004 in Anna Mauranen and Pekka Kujamäki (eds), *Translation Universals. Do they exist?* Amsterdam/Philadelphia: Benjamins, 33–49. Reprinted with kind permission from John Benjamins Publishing Company [www.benjamins.com]. The keywords have been added.

relate translations to (a) the source text and (b) the target language. I will refer to these routes as (i) the prescriptive route, (ii) the pejorative route, and (iii) the descriptive route. Along the prescriptive route we find statements about various features which all translations, or all translations of a given sort, should or should not manifest, ideally. Along the pejorative route we find statements about undesirable features which all, or most, or some type of, translations are thought to manifest, in reality. Along the descriptive route we find statements about possible universal features of translations or subsets of translations, without overt value judgements.

Each route has its problems, and each has made contributions.

2. The prescriptive route

The oldest, traditional route away from the particular has been the stating of prescriptive generalities that purport to hold for all translations. These statements typically have the form: "All translations should have feature X / should not have feature Y", and thus reflect some kind of translation ideal, universally valid. Examples abound in the early literature: Dolet's and Tytler's translation principles, for instance.* The culmination of this route is perhaps reached in Savory's famously paradoxical list of mutually contradictory principles.

> Dolet (*La manière de bien traduire d'une langue en aultre*, 1540; three of his five general principles)
>
> Translations should not be word-for-word renderings of the original.
> Translations should avoid unusual words and expressions.
> Translations should be elegant, not clumsy.
>
> Tytler (*Essay on the principles of translation*, 1797)
>
> Translations should give a complete transcript of the ideas of the original.
> Translations should be in the same style as their source texts.
> Translations should be as natural as original texts.
>
> Savory (1968: 54)
>
> 1. A translation must give the words of the original.
> 2. A translation must give the ideas of the original.
> 3. A translation should read like an original work.
> 4. A translation should read like a translation.
> 5. A translation should reflect the style of the original.
> 6. A translation should possess the style of the translation.

---

*   The points from Dolet, Tytler and Jerome are paraphrased here.

7. A translation should read as a contemporary of the original.
8. A translation should read as a contemporary of the translation.
9. A translation may add to or omit from the original.
10. A translation may never add to or omit from the original.
11. A translation of verse should be in prose.
12. A translation of verse should be in verse.

Problem: overgeneralization (neglect of differences)
The weakness of this route is of course that no account is here taken of the fact that translations are not all of a kind: some prescriptive principles may be valid for some types of translation (or types of text) and other principles for other types. As soon as this is realized, the need arises for a translation typology.

Perhaps the first attempt to make such a typology was that of Jerome, who claimed as follows:

> Jerome (*De optimo genere interpretandi*, 395)
>
> Translations of sacred texts must be literal, word-for-word (because even the word order of the original is a holy mystery and the translator cannot risk heresy).
>   Translations of other kinds of texts should be done sense-for-sense, more freely (because a literal translation would often sound absurd).

Problem: fallacy of converse accident
This is the fallacy of generalizing from a non-typical particular. Here again, differences are neglected. What we find is that statements based on translating a particular kind of text, such as a literary text or the Bible, are assumed to hold good for all kinds of texts – and indeed all kinds of translations. Traces of this fallacy are to be found in quite recent publications on translation theory. A well-known anthology of essays that came out in 1984 was entitled "Theories of Translation" (edited by Schulte and Biguenet). Most of the essays are indeed classics. But all except two deal exclusively with literary translation. The impression is given that translation theory can be more or less equated with literary translation theory – as if literary translation was typical of all translation. A similar impression is given by Venuti's recent collection of readings (2000), the great majority of which concern literary translation.

Problem: idealization
By this I mean the evident underlying belief in perfection, in a perfect translation that would be absolutely equivalent and also absolutely natural. The influence of theological myths is strong here, such as that of the 72 translators of the Septuagint who all arrived miraculously at the same solutions…

Contribution: first attempts to generalize
These early prescriptive statements were at least a first attempt to get beyond the particular, to establish more general principles and parameters. The statements were based on implicit predictive hypotheses based on the following argument:

- A given translation X is a good translation (i.e. this is someone's reaction to it, its effect on their judgement).
- This quality judgement is based on the presence of features ABC in the translation X.
- Therefore, all translations with features ABC will be good, people will react to them in this way.

The argument only works, of course, if we accept three assumptions: that the quality assessment of translation X really is caused by the presence of features ABC and not something else; that all translations are of the same type as X; and that features ABC are universal indicators of high quality.

Contribution: subsequent attempts at typologies
Since Jerome, there have been many attempts to set up typologies of translation (see e.g. Chesterman 1999b for a brief survey). None have yet become generally accepted.

Contribution: concern with translation quality
Quality is a central concern of all those who are involved in the practical work of translation. The descriptivists have perhaps over-reacted against traditional prescriptivism in their desire to place Translation Studies on a more scientific basis. However, if quality assessments are seen as part of the effects that a translation has, they need not be excluded from empirical analysis. Defining quality, and devising reliable measures of it, are genuine research problems that should form part of research into translation effects.

3. The pejorative route

The second route away from the particular is related to the first, but takes a different direction. Here, all translations (or: all translations of a certain kind) are regarded as being deficient in some way. That is, an attempt is made to characterize a set of translations in terms of certain negative features. Along this route we find the traditional tropes of loss and betrayal, the view of translations as merely secondary texts, as necessarily either not faithful or not beautiful.

They are not faithful because they are too free, too fluent, too much naturalized, too domesticated: these deficiencies are often noted by literary critics. Translations are not beautiful if they contain unnatural target language, such as that frequently noticed in tourist brochures, menus, etc. (For dozens of examples, surf the web for Tourist English.)

Along this pejorative path, we find hundreds of statements to the effect that translators are doomed to eternal failure, they are objects of scorn or laughter. The literature abounds in critics' lists of typical translation weaknesses. One of the most recent examples is represented by Antoine Berman, with respect to literary translation: in brief, he claims that these are typically too free. Here is his list of the "deforming tendencies" of literary translation (A. Berman 1985; see also Munday 2001: 149–151).

> Rationalization (making more coherent)
> Clarification (explicitation)
> Expansion
> Ennoblement (more elegant style)
> Qualitative impoverishment (flatter style)
> Quantitative impoverishment (loss of lexical variation)
> Destruction of rhythms
> Destruction of underlying networks of signification
> Destruction of linguistic patternings (more homogeneous)
> Destruction of vernacular networks or their exoticization
>   (dialect loss or highlighting)
> Destruction of expressions and idioms (should not be replaced
>   by TL equivalent idioms)
> Effacement of the superimposition of languages (multilingual source texts)

A similar line of argument is to be found in Kundera's ideas about translation, particularly the translations of his own works (Kundera 1993a: 123f.).[*] He complains about the way translators violate metaphors, seek to enrich simple vocabulary, reduce repetition, spoil sentence rhythms by altering punctuation, even change the typography.

Some of these putative deficiencies reoccur in the descriptive work we shall come to below.

---

[*] See Paper 22 below.

Problem: assumptions about quality – overgeneralization again
The weakness of this kind of approach is not so much a failure to develop a translation typology; rather, it is a very restricted *a priori* view of what constitutes an acceptable translation in the first place. This view is so narrow that a great many translations are automatically criticized, although they might be perfectly acceptable according to other criteria than those selected by the critic in question, e.g. relating to strict formal equivalence or flawless target language. After all, not all translations *need* to be perfectly natural TL. (By "natural" here I mean 'unmarked', in the sense that readers typically do not react *de dicto*, to the linguistic form itself.) We usually understand the funny menus and notices – they are often part of the amusement of a holiday, we may even expect them. And unnatural (marked) language will be less noticed by non-natives anyway. With respect to the alleged weaknesses of much literary translation, one can point out that most readers of literary translations may well prefer a freer, more natural version. The criticism may boil down to no more than personal preference.

Problem: assumption of the universality of formal stylistic universals
This is a different kind of problem. The literary critics I referred to above seem to overlook the fact that a given formal feature (repetition, say) may have quite different effects on readers in different cultures, where there may be quite different rhetorical and stylistic norms. These critics thus neglect the possibility of cultural relativity, in favour of a belief in form for form's sake, a belief in the existence, distribution and frequency of formal stylistic universals that have yet to be demonstrated. Formal equivalence is valued, dynamic equivalence is not.

Problem: socio-cultural effect on translator status
One highly undesirable effect of these pejorative generalizations is of course the depressing impact it has on the public perception of the translator's role, and indeed on translators' own perception of themselves, as poor creatures doomed to sin.

Contribution: concern with quality
These pejorative views do nevertheless reveal a concern with translation quality, albeit narrowly understood. From this route away from the particular we learn the need to develop more sophisticated and varied criteria for assessing translation quality. (For a recent selection of views on quality assessment, see Schäffner (1998) and the special issue of *The Translator*, 6 (2), 2000.)

Contribution: awareness of ethical issues
Another contribution worth mentioning is the way in which critics such as Berman foreground issues concerning ethnocentrism and more generally the representation of the Other. This helps us to see the wider philosophical context in which translation takes place, and has fuelled quite a bit of later research on translation ethics (see the special issue of *The Translator,* 7 (1), 2001).

4. The descriptive route

The third route away from the particular is represented by recent corpus-based work on what some call translation universals. One of the origins of such work has been Frawley's notion (1984) of translations as constituting a third code, distinct from the source-language and target-language codes. Another origin has been hypotheses like that of Blum-Kulka (1986) on explicitation, and yet another has been Toury's (1995) proposals about translation laws. We should also mention the background of work in linguistics on language universals, and in sociolinguistics on language variation.

Progress along this descriptive route seems to be moving along two roads simultaneously: the high road and the low road. On the high road, we find claims that indeed purport to cover all translations, and so they can fairly be said to be claims about universal features. These claims fall into two classes, corresponding to the two contrastive textlinguistic relations that form the core of linguistic research on translation: the equivalence relation with the source text, and the relation of textual fit with comparable non-translated texts in the target language. In other words, use is made of two different reference corpora. Some hypotheses claim to capture universal differences between translations and their source texts, i.e. characteristics of the way in which translators process the source text; I call these *S-universals* (S for source). Others make claims about universal differences between translations and comparable non-translated texts, i.e. characteristics of the way translators use the target language; I call these *T-universals* (T for target). T-universals are the descriptive equivalent to the criticisms of unnaturalness, of translationese, made in the pejorative approach.

Below are some examples of both types of proposed universals. Note that these claims are hypotheses only; some have been corroborated more than others, and some tests have produced contrary evidence, so in most cases the jury is still out.

Potential S-universals

- Lengthening: translations tend to be longer than their source texts (cf. Berman's expansion; also Vinay and Darbelnet 1958: 185; et al.)
- The law of interference (Toury 1995)
- The law of standardization (Toury 1995)
- Dialect normalization (Englund Dimitrova 1997)
- Reduction of complex narrative voices (Taivalkoski-Shilov 2002)
- The explicitation hypothesis (Blum-Kulka 1986, Klaudy 1996, Øverås 1998) (e.g. there is more cohesion in translations)
- Sanitization (Kenny 1998) (more conventional collocations)
- The retranslation hypothesis (later translations tend to be closer to the source text; see *Palimpsestes* 4, 1990)
- Reduction of repetition (Baker 1993)

Potential T-universals

- Simplification (Laviosa-Braithwaite 1996)
    Less lexical variety
    Lower lexical density
    More use of high-frequency items
- Conventionalization (Baker 1993)
- Untypical lexical patterning (and less stable) (Mauranen 2000)
- Under-representation of TL-specific items (Tirkkonen-Condit 2000)

Research then proceeds by operationalizing these general claims, i.e. interpreting them in concrete terms, and then testing them on various kinds of data in order to see how universal they actually are. Do they, for instance, apply to some subset of all translations rather than the total set? This leads us to consider the second direction pursued by modern descriptive research, the low road.

Here, research moves in more modest steps, generalizing more gradually away from particular cases towards claims applying to a group of cases, then perhaps to a wider group, and so on. The movement is bottom-up (starting with the particular) rather than top-down (starting with the general). True, a universal hypothesis might also be tentatively proposed on the basis of empirical results pertaining only to a subset. Subset generalizations fall into the same two classes as the universal claims mentioned above: claims about the source/target relation, and claims about the translated/non-translated relation. A crucial point in this bottom-up approach is the criteria on which the subset is defined. These criteria in effect define the conditions that determine and limit the scope of the claim. Several have been used, either separately or in combination, such as the following:

- *Language-bound criteria*: claims pertain to translations between a given language pair and a given translation direction. See e.g. classics like Vinay and Darbelnet (1958) on French and English, Malblanc (1963) on French and German. The results of traditional contrastive analysis and contrastive rhetoric come in useful here, at the explanatory level, when we look for the language-bound causes of translation features (e.g. Doherty 1996). Maia (1998), for instance, considers features of English word order that appear to affect Portuguese word order in translations from English: these translations show a different distribution of word order variants from that found in untranslated Portuguese texts.
- *Time-bound and place-bound criteria*: claims pertain to a particular period, in a particular culture. See e.g. Toury (1995: 113f.) on early 20th-century Hebrew norms for poetry translation.
- *Type-bound criteria*: claims pertain to a particular type of translation (characterized e.g. by a given text-type or skopos-type). Many examples: Bible translation, subtitling, technical, poetry, comic strips, gist translation... E.g. Mauranen (2000) found that translations of popular non-fiction deviated more from lexical patterning norms than did translations of academic texts.
- *Translator-bound criteria*: claims pertain to translations done by a particular translator. See e.g. Baker (2000) on translators' individual styles). Or by translators of a particular kind (trainees; men/women; to L1 or L2; ...).
- *Situation-bound criteria*: claims pertain to particular conditions of the publishing or editorial process, in-house stylistics conventions and the like. E.g. Milton (2001).

In this kind of research, we might find that given features are typical (or not typical) of some subset of translations; or that given features seem to be typical (or not typical) of more than one subset.

This third, descriptive, route away from the particular is not without its problems, either. Indeed, some scholars have preferred to reject this route altogether and restrict their attention to what makes any given translation unique, rather than focus on its similarities with other translations.

Problem: testing
Tests of these claims sometimes produce confirmatory evidence, sometimes not. But how rigorous are the tests? If you are investigating, say, explicitation or standardization, you can usually find *some* evidence of it in any translation; but how meaningful is such a finding? It would be more challenging to propose and test generalizations about *what* is explicitated or standardized, under what

circumstances, and test those. To find *no* evidence of explicitation or standardization would be a surprising and therefore strong result. Stronger still would be confirmation in a predictive classification test, as follows (based on a suggestion by Emma Wagner, personal communication). If these universals are supposed to be distinctive features of translations, they can presumably be used to identify translations. So you could take pairs of source and target texts, and see whether an analysis of some S-universal features allows you to predict which text in each pair is the source and which the target text. For each pair you would have to do the analysis in two directions, assuming that each text in turn is source and target, to see which direction supports a given universal tendency best. Or you could take a mixed set of texts consisting of translations and non-translations and analyse them for a given T-universal feature, and use the results to predict the category assignment of each text (= translation or not). Some universals might turn out to be much more accurate predictors than others.[*]

Problem: representativeness
Since we can never study all translations, nor even all translations of a certain type, we must take a sample. The more representative the sample, the more confidence we can have that our results and claims are valid more generally. Measuring representativeness is easier if we have access to large machine-readable corpora, but there always remains a degree of doubt. Our data may still be biased in some way that we have not realized. This is often the case with non-translated texts that are selected as a reference corpus. Representativeness is an even more fundamental problem with respect to the translation part of a comparable corpus. It is not *a priori* obvious what we should count as corpus-valid translations in the first place: there is not only the tricky borderline with adaptations etc., but also the issue of including or excluding non-professional translations or non-native translations, and even defining what a professional translation is (see Halverson 1998b). Should we even include "bad" translations? They too are translations, of a kind.

Problem: universality
Claims may be made that a given feature is universal, but sometimes the data may only warrant a subset claim, if the data are not representative of all translations. Many "universal" claims have been made that actually seem to pertain only to literary or to Bible translation. More fundamentally, though: since we can ever only study a subset of all translations past and present, there is always the

---

[*] In retrospect, I think these points could be more clearly expressed in terms of testing for correlations rather than predictions.

risk that our results will be culture-bound rather than truly universal (Tymoczko 1998). Concepts of translation itself are culture-bound, for a start; even prototype concepts may be, too. We can perhaps never totally escape the limits of our own culture-boundness, even if this might be extended e.g. to a general "Western culture". This means that claims of universality can perhaps never be truly universal.

In the light of these problems and reservations, it is obvious that any claim about a translation universal can really only be an approximation. But this does not matter, as long as scholars are aware of what they are claiming. After all, what these corpus scholars are basically doing is seeking generalizations. We seek generalizations that are as extensive as possible. Less-than-universal claims can still be interesting and valuable Any level of generalization can increase understanding.

Problem: conceptualization and terminology
Here there is still a great deal to be clarified. I made one proposal above, about distinguishing between S and T-universals. Baker's original use (1993) of the term "universal" seems to have to refer to T-universals, since her point of comparison is non-translated, original texts; however, several of the examples of previous research that she mentions are based on evidence from a comparison with source texts, and hence concern S-universals (such as the reduction of repetition). If your corpus does not actually contain source texts, you surely cannot study S-universals. Other scholars have, however, used the term to apply either to S-universals alone, or more generally to both S and T types. I think that the use of the term "universal" itself is valid and useful, provided it is kept for claims that are actually hypothesized to be universal, not specific to some subset of translations.[*]

Some scholars prefer to refer to these claims as hypotheses, such as the explicitation hypothesis (Blum-Kulka and others) or the simplification hypothesis (Laviosa-Braithwaite 1996), or the retranslation hypothesis. Others speak of laws: cf. Toury's proposed laws of interference and standardization. Chevalier (1995) writes about "figures of translation", comparable to rhetorical figures; the occurrence of these figures is contrasted with translation alternatives that are more neutral or natural or "orthonymic", in the same way that in rhetorical analysis one can distinguish between utterances with or without rhetorical embellishment. Still other scholars prefer to look for core patterns, or simply widespread regularities.

---

[*] I am now (2016) more critical of this term, as mentioned in the introduction to this section on "universals".

Claims about universals are in fact examples of descriptive hypotheses – unrestricted descriptive hypotheses, with no scope conditions. As soon as we limit the scope of the claims to some subset of translations, we are proposing restricted descriptive hypotheses.

When it comes to the hypotheses themselves we find a plethora of terms that appear at first sight to mean more or less the same thing (e.g. standardization, simplification, levelling, normalization, conventionalization). Sometimes these are used to refer to a feature of difference between translations and their source texts, and sometimes to a feature of difference between translations and non-translated texts. These latter are called 'parallel' texts by some scholars, 'comparable' texts by others, and 'original' texts by still others. I now use 'non-translated' to avoid confusion: this also gives the convenient abbreviation NT, to go with ST and TT.

And further: some of the terms appear to be ambiguous between a process reading (from source text to translation) and a product reading: e.g. those ending in *-tion* in English. We do need to standardize our terminology here.

Problem: operationalization
Different scholars often operationalize these abstract notions in different ways – which again makes it difficult to compare research results. We need more replication, and this means explicit descriptions of methodology.

Problem: causality
A final major problem has to do with causality and how to study it. To claim that a given linguistic feature is universal is one thing. But we would also like to know its cause or causes. Here, we can currently do little more than speculate as rationally as possible. The immediate causes of whatever universals there may be must be sought in human cognition – to be precise, in the kind of cognitive processing that produces translations. Translations arise, after all, in the minds of translators, under certain causal constraints. One source of these constraints is the source text, or rather its meaning or intended message.* The translator is constrained by "what was said" in the earlier text. More precisely, translators are constrained by what they *understand* was said in the source text. This inevitable interpretation process acts as a filter; and it is precisely this filtering that seems to offer a site for the explanation for some of the S-universals that have been claimed, such as those concerning standardization and explicitation. Filtering involves reducing the irrelevant or unclear, purifying, selecting the essence. How it works in detail remains to be seen.

---

* And, I should add, its form.

Constraints on cognitive processing in translation may also be present in other kinds of constrained communication, such as communicating in a non-native language or under special channel restrictions, or any form of communication that involves relaying messages, such as reporting discourse, even journalism. It may be problematic, eventually, to differentiate factors that are pertinent to translation in particular from those that are pertinent to constrained communication in general.

Other kinds of explanations may be sought in the nature of translation as a communicative act, and in translators' awareness of their socio-cultural role as mediators of messages for new readers (see e.g. Klaudy 1996). Translators tend to want to reduce entropy, to increase orderliness. They tend to want to write clearly, insofar as the skopos allows, because they can easily see their role metaphorically as shedding light on an original text that is obscure – usually unreadable in fact – to their target readers: hence the need for a translation. Their conception of their role may give a prominent position to the future readers of their texts; this may have been emphasized in their training, for instance. It is this conception of their mediating role that may offer some explanation for the tendency towards explicitation, towards simplification, and towards reducing what is thought to be unnecessary repetition – to save the readers' processing effort. In terms of relevance theory (which defines relevance as the optimum cost-benefit ratio between processing effort needed and cognitive effect produced – see Gutt 2000), translators as a profession are perhaps more aware than other writers of the cost side of the relevance equation. It may be that translators see explicitation in some sense as a norm; perhaps it was even presented as such in their training.

This raises the interesting question of whether there might exist universal norms of communication which could provide explanatory principles for possible translation universals, perhaps along the lines of Grice's maxims (Grice 1975) or notions of politeness. However, these will have to be modified somewhat if they are to be made appropriate to non-Anglo-Saxon cultures.

Research into the *effects* caused by potential universals is still in its infancy. Effects on readers, on translator trainers, and on translators themselves would all be worth studying. It may be that the more we know about T-universals, for instance, the more scholars or trainers will be tempted to see them as undesirable features that should be avoided – at least in translations whose skopos includes optimum naturalness. On the other hand, as the sheer quantity of translations grows and target-language norms become blurred, it may be that readers will become more tolerant of apparent non-nativeness; different cultures might differ considerably in this respect. One long-term effect of knowledge about S-universals on source-text writers might even be a greater concern for the clarity of the source text, in order to facilitate the translator's task and lessen the need for explicitation. This in turn could lead to greater fidelity to the original.

Contribution: methodological
The prime benefit so far of this kind of descriptive research has, I think, been methodological. Corpus-based research into translation universals has been one of the most important methodological advances in Translation Studies during the past decade or so, in that it has encouraged researchers to adopt standard scientific methods of hypothesis generation and testing. This kind of research also makes it obvious that we need to compare research results across studies and take more account of what others have done. The application of methods from corpus linguistics has encouraged more use of quantitative research. Research on descriptive hypotheses has also brought new knowledge about translation, and a host of new hypotheses to be tested. It has thus helped to push Translation Studies in a more empirical direction.

Contribution: interdisciplinarity
Another benefit has been the highlighting of interdisciplinarity. Descriptive research on universals shows how Translation Studies must be linked to other fields, not only within linguistics but within the human sciences more generally (cognitive science, for example, and cultural anthropology).

Contribution: concern with translation quality
Perhaps paradoxically, this descriptive approach has also drawn our attention to subtle aspects of text and translation quality. There are many potential applications here: translators who are aware of these general tendencies (even if they may not be universal ones) can choose to resist them. Non-native translators can make good use of quantitative information, banks of comparable non-translated texts, to make their own use of the target language more natural, and they can run tests to check the naturalness of aspects of their translations. This facility may lead to the gradual blurring of the distinction between native and non-native translators at the professional level, which in turn should have an influence on assumptions held by many translation theorists about the exclusive status of translation into the native language. (This issue is discussed e.g. in Campbell 1998 and Pokorn 2000.)

What we need, therefore is much more replicated work on testing different restricted and unrestricted hypotheses on different corpora. We need to standardize our main concepts and ways of operationalizing, for greater research cooperation. We need to relate descriptive hypotheses to each other, at still more abstract levels. We need to develop electronic corpus tools. We need to generate new descriptive hypotheses. And we need to work on testable explanatory hypotheses in order to account for the evidence we find.[1]

Note

1. This article is based on three conference presentations, during which my ideas on the topic have developed. One paper was read at the Third EST Congress in Copenhagen in August-September 2001, as part of the session on universals; another was read at the Symposium on Contrastive Analysis and Linguistic Theory at Ghent in September 2001; and a third at the Conference on Universals at Savonlinna in October 2001. There is some overlap between the published versions of all three presentations. I am grateful for all the critical comments and feedback I have had at these meetings.

PAPER 21

What is a unique item?*

The so-called unique items hypothesis claims that translations tend to contain fewer "unique items" than comparable non-translated texts. This is proposed as a potential translation universal, or at least a general tendency. A unique item is one that is in some sense specific to the target language and is presumably not so easily triggered by a source-language item that is formally different; it thus tends to be under-represented in translations. The concept of a unique item is not well-defined, however. Drawing on some earlier work on transfer, contrastive and error analysis, this article offers a critical analysis of the concept, and raises a number of methodological issues concerning research on the topic.

Keywords: unique items hypothesis, Tirkkonen-Condit, under-representation, universals

1. Introducing the hypothesis

In the context of research on what are often called translation universals, i.e. regular tendencies or recurring patterns in translations, Sonja Tirkkonen-Condit (2002) has proposed a "unique items hypothesis" according to which translations tend to contain fewer unique items than comparable non-translated texts.[1] The hypothesis seems intuitively reasonable, and preliminary research results seem to support it (see also Tirkkonen-Condit 2004), at least with respect to certain items.

Tirkkonen-Condit relates the hypothesis to two wider issues. One is the question of whether the language of translations is more normalized than that of non-translations: a lower-than-normal frequency of unique items would suggest that translations are not "normal" in this respect. This is a textlinguistic matter. The second issue is a psychological one, having to do with people's intuitions about, and reactions to, texts, and in particular about their ability to recognize certain texts as being translations or not. The question here is whether informants use intuitions about unexpectedly low frequencies of certain items when they are

---

* First published in 2007 in Yves Gambier, Miriam Shlesinger and Radegundis Stolze (eds), *Doubts and Directions in Translation Studies*. Amsterdam/Philadelphia: Benjamins, 3–13. Reprinted with kind permission from John Benjamins Publishing Company [www.benjamins.com]. The keywords have been added.

asked to distinguish translations from original texts – and to what extent they are successful in making such judgements.

However, it is not clear what exactly is meant by a "unique item". There are several problems in the way the concept is currently used. Here is how Tirkkonen-Condit introduces the idea (2002: 208–9):

> Katharina Reiß suggested some thirty years ago that translations may not fully exploit the linguistic resources of the target language. In discussing the devices of evaluating translation quality without recourse to the source text, Reiß (1971), following Güttinger (1963: 219), suggests a simple test: take the most frequent words in the target language that do not exist in the source language and check the extent to which these appear in the translation. These "missing words" will reveal whether the translator knows the target language well enough to attain good translation quality. This rule of thumb, according to Reiß (1971: 19) applies not only to the "missing words" but also to "alle Begriffe und Wendungen, die in der anderen Sprache mit unterschiedlichen sprachlichen Mitteln zum Ausdruck gebracht werden". This discussion gives rise to another, potentially universal hypothesis [i.e. in addition to those concerning simplification etc.], which I will call *the unique items hypothesis*.
>
> This means that translated texts would manifest lower frequencies of linguistic elements that lack linguistic counterparts in the source languages such that these could also be used as translation equivalents. I will refer to these as unique items or unique elements. The unique elements are not untranslatable, and they may be frequent, typical and entirely normal phenomena in the language; they are unique only in respect of their translation potential, as they are not similarly manifested in other languages, or at least not similarly manifested in the source languages of the translations.   (Square brackets added, emphasis original.)

As examples of unique items in Finnish she cites Finnish verbs like *jaksaa, ehtiä, viitsiä*; these could be translated into English as 'be strong enough / have enough energy (to do something)', 'have enough time', 'have enough initiative / be interested enough'. These sufficiency verbs have traditionally been regarded as rather special to Finnish. Other languages seem to lack lexicalized equivalents and use phrasal expressions of some kind. And this is the point: the claim is that verbs like this are under-used in translations into Finnish, precisely because there is not a similar lexicalized verb in the source text which would "trigger" them in the translator's mind. In a later paper (Tirkkonen-Condit 2004) she explains the notion of a unique item thus:

> Every language has linguistic elements that are unique in the sense that they lack straightforward linguistic counterparts in other languages. These elements may be lexical, phrasal, syntactic or textual, and they need not be in any sense untranslatable; they are simply not similarly manifested (e.g. lexicalized) in other languages.
> (2004: 177)

I want to focus here on the concept of the "unique item" itself. The hypothesis may be a fruitful one, well worth testing under different conditions; but there are a number of conceptual problems in the way it has been formulated that need to be sorted out first.

2. Unique with respect to what languages?

The first problem is the context in which uniqueness is defined. Is the "uniqueness" defined with respect to a given source language, to several languages, or to all languages? The formulations cited above are slippery in this respect. In the 2002 article, the context is defined as "other languages, or at least ... the source languages of the translations". In 2004, it is "other languages". In an email to me, Tirkkonen-Condit specifies that she is really focusing on the source languages of specific translations. In other words, no claim is being made about the uniqueness of, say, Finnish sufficiency verbs with respect to all other human languages. Testing such a claim would indeed be quite a task. We should therefore conclude that "unique" means "present in the target language, but not present in a similar way in a given source language".

This solution is exactly parallel to the definition of a cultureme (or culture-specific item) used by Nord (1997: 34) and other skopos theorists. A cultureme is a cultural phenomenon that is present in culture X but not present (in the same way) in culture Y.

"Unique" is thus the opposite of "universal" only in a very weak sense. An item that is unique is one that does not appear (in the same way) in at least one other language: the source language. It might of course appear in any number of other languages, but that is not the point at issue, since the other languages are not involved in the particular translation at hand.

3. Absolutely unique?

Is uniqueness an absolute property (i.e. given items either are, or are not, unique) or a relative one (i.e. some items can be more unique than others)? Despite the absoluteness that is perhaps implied in Reiß's formulation, to which I shall return shortly, Tirkkonen-Condit's incorporation of the notion of similarity in her definition surely forces the conclusion that this uniqueness can only be understood in a relative sense. Translationally equivalent items in two languages can be more or less similar, and moreover more or less similar in an infinite number of different ways. The less similar they are, the more unique a given target item is said to be; the degree of uniqueness depends inversely on the degree of similarity.

For instance, consider the following heading in my Finnish telephone book (both Finnish and Swedish are official languages in Finland):

Finnish: Soittaminen hätänumeroon 112
         'ringing to-emergency-number 112'

Swedish: Så här ringer du till nödnumret 112
         'in this way you ring to emergency-number 112'

The headings are printed one below the other, and are followed by detailed and equivalent instructions in both languages. Consider the kinds and levels of similarity or equivalence that are involved here. Apart from the obvious pragmatic/functional similarity, there are large formal differences: Finnish non-finite vs. Swedish finite clause; Swedish mention of the addressee, in second person singular; Swedish initial adverb; Finnish use of the illative case ('to') vs. Swedish preposition (*till* 'to'). Both use a compound noun for 'emergency number', though. And both share the same thematic order "ring – emergency number – 112".

Now imagine that the source text for these instructions was Swedish, and that it is being translated into Finnish. Our Finnish translator could have followed the Swedish structure fairly closely, and written:

Näin soitat hätänumeroon.
'thus you-ring to-emergency-number'

This solution is quite acceptable. It would have been readily prompted by the Swedish original. The printed Finnish version, however, uses the verbal noun construction with *soittaminen* 'ringing'. This is very different from the Swedish structure in our imagined source text. In standard Swedish the use of a formally similar structure with a verbal noun (*ringande*) would not be acceptable here. But Swedish does allow the nominal use of an infinitive: *att ringa* 'to ring' could be used, although it would be less natural. So: is the Finnish verbal noun construction a unique item? Is it "more unique" to Finnish than the use of the illative case, which is also not available as such in Swedish? The answer will depend on the criteria chosen to measure uniqueness.

The point of this example is simply to underline that the uniqueness under discussion here must be understood in a relative sense, as 'relative dissimilarity'. This means that we are already weakening the semantic content of the term.

4. How do we identify uniqueness?

The suggestion made by Reiß (1971), that we should look for "words" in the target language that do not exist in the source language, can hardly be taken at its face value: of course, *all* the words in a given target language "do not exist" in a given source language, except for possible loanwords from the same source language. In the passages cited above, Tirkkonen-Condit wrote of "elements that lack linguistic counterparts", or "that lack straightforward linguistic counterparts". This is loosely glossed as "elements that are not similarly manifested" or not "lexicalized".

This gloss, and the preceding definitions, are much too loose, because the nature of the required similarity is not made explicit. If we identify a unique item in terms of the non-existence of a straightforward, one-to-one equivalent in some other language(s), this depends in turn on what we mean by equivalence, and by this particular kind of equivalence. We are presumably talking about some kind of formal equivalence here, but at what level of delicacy?

If a verb (such as a Finnish sufficiency verb, such as *ehtiä*) is translated into English as a phrase (e.g. verb+object+adverb: 'have time enough'), we have an instance of what Catford (1965: 79) called a unit shift. The units are morpheme, word, group (phrase), clause, sentence. (We might also add higher units such as paragraph, section or chapter, text.) In this case, the shift is from word to group (phrase). Formal shifts of a more delicate kind occur when a translator shifts from one source-text verb class (say, transitive) to a different one in the target text (intransitive), or from a mass noun to a count noun (examples of Catford's class shifts), or from e.g. singular to plural (Catford's intra-system shift). However, shifts of these kinds do not seem to be among those suggesting the existence of unique items, in the sense described by Tirkkonen-Condit. Nor do cruder kinds of shifts involving major restructuring, omissions or additions. Nor even higher-level unit shifts, such as those from sentence to clause or clause to group, or vice versa.

The key level seems to be that of the word or the morpheme. Tirkkonen-Condit's other main examples concern certain Finnish particles. However, she also mentions idioms, which may be manifested as strings as long as a clause. Her examples include the following types of unique items for Finnish (2002: 215):

- clitic and other particles (e.g. *-pa/pä* signifiying emphasis)
- colloquial lexical items, sufficiency verbs (e.g. *viitsiä* 'have enough initiative')
- idioms, fixed collocations, set phrases (e.g. *kaikki on katoavaista* 'everything is ephemeral')
- word order (idiomatic use of clause-initial copula in the possessive structure: *on teillä* 'is at-you' – i.e. 'you have' – instead of *teillä on* 'at-you is')
- use of impersonal reference (impersonal verb: *täytyy muistaa* '(one) must remember')

My preliminary answer to the question of how to identify uniqueness is that an item counts as unique if it cannot be readily translated back into a given source language without a unit shift. "Readily" is slippery, I admit. But so, I am arguing, is the whole concept of a unique item. This answer also allows the inclusion of (most) idioms as unique items, for their translation usually requires unit shifts at some level. One problem with this answer is that the definition of the basic units themselves may not be so obvious if we turn to less commonly studied languages outside Standard Average European.

This preliminary answer derives from early research of a very similar kind in contrastive and error analysis. In a classic paper on "Over-indulgence and under-representation – aspects of mother-tongue interference", Levenston (1971: 115) wrote:

> One feature of non-native use of a second language, or L2, is the excessive use ('over-indulgence') of clause (or group) structures which closely resemble translation equivalents in the mother tongue, or L1, to the exclusion of other structures ('under-representation') which are less like anything in L1. 'Closely resemble' can be more precisely defined as 'with translation equivalents which correspond at the level of group (or word) as well as clause'; 'less like' means with translation equivalents which correspond at the level of clause (or group) only.

Levenston was not studying translations as such, but non-native use of a language (English as used by Hebrew speakers). But he used translation equivalence in his conceptualization of elements that appear more or less frequently than expected in L2 [usage]. He defines his notion of relevant similarity in terms of unit correspondence at different levels. This might offer us an alternative formulation of a unique item (cf. Levenston's under-represented item): it is one for which the translation equivalent only maintains unit correspondence at some higher level or levels, not at given lower levels. The higher the lowest possible level of unit correspondence, the less the similarity. For instance, a translation equivalent preserving unit correspondence only at sentence level, but not lower, would be less similar than an equivalent preserving unit correspondence also at group or word level. Consider the translation of proverbs, for example, for which unit correspondence is usually only maintained at the sentence level, not below. Translations that preserve unit correspondence only at higher levels are of course freer translations.

5. Linguistically or perceptually unique?

Is the uniqueness assumed to exist in some psychological sense, as part of the translator's perception of the languages concerned, or in a linguistic sense, as part of the lexico-grammatical systems of the given languages? In other words, are the items really unique (in the sense specified above), or does the translator just think they are? I shall refer to these two interpretations as linguistic difference (i.e. one that is objectively proved by contrastive evidence) and perceived difference (which may or may not also be objectively substantiated).

Levenston's paper combines these two interpretations, in that he brings in the psychological notion of interference from the native language to explain why over-indulgence and under-representation occur. But they should perhaps be kept separate. Speakers of a given language, especially non-native speakers, may not have an accurate perception of what is "unique" to that language in the sense I suggested above, i.e. with respect to some other given language. Levenston was studying non-native usage; but it is also worth recalling that translators may also be working into a non-native language. Here too, early work in contrastive analysis may be revealing. I am thinking in particular of work by Eric Kellerman (e.g. 1986) and Terence Odlin (e.g. 1991) on speakers' perceptions of the languages they use. Kellerman's studies examined whether Dutch students would be willing to transfer Dutch idioms literally into English in cases where such a translation would in fact have been acceptable. His results suggested that native speakers may overestimate the degree of linguistic uniqueness of items in their native language: there were many examples of idioms that could have been transferred verbatim, but these students did not feel that it would be possible because they were felt to be typically Dutch and hence non-transferable. Odlin (1991) queries Kellerman's interpretation of these results, and provides rather different kinds of evidence from his study of language mixing by bilinguals in Ireland. He found plenty of evidence of the direct transfer of Irish idioms into English, but proposed to account for these in terms of environmental and sociological factors such as the number of bilinguals in the community.

Other scholars in contrastive and error analysis have proposed an avoidance strategy (see Faerch and Kasper 1983), whereby L2-learners or users tend to avoid items that are difficult; these difficult items are often those that are "different" in the two languages. We are in fact not too far from Lado's initial contrastive hypothesis (1957: 2) that differences between L1 and L2 will cause learning difficulties whereas similarities will facilitate learning. However, the avoidance strategy depends on perceived difference whereas Lado's hypothesis is based on linguistic difference.

In the case of the unique items hypothesis, we are not dealing with transfer. Our interest is in items that are under-used because translators tend to prefer alternative expressions that are formally closer to the source text. Thus:

ST I do not have enough time for research.

will tend to be translated into Finnish as

TT1 Minulla ei ole tarpeeksi aikaa tutkimukseen.
      'at-me is not enough time for-research'

rather than

TT2 En ehdi tehdä tutkimusta.
      'I-do-not have-enough-time to-do research'

The TT2 version uses the Finnish "unique" verb *ehtiä*, 'to have enough time', but this is evidently not readily triggered by the English, which lacks such a verb.

Moreover, we cannot appeal to notions of perception, because the whole point of the hypothesis is that the target unique items are not perceived (or at least: not perceived as belonging to the same register); they are not even triggered. My conclusion is therefore that our hypothesis must be concerned with linguistic uniqueness. However, this uniqueness is assumed to have consequences at the level of cognitive processing. It follows that research methods based on questionnaires or translation identity tasks may not be good ways of testing the hypothesis, since they tap perceived uniqueness, not linguistic uniqueness. Linguistic uniqueness can be more objectively determined with the use of grammars, dictionaries, corpora and contrastive analysis.

6. Are unique items unique to translation?

To the extent that translations can be successfully distinguished from non-translations – by naive informants, and/or by researchers using objective statistical methods –, we can infer that there may be something about (some?) translations that makes them recognizably different. The unique items hypothesis claims that translations under-use unique items, for instance, in the sense explicated above. Does this difference itself amount to a kind of uniqueness, or are the potential distinguishing features of (these) translations similar to those of certain other kinds of texts as well, such as those produced under special time constraints or language proficiency conditions?

Here again I return to earlier research in contrastive analysis and interlanguage studies, the avoidance hypothesis and the notion of simplification in learners' language. (See Faerch and Kasper 1983 again.) There is a good deal of evidence in the literature to suggest that L2-speakers tend to prefer structures that are similar to those in their L1 (cf. Levenston, above). This corresponds exactly to Tirkkonen-Condit's speculation that novice translators, even when translating into their native language, tend to prefer literal strategies whenever possible. It even agrees with the advice offered by Vinay and Darbelnet (1958), Newmark (1981: 39) and others, to the effect that literal, close translation is a good default strategy. One consequence of this strategy is of course that the risk of interference – i.e. unwanted, negative transfer – increases. Another risk is that unique items get forgotten, as predicted by the unique items hypothesis.

I thus suggest that the unique items hypothesis is not unique to translation, but also applies to other communication contexts in which extra difficulties are present, such as the need to speak or write in a second language. In other words, it implies a more general cognitive constraint on language use under certain conditions. This in turn raises questions about the structure of the linguistic repertoires in the mind, about what kinds of things might be central or more readily accessible in this repertoire and what kinds of things might be less readily accessible. It also raises questions about the status of other so-called translation universals, which may turn out not to be universal specifically to translation but rather to what we could call extra-constrained communication in general.

7. Is "unique item" a good term?

In the light of the above discussion, the answer to this question is perhaps "no". The notion of uniqueness seems to be too strong, in several respects. Uniqueness is relative rather than absolute; the hypothesis refers to particular sets of source and target languages rather than to all languages; uniqueness can be defined only rather loosely in the contrastive terms of relative formal difference; and the phenomenon in question may not be unique to translation but may also be typical of second-language usage. To phrase the hypothesis in terms of "uniqueness" thus implies stronger claims than are actually being made.

Compare the sense of the term "lacuna" (also referred to as a semantic void or lexical gap), as traditionally used in translation studies. This is usually understood as the absence in the target language of a (non-shifted) equivalent of some word or expression in the source language. What we have been calling a unique item seems to be the opposite of a lacuna, in some sense: in our case, the absence is not in the target language but in the source language, and the "gap" is formal rather than semantic. Unique items are perhaps no more than formal source lacunas. Sonja Tirkkonen-Condit (personal communication) also speaks of "linguistic asymmetry" in this respect. Such asymmetry may be quantitative as well as qualitative. Languages may simply have "preferred means" for expressing a given meaning or function. – This point admittedly argues against the term "lacuna", which indicates more of an absolute difference, the presence of a definite "gap".

8. Is the cart before the horse?

My final question returns to issues of research methodology. We have seen that there are problems with defining unique items *a priori*. However, if we are looking for instances of this category, we of course need to know in advance what we are looking for.

The best way out of this quandary is, I suggest, to adjust the research methodology. This in fact means returning to the initial intuitions and observations that gave rise to the hypothesis in the first place, and also to the insights of earlier scholars in contrastive analysis. In other words, the research process would look like this:

i. Use contrastive corpus studies to investigate which items manifest significantly different frequencies in translations (TT) vs. non-translations (NT).
ii. Divide the items manifesting significantly different frequencies into those occurring more frequently in TT and those occurring more frequently in NT. It turns out, for instance, that Finnish sufficiency verbs occur more often in non-translated Finnish than in translated Finnish. And see e.g. Olohan and Baker (2000) on the over-representation of reporting *that* in English translations.
iii. Rank the items according to degree of frequency difference. Focus on those items whose frequency differences across the two corpora (TT and NT) are highest, above some arbitrary threshold. We will thus have two sets of items. The first set contains items that are clearly *over*-represented in the translations studied, and the second set those that are clearly *under*-represented there.
iv. Then consider explanations for these results. In the case of the under-represented items (such as Finnish sufficiency verbs in Finnish translations), one explanatory hypothesis might be formulated in terms of formal distance. That is: the greater the formal (syntactic) distance between a given source-language item and an appropriate corresponding target-language item, the less likely it is to be selected by translators. (This hypothesis obviously needs a way of measuring formal distance; Catford's classification of shifts could be taken as a starting-point, as suggested above.) The under-represented items that are thus formally "very different" from their source-language equivalents will

include those that we have been calling unique items. Note, however, that the under-represented set may also include items that are not readily explained in this way; i.e. some of these items may not be unique in this sense.

This way of looking at the methodological process does not start with the idea of a unique item. Here, the uniqueness of an item is defined operationally, in overtly relative terms, and *a posteriori*. Uniqueness, in the sense explicated in this section, is here postulated as part of one possible explanation for the occurrence of under-represented items in translations.

Sonja Tirkkonen-Condit (personal communication) suggests an alternative methodology, which is in fact closer to the one she has used herself. Start from contrastive analyses of given language pairs. Select items which turn out to have the "same" semantic or pragmatic meaning, but which are formally different in the two languages (or where formal equivalents actually have different functions). Then compare the frequencies of these items in translations and non-translations. – I note nevertheless that this method needs a careful *a priori* interpretation of levels of formal equivalence, as argued above.

9. What's the point?

One reason to study potential translation universals is simply to understand more about translation in general, about the nature of translating. This research may also tell us something about the varying tolerance for interference. For those with psycholinguistic research goals, work on these potential universals may also bring new insights into what goes on in the translator's mind.

For scholars looking for practical applications, and for trainers of translators, research on universals may suggest ways to improve the quality of translations. By explicitly drawing the attention of trainees to items that are typically under- or over-represented in translations, we can encourage future translators to use these items more or less frequently than they might otherwise have done. In so doing, in the long term, we may even have some effect on these tendencies themselves. They might even become less universal…

Note

1. I am grateful for Sonja Tirkkonen-Condit's helpful comments on an earlier version of this paper.

PAPER 22

Kundera's sentence[*]

This paper is an analysis of Kundera's essay "Une phrase" ('A sentence'), where he criticizes French translations of a sentence in Kafka's novel *Das Schloß* ('The castle'). Kundera argues that literary translators must be as literal as possible, sticking close to every detail of the author's style. I suggest that this position is based on a dubious assumption about the universal effects of stylistic features. I then relate Kundera's view to some aspects of his life, with reference to Simmel's sociological concept of the stranger.

Keywords: Kundera, Kafka, style, literal translation, universals, Simmel's stranger

1. Kundera's criticism

Milan Kundera published *Les testaments trahis* in 1993. This collection of essays has since been translated into English (by Linda Asher: *Testaments betrayed. An essay in nine parts.* London: Faber and Faber 1995). The essays are about the art of literature, especially the novel; about the relations between literature, music and time. One of the essays, entitled "Une phrase" (pp. 123–144) deals with translation. More specifically, it deals with three French translations of a single German sentence from Kafka's *Das Schloß* ([1926] 1935). I shall first summarize Kundera's critical analysis and argument, and then consider how his beliefs about translation, and the form of his own discourse, can be understood against the background of his own life-history.

The sentence in question comes from Chapter 3 of Kafka's novel, and describes an act of love experienced by the protagonist, K. Here is the original German:

---

[*] First published in 2004 in Juliane House, Werner Koller and Klaus Schubert (eds), *Neue Perspektiven in der Übersetzungs- und Dolmetscherwissenschaft.* Bochum: AKS-Verlag, 73–86. The paper is reprinted here by kind permission of the publisher. This text includes a couple of minor revisions. The abstract and keywords have been added.

> Dort vergingen Stunden, Stunden gemeinsamen Atems, gemeinsamen Herzschlags, Stunden, in denen K. immerfort das Gefühl hatte, er verirre sich oder er sei so weit in der Fremde, wie vor ihm noch kein Mensch, einer Fremde, in der selbst die Luft keinen Bestandteil der Heimatluft habe, in der man vor Fremdheit ersticken müsse und in deren unsinnigen Verlockungen man doch nichts tun könne als weiter gehen, weiter sich verirren.

Kundera takes three published French translations for analysis. The first is by Vialatte, from 1938, and runs as follows:

> (1) Des heures passèrent là, des heures d'haleines mêlées, de battements de cœur communs, des heures durant lesquelles K. ne cessa d'éprouver l'impression qu'il se perdait, qu'il s'était enfoncé si loin que nul être avant lui n'avait fait plus de chemin ; à l'étranger, dans un pays où l'air même n'avait plus rien des éléments de l'air natal, où l'on devait étouffer d'exil et où l'on ne pouvait plus rien faire, au milieu d'insanes séductions, que continuer à marcher, que continuer à se perdre.

The second is a revised version of Vialatte by David, reproduced by Kundera from David's corrections (1976).

> (2) Des heures passèrent là, des heures d'haleines mêlées, de battements de cœur confondus, des heures durant lesquelles K. ne cessa d'éprouver l'impression qu'il s'égarait, qu'il s'enfonçait plus loin qu'aucun être avant lui ; il était dans un pays étranger, où l'air même n'avait plus rien de commun avec l'air du pays natal ; l'étrangeté de ce pays faisait suffoquer et pourtant, parmi de folles séductions, on ne pouvait que marcher toujours plus loin, s'égarer toujours plus avant.

The third translation is by Lortholary, from 1984.

> (3) Là passèrent des heures, des heures de respirations mêlées, de cœurs battant ensemble, des heures durant lesquelles K. avait le sentiment constant de s'égarer, ou bien de s'être avancé plus loin que jamais aucun homme dans des contrées étrangères, où l'air lui-même n'avait pas un seul élément qu'on retrouvât dans l'air du pays natal, où l'on ne pouvait qu'étouffer à force d'étrangeté, sans pouvoir pourtant faire autre chose, au milieu de ces séductions insensées, que de continuer et de s'égarer davantage.

The translation offered by Kundera himself, as "une traduction fidèle", is as follows:

> (4) Là, s'en allaient des heures, des heures d'haleines communes, de battements de cœur communs, des heures durant lesquelles K. avait sans cesse le sentiment qu'il s'égarait, ou bien qu'il était plus loin dans le monde étranger qu'aucun être avant lui, dans un monde étranger où l'air même n'avait aucun élément de l'air natal, où l'on devait étouffer d'étrangeté et où l'on ne pouvait rien faire, au milieu de séductions insensées, que continuer à aller, que continuer à s'égarer.

For interest, I also add here the English translation by Willa and Edwin Muir (1930).

(5) There, hours went past, hours in which they breathed as one, in which their hearts beat as one, hours in which K. was haunted by the feeling that he was losing himself or wandering into a strange country, farther than ever man had wandered before, a country so strange that not even the air had anything in common with his native air, where one might die of strangeness, and yet whose enchantment was such that one could only go on and lose oneself further.

Kundera then proceeds to criticize the first three translations, and implicitly to justify his own, in the following way. His underlying statement of belief, of value, of the relative authority of author and translator, comes halfway through the essay (p. 133–4):

> L'autorité suprême, pour un traducteur, devrait être le *style personnel* de l'auteur. Mais la plupart des traducteurs obéissent à une autre autorité : à celle du *style commun* du « beau français » (du bel allemand, du bel anglais, etc.), à savoir du français (de l'allemand, etc.) tel qu'on l'apprend au lycée. Le traducteur se considère comme l'ambassadeur de cette autorité auprès de l'auteur étranger. Voilà l'erreur : tout auteur d'une certain valeur *transgresse* le « beau style » et c'est dans cette transgression que se trouve l'originalité (et, partant, la raison d'être) de son art. Le premier effort du traducteur devrait être la compréhension de cette transgression. Ce n'est pas difficile lorsque celle-ci est évidente, comme, par exemple, chez Rabelais, chez Joyce, chez Céline. Mais il y a des auteurs dont la transgression du « beau style » est délicate, à peine visible, cachée, discrète ; en ce cas, il n'est pas facile de la saisir. N'empêche que c'est d'autant plus important.

Kundera illustrates this argument from various angles, beginning with the metaphorical level. He rejects translations that add something metaphorical where the original is plain and literal (*s'enfoncer* in (1) and (2), as opposed to Kafka's *sein*); translations that introduce a different metaphor (*exil* in (1)); translations that heighten a source-text metaphor (*marcher* in (1) and (2), as opposed to Kafka's *gehen*); translations which affect the level of abstraction of the original (*pays, contrée* for *die Fremde*).

Kundera is critical of the tendency of translators in general to avoid the obvious word, the most neutral one, and prefer a semantically richer one, in accordance with the requirements of elegant French rhetoric. He calls this tendency a need to synonymize, and explains it with reference to the translator's need to find an outlet for his/her own creativity and a pathway to social recognition: how else will a translator's skill be acknowledged, after all, since readers do not normally compare translations with originals? Examples here are *rien des éléments* (1), *rien de commun* (2), *pas un seul élément* (3), for Kafka's *keinen Bestandteil*; *éprouver l'impression* (1, 2) for *das Gefühl haben*. Kundera rejects these, in other words, as unnecessary overtranslations. Wherever Kafka chooses a simple word, the translators seem to avoid one in their search for a richer vocabulary. Kundera accuses these translators of neglecting Kafka's own ascetic aesthetic.

His next examples concern Kafka's uses of repetition. Some of these have been kept in the translations, (*Die Stunden, die Luft*), but Kundera is critical of the translations that do not preserve exactly the same number of repetitions: Kafka uses *gemeinsamen* twice, none of the French translations reflect this; the same goes for *haben, weiter*, and *vergehen/gehen*. A key concept is of course *die Fremde* (twice) / *die Fremdheit*. Kundera argues that *die Fremde* is in fact the only item that cannot be translated "*mot à mot*" into French, and so a two-word solution is acceptable, but the concrete solutions offered by the three French versions (*pays, contrée*) lose Kafka's sense of abstraction, and the *exil* in (1) is quite wrong: Kundera's choice is *monde*. Kundera's main point here is that all instances of repetition should be strictly preserved, just as a translator of Heidegger's *das Sein* would not use sometimes *l'être*, sometimes *l'existence*, sometimes *la vie*, etc. In other words, Kundera wants verbal consistency, not contextual consistency, because he argues that Kafka's repetition is motivated, it has a semantic and aesthetic function; it is in fact iconic here (my observation, not Kundera's specifically).

A further point concerns punctuation: this too is functional, iconic. Translation (1) thus sins by introducing a semi-colon and breaking the rhythm of the sentence; (2) is even worse, with two semi-colons. In the French translations as a whole, too, there are many more paragraph breaks than in the original, which is unfaithful to Kafka's original intention: Kafka wanted a big font and few paragraphs; what he gets in these translations is a small font and lots of paragraphs. The text as a physical document has thus changed its nature, unnecessarily. Kundera concludes (p. 144): "Dans cette indifférence à la volonté esthétique de l'auteur, toute la tristesse du destin posthume de l'œuvre de Kafka se reflète."

In this light, it seems strange that Kundera himself should have added a comma after the first word *Là*, and another after *s'égarait*; and that he has not preserved the phrase order at the end: *au milieu de séductions insensées* could come (again iconically, surely?) before *l'on ne pouvait rien faire*, as in the German.

2. Kundera's rationale

Kundera's position on the desirable relation between source and target text is thus one that gives a near-absolute priority to formal/aesthetic/stylistic equivalence. There is no discussion of equivalence of reader-reactions, or of the relation between the target text and other literary texts in the target culture polysystem. Rather, underlying Kundera's whole argument is the assumption that a given formal feature *will produce* the same reaction, that it *has* the same aesthetic value, in any culture at any time; a writer's uses of rhetorical schemes and tropes are universal in effect, they work in the same way for every reader, in any language. Style is thus a value *an sich*, not something related to readers' perceptions. It exists as an objective truth. This view is also evident in the priority Kundera gives to formal structure in his own novels.

It is if a work of art is to be translated "in a vacuum", the only relevant connection being that between the two texts themselves. In this respect, Kundera of course identifies himself with a long and respectable tradition, going back through Berman and Meschonnic to Benjamin and then further to the German Romantics. It is the tradition of *l'art pour l'art*, of the glorification of the artist and the magnification of the art critic as privileged interpreter of mysteries. It is a tradition that overtly rejects that of the *belles infidèles* which has been so influential in (e.g.) French translation history, a tradition that rejects all tendencies to domesticate.

For Kundera, it appears not to matter (in fact, not to be conceivable) that a repetition in a source text might actually have a different effect on source-text readers, compared with the effect that the same repetition in the translation might have on target-text readers. There might, after all, be quite different norms concerning repetition in the two languages, different threshold levels above which repetition was not easily tolerated. Similarly, it does not matter that the two languages concerned might have different norms concerning the use of "simple" vocabulary, or sentence length, or the use of semi-colons. Different norms such as those that might presumably have motivated some of the translation decisions that Kundera criticizes. But for Kundera there are no different norms, it seems. What counts is the *"style personnel de l'auteur"*, not the *"style commun"*. If Kafka repeats a word, translators of Kafka (in any language, presumably) should repeat it, regardless of readers' expectations, regardless of how this repetition might affect readers, regardless of how this particular artistic, rhetorical device might be understood.

For Kundera, then, aesthetic responses are universal, not affected by e.g. mother-tongue background or general cognitive experience; what is important is that the text itself, the translation, should be formally as close as possible to the original. What we therefore find is a kind of distancing: for Kundera, texts do not exist (primarily) for readers, or in relation to other surrounding texts in their language; they have an existence of their own and are to be respected as such. Literary texts do not exist in what we might call a culture-bound state, in a particular cultural polysystem; they are not subject to language-specific norms or expectations (beyond basic grammaticality, of course). They exist in a kind of no-man's land, subject only to the norms they create themselves or that are established by the authors themselves. (For a more realistic view, see Gerzymisch-Arbogast 2001.)

We can further infer that for Kundera, the existence of literary texts is timeless, beyond the reach of historical change: translations of Kafka should always exploit precisely the same schemes and tropes that Kafka did, regardless of the period of the translation, regardless of any possible diachronic developments in both source and target languages, regardless of any gap between the time when Kafka wrote and the time of the translation.

In this a-historical no-man's land the only authority is the source-text author, whose intentions are assumed to be directly accessible via their expression in aesthetic form. In such a situation, translators are "sentenced" to play a very subordinate and restricted role.

3. Some discourse analysis

Kundera's book is in French, not his native language Czech; the following comments should therefore be seen in the light of someone writing in a non-native language. Kundera's discourse here, his own personal style, has a number of interesting features. The book is a collection of essays, not a "strictly academic" kind of text-type, and free use is made of the first person *je*, emphasizing the personal aspect of the various claims and arguments.

One key concept that occurs repeatedly is that of *fidelité*. His own translation (number 4 above) is first mentioned in the introductory paragraph, as "le plus fidèle possible" (p. 123). Then, after presenting the previous French versions, Kundera quotes the German original, and follows it immediately with this clause: "*Ce qui, dans une traduction fidèle, donne ceci :*" – i.e. his own translation. Two points are of interest here. First, in terms of textual syntax, Kundera introduces his own translation in the same virtual sentence as the German: the German original is the antecedent of Kundera's relative clause *Ce qui...*, and Kundera's own translation follows the colon after *ceci*. The very syntax here thus binds Kundera's own translation more closely to the original than any of the other French versions. Kundera is using a formal device to reinforce his actual argument: iconicity yet again. On the other hand, this formal trick immediately puts the other translations at a disadvantage: even before any analytical discussion, they are already further from the original. Secondly, note the laconic presentation, in parentheses, of *dans une traduction fidèle*: it as if there is nothing to be questioned here, no argument possible that might characterize one or more of the other translations as "faithful"; as if none of the others, in contrast, have any right to be called faithful. Kundera thus presents himself as one who knows the answer, who *knows* what a faithful translation is.

In discussing the other translations, Kundera makes much use of evaluative terms that presume a strong notion of correctness. Possible translations of a particular source item are not better or worse, but clearly right or wrong. Errors are thus automatically binary (compare Pym 1992c), so that there is no space for counter-arguments. Commenting on one of Vialatte's solutions, Kundera writes: "*Le mot par lequel Vialatte a fauté est d'abord le verbe [...]*" (p. 126). Note: *a fauté*. Vialatte *should not* have translated *sei* as *s'était enfoncé*. Similarly, David "*corrige*" Vialatte at some points. We get the impression that there is only one possible acceptable translation, others are simply wrong. We are a long way from Quine's (1960) implication that translators can always disagree, there are always alternatives. Further: wrong translations are wrong because Kafka would not have liked them.

Kundera *knows* what kind of style Kafka wanted, he knows that, for instance, Kafka was not aiming at something grotesque in this description. Kundera thus (believes he) has access to Kafka's intentions, that these intentions are indeed unambiguous and intelligible, that they are either faithfully reflected in a translation or else they are betrayed. In arguing against other views, Kundera "corrects" these views rather than presents counter-evidence. "*Il faut corriger l'idée affirmant que Kafka n'aimait pas les métaphores*" (p. 128); "*ce que Kafka n'aimait pas, c'était la lyrisation de la prose romanesque*" (p. 128). We get the impression that writers understand each other, they have a kind of privileged access to each others' intentions, an access that translators cannot hope to achieve.

Writers are in fact a class apart. As guardians of aesthetic truth, they can tell translators what to do. Poor translators: how can they remain themselves and at the same time be faithful to their source-text authors? The only solution, says Kundera, is for translators to invest their own creativity in their work, to take some responsibility for stylistic and lexical choices, writing *mélancolie* where the author has written *tristesse*, even without the pressures of repetition, and so on. Kundera appeals to his own experience here, when revising translations of his own texts. The tone becomes exasperated: I (Kundera) write *auteur*, the translator chooses *écrivain*, I write *écrivain* and the translator writes *romancier*, etc. But: this love of synonyms is the great sin of translators. "*Ô messieurs les traducteurs, ne nous sodonymisez pas !*" (p. 132).

So what are translators to do, according to Kundera? The implication is that they should *not* make (such) use of their own creativity, that they should not try to usurp the creative role of the original writer, that they should subject their own identities to that of their authors. Kundera understands the translators' desire to enrich the style, to translate in a way that will be appreciated by the target-text-reading public, because this is the (only?) way for translators to gain any public recognition of their competence; but he condemns this desire nonetheless. Ideal translators are thus sentenced to invisibility.

Kundera is particularly annoyed about the added semi-colons and the breaking-up of the paragraphs, because this radically alters Kafka's *"souffle"*, the long breath of the prose. Other translations, in other languages, have not done this, changing the articulation of the original (Kundera claims). Why have all the French translators done so? He finds no answer. – Kundera's underlying assumption here is, again, a revealing one. There is assumed to be a universal method of translation, applicable in all cultures; it is not conceivable that there might exist culture-specific translation norms that would tend to give rise to different kinds of translation, a different use of various translation strategies in different cultures and at different times. There is no "specifically French" translation tradition, no *belles infidèles* in the past that might help to explain a contemporary French translator's behaviour. There is one absolutely and universally correct method for translating Kafka, and one only. Why? Because to do anything else would be to betray the author's wishes, to be indifferent to the author's aesthetic will (p. 144).

Moreover, there is no recognition of any kind of descriptive universals of translation, such as the well-known and widespread tendency of translators to reduce repetition, regardless of language or text-type. Translators do tend to do this; Kundera simply prescribes that they should not.

In sum, as mentioned above, Kundera's whole position is explicitly against the domesticating approach taken by the French *belles infidèles*; he overtly resists the dominant, mainstream translation tradition of the culture in which he lives, and aligns himself with the opposing, resistant tradition.

4. Some biographical data[1]

Kundera (born 1929) took up a visiting lectureship in France in 1975. In 1979 he was deprived of his Czech nationality and *de facto* sentenced to exile. He was granted French nationality in 1981 and has lived in France ever since, shifting to French as his language of literary expression, and publishing work in French that has not even been translated yet into Czech. He no longer publishes directly in Czech.

The last work he wrote initially in Czech was *Nesmrtelmost* ('Immortality'); this was actually published first in French translation in 1990, and appeared later in Czech in 1993[b]. At the end of the Czech edition there is an Afterword (dated 1992), where Kundera explains that the French version of this work was heavily edited and revised from the original Czech manuscript. Since 1985 he has made a point of checking translations of his work himself as far as possible, especially those [of his earlier works] into French. Why? Because, says Kundera, he knows that most of his readers will not read his books in Czech but in some other language, i.e. in translation, and so he wishes to ensure that at least one of these translations – the French one – will be in a form that he, as the author, can identify with and be personally responsible for. "My books live as translations" (1993b: 346), he acknowledges; it is as translations that they are read, criticized, reviewed, accepted or rejected. It is a matter of pride for him that he can now claim that since 1987 all of his works published by Gallimard have a note to the effect that the French text has "la même valeur d'authenticité que le texte tchèque" (*ibid*.). The published Czech version of this book also meant a lot of revision on the basis of the French version, which had superseded the original Czech manuscript. From now on, Kundera's books enter the Czech literary world only as "echos" of original texts.

Kundera thus insists on his right to set the author's opinion above that of the translator's, making it quite clear that it is the author who is in charge. His own Czech style had the reputation of being clear, not complicated, in fact easy to translate.

In a radio interview in 1995 he had this to say in response to a question about whether he had lost his native language (I paraphrase from the published Czech transcript that appeared in Lidové Noviny, Oct. 30, 1995):

> There is one thing that people do not seem to understand. To begin a totally new life at the age of 45 in a new country demands all one's strength – yes, you heard right, all one's strength. During the last twenty years I have read very few Czech books. Don't blame me for that. No-one can manage to live completely [or: fully] in two countries, two cultures. Even though I speak only Czech with my wife, I am surrounded by French books, I relate to things from a French point of view, with French sentences, just as you [the Czech interviewer] live in a Czech environment with the Czech language. And so one day it became necessary for me to choose what language to write in. I was just as surprised [by that choice] as you. Will I ever return to Czech? Will I return, even partly, to the Czech Republic? I don't know. I'll let it be a surprise. Everything that has happened to me since I left Czechoslovakia has been nothing but surprises, and they haven't stopped yet.

It is perhaps of significance that in this short extract Kundera twice uses the concept "totally", "completely" – "To begin a totally new life", "No-one can [...] live completely in two countries". (In Czech the words are also different, but they are derivationally related: *úplnû* and *naplno*.) The implication seems to be that, given Kundera's life situation, there is no possibility of compromising, of sharing two cultures, of being able to choose to be partly Czech and partly French, of living on a borderline, of both-and. No, the situation is either/or, the distinction is absolute.

5. Simmel's stranger

I now broaden the focus from Kundera and his views on translation to include a sociological angle: how a scholar's conception of the research object is constructed partly on the basis of the scholar's mode of discourse, and how that in turn is based on the scholar's personal beliefs and life situation.[2] My source of inspiration is Georg Simmel's concept of the stranger (Simmel [1908] 1950). I will outline this highly influential notion, and then consider how it may help us to understand Kundera's position on translation.

Simmel's figure of the stranger describes a recognizable sociological type. The archetypical stranger is someone who comes from somewhere else but does not move on; he is a "*potential* wanderer" (Simmel [1908] 1950: p. 402; italics original), because he has wandered but has currently stopped wandering. He has left the group to which he originally belonged, and become a member of a new group, but because he has not belonged to this new group from the beginning his place in it remains in a sense peripheral; he belongs, but does not belong. As a stranger, he represents the unknown and therefore the potentially threatening. On the other hand, he brings into the new group qualities that are not endemic to it, and hence stimulates its development. Being a stranger is a particular form of interaction, an interaction that paradoxically combines elements of nearness and of distance: the stranger is near, for otherwise we would not perceive him at all; yet he is at the same time distant.

To be a stranger, in Simmel's sense, is not the same as to be a foreigner: foreigners are forever distant, they are never integrated into the new group, as the Barbarians were foreign to the Greeks. Strangers have become integrated, albeit only to some extent. On the other hand, "stranger" does not mean the same as "exile", either. To say that someone is an exile is to define a relationship to a previous group, from which a person has fled or been expelled, under some compulsion. To describe the same person as a stranger is to describe a relation vis-à-vis a new culture. Yet the state of being a stranger is a precarious one: partial integration in the new culture may be only temporary, since the first uprooting may not be the last.

Some strangers began by being traders, who settled in the new group instead of leaving it. Strangers are not "owners of soil" (p. 403), but are typically more mobile within the new group than native soil-owners. They are also more objective than the natives, and can therefore participate more effectively in certain situations (such as playing the role of judge); they are freer to see more points of view. Their relation to other members of the new group is more abstract, too: "with the stranger one has only certain *more general* qualities in common, whereas the relation to more organically connected persons is based on the commonness of specific differences from merely general features" (p. 405; italics original). "The stranger is close to us, insofar as we feel between him and ourselves common features of a national, social, occupational, or generally human nature. He is far from us, insofar as these common features extend beyond him or us, and connect us only because they connect a great many people" p. 406).

Traditional examples of strangers are immigrants, expatriates, or (in many cultures) Jews. Translators, too, are frequently outsiders, marginal people, in the culture in which they work. (I am an immigrant myself, born in England but now based in Finland.) Pym (1997) has suggested that this peripheral situation in which many translators find themselves provides the basis for a translation ethics, with a primary loyalty not to one culture or another but to the intercultural space between them. Other examples of strangers are anthropologists who make extensive field-studies of a group that they were not born into: their relationship with the people they are studying is marked precisely by the specific synthesis of nearness and distance which Simmel sees as characterizing the position of the stranger. They can describe the Other, by virtue of the nearness; but they cannot truly know the Other, because of the distance.

Initially, Kundera chose to become a stranger when he left to teach in France. When his Czech nationality was removed, he had no choice but to remain a stranger. Since the downfall of the Communist regime, however, he has not *had* to stay in France: this appears to be more of a free choice, albeit under some pressure deriving from his very success in settling in France. He greeted the downfall of the old regime in 1989 with joy, but also with melancholy, feeling that the change had come too late for him to uproot himself yet again and return.

One may react in different ways to being a stranger. You may accept this status, deciding to be a stranger by free choice or even as an act of will under compulsion. If you thus accept this new status as marginal man, you align yourself with masses of people in many societies at all periods of history who have likewise lived on an edge, between two or more cultures, whose psychological home is some kind of intercultural terrain. You accept a bilingual existence, and you accept an approximate bilingualism, despite the costs to your proficiency in both languages. You accept the imperfection of communication and understanding, perhaps with the belief that your status is only relatively, not absolutely, different from that of anyone else, even monolingual monocultural insiders, for we are ultimately all different people. You keep in touch with both cultures, and do not feel cut off from your first culture. Such expatriates are happy strangers.

But suppose you do not accept this status of being a stranger: you cannot stand living betwixt and between, you want a "proper" home somewhere, you want roots in one place. You then have two main choices. One solution is to remain as far as possible rooted in your source culture, refusing to adapt to the new, refusing to learn the new language beyond minimum proficiency etc. You choose to live in a social and psychological ghetto, an enclave of people who are just like you, strangers from the same original homeland, in a world within a world. The second solution is to go native, to refuse to speak the first home language, refuse to associate with other strangers like yourself, and submerge yourself totally in the target culture. In so doing, you attempt to deny or conceal the fact that you are in fact a stranger; you wish to be taken as a native. These two solutions are those available to unhappy strangers.

It seems to me that Kundera's position on translation may be partly explained by his rejection of the stranger's status, or at least by the assumption that he is unhappy with it – for whatever reasons, no doubt especially because of the period in which he was forceably cut off from his Czech roots. And to the extent that he now writes primarily in French, his reaction to living in a second culture is more like the second solution above. This rejection of the stranger's relativistic status may also explain Kundera's continued need for an absolute: aesthetic form, the writer's art. True, this concern was already evident in his early Czech writing, but its foregrounding in his ideas on translation is done with a passion that may also stem from a life experience outside art.

In Kundera's critique of the French translations of Kafka we find a craving for something to hold on to, something constant that *must* be held on to: some kind of stylistic anchor for a ship adrift. We find a refusal to entertain any kind of idea of cultural relativity, in which given forms might have different effects on different people. We find an insistence on originary authorial authority, a refusal of any kind of translatorial licence, for any licence means a betrayal of origin. Kundera has shifted his own authorial original form from Czech to French, and the passion with which he clings to Kafka's original text-form is perhaps partly to be understood as an expression of the bitterness of Kundera's own personal loss, the loss of originary Czech text-form.

Some circumstantial support for this possible explanation might even be seen in Kundera's use of "totally" and "completely" in the quotation given above. The only way is to be totally this or totally that, no middle path is possible. The stranger, of course, is a stranger precisely because he *is* partly this and partly that. Kundera seems to view cultures here as classical categories, but the stranger's world is inherently fuzzy.

Underlying Kundera's position, both in his life and in his views of translation, there is a single common theme, one that lurks at the roots of all translating: the problem of identity (this is in fact the explicit theme of a later book, *L'identité*). For some, the key question is: how to preserve identity under conditions of change?

Here, identity is something absolute and must be preserved absolutely. Kundera's artistic and cultural identity have come under threat, and he resorts to an absolute authorial identity, perhaps by way of compensation. For others (the happy strangers), the key point is rather: identities always change over time, so what is the most appropriate direction and pace of this change? Here, identity is never absolute, it is always in a state of flux, change is assumed to be part of life. Some change is inevitable, although too much change too fast may of course provoke counter-reactions.

Kundera's most recent[*] novel, *L'ignorance* (first published in Spanish, then in French in 2003), is a sad meditation on the theme of emigration and the impossibility of a return to an original identity. It is about the pain of experiencing that what was once familiar has become strange.

6. A tentative hypothesis

If this suggested link between Kundera's life experience and his views on translation stands up to criticism, the question arises as to whether this situation is specific to Kundera alone, or whether we can generalize from it. A generalization might take the form of the following tentative hypothesis: that there is a causal relation between certain aspects of the life experience of expatriate writers – including their attitudes towards this experience – and their views on translation. In particular: that such writers who have accepted the status of a stranger and are happy with it, who are happy with a bicultural existence in an intercultural space, – such writers will tend to exert less authorial control over translations of their works, and will be less inclined to set up aesthetic absolutes such as total formal or stylistic equivalence. These happy strangers will tend to grant their translators more freedom, and also more status.

On the other hand, expatriate writers who, for whatever reason, have not accepted their stranger's status will tend to react more like Kundera, and treat their translators as potential threats to their identity.

Further, the views of writers who are not strangers at all, who remain within their original home cultures, might be expected to contrast with Kundera's, along the same lines as the views of happy strangers.

An obvious problematic factor in any follow-up research aiming to test this hypothesis will be the difficulty of distinguishing the stranger-status variable

---

[*] "Most recent" when this paper was originally published, in 2004. Since then, *La Fête de l'insignifiance* has appeared, in 2014.

from other relevant variables. One such variable might be the relative statuses of the languages/cultures involved: for instance, in moving from Czech to French, Kundera is in some way moving from a "smaller" culture to a "larger" one. Another variable might be the actual target-language proficiency of the writers concerned: you might tend to be less authoritarian if you do not really command the target language so well yourself.

Notes

1. I am most grateful to Helena Lehečková for her help with the details of this section, including translation from Czech.

2. My thanks to Philip Riley for a stimulating conversation on this theme, and many helpful suggestions.

PAPER 23

Universalism in Translation Studies[*]

It is sometimes said that the way to develop current translation theory is to look at specifically non-Euro-centric and non-Western approaches and learn from them. Against such a position I take a Popperian view. I argue that this proposal is flawed because it commits the genetic fallacy, where an idea or hypothesis is assessed according to its origin. Rather, any hypothesis should be tested as widely as possible, regardless of where it comes from. This includes taking account of the context of discovery. I illustrate my main point with reference to some basic conceptualizations of translation (such as the transfer metaphor), so-called translation universals, and the debate about whether translation studies should have a standardized terminology.

Keywords: hypothesis testing, metaphor, universals, generalization, terminology, Popper

---

There is a view in contemporary translation studies (TS) that our field is too Euro-centric, or too Western, and therefore needs to expand to incorporate non-Western approaches. Such an expansion is seen as offering solutions to some current trends that challenge the development of translation theory. These include the rapid spread of translation technology and the increase of non-professional and group translation practices, seen for instance in crowdsourcing and fan translation. It is also argued that current Euro-centric views cannot account adequately for some translation practices in non-Western cultures. Underlying this general view there seems to be the assumption that TS as a research field is particularly affected by cultural relativity, and has been dominated for too long by European culture; it needs shaking up. I shall argue that the terms in which this relativist view is commonly presented are wrong and misleading, although there is a good point to be made from the evidence alluded to in the discussions of this issue in the literature.

---

[*] First published in 2014 as a Forum opener in *Translation Studies* 7, 1: 82–90. Reprinted by kind permission of the Editor, and Taylor and Francis Group (http://www.tandfonline.com). The text includes some minor revisions prompted by some of the Responses, and a reference has been added.

1. **Kuhn vs. Popper again?**

At a philosophical level, the situation outlined in the previous paragraph recalls the famous debate in the 1960s between Thomas Kuhn and Karl Popper (see e.g. Popper 1959 and Kuhn 1962). Fuller (2003) argues that although Kuhn seems to have won this debate, he should have lost. I agree. According to the relativist view we seem to have a kind of Kuhnian "paradigm": a "Western", socio-culturally determined conceptualization of translation, let us say, which (so the argument goes) Western scholars have assumed is universal but is not, because non-Western conceptualizations are different (see e.g. Hermans 2006, Tymoczko 2007b, Wakabayashi and Kothari 2009). This paradigm has arisen (partly) as a result of the colonial dominance of the West and the hegemony of some of its major languages, notably English. The paradigm persists (partly) because of the entrenched and institutionalized nature of this hegemony, and ultimately reflects a continuing cultural imperialism. On this view, TS will advance by overthrowing its Western paradigm, or by expanding it to incorporate non-Western concepts and theories. Western scholars therefore need to know more about Chinese or Indian theories, for instance, in order to make TS more universally applicable. By including non-Western ideas TS will also improve its ethical standing (see e.g. Tymoczko 2007a). Note that this relativist view *seeks* universality, but argues that this cannot be achieved with our current Western-centric theories.

Against this position, I set a Popperian view. Here, the initial assumption is that all scientific endeavour is intrinsically universalist. Hypotheses and theories can emerge anywhere, in a given context of discovery, but they are assessed anywhere they can be assessed, in a universalist context of justification. There is no added value in assessing them specifically in country or culture X, any more than there is added value in the fact that they were first formulated in country or culture Y. Applied to translation, this implies that while a local theory of translation – a putative Finnish theory, say – might contribute to an understanding of translation practices in Finland, for instance as a case study in the history of translation, it would only have wider value insofar as it could also shed useful light on translation practices elsewhere. For universalists, the above-mentioned relativist position commits the genetic fallacy, according to which an idea, hypothesis or theory is valued (or not) according to its origin. In other words, to claim that TS would be enriched by ideas, etc., that originate in non-Western cultures *because* they arise there, is a bad argument.

It is of course valuable to take a given context of discovery into account when examining a hypothesis, etc., since we know that all our thinking is affected by our culture. It thus makes sense to check out the cultural origins of hypotheses, in order to evaluate the influence of these particular origins on the hypotheses in question. For instance, as Pym (2011) has recently argued, several of the main Western theories of translation can be seen as having arisen as responses to "Western" problems. Nida's concept of dynamic equivalence was evidently influenced by the (largely American) evangelical concern to propagate the Bible in new languages; Skopos Theory was probably motivated by the need to raise the academic status of translator training in German universities; and translation corpus studies were stimulated by the growing numbers of overseas students studying translation and/or applied linguistics in the UK. These motivations were not necessarily the only ones, of course, but they were surely important contributory factors in the development of these ideas. A Popperian would add that a critical examination of the context of discovery of a given hypothesis follows naturally from the critical attitude that is basic to scientific methodology in general.

Now, the relativists are surely right in pointing out that some of the current Western assumptions in TS look doubtful in the face of evidence from translation practices that have so far been little studied, whether in the West (e.g. the study of non-professional translation) or elsewhere. But then the Popperian response would be: let us then test these assumptions on whatever relevant data we can find, wherever we find some, and the more widely the better. Conversely, ideas that originate in non-Western cultures should also be tested, on any relevant data available, in whatever culture, to check whether they apply more generally. If the assumptions and ideas are supposed to be valid for translation universally, we can test them anywhere. To repeat: there is no particular geographical virtue in privileging an idea *because* it comes from the West or the non-West (see further Fuller 2003: 182–3).

It is obvious that groups of scholars within a particular country or area do sometimes influence each other, so that ideas of a certain kind sometimes merge around particular approaches or major projects. It is well known that much of the literature on functional approaches in TS stems from scholars in German-speaking countries. Brazilian ideas about translation as cannibalism have nourished both translation and its research especially in that country (see e.g. Vieira 1994). In Finland, the quest for translation universals has stimulated many projects (see e.g. the papers in Mauranen and Kujamäki 2004), and still does. But this is not evidence against what I am calling the universalist, Popperian position. Any fruits of local theoretical schools can, and should, be tested wherever possible. And this is where we have often appeared to be premature: there is a tendency in TS to make claims about universality without actually testing these claims adequately.

It should also be mentioned that some TS scholars seem to resist all attempts at generalization or universalism, seeking instead to uncover the context-bound contingencies of particular translations rather than make claims about general tendencies. For instance, Hermans calls not for general hypotheses but "thick", detailed analyses of individual cases (Hermans 2007a: 145–50); this would serve, he says, to keep in check the "universalizing urge of theory". I agree that any theory of anything – if it aims to be a general theory – must claim to "universalize"; but I do not agree that this is a tendency that must be kept in check. A theory that did not aspire to universalize, i.e. to generalize as far as possible, would not take us beyond particular cases, or particular sets of cases. What matters is that any general claim needs to be tested, on particular cases of all relevant kinds. Conversely, thick case studies can generate hypotheses whose generality can be tested on other data. We can work top-down (testing general claims against particular cases) or bottom-up (generating potential generalizations from particular cases); both directions are surely needed in the field as a whole.

2. A non-universal metaphor?

Another point concerns the terms and metaphors we use to conceptualize our subject, how we interpret it. It has been argued, for instance, that because of the etymology of the English term *translation* and its Indo-European cognates, TS scholars (many of whom have been in the West, yes) have traditionally over-valued the cognitive metaphor of transfer, carrying something across, and the concomitant notion of equivalence, at the expense of other conceptualizations of translation (see e.g. Chesterman 2006a; Tymoczko 2007a, b). The result has been an overgeneralization: the transfer metaphor has been assumed to be universal, which may have influenced the selection of texts in translation corpora in different languages, and also the quality assessment of these texts. The solution, in my view, is not to compare the Western notion of translation to non-Western ones because these others are non-Western, but because they are, quite simply, *different*. One tests the usefulness and applicability of a conceptualization (among other ways) by comparing it with competing conceptualizations. It matters not a hoot where these competing conceptualizations come from. So it makes good sense to look at alternative etymologies of words that seem to mean something like 'translation' in different languages, in an attempt to arrive at a concept that might be more general than one rooted only in the idea of transfer.

One might for instance work towards a cluster concept, as argued by Tymoczko (e.g. 2006).[*] She argues that translation can be usefully conceptualized together with the notions of transference (involving material movement), representation, and transculturation (the transmission of cultural characteristics, such as art

---

[*] In her Response (2014, *Translation Studies* 7, 1: 101–105) Tymoczko points out that I have misunderstood something here: cluster concepts cannot be fully characterized in terms of any set of features, as they are open-ended.

forms). In this conceptual cluster, the idea of semantic equivalence (i.e. transfer) is not foregrounded. Another possibility is suggested in Chesterman (2006a), based on a semantic cluster of the three central notions of equivalence, difference and mediation, following Stecconi (2004); admittedly limited evidence from a small number of languages suggests that these three central notions can be manifested with varying degrees of relative priority in the terms for 'translation' in different languages. It remains to be seen, however, whether any such cluster concept will prove to have sufficient added value to become widely adopted.

The point here is that if Western scholars have been too hasty to assume the universality of the transfer metaphor, this assumption can be tested and refined or rejected according to the usual criteria for testing a hypothesis. In this case, we are dealing with an *interpretive* hypothesis. (An interpretive hypothesis claims that X can be usefully interpreted as Y; see further, e.g., Chesterman 2008a[*].) Maybe its range of useful application will be found to be narrower than we have thought. The consequent adjustment to the theory would thus reflect a very typical progression in science: a general, or even universal hypothesis (of any kind, empirical or interpretive) is proposed, then tested and found to be less general than was previously thought, so conditions are determined which define its more limited scope of application. The contrary procedure, which is also standard, is to start with a limited, conditioned claim and then discover that its range of application is wider than assumed. Top-down and bottom-up, again.

Given that conceptual metaphors are interpretive, not empirical hypotheses, it might be thought that they are particularly culture-bound; it would therefore be naïve and unjustified to extend them to universal application. I think there is some support for this view, especially because there is a tendency to neglect the testing of interpretive hypotheses: they tend to be proposed and defended, and illustrated with selected examples, rather than critically tested. (Interpretations cannot in principle be falsified – for an interpretation is always *possible* – but they can certainly be assessed in comparison with alternatives, and their usefulness can be tested in practice. See further Føllesdal 1979.) Assessing the potential universal applicability of our interpretive hypotheses requires not only wide-ranging data of all kinds but also an imaginative openness to alternative hypotheses, alternative interpretations, a willingness to see our "X" (translation) in terms of other "Y's", seeing it differently. This is a considerable epistemological challenge, but it does not mean abandoning a critical attitude to any of the alternatives. A cultural evolutionist might observe that the larger the population of available conceptualizations, and the more variation there is in that population, the better the conditions will be for the eventual emergence of a robust theory.

---

[*] Paper 18 in this volume.

3. Universal features of translations?

The problems of finding the appropriate scope of an *empirical* hypothesis, on the other hand, and also some of the different attitudes to universalism, are illustrated in what is perhaps the most obvious recent manifestation of universalism in TS: the research on translation universals, already mentioned above.

The idea that there are (or might be) "universal" features of translations is an old one, although it is only during the past couple of decades or so that serious research has been done on this topic. It has long been realized that there are always differences between translations and their originals (i.e. there are always shifts). Typical differences between source and target texts include interference, explicitation, or increasing standardization. In addition, translations often show evidence of "translationese", i.e. non-natural target language. Differences between the target text and non-translated texts in the target language include simplification and the under-representation of target-language-specific (so-called unique) items. (For references and more details, see e.g. the papers in Mauranen and Kujamäki 2004.)

At first sight, this line of research makes intuitive sense, although the general hypothesis that "translations are different" makes only a cautious, unsurprising claim. However, it is a claim that has given rise to some heated debate. In a polemical piece against the whole notion of universals, Juliane House argues that "the quest for translation universals is in essence futile" (2008: 11), mainly because she sees the only valid universals as those pertaining to language pragmatics in general, not translation in particular.

So what is so controversial about the idea? In the first place, critics have not liked the term "universals" itself, which was popularized (though not invented) by Mona Baker (1993). It does indeed seem misleading, if it is interpreted as being analogous to the sense in which it is used in "linguistic universals". In language typology, the search for universals, later influenced by Chomsky's theory of Universal Grammar, has meant formulating generalizations about language structure that are claimed to be based on the constraints of human cognition, and underlie (or are manifested in) the structures of individual languages. Claims about such universals have been tested on hundreds of languages, and could in principle be tested on all known languages, since these amount only to six or seven thousand. Some such universals are claimed to be absolute, occurring in all possible natural languages; others are probabilistic, e.g. of the form: if a language has feature A, it probably also has feature B (for a general account, see, e.g., Croft 2003). But with respect to translation, the term must be interpreted differently, more loosely, for several reasons.

The notion "translation" is categorically different from that of "language". Translations are instances of *parole*, not *langue*, and as such they come in very different forms and sizes, from a single spoken word to a whole book, for instance, not to mention all kinds of multi-modal variants. There is enormous variation of usage and interpretation here, both culturally and historically; and we do not even have access to much of the relevant evidence from the past, or from oral translation (i.e. interpreting). Maria Tymoczko (1998) is one scholar who has drawn particular attention to this problem, and to how seriously it affects the construction of corpora in projects that set out to generate or test hypotheses about translation universals.

In my view, what all this implies is that the term "universal" has been an unfortunate and misleading choice in this context, as applied to linguistic features of translations. Some scholars have preferred to speak of tendencies, or probabilistic translation laws, such as those of interference and growing standardization (Toury 1995). But ultimately, the quest for universals is no more than the usual search for patterns and generalizations that guides empirical research in general. Our mistake has been to assume too quickly that the tendencies or regularities we have found might really be "universal". True, to state a hypothesis in a maximally general form exposes it rapidly – and usefully – to the risk of counter-evidence, which should then lead to the increasing limitation of the scope of the hypothesis, or indeed to its rejection. Claims about the tendency of translators to explicitate, for instance (going back to Blum-Kulka 1986), obviously cannot apply so much to translation types such as subtitling or the translation of comic strips, or to gist translation, owing to the constraint of available space, so it cannot be a uniformly "universal" tendency.

On the other hand, hypotheses have been proposed that may not be general enough. All translations may well tend to show signs of interference, and of shifts; and causes for these signs can be inferred to lie somewhere in human cognition processes (see e.g. Halverson 2003). However, such tendencies might not be specific to translation and may also be found in other forms of discourse mediation, as argued for example by Ulrych (2009). Along similar lines, Lanstyák and Heltai (2012, 100) make a good case for the view that (potential) translation universals are a form of "language contact universals", which are also manifested in the language performance of bilinguals. These language contact universals are in turn a subset of more general "universals of constrained communication" (2012: 100).

It is thus essential to specify the scope of a hypothesis, and to be open to the need to extend or restrict this scope. Conditioned generalizations, at a lower level of generality, specific to particular languages, genres, translator profiles, working conditions, and so on, may bring a wealth of new information about translation, although they appear less ambitious than grand claims of universality. As our knowledge accumulates about how these *conditioned* hypotheses fare in different tests, we may be able to generate more general correlative or causal hypotheses. It is less the individual translation features themselves that might justify this kind of universality claim, I suspect, but rather the relations between types of features and types of contextual conditions. We are not there yet, but it may well be *these* hypotheses that can claim to be generally valid, applying to any case where a given set of conditions is met. For instance, we might develop hypotheses about the way in which space or time constraints affect translator decisions under different circumstances. But it's always the testing of the hypotheses – the context of justification – that matters.

4. Standardized terms?

At bottom, as Tymoczko (1998) has stressed, we still lack a generally accepted definition of "translation" itself. Although there are also fuzzy borders in linguistics between what we want to call a language and what we want to call a dialect, this is nothing compared to the problematic terminological mess around translation, version, adaptation, and so on. How free, or indeed how bad, does a claimed translation have to be before it is felt (by whom?) *not* to be a translation at all? Isn't a really bad translation nevertheless still a translation, of a kind? Should "bad" (or indeed non-native) translations be included in a representative corpus of translations in general, on which hypotheses about universals could be tested? – I think the answer to this last question must be yes, *unless* the scope of the hypothesis in question is restricted to competent, published professional native translations only, not claimed to apply universally to *all* translations. (Is there a corpus somewhere that explicitly includes "bad" translations?)

One solution to the definition problem might be to resort to formalization, in an attempt to get beyond the limitations of a single natural language and take refuge in the universal language of mathematics. Very few TS scholars have taken this route, however. A notable exception is García-Landa (1990), but he has not been followed, as far as I know, perhaps because even if one formulates one's theory in mathematical symbols these still need to be defined and interpreted in natural language(s). If anyone comes up with a solution that gains wide acceptance, I think the TS field would only benefit, at least as a field of empirical research.

A more important issue is the need (or not, according to your view) for a standardized terminology. "Universalists" have been arguing for more agreement on TS terminology (see e.g. the special issue of *Target*, volume 19, 2, 2007), and some practical steps have been taken in the work on the Benjamins online Bibliography of Translation Studies (see <http://benjamins.com/online/tsb/>). But there are still many who find that such a project limits their freedom to interpret terms and concepts in ways they find most appropriate, who feel that a standardized terminology would be a straitjacket for TS, not an advantage. Here I think the difference is between those who see TS as an empirical human science (which therefore needs some standardized terminology, like any other science), and those who see it as a hermeneutic discipline (where conceptual argument about meaning and interpretation is more central). If we agree that it can be both, the consequence may be even more of a split in the field than we have at present.

The terminology problem is one that still remains without a generally agreed solution. The debate on the issue has of course raised matters of language policy, institutional power and democracy, and the argument will no doubt continue. If any standardized terms are to be agreed for, say, English, this still leaves open the problem of their standardized translations in other languages. There are several multilingual glossaries of the field available, but none has yet been generally accepted as standard.

5. Concluding remarks

I have argued that the proper assessment of ideas, theories and hypotheses has nothing to do with their geographical origin in the West or non-West. As Pym puts it, "no idea is going to be superior simply because it came from a particular direction" (2011: 60). As translation is a cultural phenomenon, we can expect a huge variety of views and approaches. The more the merrier, indeed. But this does not mean that we have to subscribe to a naïve relativism (where all we see is differences, and similarities are ignored), any more than we need to subscribe to a naïve universalism (where all differences are ignored). After all, is this not what translation itself is all about: creating similarity alongside difference?

So if we are working towards a general theoretical framework that can describe and explain translation in its widest sense, all potential components of such a framework need to be tested as widely as possible, regardless of their culture of origin. What matters is whether a concept, model, hypothesis or theory turns out to be useful or not, in solving a given problem and/or in bringing deeper understanding. Or, indeed, in generating further fruitful questions.

SECTION VIII

The sociological turn

The increasing interest in sociological approaches to translation raises again the idea of consilience in TS, as a counter-balance to the spreading fragmentation of the field (see Paper 4 above, and also Chesterman 2007c). Translation sociology has obvious relevance for research with a direct social impact, such as issues of quality that are sometimes sidelined in purely descriptive work, reception studies of various kinds, and questions concerning language and translation policy. It has contributed methodologically to the spread of causal models in translation research (see e.g. Pym 2006).

Paper 24 introduces some of the main research trends that have led to the so-called sociological turn, and distinguishes three main areas for future research: the sociology of translation in terms of national and international publication flows, sociological research on translators themselves, and the sociology of the translation process. There has been, of course, a good deal of work on translation sociology since this paper was first published. See for instance Wolf and Fukari (2007), and several relevant entries in the Benjamins *Handbook of Translation Studies*. The relation between Bourdieu's theory and Actor Network Theory has been interestingly discussed in Hekkanen (2009).

Paper 25 is a revised version of James Holmes' famous map of Translation Studies, giving pride of place not to texts (translations) but to people (translators). It also draws attention to an often overlooked branch of Holmes' map, that of translation policy. This subfield of TS has certainly boomed in recent years (see e.g. Meylaerts 2011 and González Núñez 2016). There is some overlap with Paper 24.

Paper 26 returns to one of Gideon Toury's insights into the difference between translation acts (cognitive) and events (sociological), and extends his analysis of kinds of translation problem in order to shed light on different translation process models. For an interesting critical response to this paper, see Muñoz Martín (2016).

PAPER 24

Questions in the sociology of translation[*]

This paper welcomes the current interest in a sociological approach in Translation Studies, as a way of focusing on part of the wider context of translation. Three sub-areas are distinguished: the sociology of translations as products, the sociology of translators, and the sociology of the translation process. Some current sociological models are outlined, and the notion of a 'translation practice' is introduced as a central component in a sociological approach. Actor Network Theory is outlined as a potentially useful framework, and a number of possible research questions are suggested.

Keywords: context, sociology, culture, model, translation practice, Actor Network Theory, research questions

1. The sociocultural context

In his critical review of the selected proceedings of the 1998 Granada EST conference (Chesterman et al. 2000), Albrecht Neubert (2001) makes a valid point. Although we entitled the volume in question "Translation in Context," neither the book as a whole nor any of the contributions as such really offers an adequate analysis of the key notion of context itself. It is a truism to point out that in the past few decades Translation Studies has hugely expanded its focus, from the narrowly linguistic to contexts of all kinds. But we lack a shared understanding of precisely how this total context is best delineated. This paper is, in part, an attempt to respond to Neubert's criticism.

Let us start with the opposition, current especially in the 1990's, between the linguistic context and the cultural context. Scholars began proclaiming the "cultural turn" that would soon replace the purely linguistic analysis of texts (see e.g. Bassnett and Lefevere 1996). Early cultural studies of translation made much use of polysystem theory, which was indeed originally developed as a theory of culture

---

[*] First published in 2006 in João Ferreira Duarte, Alexandra Assis Rosa and Teresa Seruya (eds), *Translation Studies at the Interface of Disciplines*. Amsterdam/Philadelphia: Benjamins, 9–27. Reprinted with kind permission from John Benjamins Publishing Company [www.benjamins.com]. A link has been updated. The abstract and keywords have been added.

and cultural transfer. (For some critical views on this division, see e.g. Baker 1996, Pym 1999, Tymoczko 2002.)

However, this oversimplified dichotomy not only overlooked the fact that linguistics itself had at that time already expanded far beyond mere syntactic analysis, into textlinguistics and discourse analysis, pragmatics, and cognitive grammar. It also neglected the growing interest among some translation scholars in cognitive processes (for a recent survey, see *Across Languages and Cultures* 3.1 [2002]).

Furthermore, much of the work grouped under the cultural turn actually seems closer to sociology than to culture studies. We have, for instance, seen an increasing interest in historical studies: witness the series of publications from the Göttingen project, and Anthony Pym's work on the methodology of historical research on translation (1998). This kind of research has included an interest in the physical movement of people and texts across cultural borders, the influence of publishers and patrons, and economic as well as textual factors. Maria Tymoczko and Edwin Gentzler (2002) speak of "the power turn" in referring to a whole range of research on ideological aspects of translation: this covers themes such as postcolonial issues, gender issues, the manipulation of national identities and their perception, and the illusion of the translator's total neutrality. Here too, the subjects covered are at least as sociological as they are cultural. Hence perhaps the tendency of many scholars, including myself, to resort to the compound concept of the "sociocultural".

This is a bit lazy, though. It ought to be possible to draw a rough line down the middle of this concept, with (mainly) sociological issues on one side and (mainly) cultural ones on the other. One reason for doing this, for attempting to clarify the concept in this way, is the view we might then have of apparent research gaps – as I will try to show in what follows.

There has long been disagreement about precisely how culture is best defined, but recent decades have seen something of a growing consensus (for a useful summary of these developments, see Katan 1999). A good starting place is the proposed definition by Kroeber and Kluckhohn (1952: 181), given as their conclusion to a list of 164 previous definitions. (I cite it from Katan 1999: 16.)

> Culture consists of patterns, explicit and implicit, of and for behaviour acquired and transmitted by symbols, constituting the distinctive element of human groups, including their embodiment in artifacts; the essential core of culture consists of traditional (i.e. historically derived and selected) ideas and especially their attached values. Culture systems may, on the one hand, be considered as products of action, on the other hand, as conditioning elements of future action.

This definition sees culture partly as something external (visible as behaviour and as artifacts), and partly as internal (ideas and values). Of these two aspects, the internal ones are seen as more central ("core"). This centrality is represented to various extents in several well-known models of culture, such as that of Geert Hofstede (1991). Hofstede's model is an "onion model" of different layers. At the core we have values, and around this, practices. Practices include rituals, heroes and symbols. So the further out we move from the cultural core, the more we move into the realm of sociology: into the realm of social behaviour and social relations, of institutions, of the production and distribution of artifacts, etc. As the above quotation suggests, cultural systems are both produced by action – including, and especially, social action – and serve to influence future action. Put simply, we have a constant interplay between actions and ideas, with the causality working both ways. The sociologists focus more on the actions, and the cultural studies people on the ideas.

With respect to translation, this means that we can now map out the main regions of our "spatial" context as follows (in addition to the immediate textual context):

- *Cultural context*: focus on values, ideas, ideologies, traditions etc.
- *Sociological context*: focus on people (especially translators), their observable group behaviour, their institutions etc.
- *Cognitive context*: focus on mental processes, decision-making etc.

Some of the concepts we use in Translation Studies fall on borderline areas, and this has perhaps contributed to the way these borders have become blurred. One such Janus-concept is that of the norm, which is both cultural and social; another is the fuzzy notion of discourse, which seems at least to straddle the border between the texts and their social context, and perhaps other borders as well, depending on your definition of it.

2. Current models and frameworks

In the sociological context, we find quite a variety of approaches, all competing for space and prestige. We also find gaps: clusters of interesting sociological questions that do not seem to have benefited from adequate theoretical frameworks at all.

I think we can usefully divide "the sociology of translation" into three sub-areas. They are:

a. the sociology of translations as products;
b. the sociology of translators;
c. the sociology of translating, i.e. the translation process.

The third sub-area is the one that has received the least attention, as far as I am aware, and it is the one to which I want to give the most space. Before doing so, however, I need to sketch in the background, and so what follows is first a brief survey of what I see as the main theoretical models and approaches currently used in sociological studies of translation, in the light of these three sub-areas. We will then focus specifically on the translation process itself.

2.1 Polysystems

One of the most influential models has been polysystem theory. I suggested above that polysystem theory is a cultural rather than a sociological one, and it is true that its major applications have had to do with the cultural position and status of translations – particularly literary translations – in the textual or literary polysystem of the target culture. Relations have been explored between translations and other kinds of "rewritten" texts, such as anthologies. Issues studied include such themes as the canonization of texts, the shifting status of texts, the reshuffling of relations in the target system as a result of the entrance of translations of certain kinds. However, some polysystem scholars have extended their focus to more sociological questions, such as Lefevere's interest in the institution of patronage (1992a): the influence of publishers and other sponsors in selecting texts to be translated and in setting or confirming translation norms. In its sociological applications, polysystem theory is primarily a model of the sociology of translations, my first group above; to a lesser extent it also touches on the status and role of translators themselves.

2.2 Bourdieu

A model that give more focus to the sociology of translators is that of Bourdieu. (See the special issue of *The Translator*, 11, 2, 2005.) Recall that one of his central concepts is that of the field, within which agents (i.e. for us, translators) compete for positions of status and power (see the discussion in Hermans 1999: 131f). Jean-Marc Gouanvic (1999, 2002) has used Bourdieu's model in his study of the emergence of science fiction as a new genre in France after World War II, under the influence of translation. Gouanvic looks at the roles played in this emergence by economic factors, key translators and publishers, marketing practices and book clubs. The focus is on the factors that gave rise to a new literary genre in France, not on the actual translating process itself. Heilbron (2000) also makes use of Bourdieu's general approach in analysing the international flows of translated books between core and peripheral cultures, as part of a broader globalization process. He calls for more research on the social organization of different segments of the international translation market, including segments where translations are particularly rare, such as school books, where national authorities exert a decisive influence.

Another of Bourdieu's central concepts is the habitus. This is the basic psychological-emotional disposition of agents (in a field), including notions of role model, self-image and group identity. Simeoni (1998) has drawn attention to the typical habitus of translators as one of "voluntary servitude," an expression that recalls Douglas Robinson's view (1991) of the somatics of translation. (See also Kalinowski 2002.) This kind of approach is thus directed more at the sociology (or sociopsychology) of translators themselves, rather than at translations as products or at the observable process of translating.

2.3 Luhmann

Niklas Luhmann's theory of social systems has also been applied in Translation Studies (see Hermans 1999: 137f, Poltermann 1992). Luhmann sees society as being constructed of differentiated systems (the law, the church, politics…), each being constituted of acts of communication (e.g. Luhmann 1990). These communications are the elements out of which society is built. A translation event is precisely such a communication, an element of the translation system. A translation event can be defined temporally as the duration of a translation task, from initial request to delivery and payment. Following Toury (1995: 249), we can distinguish such events from translation acts: acts take place in the translator's head, at the level of cognition, and are not observable directly.

Social systems of different kinds use different organizing codes. Like many systemic thinkers, Luhmann seems to like binary codes: thus the legal system organizes itself on the basis of the difference between legal and illegal; science works on true vs. false. Hermans suggests (1999: 143) that the translation system is structured on the difference between a valid and a non-valid representation of the source text – which raises interesting questions of interpretation and conceptual analysis that I will not go into here.

But a translation system contains more than just translation events. It also contains statements about these events: discourse on translation, including such texts as translation reviews, prefaces and other paratexts, and also scholarly research on translation: all these feed into the system, reflecting it and affecting it. These additional elements show something about people's perception of translation (at a given time and place). These perceptions are of course partly formed by translations themselves, but they also serve as expectations which affect the way translators think and work. In this sense, the translation system is self-reflective and self-developing.

Like Bourdieu's model, Luhmann's too seems more applicable to the study of factors influencing translation and translators, and to the distribution of different kinds of translations in society, than to the translating process itself. He offers a way of conceptualizing norms, for instance, as expectations within the translation system. And he also offers a way of looking at the relations between the translation system and other social systems, in terms of interference and influence.

2.4 Translation historiography

Recent research on translation (and interpreting) history has stressed the roles of individual translators, as real people living in specific circumstances. This view of history thus focuses less on the movement of ideas than on the movements of real people, and also of concrete texts and manuscripts. In terms of my tripartite division, the historical approach advocated e.g. by Pym (1998) and Delisle and Woodsworth (1995) concerns above all the sociology of translators.

Pym (1998: 5) divides translation historiography into three areas. Its "archaeology" has to do with who translated what, how, when, where, for whom, etc. – These are the basic textual and sociological facts. Then there is "historical criticism", which looks at the consequences of translations in terms of their contribution (or otherwise) to "progress". This is the ideological dimension (including the scholar's own ideology). And finally there is "explanation," which explores the causality of translation, including social causes. Pym's aim is thus to place translators and translations in a broad sociohistorical context.

2.5 Critical discourse theory, pragmatics

These frameworks have also been used in translation research that could be called sociological in approach, in the sense that they allow us to explore the relations between textual features and, for instance, political aspects of power and ideology. Annie Brisset (1990) adapted critical discourse analysis in her examination of some drama translations in Quebec. Such work draws attention to the potential political (and thus also social) effects of translation, and also to the intentions of translators, but sheds no light on the process itself.

Norman Fairclough's theory of critical discourse analysis (1992 and later publications) provides a rich framework for the analysis of what he calls the discursive practices of text production, distribution and consumption; a central notion is that of intertextuality. However, Fairclough's work aims to analyse social change in general, not translation as such. It has not yet been much applied in translation studies (but see Olk 2002), although it suggests a potentially useful model for the analysis of some aspects of translation practice.

Some scholars have adopted a pragmatic framework in their analysis of translation (see e.g. Hatim and Mason 1990, Hickey 1998). This work applies concepts such as Grice's conversational maxims, relevance theory, politeness and presupposition in the close textual analysis of translations. It takes account of the social consequences of translators' choices, and underlines the important fact that translators must be aware of their implied readers. As candidates for a general sociological theory of translation, however, these approaches are too restricted in focus. They are really extensions of textlinguistic analysis.

2.6 Sociolinguistic models

A glance at recent issues of *Translation Studies Abstracts* shows that there is quite a variety of translation research that is sociolingustic in one way or another. At the "socio" end, we find research that examines particular aspects of the social conditions of translation, such as translation to and from creole languages (Lang 2000): such a situation obviously poses special problems for a translator. At the "linguistic" end, we find many studies of particular textual features that have social causes or correlations, such as dialects and other instances of linguistic variation. (See e.g. Berthele 2000 on the translation of Jim's vernacular in Huckleberry Finn, or Mayoral Asensio 2000 on the translation of linguistic variation more generally.) Between these two ends, there are studies that could also be listed under my "pragmatics" heading, dealing e.g. with politeness and audience design. Mason (2000) uses the notion of audience design in his analysis of the causes of translation shifts.

An early attempt to draw together a number of sociolinguistic analyses is the work of Maurice Pergnier ([1978] 1993), which incorporates constraints of time, place and medium as well as more linguistic aspects. And we should not forget Eugene Nida's pioneering work in the 1960s and later, on communicative aspects of translation. His model borrows much from information theory (notions of message, noise, redundancy, recoding, channel, readability or accessibility). (See e.g. Nida 1964.)

These sociolinguistic models foreground correlations and causal connections between situational features and linguistic profile features. A much broader picture is offered by Jean Peeters (1999), who offers a sociolinguistic model based on Jean Gagnepain's theory of mediation. It is presented as an anthropological theory, in that it claims to capture what it is that makes human communication human. There are four key concepts, each corresponding to a whole theoretical level. They are the *Sign* – having to do with designation, meaning, cognition; the *Tool* – having to do with production, technology, ends and means; the *Person* – having to do with interactions, social relations; and the *Norm* – having to do with values. We can relate these quite easily to the general model I outlined above. The Sign relates to the cognitive level, and the Tool to the linguistic texts themselves; the Person is seen in social terms; and the Norm represents what I called the cultural level. Peeters' approach stresses that translation as a process is governed by the same influences that affect any exchange. Like other forms of interaction, translation is affected not only by one's own intrinsic manner of being but also by one's attitude towards and perception of others – a view that recalls Bourdieu's habitus.

2.7 Skopos theory

Skopos theory (Reiß and Vermeer 1984, Vermeer 1996, Nord 1997) could also be seen as having a sociological viewpoint, in that it gives prominence to the role of the client, to the negotiations between translator and client concerning appropriate translation strategies, and the reactions of the reader (accepting or protesting against the translation). Holz-Mänttäri's framework of action theory (1984) has a broader scope, but has been less applied outside the German-speaking world, perhaps partly because of its idiosyncratic terminology. Hanna Risku (1998) makes good use of it in her account of translatorial competence. (See also Risku and Freihoff 2000.) Risku also includes other agents in her model, such as revisers.

2.8 Quality control, the translation market, language planning

Then there is the work on quality control procedures and multilingual documentation management, mainly in the field of technical and business translation (e.g. Sprung 2000), and the development of international quality standards for translation (for a discussion of the latter, see Chesterman and Wagner 2000, ch. 6). This work is motivated by the practical requirements of business efficiency, and has not yet really become part of the mainstream of Translation Studies, which is unfortunate. Research on these procedures obviously applies many of the notions of action theory, albeit only implicitly. It is certainly focused on the concrete translating process – a feature that has been lacking or underplayed in many of the models I have mentioned.

A related area in the sociology of translations is the needs analysis of the translation market, particularly in the business world, and research on its functioning (e.g. Lambert 1996). Key concepts here include job satisfaction, conflict resolution (disagreements and clashing role perceptions between clients and translators), and translation policy. To what extent, for instance, are translation and language policies and practices integrated with the rest of a company's activities? What kind of feedback systems are available?

Finally, mention should be made of work in language planning, which is directed towards the application of research-based knowledge to particular social situations and problems. Typical issues concern language and/or translation policies in multilingual countries or institutions, or for minority languages. These issues have obvious relevance for language rights, democracy, and political development, all of which lie within the sphere of sociological interest.

Research that I have grouped under this heading covers all of my three sociological areas: translations, translators, and the translating process. It might thus offer a better foothold for future sociological research than models that have been originally developed to deal mainly with literary translation.

Each of these models or approaches allows us to ask different kinds of questions. Overall, the least attention seems to have been given to the actual process of translating, as a series of concrete tasks. With the exception of research on quality control, none of the above models seem to place the observable process of individual translation tasks at the centre of focus. There is a kind of gap here, at what might be thought of as the centre of sociological translation research: a gap between frameworks based on abstract sociocultural systems on the one hand, and extensions of text-based frameworks on the other. It is to this gap that I now turn in more detail, with a consideration of the concept of a practice.

3. Translation practices

I want to suggest that the notion of a practice fills this gap at the centre of the sociology of translation. It allows us a sociological perspective which enables us to focus on the process of translating, rather than the subsequent history of the translation product once it has been submitted to the client, or the influences that impinge on the translator before a given translation task is undertaken. I will first discuss the notion itself, and then show how it can be applied to Translation Studies.

We can start with the observation that a practice involves people (usually more than one): this in itself takes us one step up from a focus on a translator as a single agent. We have already met the term "practices" as part of Hofstede's onion model of culture. His use of the term, however, is more abstract than the sense I want to develop, as it includes symbols; besides "heroes," it also covers "rituals," but these are not appropriate for our purposes as they are defined as "technically superfluous" patterns of behaviour, such as the use of small talk in some cultures.

In his overview of sociological theory, Runciman (1998: 11–12) sees practices as units of reciprocal action. Being reciprocal, they therefore exist at the level of group or institutional behaviour. As units of action, they are socially, concretely real; not just semiotically real. They are obviously subject to constraints imposed by power relations of various kinds: norms are prime examples.

The philosopher Alasdair MacIntyre (1981), in the course of his argument in favour of an ethics based on virtues rather than rights or values, proposes a more complex definition. He writes:

> By a "practice" I am going to mean any coherent and complex form of socially established cooperative human activity through which goods internal to that course of activity are realised in the course of trying to achieve those standards of excellence which are appropriate to, and partially definitive of, that form of activity, with the result that human powers to achieve excellence, and human conceptions of the ends and goods involved, are systematically extended.
>
> (1981: 175)

There are several aspects to this definition that are highly relevant to our concerns. (For further discussion, see Chesterman 2001c*.) Note first the emphasis on cooperative human activity: shared effort towards an agreed end. If we adopt this view, we note a difference between practices and Bourdieu's fields: the latter are more characterized by competition than by cooperation, because of Bourdieu's focus on the struggle for power. The key value in MacIntyre's definition is not power but excellence. On this view, practitioners – i.e. people working in a practice – seek first of all to be good at their work, and need therefore to cooperate. Power considerations cannot be overlooked, but they are not central; and they may apply at levels other than that of the practitioners themselves, e.g. at the level of those who use their services or products. Examples of practices given by MacIntyre are football, chess, architecture, farming, physics, medicine, painting, music, politics. We can easily add translation to this list.

An emphasis on the striving for excellence thus underlines the positive side of professional work, the personal concern with quality. Actions that are seen to be of high quality may of course eventually attract status and other attributes of symbolic power, but MacIntyre is keen to stress the "internal goods" rather than external benefits. Internal goods include the good feeling you get when you know you have done something well – the translator's "ahaa!" experience, the pleasure of solving a tricky passage, of finding the right term. There may be an interesting way here of bringing back issues of quality into descriptive research.

---

* Paper 27 below.

MacIntyre points out that entering into a practice means entering into a relationship with its history and tradition (its narrative, in fact) and its contemporary practitioners. It also means accepting the authority of prevailing standards of excellence (at least initially), and striving to achieve them, even to exceed them. Novice practitioners thus need to become socialized into the practice, which often involves some kind of accreditation, so that quality control (standards of excellence) can be maintained. Practices are "socially established," i.e. more or less institutionalized. They may coincide with professions (e.g. medicine), but they may not. Whether or not translation is actually a profession proper is a moot point: perhaps not, in that we have no monopoly over a particular social value (such as health, for the medical profession), nor are there (yet) compulsory accreditation procedures (anyone can set up as a translator…). But translation is certainly a practice in MacIntyre's sense.

Summing up so far, we have an idea of a practice as an institutionalized system of social conduct in which tasks are performed by actors fulfilling roles, under contextual conditions which include a striving for quality.

With respect to translation, then, we can say that the *practice of translation* (in a given context) is made up of *tasks* whose performance takes place via *translation events* (in that context).

If we study translation as a practice in this sense – as a set of translation events – we shall be interested in many questions that are not so easily posed within most of the frameworks I listed above. These, then, are potentially interesting research problems. Some examples:

- Whom do translators work with? Which other agents cooperate? How does co-drafting work?
- What roles do these other agents play? (For instance, how do quality control systems operate? Are there different processes for different aspects of revision? Revision on screen / on paper? Different revisions for different aspects of the text?)
- What kinds of relations prevail between the various agents? (These relations are both "vertical", with the client or project manager, and "horizontal", with other team members, revisers or consultants.)
- What kinds of technical resources are used in the performance of tasks, and how? How does this use vary?
- How do translators organize their own working conditions ergonomically?
- What are the distinct phases of the task process (i.e. the translation event), from the initial need to the delivery of the translation and payment of the fee? How are the phases distributed over time?
- How are multilingual documents drafted?

- How do working conditions and processes vary according to whether the client is "exporting" or "importing" the translation?
- What constraints exist, and how do they affect the task process?

Not just abstract power relations and norms, but more concrete things like policy decisions can also directly affect working conditions. For instance:

- What are the policy decisions about the provision of source texts and the right to edit them and/or correct errors?
- What are the policy decisions about the choice of translators: native or non-native, in-house or freelance, single or team?
- What are the policy decisions about the availability of consultation, arbitration procedures in cases of unsolved queries or disagreements?
- What are the policy decisions on procedures for producing multilingual documents, in different institutions?

Some of these questions are raised by Brian Mossop (2000) in a call for more research on translators' workplace procedures. He particularly underlines the need to study revision procedures, in order to find out more about how quality is improved in professional conditions. (See also Mossop 2001, Malmkjær 1994, Hansen 2002.) Other questions are touched on in some of the approaches I have outlined above. Päivi Vehviläinen (2000) has done interesting work (in Finnish) on inferring translators' internalized role models from their discourse in interviews. None of the frameworks so far mentioned seems capable of covering all the above questions.

Other questions that seem pertinent to research on translation practice concern the relations between translators and other agents, rather than their actual actions:

- What is the status of the various agents? How is this status manifested? How do translators perceive their own status? What kinds of role models do they have? (Cf. their habitus.)
- What is the public perception of people involved in translation practice? How is this manifested? (The discourse on translation, representation of translators in literature, customer satisfaction, feedback, rates of pay…) Answers to these questions could tell us something about what we could call translators' public image or their "perceived" habitus, as opposed to their actual "experienced" habitus.
- How do rates of pay vary, how are they calculated?
- How do professional translators try to develop their own skills?
- What kinds of accreditation systems exist in different countries? How well do they work? What do professional translators think of them?

4. Actor-network theory

One sociological theory that, at first sight, might seem eminently applicable to research on translation practice is actor-network theory (developed especially by the French sociologists Bruno Latour and Michel Callon; a useful initial resource can be found at <http://www.lancaster.ac.uk/fass/centres/css/ant/antres.htm>). This has not yet, to my knowledge, been much applied in Translation Studies (but see Buzelin 2005*). I will outline some of its main ideas here, and point out briefly how it might be adapted for our purposes.

Actor-network theory (ANT) was originally developed in the late 1980s and 1990s as a tool to study technological innovation and scientific progress, as part of the sociology of science. It has been influenced by postmodernist ideas, and by the debates on the discourse of science. The central notion of an actor (or agent or actant) is understood to include both human and non-human agents: people interact with machines, computers, books etc., and all these form part of the socio-technical network in which science is done, or in which some new engineering project is undertaken. The network has no centre, all the elements are interdependent. Important roles are played by knowledge systems and by economic factors, as well as by people and by technical aids. Causality is not unidirectional: any node in the network can affect any other node. The theory distinguishes various kinds of relation between the nodes of a network, including one called "translation," which may be misleading for translation scholars as it has a somewhat different sense: it refers to the way in which each actor has to "translate" meanings into his/her/its own terms, in order to make sense of them. This then leads inevitably to compromises, without which the project cannot move forward: at some stage, debate stops after adequate consensus is reached, and issues are considered "closed" simply for the practical reason of making some progress. All actors have their own interests and values, too, which affect how they participate in the project and how they interpret their own roles. (For a critical collection of papers on ANT, see Law and Hassard 1998.)

While this theory is not applicable *in toto* to Translation Studies, largely because its main focus (as part of science and technology studies) is so different, it does offer ideas that we could develop in the study of translation practices. For instance, we might wish to establish what networks exist (in a given context): what the various nodes are, both human and non-human; what the range of the network is; what use is made of each of the nodes; the frequency of links in different directions; the flexibility of the network, the extent to which it remains stable or

---

* And now e.g. Abdallah (2012), Hekkanen (2009).

expands or contracts over time; even the ways in which compromises are born and become necessary. How do translators build and maintain their networks?

Translators too need to compromise and "satisfice" – i.e. accept solutions that are adequate even if not necessarily optimal, and shelve doubts. There comes a point at which further effort to find a better solution is simply not worth the time: the deadline looms, and other problems also need solutions. There is interesting research to be done on how the translating process reaches this satisficing point, and on how the point is recognized by the translator. This research would complement the notion of processing effort used in relevance theory (see Gutt 2000): there, the processing effort in the relevance equation is that invested by the receiver. The study of satisficing, however, would focus more on Levý's "minimax" strategy (1967), where the effort is the translator's.

However, in translation practice it is not the case that there is no central node: there is – the translator. The ANT notion of a project needs to be scaled down to refer to individual translation tasks. These tasks give rise to products that are innovations in a way, for they are new texts, but not in the wider social sense of technical or scientific inventions.

To conclude, here is a list of statements that would characterize such a sociology of the translating process. Each of the italicized terms indicates a complex concept that needs analysing in much more detail than I have had the space to do here.

- The sociology of translating focuses on translating as a social *practice*.
- The practice consists of the performance of translation *tasks* (observable as translation *events*).
- The practice is *institutionalized*, to a greater or lesser extent.
- The tasks are carried out by *translators*, as people with their own subjectivity, interests and values.
- Translators create and use *networks*, with the help of which the tasks are accomplished via cooperation.
- Networks consist of human and non-human *actors* (or *resources*).
- Each actor fulfils a *role* or function (division of labour…).
- Each role has a *status* (public perception…).
- Each task is completed under *constraints* (norms, policies, other networks…).
- Translation practice is governed by some notion of *quality*.

5. Applications

If we can build up a body of descriptive data on the sociology of translation practice under different conditions and in different cultures, its use will be twofold. In the first place, it will help us to understand more about translation causality, i.e. in explaining why translations look the way they do (see Brownlie 2003 for a good example).

In the second place, sociological research can influence our understanding of translation quality. All the research questions I posed above are descriptive ones, but they are all relevant to normative issues of quality. In fact, they are all relevant questions for research on *best* practice. If we can correlate these kinds of research results with measures of the quality of the translation, we might find interesting information about which working methods (including which revision systems) seem to lead to the best translations, under which conditions. One might start by comparing the networks (and network use) of professionals vs. amateurs or trainees, for instance. There is already research on the differing use of some non-human resources by these two groups (e.g. Jääskeläinen 1999).

In this way, research on translation sociology could also serve the needs of institutions developing their own translation services, as well as translator training programmes.[1]

Note

1. An earlier version of this paper was presented at the Third Riga Symposium on Pragmatic Aspects of Translation (November 1–2, 2002); see Chesterman 2003.

PAPER 25

The name and nature of Translator Studies[*]

A number of recent research tendencies in Translation Studies focus explicitly on the translator in some way, rather than on translations as texts. These trends might be grouped under the term "Transla*tor* Studies". The article argues that this new focus is inadequately represented in Holmes' classic map. Evidence of the recent trends is found especially in translation sociology, but also in translation history and in research into the translator's decision-making processes. A broad outline of Translator Studies would cover sociology, culture and cognition, all looking at the translator's agency, in different ways.

Keywords: translator, Holmes, sociology, policy, agent model

1. Translator studies?

James Holmes started his now classic article (1988b, original version 1972) with the observation that when science discovers a new area of ignorance, one of two things tend to happen. The new set of research questions may be incorporated into an existing domain, in which case it becomes a legitimate branch of that domain. Or the new questions may lead to the establishment of a new research field, a new interdiscipline. Holmes argued that, at the time he was writing, the new field of what we now call Translation Studies illustrated the second case, and he gave some space to a discussion of the possible names for this new field. A generation or so later, it now seems that we have an example of his first case: within the field of Translation Studies we may be witnessing the development of a new subfield, a new branch. I suggest we could call this *TranslaTOR Studies*.

As a simple preliminary definition, let us say Translator Studies is the study of translators (and of course interpreters). Of course, all research on (human) translations must surely at least imply that there are indeed translators behind the translations, people behind the texts. But not all translation research takes these people as the primary and explicit focus, the starting point, the central concept of

---

[*] First published in 2009 in *Hermes* 42, 13–22. Reprinted by kind permission of the editors. One reference has been updated. The keywords have been added.

the research question. Examples of the kinds of research that illustrate this focus are given below.

Opinions will vary on whether or not the research trends I am referring to actually constitute a distinct subfield rather than merely a kind of broad perspective on aspects of Translation Studies in general. Perhaps my sketch shows no more than an ongoing shift of emphasis within translation research as a whole. But such shifts may also merit our metatheoretical attention. – Following is an overview of what I see as this emerging subfield, in the form of a brief response to Holmes' original article and the map he discusses there.

2. Back to the map...

The famous map has circulated in many publications, such as Toury 1995: 10. However, the published version of Holmes' original article (1988b) does not actually contain it in diagram form. Curiously, some versions of the figure (such as Toury's) omit the branch on translation policy, which is nevertheless explicitly listed in the article itself. Below is a version of the map including this branch.

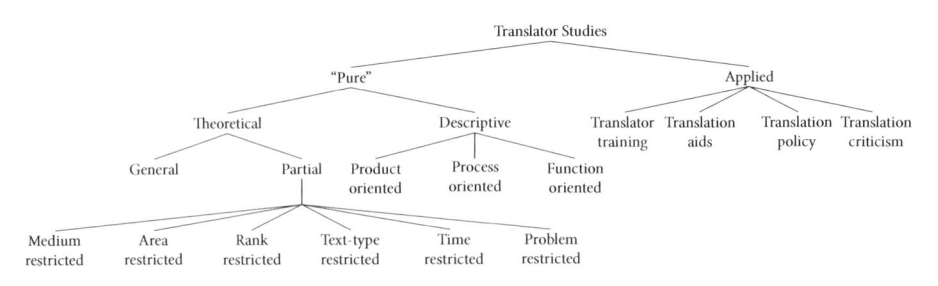

Figure 1. Holmes' map (based on Holmes 1988b).

The map has of course been widely commented on before. Toury (1995: 9f) problematizes the apparent autonomy of Holmes' major division of descriptive research into orientations of product, process and function, and also the relation between "descriptive" and "theoretical" studies. Pym (1998) points to the absence of historical research on the map (although Holmes does mention historical studies of translation, albeit not explicitly translators, in the text). Lambert (1991) argued that the map should have given more weight to contextual and pragmatic factors. Snell-Hornby (1991) argued that the categories of "partial", restricted studies are outdated, and proposed a different kind of map altogether, showing the relations between the interdiscipline of Translation Studies and its neighbouring disciplines. Gile (2005b: 341) points out several problems, particularly concerning the "descriptive" category: applied research can also be descriptive, for instance. Chesterman

(2004c) also queries some of Holmes' apparent assumptions about the relation between theory-building and description. My purpose here, however, is to see to what extent the scope of our putative Translator Studies is represented in the map.

Holmes' general distinctions between pure and applied studies, and between theoretical and descriptive ones, are not relevant to us here. I will start with his types of partial studies (as opposed to general). Holmes says that these deal with specific aspects of translation rather than translation as a whole. The first of these types is medium-restricted studies. Holmes uses the notion of a medium in two different ways. In terms of human vs. machine translation, our proposed subfield of Translator Studies is certainly implied. In terms of written vs. oral media, we can take Translator Studies to be implicitly relevant to both. The other kinds of partial studies (restricted by area or language, textlinguistic rank, text-type, time, translation problem) do not indicate any explicit relevance for Translator Studies, because the main focus of such work is textual. Under time-restricted studies, however, we can obviously place work on the history of translators and interpreters, many of whom were cultural pioneers.

Under descriptive studies Holmes lists those oriented towards product, process or function. Since the products of translation are texts (including the oral variety), this branch on the map does not primarily relate to our new subfield. In Translator Studies, texts are secondary, the translators themselves are primary; this priority leads to quite different kinds of research questions. (This is not to deny that product-oriented research can reveal interesting things about the people behind the texts.)

3. Translation sociology

The process orientation, however, is certainly relevant. Holmes relates this to cognitive studies of the translation act – an area of translation research that has expanded considerably since his time. But he makes no mention at all here of the sociological process of the translation event. True, this is partly implied by what he says on the topic of function-oriented research, which has to do with the reception of translations in the target socio-culture. Holmes even suggests the possibility of what he calls "translation sociology" as a future area of research. This is indeed a prophetic statement, in the light of the recent "sociological turn" in Translation Studies. I have suggested elsewhere (Chesterman 2006b[*]) that such a translation sociology comprises three strands:

---

[*] Paper 24 above.

- the sociology of *translations*, as products in an international market;
- the sociology of *translators*; and
- the sociology of *translating*, i.e. the translating process.

Holmes seems to have foreseen only the first of these strands. The second and third strands are obviously central areas of Translation Studies nowadays. (For examples dealing with both translators and interpreters, see e.g. Heilbron 2000; Bachleiter and Wolf 2004; Diriker 2004; Inghilleri 2005; Wolf and Fukari 2007; Koskinen 2008; van Dam and Zethsen 2008; the special issue (2002) of the sociological journal *Actes de la recherche en sciences sociales,* 144; and the new journal *Translation Studies*.)

The *sociology of translators* covers such issues as the status of (different kinds of) translators in different cultures, rates of pay, working conditions, role models and the translator's habitus, professional organizations, accreditation systems, translators' networks, copyright, and so on. Questions of a different kind under this heading are those relating to gender and sexual orientation, and to power relations, and how these factors affect a translator's work and attitudes. The sociology of translators also covers the public discourse of translation, i.e. evidence of the public image of the translator's profession, as seen e.g. in the press, or in literary works in which one of the central characters is a translator or interpreter (see e.g. Maier 2006, Kurz and Kaindl 2005). Under the same heading I would place research on translators' attitudes to their work, as revealed in essays, interviews, translators' prefaces and notes, etc. Here too I would place the wide field of translators' ideologies and translation ethics: curiously, this is entirely absent from Holmes' map. An extension of this strand would include the study of voluntary, activist translators (see e.g. Baker 2006, especially Chapter 7; Munday 2007).

In this connection, I would like to draw attention to an idea which is given a preliminary airing in Chesterman and Baker (2008). We have become accustomed to use the term "skopos" to denote the intended effect of a translation. We might also make use of the companion term "telos" to denote the personal movation of translators. This would include the reasons why they work in this field in general, and also the reasons why they translate a given text. Voluntary translators in particular, such as activist translators, may have teloi that are specially interesting. Sociological work on the teloi of translators (and of course interpreters) might make worthwhile contributions to a better understanding of their attitudes and personal goals and ethics, and how these are realized in what and how they translate.

A recent incident in Finland illustrates other dimensions of sociological research on translators. An employment advertisement appeared in a newspaper, asking for applications for the following post: "a Russian-speaking translator / interpreter / cleaner" [sic!]. The Finnish translation community reacted immediately, with horror, and protests followed. But the incident reveals worrying aspects of the public perception of the translator's / interpreter's status, attitudes to Russian speakers (the advert was probably targeted at immigrants), and commercial exploitation. It also raised issues concerning employer's ethics. I wonder how typical such advertisements might be?

The *sociology of the translating process*, on the other hand, has to do with the study of the phases of the translation event: translation practices and working procedures, quality control procedures and the revision process, co-operation in team translation, multiple drafting, relations with other agents including the client, and the like. A central concept is that of translation norms, which have been much in evidence in translation research especially since Toury (1995). (For further discussion and references, see e.g. Mossop 2001 and Chesterman 2006b.)

Moving now to the applied branch of Holmes' map, we find three sub-types that are relevant to Translator Studies. One is translator training, which is so obvious that no further comment is needed here. The second is translation policy, which is certainly an area of Translator Studies. On this, Holmes writes:

> The task of the translation scholar in this area is to render informed advice to others in defining the place and role of translators, translating, and translations in society at large: such questions, for instance, as determining what works need to be translated in a given socio-cultural situation, what the social and economic position of the translator is and should be, or [...] what part translating should play in the teaching and learning of foreign languages. ([1988b] 2000: 182)

With hindsight, we may feel that the tone here is somewhat prescriptive. After all, we can also seek to describe and explain translation policies of particular institutions (such as the EU, for example, or a given company or municipality) without necessarily giving them advice. These policies might bear on questions such as whether a commissioned translation should be done by a native speaker of the target language or not, or by a professional translator or not; whether a given type of task should be done in-house or by a freelance translator; what kinds of arbitration procedures are available in cases of dispute; or what kinds of consultation services are available to the translator. This research topic thus extends into Holmes' descriptive branch. Holmes also seems to include here some of the topics I have listed under the sociology of translators, above. Here too, the notion of norms is central, especially Toury's preliminary norms, which deal explicitly with translation policy.

Holmes' third applied sub-type is the study of translation aids. From the point of view of how translators themselves use various aids and resources, this research is clearly part of Translator Studies, being part of the study of the translator's working procedures. The development of the aids themselves, such as the improvement of translation memory systems, lies outside our subfield. Holmes' last sub-type, translation criticism, does not seem to lie within Translator Studies.

4. Towards an agent model

What can we conclude from this brief survey? First of all, Holmes vision of Translation Studies was highly weighted towards texts rather than the people that produce them. This is not surprising, in view of his own special interest in literary translation and research on it. We have found explicit or implicit acknowledgement of Translator Studies at various points on the map, but not in any consistent manner. Our points of contact have been at different levels in Holmes' hierarchy. We have also found some gaps in the map, especially regarding the scope of research on translation sociology, history and ethics. To be fair, such research topics had scarcely yet appeared in 1972. Using Holmes' map, it is difficult to provide a coherent picture of the new subfield, so here is an alternative (from Chesterman 2006b and elsewhere).

Assume that Translation Studies consists of four big branches: textual, cultural, cognitive and sociological. The textual branch deals with all matters textual, and thus by definition lies outside Translator Studies. But the three other branches are all relevant to us here, and indeed offer one way of conceptualizing this subfield of Translation Studies. The cultural branch deals with values, ethics, ideologies, traditions, history, examining the roles and influences of translators and interpreters through history, as agents of cultural evolution. The cognitive branch deals with mental processes, decision-making, the impact of emotions, attitudes to norms, personality, etc. The sociological branch deals with translators'/interpreters' observable behaviour as individuals or groups or institutions, their social networks, status and working processes, their relations with other groups and with relevant technology, and so on. All three branches comprise both theoretical and descriptive studies, and also pure and applied studies.

```
                        Translator Studies
                               |
         ┌─────────────────────┼─────────────────────┐
      Cultural              Cognitive            Sociological
         |                     |                     |
  ideologies, ethics,    mental processes,    networks, institutions,
      history...        emotions, attitudes...  status, workplace processes...
```

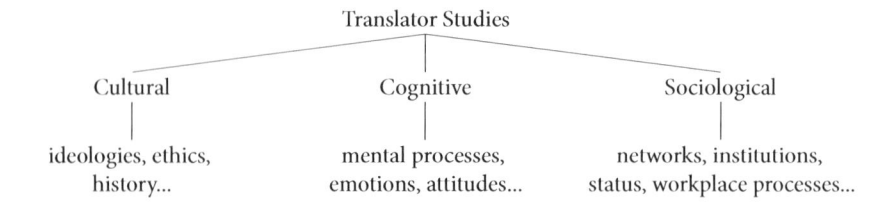

Figure 2. Sketch of Translator Studies.

In terms of Popper's three ontological worlds (e.g. Popper 1972), the objects of study of the cultural branch lie mainly in World 3, the world of objective contents of thought which are in the public domain. The objects of study of the cognitive branch lie in World 2, the sphere of mental states. The objects of study of the sociological branch lie partly in World 1, the world of observable physical phenomena (e.g. actions, behaviours) but partly also in World 2 (subjective ideologies and attitudes) and partly in World 3 (status, public image). The sociological branch is thus ontologically the most complex. It may thus be the most prone to further fragmentation.

A sociological perspective also forces us to adjust our traditional models of the object of our research. I have elsewhere (e.g. Chesterman 2000a[*]) suggested that TS has typically made use of three general models of translation. The first is a comparative model, based on comparing two bodies of text, such as source text and target text or translations and non-translations. The second is a process model, looking at phases of the translation process over time, either at the cognitive level of decision-making or at the observable level of translator behaviour and workplace procedures. The third is a causal model, with many variants. However, the kind of work cited above suggests that some scholars are now using an additional general model focusing not on translations as texts, nor even on the translation process, but on the translators themselves and the other agents involved. Perhaps we could call this the *agent model*.

In the light of the foregoing sketch, we can now return to our preliminary definition of Translator Studies and offer an expanded version: Translator Studies covers research which focuses primarily and explicitly on the agents involved in translation, for instance on their activities or attitudes, their interaction with their social and technical environment, or their history and influence.

---

[*] Paper 10 in this volume.

PAPER 26

Models of what processes?[*]

Toury (1995, 2012) distinguishes between cognitive translation acts on the one hand, and sociological translation events on the other; a translation act is embedded in a translation event, and both acts and events are seen as processes. He also explains three senses of 'translation problem', which relate to different notions of the processes involved in the translation act.

The present paper analyses and develops these ideas. It distinguishes between what are here labelled virtual, reverse-engineered and actual processes of translation acts or events, which correlate with Toury's three senses of 'translation problem'. A few examples are given of models of each kind of process, both classical and more recent ones. Also discussed is the extent to which the various models are predictive and hence testable. To designate the translation process at the historical and cultural level, alongside the mental act and the situational event, the term 'translation practice' is suggested.[1]

Keywords: translation process, translation model, translation act, translation event, translation practice

1. Act and event

Most process research on translation has so far focused on the cognitive dimension; the investigation of sociological processes has not attracted so much attention, although the recent "sociological turn" in translation studies may influence future tendencies (see e.g. Wolf and Fukari 2007). The distinction between these two basic dimensions was already implied by Gideon Toury (1995), in his discussion of natural translation and sources of feedback. Feedback, he wrote, may come from the translation recipients, and also from

---

[*] First published in 2013 in *Translation and Interpreting Studies* 8, 2, 155–168. Reprinted (2015) in Maureen Ehrensberger-Dow, Birgitta Englund Dimitrova, Séverine Hubscher-Davidson and Ulf Norberg (eds), *Describing Cognitive Processes in Translation. Acts and events*. Amsterdam/Philadelphia: Benjamins, 7–20. Reprinted in the present volume with kind permission from John Benjamins Publishing Company [www.benjamins.com].

those who have commissioned the act of translating, and sometimes from the originator of the utterance to be translated as well. When realized by actual persons, these roles (in the sociological sense) – all parts of the interactional makeup of a translating *event* – may, of course, partially overlap.

(1995: 249, emphasis original)

Reading somewhat between the lines here, many scholars (including myself) have taken "act of translating" – or translation *act* – to refer to the cognitive process, whereas the translation *event* is the observable sociological framework in which the cognitive translation act takes place. In the revised version of the book (Toury 2012: 67–68), this distinction is drawn more clearly and developed at some length. The locus of the translation act is said to be "the human brain". Yet Toury insists there that the cognitive cannot be completely separated from the environmental. The relation between the mental act and the situational event is one of "complementarity and containment". This is a position that has also been taken by other scholars such as Risku (2010), who have explored the relevance of the notion of situated cognition to Translation Studies. Toury calls for research on the interaction between these two levels, the mental and the situational. A recent example of how this interaction might be studied is Jones (2011), on poetry translation; this study combines TAPs, interviews, and agent networks.

An act is thus embedded in an event: the event is the sociological or situational context of the act. The event is directly observable: one can follow a translator's overt behaviour, observe phone calls, emails, use of the internet, physical movements, and so on. But the act is not directly observable, one can only make inferences from the behaviour one can see. Even the insertion of electrodes in the brain does not provide direct access to cognition itself, only to the electric pulses and neuron activities etc. which manifest it. A translation event normally involves other actors too, of course, who also perform relevant cognitive acts.

In principle, the distinction between the cognitive translation act and the sociological translation event seems clear, although both terms refer to processes taking place in time; moreover, some models appear to incorporate aspects of both dimensions. In translation, these time scales are very different: one is measured in seconds or microseconds, the other in hours or days, or even months. There does not yet seem to be agreement about how to define precise starting and ending points of a translation act or event, however, or how to conceptualize the overlap between them. Aspects of the event, for instance, such as the details of the brief and the definition of the intended addressees, presumably influence the mindset of the translator and hence the cognitive translation act, perhaps even before he/she even receives the source text. Let us nevertheless suggest that a translation act begins when the translator begins to read the source text, and ends when the translator decides to take no further action in revising the translation (although there might still be further thought on the subject). The act may of course be interrupted. A translation event, on the other hand, could be said to begin when the translator accepts the job (or perhaps when the client begins to look for a translator?), and ends with, say, payment of the bill (or perhaps when the first recipient reads the translation?). Translation events have been investigated in different ways, via workplace studies, revision procedures, the analysis of translator teams and networks, translator agency, and so on (see e.g. Kinnunen and Koskinen 2010). Here too, interruptions are common.

This paper mainly concerns translation, but it is worth noting that, in interpreting, the distinction between act and event often seems less clear-cut. But the interpreting act and event can still be studied separately, as indeed they are, using different kinds of methods and models.

2. Models and problems

The term "model" is significantly polysemous in the philosophy of science, where debates range about what a model is ontologically, what kinds of models there are, and how models relate to theories. For instance, some models aim to be representations of a phenomenon, in some way or other, while others have the form of an explanation (like a law). Some models are more explicit than others; some are formulated in mathematical terms, others are based on analogy (such as the computer model of the mind). Within Translation Studies, too, there are many different views. I take a model here to be a preliminary kind of theory, one which claims some relation of similarity with the object that is modelled; a model, on this definition, purports to be isomorphic with its object, in some way. In some kinds of models this isomorphism is obvious. Think of those models of the solar system, before and after Copernicus, that you saw at school. In others, such as mathematical or computational models, the isomorphism is more abstract. Models in this sense show what are thought to be the main components or elements of a phenomenon, what are thought to be the main relations between them and their main functions. I shall assume here that models are basically systematic descriptions, descriptive hypotheses, which claim to *represent* something. True, such a model may also imply an explanation, for instance if the relations included are causal. Consider for instance a simple model of a primitive steam engine, showing how increasing the temperature of water in a container eventually causes an increase of pressure when the water boils, and this pressure then causes something to move somewhere else in the modelled system; the resulting movement is thus explained by the model.

Explanations of various kinds are also implied by the predictiveness of models, insofar as they are indeed predictive. In a weak sense, a general descriptive model implicitly predicts that it will also apply to yet-to-be-studied instances of the phenomenon in question, indeed to all possible instances belonging to the same set. In this weak sense, a descriptive model could be said to be explanatory in that it generalizes, by predicting applicability to unknown instances (on explaining via generalization, see Chesterman 2008b[*]). However, explanations and predictions do not inevitably go hand in hand, as is well known.

In a stronger sense, a model can be predictive of consequences that can themselves be tested empirically. A classic example from chemistry is Mendeleev's 19th-century model of the elements, the periodic table, which arranged the elements by group and by atomic weight. The first versions of this model had gaps at certain points; the model predicted that these gaps would eventually be filled, as new elements were discovered. And they were. As we shall see, not many models of the translation process appear to be particularly predictive.

In what follows I will distinguish between different kinds of models of the cognitive translation process according to the ontological status of what is being modelled. These different kinds of models actually represent different senses of 'translation process', although all are concerned with the cognitive translation act, not the sociological event. My presentation of model types is based on Toury's discussion (2002; and 2012, Chapter 2) of three different senses of the term 'translation problem'. Toury does not give labels to these different senses, but refers to them as problem$_1$, problem$_2$ and problem$_3$. In brief, Toury's distinction is as follows. The first sense is the potential problem of the translatability of a given source-text item into a given target language, under given conditions: how might this ST item be translated here? A problem in the second sense is identified by starting with a given target-text item that functions as a factual translation solution, and then attempting in retrospect to reconstruct the translation problem for which it has been selected as a solution, and also to reconstruct the thinking that led the translator to this solution. And the third sense is the notion of a problem as it is observed to be experienced by the translator, during the process of a given act of translation, via traces left e.g. by interim solutions, by verbal reflection, or by pauses in the process. In Toury's revised version of his book (2012), these three senses of 'translation problem' are argued to correspond to different senses of the translation act.

With these senses in mind, consider what they imply for an understanding of different models of the process of the translation act. I propose to distinguish three kinds of models: models of *virtual processes*, corresponding to Toury's first

---

[*] Paper 12 in this volume.

sense of 'problem'; those of *reverse-engineered processes*, corresponding to Toury's second sense; and those of *actual processes*, corresponding to his third sense. I now look at these types in more detail, and give some examples.

3. Models of virtual processes

First, consider a model of what I will call a *virtual process*: this would be the potential path from one sense of 'translation problem' to a potential solution, showing for instance the possible strategies for the translation of an allusion or a pun (taken as translation problems, in Toury's sense 1). Such a model is pedagogical or advisory/prescriptive in nature, and starts with something in the source text that is treated as a translation problem, or as we saw Toury put it, a problem of translatability. It thus takes a prospective approach. Based on intuition, or experience, or on the analysis of many translations, the model then outlines possible courses of action leading to possible solutions, in theory. It is a simplified, idealized model, of possible decision processes leading to acceptable solutions (although, clearly, real translators might not behave optimally). Such a model might also purport to represent the translation process in general, not just the solution of a given problem. Models of the virtual process are predictive in the weak sense that if translators follow the advice illustrated by the model, it is presumably assumed that the results will tend to be more acceptable than if the advice is not followed. In other words, the model implies a prediction that its use will lead to beneficial effects: hence its usefulness in the classroom. In principle, therefore, these models are testable: we can test whether their use really does lead to better translations than cases where they are not used. (But do we have any such tests?)

An early example of such a virtual model is Nida's (e.g. 1969) well-known three-stage model, comprising analysis, transfer and restructuring, with obvious pedagogical aims. Nord's "looping model" (1991a) takes Nida's pedagogical approach a step further. She starts with the analysis of the skopos, then the analysis of the source text, followed by the production of the translation. The model loops back and forth between these three. Feedback comes from the emerging target text itself, too, as later decisions affect earlier ones. Hönig (1995) proposes an "ideal" flow-chart model (1995: 51), including the translator's macro- and micro-strategies, monitoring, etc. Interestingly, he explicitly compares his virtual model with Krings' actual one (see below).

Levý's game-theoretical model (1967) takes a teleological point of view of the virtual translation process, in which the translation act is represented as a series of decisions, which are like moves in a game. Alternative solutions to a given ST segment are generated, assessed according to specified criteria (such as stylistic naturalness vs. semantic closeness, or type of implied audience). Most of the examples he analyses are modelled in terms of binary decisions. Levý takes the process of translating to be "a game with complete information"; this means a game where every decision and move is influenced by the knowledge of previous decisions and their consequences.

Along similar lines, but focusing on a particular translation problem (in Toury's sense 1) rather than translation in general, Leppihalme's study (1997) offers a model of a decision-making tree, incorporating an implicit suggestion that this is a helpful way to arrive at a possible, or optimal, solution for the translation of different kinds of allusions.

4. Models of reverse-engineered processes

Corresponding to Toury's second sense of 'problem', there are models of what I will call a *reverse-engineered process*. These aim to reconstruct the possible or even probable route taken to a given factual solution (or set of solutions), as in reverse engineering. For instance, as outlined above, from a target-text segment we infer a possible translation problem in the corresponding source segment, and then speculate on the most plausible sequence of actions or decisions leading to the given solution, considering linguistic factors, likely motivations, available resources and constraints and so on. In other words, we ask "how could the translator have arrived at this solution?"

Such models are often implied in studies focusing on translation or interpreting errors (however these are defined): given the error, the possible or probable antecedent decision-making stages are inferred, with the aim of determining likely causes of the error. They are thus potentially predictive, in that they can in principle predict that the presence of certain conditions or aspects of the decision-making process will increase the probability of such errors. In pedagogical use, such models are also used in the retrospective reconstruction of (probable) decisions leading to successful translations (see e.g. many examples in Kußmaul 2007, and similar translation manuals).

Gile's Effort Model for simultaneous interpreting (revised in Gile 2009) can be interpreted as one example of this kind of model, because it looks like a possible representation of conditions for a reverse-engineered process, rather than a model of the actual process itself. It infers the existence of three basic 'Efforts': the Listening and Analysis Effort, the Production Effort (including self-monitoring) and the short-term Memory Effort, plus a Coordination Effort for processing capacity management. Errors are predicted when one or another of these Efforts is overburdened.

Another example of this kind of model is illustrated in a study by Shreve et al. (2011). Looking at speech disfluencies in sight translation, the authors infer that these may be caused by what they call visual interference. This study does not set out an explicit model, but appears to assume that such a model would comprise components such as comprehension, transfer, production, and in this case also reading. Like other TAP researchers, Shreve et al. assume in general that (longer) pauses indicate problems or points where special efforts are needed.

5. Models of actual processes

The third kind of model aims to represent a process in real time. We could call it a concurrent model, of an *actual process*. Such models make use of data derived from observation of the process as it takes place, using such methods as think-aloud protocols, keyboard logs, eye-tracking, and the like. They are thus different from reverse-engineered models in that they observe the process as it unfolds, rather than retrospectively inferring from the end-result how this result might have arisen. (True, a model of an actual process also involves inferences concerning the nature of the unobservable cognitive activities presumably taking place.) Models of an actual process are different from virtual models in that they are descriptive, not prescriptive (see e.g. Kußmaul 2007: 91).

Krings' model of the actual process (1986), based on TAP data, is a grouping of types of strategies (of comprehension, retrieval, decision-making, monitoring and reduction) to solve problems of different kinds. Lörscher's model (1991) aimed to represent the abstract kinds of "strategies" translators use when they come to a segment of source text that they cannot translate routinely: they have to stop and think. Lörscher's strategies are thus problem-solving ones, and do not represent the whole of the translation act. Examples of such strategies are: the realization of a translation problem; its verbalization; formulation of a tentative solution; assessing this solution. The classification is based on TAP data, with a few non-professional translators. What is modelled is part of an observed process, at a very general level. He concludes that the strategies he discusses are unlikely to be specific to translation itself, but pertain to text-processing generally. Jakobsen's recent work with Translog and eye-tracking (e.g. 2011) is of considerable interest as an approach to the observed cognitive process, i.e. what I have called the actual process. Among his results he cites data (2011, 40) suggesting that at least on some occasions, comprehension, formulation of a translation and actual typing could not possibly always be in sequence, linearly, but overlap; this is because some recorded chunks are so long they could not possibly have been held in short-term memory. In other words, there must have been some parallel processing going on. An alternative interpretation of these results might argue that they go against the assumption that there are separate "modules" for memory, formulation and physical execution (typing) in the first place.

On the basis of his eye-tracking and keystroke data, Jakobsen summarizes the translation "micro-cycle" as a series of six steps, which he presents as a "small algorithm" (2011: 48).

1. Moving the gaze to read the next chunk of new source text (and constructing a translation of it)
2. Shifting the gaze to the target text to locate the input area and read the current target-text anchor word(s)
3. Typing the translation of the source-text chunk
4. Monitoring the typing process and the screen outcome
5. Shifting the gaze to the source text to locate the relevant reading area
6. Reading the current source-text anchor word(s)

As thus formulated, these steps partly refer to the translation act and partly to the event. Typing is an observable feature, and hence pertains to the translation event; constructing a translation and monitoring, however, are cognitive acts. Jakobsen adds that specifically steps 3 and 4 are not necessarily in linear sequence; that there may be a good deal of recursion; and that steps can be skipped. Steps move sometimes from source to target and sometimes from target to source.

When models of actual processes are sufficiently formalized, computational models of the translation act can be developed, with the goal of improving interactive Machine Translation systems. Carl (2012), for example, reports research of this kind, based on the actual behaviour of expert translators. This behaviour is studied via keystroke logging and eye-tracking, but the derived "production rules" include inferred mental operations such as shifting attention and actually translating, as well as the observable actions of shifting gaze and typing. Carl also outlines a statistical model of the process studied, which appears to match actual human behaviour more closely. This model so far only deals with "unchallenged" (i.e. problem-free, routine) translation.

6. Relations between types of models

The relations between models of these three kinds of processes prompt a number of questions. In the first place, whose processes are being studied? Much of the research on actual processes has compared novice translators to professionals or experts, on the assumption that something can thus be learned about the development of translation competence, or about potential application in translator training (see e.g. Jääskeläinen 1999, Englund Dimitrova 2005). There has thus been an implicit or explicit quality variable involved: it is often the cognitive processes of *good* translators that we are really interested in. Kußmaul (2007), for instance, is particularly interested in successful, creative translation solutions.

There is a potential problem here, concerning the relation between virtual processes and actual ones: our simplified models of virtual processes may be pedagogically useful, but they may not in fact correspond to what professionals actually do. (For an early discussion of this issue, see Lörscher 1989.) Is there evidence, for instance, that translators proceed through a logical series of binary decisions, as suggested by some virtual models? (All translators? Or just some types?) Models of virtual processes can thus generate predictions that can be tested.

Similarly, if reverse-engineered processes can be shown to lead, in theory, to a given solution, to what extent might such a process correspond to an actual process which did lead to this solution? What might be the significance of the realization that two or more different processes might arrive at the same solution? Might reverse-engineering even suggest more efficient ways of proceeding? Or is the point of reverse-engineering models only to generate questions and then perhaps hypotheses: *could* the process have been like this? And how might reverse-engineered models relate to virtual ones?

Models of actual processes are likely to prove a good deal more complex, and involve much more variation, than models of the first two process types, which naturally tend to be idealized and simplified. Of course, any model may turn out to be inaccurate, incomplete, or simply wrong, if it makes false predictions. Most of the examples mentioned do not score highly on predictiveness, except in the pedagogical sense of predicting their own usefulness in training, and in the weak descriptive sense of purporting to be general models. None seem to be strongly predictive, in the sense of a model exposing itself to the risk of being falsified by predictions that are not realized.

In terms of testability, we could say that models of reverse-engineered processes could be checked to some extent by retrospective interviews, or tested against other kinds of triangulated data elicited during the process itself, as indeed is done (e.g. Englund Dimitrova 2005). However, there is no guarantee that models of a reconstructed process necessarily represent the *actual process* which terminated in a given translation.

7. Some models of the translation event

Models of the sociological event have been rarer than those of the translation act; in many cases they are only implicit. My first, simple example is from the professional translator Robert Bly (1984), who wrote a classic essay about his own way of translating poetry (specifically, a Rilke poem). He summarized this as eight steps.

1. Make a literal version of the poem.
2. Check the meaning in depth.
3. Polish the English.
4. Naturalize the language to spoken English.
5. Check that the translation is still true to the mood of the original.
6. Pay attention to the sound. Read the translation aloud.
7. Get a native speaker to react to the translation.
8. Re-read all previous drafts; check other people's translations; do the final draft.

As a representation of what Bly says he himself does, the stages represent a generalized report of actual empirical processes, but as prescriptive "advice" they describe an ideal, virtual process.

One of the earliest and simplest event models proposed by a TS scholar was Sager's (1994) four-stage one: specification (understanding the client's instructions, checking that the brief is appropriate and feasible); preparation (finding the necessary resources, terminology, and so on); translation; and evaluation (revision). This model of the translation working procedure interestingly places translation itself (presumably that phase of the event that represents the translation act) as a separate stage, distinct from other activities. Sager's stages are in an obvious linear sequence, and also seem to represent an ideal type of process: a virtual process. In real life, for instance, a professional translator may start translating at once, before even reading the whole of the source text and before any preparation: it would depend on the text in question and how routine the task was. Admittedly, Sager's stages are formulated at a very general level of delicacy or granularity, and thus hide much potential variation.

Skopos Theory (Reiß and Vermeer 1984) and its close relative, the Theory of Translational Action (Holz-Mänttäri 1984) are also implicitly event models. They incorporate a number of actors, not just the translator. In Holz-Mänttäri's model, the stage even begins to look crowded: we find the Initiator, the Commissioner, the ST Producer, the TT Producer (i.e. the translator), the TT User, and the TT Receiver. And they view translation as an act of communication in a sociological or situational context: hence the importance of the skopos.

Studies of interim solutions and the revision process map sequences of changes made at different stages, as one could do with Bly's evolving versions of his Rilke translation. Englund Dimitrova's (2005) model of the translation event has three phases: initial planning, text generation, and revising. Self-revision is seen to occur both during the writing phase and after it. Englund Dimitrova notes that the advent of computers has probably altered revision routines, as it allows easy and instant revision, with more scope for non-linear working procedures (2005: 136).

Revision by others obviously occurs at the post-writing phase. Bly's model includes "another native speaker". If there are several "others", as in Nordman's (2009) study of legal translation from Swedish to Finnish, the whole translation event can be plotted as a chain involving different actors in sequence: the initial translator (or translator team), then various legal and language revisers in turn.

The various "others" involved in the translation event can be naturally mapped as nodes in a network, resulting in a nexus model of the sociological process (cf. e.g. Koskinen 2008, Kinnunen and Koskinen 2010). Actor Network Theory has been used by a number of scholars, as a way of formalizing some aspects of such networks (see e.g. Buzelin 2005, Jones 2011). Such models show multiple connections between nodes, with some nodes becoming more dominant than others. And nodes do not have to be animate (in Actor Network Theory at least), which allows the possibility of incorporating all kinds of electronic resources into the model.

Some research using an implicit event model highlights the difficulty of determining when a translation event ends. For instance, Künzli and Ehrensberger-Dow (2011) study the effects of a particular kind of subtitling on audiences. Earlier, I suggested that an end-point might be specified when the translator receives payment, or perhaps when the first recipient reads the translation. But suppose the translation is never read? Studies of reader response and reception nevertheless seem highly relevant to the translation event, if only because of the way the translator's knowledge or beliefs about implied readers can affect translation decisions. This is in fact the point of the article in question: it appears that readers, or at least some readers, may be able to cope with longer and more complex subtitles than the current norms suppose, which would then allow the subtitler to translate more fully.

In terms of testability, none of the event models mentioned is strongly predictive.

8. The translation practice?

In addition to cognitive and sociological processes, we can also see Translation Studies in the context of a larger process of historical and cultural evolution, marked by changing traditions, norms and fashions, the careers of major influential translators, and so on. Translation Studies does not seem to have an accepted term to describe translation as a phenomenon on this level, a term that would match 'act' and 'event'. Perhaps 'practice' might do. Long-term trends in this historical process seem to include deprofessionalization and dehumanization: cf. the increasing use of crowd-sourcing and of machine translation. Shorter-term "historical" processes have been studied in terms of the acquisition of translator competence or expertise, in longitudinal developmental studies (e.g. Schmidt 2005, Göpferich 2009.) In the longer time-scale of human evolution, the practice of translation can be seen as one means developed by homo sapiens for managing a kind of heterogeneity, coping with communication across linguistic difference.

In terms of process modelling, it is worth noting that historical and cultural studies tend not to aim at, or stop with, temporal models of processes: history is more than just one damn thing after another… Such studies may set out to build descriptive networks, like those used to represent the translation event (see e.g. Pym 1998: 86ff). But the aim is usually to find cause and effect relations (cf. Pym 1998: 143ff).

9. Concluding remarks

If models incorporate causality in some way, they can make strong predictions and thus be tested. Some of the cognitive models we glanced at above do include causal factors: Gile's Effort Model, for instance; and to some extent Levý's decision-making model, in that decisions are seen to be partly based on (i.e. caused by) cost-benefit calculations on the pros and cons of various alternatives. But most of the ones we have looked at are non-causal, so far; at least, they are not *explicitly* causal. Retrospective methods such as interviews or error analysis may suggest causal factors, but these are inferred via the logic of reverse engineering. The challenge is then to test a reverse-engineered model against real-life translation, against an actual process.

A similar challenge faces scholars who draw pedagogical inferences from their descriptive models, as these inferences also imply a cause-and-effect dimension. But we need more empirical tests of the validity of such inferences: whether, for instance, translation quality would be improved by the adoption of such-and-such a model as a basis for translator training. We do not know enough about how predictive our models might be.

Indeed, some scholars may feel that we are not at all ready yet to build anything more than very simple models, and that research should proceed by generating and testing specific hypotheses: if supported, these hypotheses may then be synthesized into a complex (and causal) model. One recurring observation is that many studies indicate a great deal of variation across subjects, both in translation and in interpreting. This makes generalization risky; but without generalizations we cannot build models.

If one does set out to construct a model, I conclude, it is important to be clear about what kind of process one is seeking to model; i.e. about what kind of model one is building, based on what facts and/or hypotheses, and what assumptions. What testable hypotheses might the model generate? What kind of predictions is the model capable of making, if any? If it can make explicit predictions, it can be tested, and maybe progress can be made.[1]

Note

1. My sincere thanks are due to the two critical referees who made many helpful suggestions on the initial version of this paper. I should undoubtedly have taken more of them on board than I have been able to.

SECTION IX

Translation ethics

The last couple of decades have seen renewed interest in translation ethics (see e.g. these special issues of *The Translator*: 2001, 7 (2), The Return to Ethics; 2012, 18 (2), Non-professionals Translating and Interpreting: participatory and engaged perspectives; and 2010, 16 (2), Translation and Violent Conflict). We have moved beyond the traditional ethics of sameness, via an ethics of difference (e.g. Venuti 1998), to propose broader and more complex viewpoints. Anthony Pym (1997, 2012) helped to shift the focus from texts to people, and other scholars have further extended ethical analyses to the way quality is affected by working conditions (e.g. Abdallah 2012), an approach some are beginning to refer to as the ergonomics of translation (e.g. Ehrensberger-Dow and O'Brien 2015). Others have investigated ethical aspects of the work and treatment of translators and interpreters under wartime conditions (Baker 2006, Footit and M. Kelly 2012). Yet another new focus has been the ethical questions concerned with non-professional translators such as activist translators and crowdsourced translators (e.g. McDonough Dolmaya 2011a). Philosophical and historical perspectives on translation ethics are represented in different ways by Koskinen (2000b), S. Berman and Wood (2005) and Campbell and Mills (2012). Court interpreting raises its own special problems as well: Inghilleri (2012) argues that an interpreter's personal ethics also has a role to play in professional work. For a critical survey of seventeen codes of professional ethics, see McDonough Dolmaja (2011b) – this is particularly relevant to Paper 27.

Paper 27 comes from the 2001 special issue of *The Translator* on translation ethics.

Paper 28 illustrates how the four models introduced there can be applied to a particular case. I have discussed this case in a number of seminars on translation ethics, as an illustrative example of an ethical problem, and participants have sometimes wondered why the offending date was not simply translated as "in the spring" or "in April". A good point!

PAPER 27

Proposal for a Hieronymic Oath[*]

Four current models of translation ethics are described, based on the ideas of representation, service, communication, and norms. There are problems with all these models: they are in several respects incompatible, and have different ranges of application. An alternative approach is therefore offered based on Alasdair MacIntyre's ideas about virtues and the deontic force of excellence in a social practice. This leads to a fifth possible model, an ethics of professional commitment: cf. Maria Tymoczko's suggestion that translation is a commissive act. At the centre of such a model there might be an official oath, comparable e.g. to the Hippocratic Oath for the medical profession. I end with a proposal for a Hieronymic Oath for translators.

Keywords: ethics, values, virtues, MacIntyre, excellence, commitment, oath

In the Hopi Indian culture, the Spider Grandmother is the mythical figure who oversees the spiritual development of mankind. She gave two basic ethical rules, not just to Hopis but to all men. "She said, 'Don't go around hurting each other,' and she said, 'Try to understand things'" (Heat-Moon 1984: 187).

These two ethical principles – one negative and one positive – may take us a long way towards an ethics of translation. This paper first offers an analysis of the current state of affairs, and then offers an alternative proposal.

1. **Four current models of translation ethics**

I will start by crystallizing the multiplicity of ideas about translation ethics into four basic models. There are overlaps between some aspects of these models, but I will mostly disregard them here.

---

[*] First published in 2001 in *The Translator* 7, 2: 139–154. Reprinted by kind permission of the journal's current copyright holders, Taylor and Francis Group. See http://www.tandfonline.com/toc/rtrn20/current. The reference to the EU *Fight the Fog* campaign has been updated, and a couple of reference dates have been added. One cut has been made: the section originally dealing with the Code of Practice of the American Translators Association is no longer valid, as their current code (dating from 2010) is formulated rather differently and would require different comments. The keywords have been added.

Ethics of representation

This model of translation ethics goes way back to the ideal of the faithful interpreter, and to the translation of sacred texts. The ethical imperative is to represent the source text, or the source author's intention, accurately, without adding, omitting or changing anything. A contemporary manifestation of this ethic is to be found in the EU translation services: political reasons dictate that EU documents in whatever official EU language are legally equivalent to any other language version, perfect representatives of each other, and that no single version is privileged as a source text, in theory. (For a detailed discussion of the EU translation situation, see Koskinen 2000a.)

Another line of inheritance of this ethic has to do with the long tradition of representing the Other, the relation with alterity. It comes to the fore particularly during the German Romantic movement, and in subsequent theoretical contributions stressing the value of allowing the Other to appear in its own light, without being domesticated: cf. the general arguments of Schleiermacher, Berman (e.g. 1984) and Venuti (e.g. 1995). These theoretical positions stress that every translation is an interpretation, and inevitably incorporates difference. The translator's ethical dilemma is then how to choose and transmit a good – or the best – interpretation. To represent is to interpret.

If a translation *mis*represents the Other, the result may be a prejudiced, biased, ideologically suspect version, which has unethical consequences for intercultural perceptions and relations. An ethics of representation thus highlights the values of fidelity and truth: the translator must represent the source text, or source author's intention, or even the source culture, faithfully and truly, like a good mirror. So-called abusive fidelity (P. Lewis 1985) allows the Other to appear as Other, as different, in a foreignizing or minoritizing translation. Postmodern approaches problematize the possibility of faithful representation and stress the ambivalence of the relations between source and target texts and cultures (see e.g. Koskinen 2000b), but here too the central ethical problem is fundamentally one of representation, of something "standing for" something else. In this sense, the representation model of ethics is actually a semiotic one: a translation is a sign of the original.

Ethics of service

A very different kind of approach is based on the concept of translation as a commercial service, performed for a client. This is the kind of ethics that underlies (usually implicitly) much of the thinking on functional models of translation, especially those of Holz-Mänttäri (1984) and the skopos theorists. A translator is deemed to act ethically if the translation complies with the instructions set by the client, and fulfils the aim of the translation as set by the client and accepted or negotiated by the translator. A prime quality of good translator-servants is thus loyalty; they are loyal above all to the client, but also to the target readers and to the original writer (cf. Nord 1991a: 29). They are also efficient (they do not waste time or money – especially the client's); and perhaps also as invisible as possible. They provide a commercial service, and clients expect value for money. An ethics of service also underlines the value of time, of meeting deadlines etc.

Ethics of communication

This general model of ethics has received more attention during the late 20th century, e.g. in the work of Levinas. Here, the emphasis is not on representing the Other but on communicating with him/her. To recognize the Other as a "subject", with whom one can indeed communicate, is a primary ethical act, for Levinas, because this step takes you out of your own ego-confined world. (For an accessible but very brief introduction to Levinas, see Melby 1995: 119f. See also Levinas 1982, 1987.) In translation theory, the focus is naturally on communicating across linguistic or cultural boundaries.

A recent contribution which highlights the ethical aspects of such communication is that of Pym (1997, 2000; for a detailed critique, see Koskinen 2000b). For Pym, the goal of intercultural communication is the mutual benefit deriving from cooperation, and the ethical goal of translation is to further intercultural cooperation between parties who are "Other" to each other. An ethical translator therefore translates in such a way as to optimize this cooperation. (An ethical translator might also decide, notes Pym, that it would sometimes be more beneficial not to translate at all, but recommend some other means of eventually communicating, such as learning the other language.) An ethical translator's primary loyalty, on this view, is to the translator's profession, situated in an intercultural space, and hence to the whole system that makes intercultural communication possible, rather than to source text or culture or to target readers or culture. For Pym, the investment in translation (by client or translator) should not exceed the eventual mutual benefits accruing – here, his position is similar to that taken by an ethics of service.

From the point of view of communication, the ethical translator is a mediator working to achieve cross-cultural understanding. Understanding of what? Of each other, ultimately. But this is achieved via an understanding of texts, messages, signs, intentions, meanings, etc. There is a well-known conceptual minefield here, which I will not explore in this context, but with respect to translation we can usefully speak of understanding in the following sense: understanding a translation means arriving at an interpretation that is compatible with the communicative intention of the author and the translator (and in some cases also the client), to a degree sufficient for a given purpose.

Norm-based ethics

This model of translation ethics has arisen either explicitly or implicitly from descriptive translation studies and norm theory. Following Toury (e.g. 1995), descriptive translation studies investigates the norms that determine or influence translation production and reception. These norms state what acceptable translation products should look like, and they vary from period to period and from culture to culture. The norms thus represent expectations, mainly in the target culture, about what translations are supposed to be like in that culture at that time. The norms are generally accepted (in a particular culture) insofar as they appear to serve prevailing values, including ethical values such as truth and trust (see Chesterman 1997a: 169f.). Behaving ethically thus means behaving as one is expected to behave, in accordance with the norms; not surprising the reader or client. Any major breach of these expectations – for instance, a translation that is clearly more literal than the reader might expect, or one that has a specific ideological slant, or is abridged or extensively adapted – should, on this view, be signalled overtly by the translator, e.g. in a preface. One of the central values underlying this model is that of trust: if translators behave in predictable, norm-conforming ways, it is easier to trust them – and the profession as a whole.

2. **Problems**

There are several reasons for the current unease in translation studies about questions of ethics. One is the lack of compatibility between available models. Each of the four models outlined above highlights different ethical values: truth (representation), loyalty (service), understanding (communication), trust (norm-based). Are some values higher than others? In the sense that some may depend on or promote others, the answer to this question is perhaps "yes". People who speak the truth are more likely to be trusted than those who do not. People who are loyal are also likely to be trusted by those whom they are loyal to (but not necessarily by outsiders; indeed, an outsider might have good reason *not* to trust them). Truth and trust may lead to understanding. However, none of the models is very clear about what the appropriately ethical action might be in a situation where values (or loyalties) clash. On what grounds can we simply say: choose this model when it seems appropriate, and that model at other times? Would such a solution itself be ethical?

The different models do nevertheless have different scopes and limitations of application: some models have been applied more to literary or Biblical translation, others to technical or administrative translation. The representation model is vulnerable to arguments about the impossibility of totally true representation; about the relative status of originals and translations; about the illusion of perfect equivalence. How might it be applied to translation tasks that call for radical rewriting or adaptation or improvement to the text? For some scholars, the representation model nevertheless seems to be the only one, since ethical problems are sometimes discussed almost entirely from this angle (e.g. Lane-Mercier 1997).

The service model stresses the translator's expertise, but also seems to make a virtue of translatorial invisibility, weakening the translator's autonomy to some extent; it might even be argued that it can promote a mercenary attitude and a meek and passive habitus. How might it be applied to a freelance translator initiating the translation of an avant-garde Italian poet?

The communication model risks expanding the translator's responsibility to cover aspects of intercultural relations that may have more to do with clients and readers than with the translator. Suppose the intercultural understanding and cooperation is successful, but promotes evidently unethical ends, as for instance in the task of translating instructions for making a cheap nail-bomb? Is this also the translator's responsibility? How do we apply a communication ethics to an EU situation in which a document may not be translated in order to be actually read by anyone, but simply in order to legitimately exist, for political and ideological reasons, in another language?

The norm-based model seems unduly conservative, underplaying the possibility of change or improvement; but norms do change over time, partly as a result of translatorial action. How might it be applied to a situation where a translator – perhaps even as requested by the client – seeks to surprise the readers, to challenge their expectations, and wishes to strengthen this effect by declining to include a warning preface?

A further difficulty is the way in which different models focus on different levels of ethics. The norm-based model and to some extent the representation model operate mainly on the micro-ethical level, concerning the relation between the translator and the text. The other models look more to the macro-ethical level, at the relation between the translator and the wider world. How are we to decide where the ethical responsibility of the translator stops – or does it stop at all? Translators are of course responsible for the words they choose to write, but to what extent are they responsible for the effects these words may have? On what readers? Readers may be other than intended ones, after all; and readers of some future generation may react very differently to the same words. Many scholars over the past few years have pointed to the wider cultural and ideological implications of translatorial decisions. How do we define the limits of the translator's responsibility?

And what of the world's responsibility towards translators? This aspect too might be considered to belong to a general ethics of translation and translatorial behaviour. (See, for instance, UNESCO's Nairobi Recommendation.) However, I shall not pursue this theme in this article.

Our four models also differ with respect to the basic kinds of ethics they espouse. The service and norm-based models are both examples of contractual ethics. That is, ethical decisions here are based on prior agreements, contracts, expectations, either explicit or internalized; unethical decisions are criticized because they break a norm or contract. So I act like this because this is the norm, because this is the way the provider of a service should behave, this is what the translation instructions say. On the other hand, the representation and especially the communication models are examples of utilitarian ethics. That is, ethical decisions are based on their predicted results; unethical decisions can be criticized because of their undesired results. So I act like this because I want to facilitate communication, or to improve intercultural relations: I want to have this kind of effect on you, the reader.

A good illustration of the problem of incompatible ethical models is to be found in the different interpretations of the value of clarity. For many translators, clarity is an ethical value which they seek to promote in their work. It is an ethical value for many theorists too, myself included; and even for translation service administrators – see e.g. the *Fight the Fog* campaign in the EU, which sought to promote clarity both in original documents and in translations.[*] To be unclear is felt to be a betrayal of loyalty to the reader, and also to the client, who presumably wishes readers to understand a translation. Popper ([1945] 1962: 308) has even argued that clarity is a precondition for all rational communication, without which society cannot exist. But what is meant by clarity?

Different interpretations are offered by our different models of ethics. In the representation model, clarity means transparency: the translation should be such that the original is clearly visible, the Other is clearly present, represented as such, undistorted. This would usually lead to some kind of foreignizing translation. On

---

[*] See now (2016) <http://ec.europa.eu/dgs/translation/publications/magazines/languagestranslation/documents/issue_01_en.pdf>

the other hand, if the desired representation is of the author's intention rather than the source text as such, it is this intention that should presumably be made transparently visible, and the result might well be a domesticating translation. Returning to the mirror metaphor: clarity means that the mirror must be clean and non-distorting, reflecting whatever it is intended to reflect. (Intended by whom?)

In the service and communication models, clarity is interpreted as accessibility. This is a textual quality determining the ease with which readers can understand a text, its meaning, the message, the author's intention. A clear translation, in this sense, is one that can be understood without undue time and effort. Here, the degree of clarity affects the relation between translation and reader, not translation and original.

In the norm-based model, clarity is relativized to target culture expectations: the form and degree of the required clarity depends on these expectations. Critics of suggestions that clarity is a universal communication value usually interpret clarity as meaning 'directness', i.e. the absence of e.g. irony or understatement. These critics then accuse Grice [1975] or Leech [1983], for instance, of making Western Protestant discourse values into universals. None of our ethical models seem to take this view of clarity, however. Indeed, the norm-based model specifically rejects it. This model says: be as clear as the situation demands, in the way that your readers will expect. In other words, do not be so unclear that your text is unacceptably inaccessible to the people whom you would like to read it. The model stresses that the implementation of the value of clarity is context-bound and also culture-bound.

All in all, these four models are thus only partial ones; each one covers only part of the general ethical field of translation, and each seems therefore inadequate on its own. Maybe we should go back to the beginning and start again. The following section explores an alternative route to an ethics of translation.

3. The deontic force of excellence

We might start with virtues rather than values. This is the position taken by the philosopher Alasdair MacIntyre (1981), who argues interestingly against founding a general ethics on values, or indeed on rights, because of the irreconcilable conflicts between values and the lack of any rational way of prioritizing one right over another. MacIntyre's suggestion is to return to the notion of a virtue, which he analyses in terms of social roles. Social roles, in turn, are embedded in social practices – and this is where his ideas seem highly relevant to any attempt to construct an ethics for a profession.

MacIntyre defines a practice (not, it must be admitted, very clearly), as follows:

> By a 'practice' I am going to mean any coherent and complex form of socially established cooperative human activity though which goods internal to that course of activity are realised in the course of trying to achieve those standards of excellence which are appropriate to, and partially definitive of, that form of activity, with the result that human powers to achieve excellence, and human conceptions of the ends and goods involved, are systematically extended. (1981:175)

Let's unpack that a bit. The key ideas are: *cooperative human activity* and a striving for *excellence*. Paraphrasing, we could say that a practice is the kind of cooperative activity which involves the desire to get better and better at it. Examples given by MacIntyre are football, chess, architecture, farming, physics, medicine, painting, music, politics. Thus defined, all practices involve human relationships.

Excelling in a practice brings a sense of satisfaction in its own right (what MacIntyre calls "internal goods"), quite apart from any external benefits. Entering into a practice means entering into a relationship with its history and tradition (its narrative, in fact) and its contemporary practitioners. It also means accepting the authority of prevailing standards of excellence (at least initially), and striving to achieve them, even to exceed them. Achieving this excellence not only enriches the person involved, but also the community at large. Roughly speaking, a virtue can then be defined as an acquired human quality which helps a person to strive for excellence in a practice (178). Such virtues include trustworthiness, truthfulness, fairness, and the courage to take risks in caring for others. Apart from virtues, practices also involve purely technical skills. And they need institutions to support them.

How does this point of view help us in searching for a professional ethics of translation? Some would argue that translation is not a true profession in the first place, because it does not seem to have a monopoly on a value goal that is not shared by other groups (compare medicine, with the value goal of health; law, for justice; teaching, for human growth; and the police, for security) (Airaksinen 1993). After all, the values of cross-cultural understanding and cooperation are shared also e.g. by diplomats and language-teachers. But translation is clearly a practice. As such, it is cooperative, involves technical skills, is increasingly institutionalized, and seeks its own improvement via quality control systems and the training and accrediting of recruits. Its institutionalization serves to some extent to protect it and limit its legal accountability.

On the other hand, its authority to restrict accreditation is very limited: anyone can set themselves up as a translator – another reason why it is difficult to speak of translation as a true profession. When we speak of an ethics of translation, do we mean to include amateurs as well as "professionals"? One way of answering this question would be to distinguish between someone "who is a translator" and someone "who does translations (sometimes)". I will focus in what follows on the first category, on the practitioner rather than the practice.

Consider now how this notion of a practitioner naturally leads to the deontic level. If I say that Louis is a translator, I imply that Louis therefore ought to do what a translator ought to do. I further imply that Louis should know what a translator ought to do, i.e. what a good translator would in fact do; Louis thus must have some conception of excellence in the practice of translation, some mental image of 'a good translator'. If I wanted to deny this further implication, I would need to say explicitly that Louis is a *bad* translator. MacIntyre argues that in this way, with respect to "functional concepts", 'ought' can indeed be derived from 'is' (see also Chesterman 1993[*]). Different translators might of course have different mental images of 'a good translator', but anyone who calls himself/herself a translator must have some idea of what translators ought to do.

In Chesterman (1997a: 172f) I showed how a simple deontic logic can be applied to translation ethics. Roughly speaking, you discover what you ought to do by assessing the outcome of a possible action in terms of the values that are thereby promoted, and comparing this outcome to what would probably happen if you did *not* take the action in question. You then do whatever leads to the best prospective result: either that particular action, or not. In that analysis, I proposed that the relevant values which guided translatorial decisions were truth, clarity, understanding and trust; and I showed how each of these values governed a general translation norm. In the present context, I would like to focus not on the values themselves, which act as regulative ideas steering the process of ethical decision-making, but on the qualities of the decision-maker.

What virtues must our ethical decision-making translator possess, in order to make the best ethical decisions? Following MacIntyre, I suggest that the most important virtue is simply the desire to make the right decision; that is, the translator must *want* to be a *good* translator, must strive for excellence in the practice of translation. It is interesting to compare this point to the answer MacIntyre (like many others) gives to the perennial question about how to lead a good life: the good life is a life spent seeking the good.

Then there are the general virtues I have already mentioned, such as fairness (the comparative value assessment of alternative actions must not be deliberately biased); truthfulness (the assessment must be as honest as possible); and trustworthiness (the translator must be able to defend the decisions taken, to give evidence of reliability). To these we might also add empathy, i.e. the ability to put oneself

---

[*] Paper 13 in this volume.

in someone else's place – the reader's, the original author's, the client's – so as to imagine the possible effects of alternative actions. Then there are the virtues of courage and determination not to give up until a good solution to a translation problem is found.

Other necessary qualities are not virtues as such, but play a supportive role in the striving for excellence. The translator must have adequate knowledge of the alternatives available: this means obvious language skills, including contrastive linguistic and cultural knowledge, in order to assess the potential effects of different choices, in the widest sense. The translator must also have adequate technical and research skills, in order to discover and evaluate possible alternatives.

A first conclusion to be drawn from this approach is that it allows us to restrict the scope of professional ethics to the practice in question. Louis can be an ethically good translator even if he is not a member of Amnesty International, Animal Rights, or the Labour Party. This means that the political engagement of the translator, which may affect the choice of texts to be translated and also ways of translating them (see Tymoczko 2000), lies outside the realm of professional ethics. A translator may be actively engaged in support of a worthy cause, and may translate in such a way as to support this cause; but these are factors that are additional to professional ethics proper, not part of them. If Louis is an anti-fascist, and subverts the fascist texts he translates, he is allowing his personal ethics to dominate his professional ethics. Fair enough: we must acknowledge that there may sometimes be more important things than professional ethics. It is part of a bus-driver's professional ethics to observe the Highway Code of traffic rules; but in an emergency, to save a life, these might be broken. Professional ethics, thus understood, govern a translator's activities *qua* translator, not *qua* political activist or life-saver.

A second conclusion is that translation ethics might be defined in terms of excellence in this practice. I now want to explore a further aspect of this excellence, an aspect that characterizes the relation between the practitioner and the values that inspire the practice. This is the notion of commitment.

4. An ethics of commitment

I take commitment to be the glue that binds practitioners to the values of the practice. It is thus also a virtue, supporting the striving for excellence, the *wanting* to be a good translator. A commitment is often stated overtly, as a promise or oath – in the marriage service, for instance. Oaths are quintessentially statements of contractual ethics: they constitute contracts, binding promises; but they may also have utilitarian aspects, such as reference to desirable or undesirable results.

Let us look at two examples of oaths of commitment to a practice. The first example is one of the oldest of all – the medical profession's Hippocratic Oath. Here it is in full, with paragraph numbers added:

The Hippocratic Oath

1. I swear by Apollo the healer, by Aesculapius, by Health and all the powers of healing, and call to witness all the gods and goddesses that I may keep this Oath and Promise to the best of my ability and judgment.
2. I will pay the same respect to my master in the Science as to my parents and share my life with him and pay all my debts to him. I will regard his sons as my brothers and teach them the Science, if they desire to learn it, without fee or contract. I will hand on precepts, lectures, and all other learning to my sons, to those of my master and to those pupils duly apprenticed and sworn, and to none other.
3. I will use my power to help the sick to the best of my ability and judgment; I will abstain from harming or wrongdoing any man by it.
4. I will not give a fatal draught to anyone if I am asked, nor will I suggest any such thing. Neither will I give a woman means to procure an abortion.
5. I will be chaste and religious in my life and in my practice. I will not cut, even for the stone, but I will leave such procedures to the practitioners of that craft.
6. Whenever I go into a house, I will go to help the sick and never with the intention of doing harm or injury. I will not abuse my position to indulge in sexual contacts with the bodies of women or of men, whether they be freemen or slaves.
7. Whatever I see or hear, professionally or privately, which ought not to be divulged, I will keep secret and tell no one.
8. If, therefore, I observe this Oath and do not violate it, may I prosper both in my life and in my profession, earning good repute among all men for all time. If I transgress and forswear this Oath, may my lot be otherwise. (Translated by J. Chadwick and W. N. Mann, in *Hippocratic Writings*, Penguin Books, 1950.)

The oath starts and ends with a statement of commitment. Paragraph 2 states the first object of this commitment: the profession, both past and future. (Recall Pym's point about translators' first loyalty being to the translation profession.) Paragraphs 3 and 4 formulate promises in both positive and negative terms: I will do this, I will not do that. We shall return to this below. Paragraph 5 links professional ethics to personal ethics. The reference to cutting for the stone means a promise not to do things the promiser is not qualified to do: surgical operations to remove kidney or gall stones were the tasks of other professionals in Ancient Greece. Paragraphs 6 and 7 formulate positive and negative promises about the abuse of one's professional position and the importance of professional secrets.

My second example is a modern one – in fact, it is no more than a proposal for an oath. It has been suggested as a possible professional oath for engineers, by Arto Siitonen ([1991] 1993: 279), in a Finnish collection of articles on professional ethics. He calls it the Archimedean Oath.* This is my translation:

> *The Archimedean Oath (proposal)*
> An engineer is involved in creating technology for the benefit of nature and humankind. In all his/her actions, an engineer should protect the life of plants, animals and people. An engineer avoids dishonesty and discord and seeks to develop him/herself in order to become ever more skilful at solving technical problems. An engineer ponders the trends of technological development and seeks to avoid harmful effects [literally: seeks to avoid the realization of harmful objectives].

This is no more than a proposal, and much might be said about the details of the formulation: the text does not have the form of an oath, for instance. But certain points of content are of interest. The proposal starts with a statement of the general aim of engineering. It contains both positive and implied negative prescriptions. It includes an overt statement about striving for further development, i.e. towards excellence. And it suggests that engineers should reflect on what they do, in addition to being good at it.

In the light of these examples and the preceding discussion, suppose we now try to formulate a similar oath for professional translators: a Hieronymic Oath. It is perhaps surprising that no such international oath exists.† After all, translation itself is what Maria Tymoczko (1999: 110) calls a "commissive act". When submitting a translation, a translator in effect makes a promise: I hereby promise that this text represents the original in some relevant way. (Let us not get bogged down here in arguments about definitions of equivalence. The translator claims that the translation is, in some way, equivalent; in fact, he/she implictly promises this. If the client and readers trust the translator, the claim is believed.) This act of commitment reminds us of the etymology of the words "profession" and "professional": they derive from the idea of "professing", of publicly affirming something, in the form of a public vow.

---

* The idea of an Engineers' Creed or Pledge or a Scientists' Code of Ethics is in fact a bit older, and is now (2016) already being put into practice, in some form, in several engineering schools. The first actual "Archimedean Oath" was apparently formulated by students at the Lausanne Institute of Technology in 1990: see e.g. <http://www.onlineethics.org/Resources/ethcodes/Pledges/38126.aspx>.

† But see the Translator's Charter and the Nairobi Declaration, e.g. via the FIT website (<http://www.fit-ift.org/translators-charter/>), and the AIIC Code of Professional Ethics for Conference Iterpreters at <http://aiic.net/page/6724>.

At the national level we can find examples of such oaths. Many countries have a national accreditation system of "sworn translators" or licensed translators who commit themselves to a basic code of conduct. The current Finnish statement that must be signed by officially licensed translators runs as follows (my translation):

> I, N. N., promise and swear on my honour and conscience that in my work as a licensed translator I will carry out the tasks given to me conscientiously and to the best of my ability, and that I will not use for my own benefit nor divulge without permission any information I may gain in the course of my work.

This statement is laid down by Finnish law, in the statute on licensed translators and their accreditation (statute 626, dating from 1989).* It highlights the virtues of loyalty and trustworthiness, but does not enter into any of the specificities of the translator's task. Indeed, it is so general that it might be applied to practically any occupation at all, just by changing the reference to the profession in question.

[The original text here commented on the then current Code of Practice of the American Translators Association. A new Code was approved in 2010, which is formulated rather differently. It is available at <https://www.atanet.org/governance/code_of_ethics.php>.]

I will now draw on all the foregoing discussion and examples in proposing a possible Hieronymic Oath. But before I do so, let me return to the Hopis' Spider Grandmother. Note that of her two ethical principles, one is negative and one positive. The negative one is given prominence, as it comes first. It is very similar to the commitment made in the Hippocratic Oath: do no harm. Compare also the Archimedean Oath: avoid harmful effects. Why this emphasis on the negative? Most of the Old Testament's Ten Commandments are negative, too. I suspect one reason is that it is easier to define and agree about harm and suffering than about happiness or other values. There is something obvious about suffering or harm: you can see immediately that it is "not good". Injustice is easier to see than justice. "Negative ethics" enables us to be more practical, working for the elimination or reduction of the obviously bad, rather than building utopian castles in the air.

What is the harm that ethical translators seek to reduce? Maybe we could call it "communicative suffering" (Chesterman 1997a: 184–6). Communicative suffering arises from not understanding something that you want to understand, from misunderstanding or inadequate understanding, and from not being able to get your own message across. It also arises from a lack of communication at all. Translators are like doctors in that their task is to intervene in certain cases of communicative suffering: those involving language and culture boundaries. Not *all* cases of

---

* The Finnish system of certifying authorized translators changed in 2007, but the affirmation remains the same. The new statute number is 2007/1232.

communicative suffering, note (just as Greek doctors were not competent to cure all diseases); just some. Their job is to cure or alleviate these particular kinds of communicative suffering. Their intervention may not always lead to "perfect communicative health", any more than a doctor's intervention always leads to a perfect cure. But the aim is at least to reduce this suffering.

One might even call this a Buddhist attitude to translation, in that it takes a kind of suffering as its starting point, as a fundamental fact, and tries to do something about it. Compare the Christian alternative of starting with sin, with the impossibility of perfection (ideal equivalence), and the resulting implication of permanent failure. Devy (1999) makes a related point about a difference between Western and Indian metaphysics. In the West, translation has been metaphorically linked to the fall from an original state, and hence to the secondary status of derived, non-original production. In India, on the other hand, translation is readily associated with the migration of the soul from one incarnation to another. During this cycle of rebirths the soul does not lose any of its original significance; on the contrary, it ideally makes some progress towards a better state, as it is revitalized over and over again.

The Spider Grandmother's second injunction is also interesting. Try to understand things – 'things' in a very general sense, of course. A similar point is made in the engineers' oath, about pondering on developmental trends. For a translator, this is naturally a primary task: to understand what the client wants, to understand the source text, to understand what the readers can be expected to understand, and so on. If communicative suffering is our negative pole, understanding is the positive one.

This brings us back to the axiological level, the discussion of values. I suggest that understanding is the highest value for translators – albeit in a wide and varied sense. All other relevant professional values – truth, clarity, loyalty, trust – are subordinate to understanding. This, I submit, is the defining limit of a translator's professional ethics, and also of his *professional* responsibility, the responsibility of his practice. He might of course feel *personally* responsible for the *consequences* of this understanding; and this feeling of personal responsibility might well affect his decisions about whether, or how, to translate. (Compare the point made above about excluding the translator's political engagement from professional ethics.) What communicating parties do with their resultant understanding is a matter of *their* own ethical principles – whether they use it in order to cooperate, for good or evil, or whatever. Furthermore, any professional ethic must be subservient to more general or universal ethics, since professions and practices only concern subsets of societies, just as societies are subsets of humankind as a whole, and humankind of organic life in general.

5. A Hieronymic Oath?

So, here is a proposal for a universal Hieronymic Oath. A first draft, submitted for responses and criticisms of all kinds, to be developed and maybe expanded, or indeed rejected. It is influenced by the above discussion of current ethics models and values, by the notion of virtues, by the examples of professional oaths we have looked at, and also by the Spider Grandmother.

1. I swear to keep this Oath to the best of my ability and judgement. [Commitment]
2. I swear to be a loyal member of the translators' profession, respecting its history. I am willing to share my expertise with colleagues and to pass it on to trainee translators. I will not work for unreasonable fees. I will always translate to the best of my ability. [Loyalty to the profession]
3. I will use my expertise to maximize communication and minimize misunderstanding across language barriers. [Understanding]
4. I swear that my translations will not represent their source texts in unfair ways. [Truth]
5. I will respect my readers by trying to make my translations as accessible as possible, according to the conditions of each translation task. [Clarity]
6. I undertake to respect the professional secrets of my clients and not to exploit clients' information for personal gain. I promise to respect deadlines and to follow clients' instructions. [Trustworthiness]
7. I will be honest about my own qualifications and limitations; I will not accept work that is outside my competence. [Truthfulness]
8. I will inform clients of unresolved problems, and agree to arbitration in cases of dispute. [Justice]
9. I will do all I can to maintain and improve my competence, including all relevant linguistic, technical and other knowledge and skills. [Striving for excellence]

An overt and explicit commitment to an oath of this kind might do something to promote genuinely ethical professional behaviour. If the profession (or practice) of translation as a whole could eventually agree on the form of such an oath, this might have several useful consequences. It would help to formalize and thus strengthen the international accreditation of translators. An internationally accepted Hieronymic Oath would help to distinguish between professionals and amateurs, and promote professionalization. It would have a good washback effect on training programmes. And it might even serve as a stimulus for a new Translator's Charter.

PAPER 28

An ethical decision*

The article presents and discusses a tricky ethical problem posed by the German translator of a Finnish novel. The case illustrates the complex ways in which potential reader reactions can affect a translator's decision. The discussion compares how different models of translation ethics would analyse this particular example. There are also implications concerning the translator's visibility, and the idea of translation as a kind of intervention.

Keywords: ethics, [Moster], responsibility, reception, visibility, intervention

Arto Paasilinna (b. 1942) is a well-known Finnish novelist who has a reputation for absurd humour and satirical social criticism. One of his novels, *Ukkosenjumalan poika* (1984), literally "Son of the Thunder God", is a satirical critique of the Lutheran establishment in Finland. The novel starts with a meeting of the pagan gods, who are worried at the way in which Finns are turning to the new Christian religion and thus heading for moral decline... The Thunder God, who chairs the meeting, decides to send his son down to Earth to check out the situation. The plan is that his son, Rutja, will change places with a mortal and thus be able to make his observations in disguise. The chosen mortal is one Sampsa Ronkainen, portrayed as a somewhat henpecked Finnish husband. During the course of many comic adventures, the son of the Thunder God, in the guise of Sampsa, falls for a Finnish lady tax inspector, and after nine months, on the last page of the novel, a son is born to her. The novel has not yet been translated into English, but here is how the story ends, in the German translation by Stefan Moster:

> Im Frühling, am 19. April, gebar Steuerprüferin Helinä Suvaskorpi einen prächtigen Knaben. Der Säugling war zur Hälfte der Enkel von Ukko Obergott und zur anderen Hälfte vom Geblüt der Steuerprüferin. Ein göttliches Kind! Durch dieses kleine Baby wurde das Geschlecht Finnlands mit der Zeit veredelt, aber bis dahin vergingen noch Hunderte von Jahren. Das ist eine Geschichte, die jetzt noch nicht erzählt werden kann, denn wir leben erst am Ende des 20. Jahrhunderts. Das

---

* Originally published in 2009 in Rodica Dimitriu and Miriam Shlesinger (eds), *Translators and their readers. In homage to Eugene Nida*. Brussels: Éditions du Hazard, 347–354. The publisher's permission to reprint is gratefully acknowledged. A couple of references have been updated.

Finnische Volk hat also nach wie vor seine Fehler. Es gibt ausgeprägte Genußsucht, Habsucht und allerlei andere Schlechtigkeiten. Aber dennoch sind die Finnen das einzige Volk der Erde, in dem es nicht einen einzigen Verrückten gibt.

(Paasilinna 1999: 253)

[My English version: In spring, on April 19, the tax inspector Helinä Suvaskorpi gave birth to a fine boy. He was half grandson of the Thunder God and the other half came from the tax inspector's lineage. A divine child! Through this little baby the Finnish stock became refined over time, but it took hundreds of years. That is a story that cannot yet be told, because we are now only at the end of the 20th century. So the Finnish people still have their defects: a marked craving for pleasure, greed, and many other kinds of wickedness. But the Finns are nevertheless the only nation on earth without a single madman.]

This gives a good idea of Paasilinna's ironic style.

But: if you look at the Finnish original, you will notice something curious. The date of birth of this promising grandson of the Thunder God is, in Finnish, April 20, not April 19. Is this a translator's error, a slip? No. The change is the result of a considered decision by the translator, who justified his change in public, in an article in the magazine *Books from Finland* (Moster 2003). This is a quarterly publication presenting the latest Finnish fiction and poetry in English, with news from the world of Finnish literary translation publishing. Moster's article is also available online (see reference).

Let us examine the reasons for Moster's decision, and then see how they can be analysed in terms of translation ethics.

First of all, there is an in-joke here, self-irony. The original date, April 20, happens to be Paasilinna's own birthday, and so the date can be seen as symbolizing the comic claim that he himself has divine ancestry, being thus the original fount of the contemporary semi-divine Finnish race… I should think that very few of his Finnish readers would know this fact, but some might; the self-irony would thus be evident to only a small minority.

But more importantly: April 20 was Hitler's birthday. Again, I imagine that few Finns would be aware of this – I was not, at least. What about the German-speaking readers of the translation? Moster's argument for changing the date is based on his belief that this birthday is an all-too-familiar fact to the majority of German and Austrian readers. So the risk is that these readers will take the date as a reference to Hitler, and interpret the ending of the novel as referring to a Nazi saviour who will improve the gene-pool of the nation… Did Paasilinna know that this day was also Hitler's birthday? Was he suggesting an ironic attitude also towards the Nazi phenomenon? Even comparing himself to Hitler? We do not know. At any rate, Moster felt that, in Nida's terms, preserving the date would have sacrificed dynamic equivalence.

This is how Moster explains and defends his decision to change the date:

> […] As the birthday of this bearer of hope Paasilinna cites 20 April. And at just this point I had to give up the translation. I rang the editor and informed her that I could not accept this date. Why?
>
> Well, 20 April is Arto Paasilinna's birthday. The author had, then, permitted himself a little joke, one might say. But: 20 April is also Adolf Hitler's birthday, and in Germany everyone knows that. At least ('old' and neo-) Nazis know that. And for them, reading Paasilinna's novel would have made something click; I did not wish to encourage that. Simply by means of this date of birth, attributed to a saviour of the people, it would have been possible to read the novel as a parafascist fantasy, which in its narrative technique reveals striking similarities with propagandistic entertainment from the 1930s and 40s: denigration of the enlightened present as decadent and degenerate, linked with an apotheosis of the *Volk's* (people's) heathen heritage and the vision of a reconstruction of the old order by a chosen leader.
>
> Quite possibly, the book had what it took to become a cult novel in right-wing circles, and I did not want to let that happen to it – or, most of all, to me – for which reason I replaced 20 April with another date. And I did not actually ask the author, as I am wont to do in similar cases, for I wanted to avoid him disallowing the (to me) essential modification.
>
> In doing so I valued my stake as originator of the text more highly than that of the author. Is that allowed? Yes, when you think you have to do it. Is it a problem? Not really, when you know what you're doing. (Moster 2003: 60)

There are a number of interesting aspects in this decision. Moster *informs* the editor of the change, he does not ask her for permission. He gives his reasons, which he feels are so compelling that he does not run the risk of asking the author's permission (and perhaps being refused permission to make the change), or even informing the author. He admits this to us, the readers of *Books from Finland*, and thus steps forward into the limelight, visible. He still believes he did the right thing, and he is happy to accept responsibility for the final version. His stake in the translation is higher than the author's.

I have presented and discussed this case in numerous lectures and seminars, and asked audiences what they think: did Moster make the right decision? The results have usually been split. Some people think he was right, others that he should have checked with the author first (but suppose the author had said no?), or gone ahead without changing the date. One student said she saw nothing wrong with the date anyway, as it was also her birthday and therefore a good day! Personally, I agree with Moster. But the issues are not easy ones. It is precisely the complexity of the pros and cons that make this an interesting ethical decision. Let us untangle some of them, in terms of four models of translation ethics which I have presented elsewhere (Chesterman 2001c[*]).

---

[*] Paper 27, above.

The classical model of translation ethics is based on the idea of representation: an ethical translation represents the source text, both in the sense of standing for it, as a proxy, and in the sense of bearing an appropriate resemblance to it (Hermans 2007b). The dominant value here is truth: the translation "tells the truth" about the source text, does not misrepresent it. This has been the model underlying most translation of sacred texts. According to this model, Moster's decision was not ethically justified.

My second model is the service model. Here, the translator is seen as performing a service for a client, and a leading value is that of loyalty to this client. An ethical translator pays attention to the client's definition of the translation's skopos (purpose), and does what is required to meet the client's needs, without wasting time or money. This model mainly applies to non-literary translation – which does indeed constitute the vast majority of all translation. In terms of this model, Moster's case seems to be more ethical, as he informed the client of his decision (although not the author); but he did not ask the client's permission. So in some sense he was loyal to the client, in realizing the need for the client to be informed. He was not acting behind the client's back.

The third model is a communication model. Here, the ethics is based on the value of promoting understanding between the people involved. Pym (1997) sees this in more concrete terms: promoting cooperation between the two sides. In this perspective, Moster acted very ethically, since he took steps to avoid a likely misunderstanding on the part of the readers. (I am assuming, like Moster, that Paasilinna did not intend to express support for neo-Nazism.) Pym's ethics of cooperation also gives priority to another kind of loyalty: the translator's loyalty to the profession itself, his fellow-translators, the professional intercultural communicators and promoters of understanding. From this point of view Moster's action is particularly interesting. First, by avoiding a potentially destructive misunderstanding he preserved the readership's trust in the profession. And second, by making his decision public, in the article cited above, he highlights both its difficulty and his own wish to act transparently. In this respect, he does his profession a great service, publicizing the image of a responsible professional able to reflect on, and justify, his own work.

My fourth model is norm-based ethics. Here, ethical actions are those that conform to the relevant norms, so that people's expectations are not disrupted. Breaking these norms may well lead to a loss of public trust in the profession. There are several kinds of relevant norms here. Moster has followed the norm of accountability (carrying responsibility), for instance, but evidently not the relation norm governing the required resemblance between source and target.

Underlying these four models are different conceptions of how ethics is best defined. They also illustrate a broader distinction that is familiar in moral philosophy: that between contractual ethics and utilitarian ethics. In contractual ethics, a "good" action is defined in terms of existing duties, obligations, laws, agreements and the like. Service ethics and norm-based ethics are contractual: there exist conditions of service and agreed norms, which should be followed. The communication model, on the other hand, is utilitarian. Here, the ethical value of an action is determined by its results, not by already-existing conditions. The representation model seems to fall between the two: there is a strong assumption that translators should translate faithfully, but behind this there must be the belief that unfaithful translation may lead to undesired consequences.

Moster's decision shows that he has given clear priority to utilitarian ethics, because his primary motivation was to avoid bad consequences. In my earlier article on these models (2001c), I suggested that a translator's duty could be described as inverse utilitarianism, as illustrated in the guiding principle [implied in] the Hippocratic Oath: "do no harm". In this light, a translator's task could be seen as the elimination or minimizing of "communicative suffering". This is precisely what Moster is evidently motivated by: the need to avoid serious "communicative" consequences. At the same time, he has not totally neglected his contractual duties, in that he has indeed informed the client. He has perhaps also taken a risk here, put his reputation on the line, as it were. Maybe the client will never employ him again... But this too illustrates the well-known point that altruistic actions may carry a cost.

Moster's decision has deeper implications for our perception of the translator's role more generally. Traditionally, we have become accustomed to seeing the translator as a mediator, a bridge-builder between cultures. The problem with this view is that it looks at translation through rose-coloured spectacles, as if translators never acted as bridge-destroyers, as if translation could never be used for destructive ends. But there is no shortage of historical examples of translations that create misunderstanding, that mislead and distort, either intentionally or accidently. (See Baker 2006, and the interview reported in Chesterman and Baker 2008.) A translator is never totally neutral. All translation is also an intervention (cf. Munday 2007). Moster has indeed intervened, not only in the translation itself but also in bringing the matter into the domain of public debate.

Intervention may have both good and bad consequences. Consider, for instance, the curious case of the "holy book" *Ruhnama*, written by the late president of Turkmenistan, and now translated into several dozen languages. The translations have been sponsored by companies that wish to do business in Turkmenistan. Without arranging a translation and thus flattering the president, they apparently had no access to the market in this closed dictatorship. The companies themselves seem embarrassed by this situation, according to Arto Halonen's recent [2008] documentary film on the subject (see <http://www.shadowoftheholybook.net/

trailer.html>). One also wonders about the motivations and ethics of the translators involved, who are thus implicitly supporting political and economic conditions in which they surely would not like to live themselves. Who gains what, in the short and the longer term, by such cooperation?

Moster's decision reflects a political intervention of a different kind. He is taking a stand against the potential risk of encouraging neo-Nazi fanaticism. Both the decision as such and its defence in the public domain are evidence of what we might call his translator's *telos* (Greek 'end, goal'). Whereas the notion of skopos (since Reiß and Vermeer 1984) refers to the intended purpose of a translation (i.e. of a text), the idea of the telos could be a way of conceptualizing the ultimate goal of a translator, the source of personal motivation, values and priorities. One's telos may affect one's choice to translate a given text in the first place (e.g. in the case of voluntary translation), one's attitude to tricky ethical problems (such as Moster's decision), and indeed one's wish to work as a translator in general. The concept of a translator's telos needs to be worked out in more detail, but it has clear ethical dimensions, and also reflects the ongoing shift in Translation Studies away from a focus on translations as texts towards one on translators as people: people who have their own goals apart from the purposes of the texts they translate, people who sometimes have to make difficult decisions. (The telos idea is introduced in Chesterman and Baker 2008.)

I referred above to Nida's notion of dynamic equivalence. The case of Moster's ethical decision also illustrates the way in which a responsible professional bears in mind the potential reactions of recipients. This, of course, has been one of the leitmotifs of Nida's work over several decades. Of all the places where he discusses this theme, here is one which I cite in conclusion: "[…] the role of the receptor is crucial, for a translation can be judged as adequate only if the response of the intended receptor is satisfactory" (Nida [1969] 1989: 94). I hope this contribution has helped to unravel some of the implications of that last word.

References

Abdallah, Kristiina. 2012. *Translators in Production Networks. Reflections on agency, quality and ethics*. Joensuu: Publications of the University of Eastern Finland. Available at: <http://urn.fi/URN:ISBN:978-952-61-0609-0>.

Airaksinen, Timo A. (ed.). [1991] 1993. *Ammattien ja ansaitsemisen etiikka*. Helsinki: Yliopistopaino.

Alvstad, Cecilia, Adelina Hild, and Elisabet Tiselius (eds). 2011. *Methods and Strategies of Process Research*. Amsterdam and Philadelphia: Benjamins. doi: 10.1075/btl.94

Amman, Margret. 1990. "Anmerkungen zu einer Theorie der Übersetzungskritik und ihrer praktischen Anwendung". *TextConText* 5: 209–250.

Andreotti, Julia Lambertini. 2016. *Comprehension of Legal Discourse in Interpreter-Mediated Judicial Proceedings*. PhD thesis, Universitat Rovira I Virgili, Tarragona. Available at http://www.tesisenred.net/bitstream/handle/10803/397782/TESI.pdf?sequence=1&isAllowed=y

Appiah, Kwame Anthony. [1993] 2000. "Thick translation". *Callaloo* 16 (4): 808–819. Reprinted in L. Venuti (ed.), 2000, *The Translation Studies Reader*, 417–429. London: Routledge.

Armstrong, Karen. 2005. *A Short History of Myth*. Edinburgh: Canongate.

Arrojo, Rosemary. 1998. "The revision of the traditional gap between theory and practice and the empowerment of translation in postmodern times". *The Translator* 4 (1): 25–48. doi: 10.1080/13556509.1998.10799005

Aunger, Robert (ed.). 2000. *Darwinizing Culture. The Status of Memetics as a Science*. Oxford: Oxford University Press.

Austin, John L. 1962. *How to Do Things with Words*. Oxford: Clarendon Press.

Bachleiter, Norbert, and Michaela Wolf (eds). 2004. *Soziologie der literarische Übersetzung*. Tübingen: Niemeyer.

Baker, Mona. 1993. "Corpus linguistics and Translation Studies: Implications and applications". In *Text and Technology: In Honour of John Sinclair*, M. Baker, G. Francis and E. Tognini-Bonelli (eds), 233–250. Amsterdam and Philadelphia: Benjamins. doi: 10.1075/z.64.15bak

Baker, Mona. 1996. "Linguistics and Cultural Studies. Complementary or competing paradigms in Translation Studies?" In *Übersetzungswissenschaft im Umbruch. Festschrift für Wolfram Wilss zum 70. Geburtstag*, A. Lauer, H. Gerzymisch-Arbogast, J. Haller and E. Steiner (eds), 9–19. Tübingen: Narr.

Baker, Mona. 2000. "Towards a methodology for investigating the style of a literary translator". *Target* 12 (2): 241–266. doi: 10.1075/target.12.2.04bak

Baker, Mona. 2006. *Translation and Conflict: A Narrative Account*. London and New York: Routledge.

Bartsch, Renate. 1987. *Norms of Language*. London: Longman.

Bassnett, Susan, and André Lefevere. 1996. *Constructing Cultures*. Clevedon: Multilingual Matters.

Berglund, Lars O. 1990. "The search for social significance". *Lebende Sprachen* 35 (4): 145–151. doi: 10.1515/les.1990.35.4.145

Berman, Antoine. 1984. *L'Épreuve de l'étranger. Culture et traduction dans l'Allemagne romantique*. Paris: Gallimard.
Berman, Antoine. 1985. *Traduction et la lettre ou l'auberge du lointain*. Paris: Seuil.
Berman, Antoine. 1990. "La retraduction comme éspace de la traduction", *Palimpsestes* 4: 1–7
Berman, Sandra, and Michael Wood (eds). 2005. *Nation, Language and the Ethics of Translation*. Princeton, N.J.: Princeton University Press. doi: 10.1515/9781400826681
Berthele, Raphaele. 2000. "Translating African-American vernacular English into German: The problem of 'Jim' in Mark Twain's Huckleberry Finn". *Journal of Sociolinguistics* 4 (4): 588–614. doi: 10.1111/1467-9481.00131
Blackmore, Susan. 1999. *The Meme Machine*. Oxford: Oxford University Press.
Blum-Kulka, Shoshana. 1986. "Shifts of cohesion and coherence in translation". In *Interlingual and Intercultural Communication: Discourse and Cognition in Translation and Second Language Acquisition Studies*, J. House and S. Blum-Kulka (eds), 17–35. Tübingen: Narr.
Bly, Robert. 1984. "The eight stages of translation". In *Translation. Literary, Linguistic and Philosophical Perspectives*, W. Frawley (ed.), 67–89. Newark: University of Delaware Press.
Boase-Beier, Jean. 2011. *A Critical Introduction to Translation Studies*. London: Continuum.
Booth, Wayne C., Gregory G. Colomb, and Joseph M. Williams. 2005. *The Craft of Research*. Chicago: University of Chicago Press.
Brems, Elke, and Sara Ramos Pinto. 2013. "Reception and translation". *Handbook of Translation Studies*, vol. 4, Y. Gambier and L. van Doorslaer (eds), 142–147. Amsterdam and Philadelphia: Benjamins. doi: 10.1075/hts.4.rec1
Brisset, Annie. 1990. *Sociocritique de la traduction. Théâtre et altérité au Québec (1968–88)*. Québec : Éditions du Préambule.
Brooke-Rose, Christine. 1968. *The Brooke-Rose Omnibus*. Manchester: Carcanet Press.
Brownlie, Siobhan. 2003. "Investigating explanations of translational phenomena: A case for multiple causality". *Target* 15 (1): 111–152. doi: 10.1075/target.15.1.06bro
Brownlie, Siobhan. 2006. "Narrative theory and retranslation theory". *Across Languages and Cultures* 7 (2): 145–170. doi: 10.1556/Acr.7.2006.2.1
Buzelin, Hélène. 2005. "Unexpected allies: How Latour's Network Theory could complement Bourdieusian analyses in Translation Studies". *The Translator* 11 (2): 193–218. doi: 10.1080/13556509.2005.10799198
Campbell, Emma, and Robert Mills. (eds). 2012. *Rethinking Medieval Translation: Ethics, Politics, Theory*. Cambridge: D. S. Brewer.
Campbell, Stuart. 1998. *Translation into the Second Language*. London: Longman.
Carl, Michael. 2012. "A computational cognitive model of human translation processes". In *Emerging Applications of Natural Language Processing: Concepts and New Research*, S. Bandyopadhyay, S. K. Naskar and A. Ekbal (eds), 110–128. Hershey, PA.: IGI Global.
Catford, John C. 1965. *A Linguistic Theory of Translation*, Oxford: Oxford University Press.
Chalmers, Alan. [1976] 1999. *What is this thing called Science?* Indianapolis: Hackett.
Chesterman, Andrew. 1993. "From 'is' to 'ought': translation laws, norms and strategies". *Target* 5 (1): 1–20. doi: 10.1075/target.5.1.02che
Chesterman, Andrew. 1996. "Teaching translation theory: the significance of memes". In *Teaching Translation and Interpreting 3. New Horizons*, C. Dollerup and V. Appel (eds), 63–71. Amsterdam and Philadelphia: Benjamins. doi: 10.1075/btl.16.10che
Chesterman, Andrew. [1997a] 2016. *Memes of Translation*. Amsterdam and Philadelphia: Benjamins. (Revised edition 2016.) doi: 10.1075/btl.22

Chesterman, Andrew. 1997b. "Explanatory adequacy and falsifiability in translation theory". In *Transferre Necesse Est. Proceedings of the Second International Conference on Current Trends in Studies of Translation and Interpreting*, K. Klaudy and J. Kohn (eds), 219–224. Budapest: Scholastica.

Chesterman, Andrew. 1998a. "Causes, translations, effects". *Target* 10 (2): 201–230. doi:10.1075/target.10.2.02che

Chesterman, Andrew. 1998b. Review of Hans J. Vermeer, *A Skopos Theory of Translation (Some arguments for and against)*. *Target* 10 (1): 155–159.

Chesterman, Andrew. 1998c. *Contrastive Functional Analysis*. Amsterdam and Philadelphia: Benjamins. doi:10.1075/pbns.47

Chesterman, Andrew. 1999a. "The empirical status of prescriptivism". *Folia Translatologica* 6: 9–19.

Chesterman, Andrew. 1999b. "Translation typology". In *The Second Riga Symposium on Pragmatic Aspects of Translation*, A. Veisbergs and I. Zauberga (eds), 49–62. Riga: University of Latvia.

Chesterman, Andrew. 2000a. "A causal model for Translation Studies". In *Intercultural Faultlines. Research Models in Translation Studies I. Textual and Cognitive Aspects*, M. Olohan (ed.), 15–27. Manchester: St. Jerome Publishing.

Chesterman, Andrew. 2000b. "Memetics and Translation Studies". *Synapse* 5 (2000) 1–17. Bergen: Norges Handelshøyskole.

Chesterman, Andrew. 2000c. "What constitutes 'progress' in Translation Studies?", in *Översättning och tolkning. Rapport från ASLA:s höstsymposium, Stockholm, 5–6 november 1998*, B. Englund Dimitrova (ed.), 33–49. Uppsala: ASLA.

Chesterman, Andrew. 2001a. "Skopos and after. An interview with Hans J. Vermeer". *Across Languages and Cultures* 2 (1): 133–138.

Chesterman, Andrew. 2001b. "Empirical research methods in Translation Studies". *Erikoiskielet ja käännösteoria* [VAKKI-symposiumi XX, Vaasa, Finland] 27: 9–22.

Chesterman, Andrew. 2001c. "Proposal for a Hieronymic Oath". *The Translator* 7 (2): 139–154. doi:10.1080/13556509.2001.10799097

Chesterman, Andrew. 2002. "On the interdisciplinarity of Translation Studies". *Logos and Language* 3 (1): 1–9.

Chesterman, Andrew. 2003. "Between text and culture". In *The Third Riga Symposium on Pragmatic Aspects of Translation. Proceedings*, A. Veisbergs (ed.), 27–47. Riga: University of Latvia / Aarhus School of Business.

Chesterman, Andrew. 2004a. "Beyond the particular". In *Translation Universals. Do they Exist?*, A. Mauranen and P. Kujamäki (eds), 33–49. Amsterdam and Philadephia: Benjamins. doi:10.1075/btl.48.04che

Chesterman, Andrew. 2004b. "Paradigm problems?" In *Translation Research and Interpreting Research. Traditions, Gaps and Synergies*, C. Schäffner (ed.), 52–56. Clevedon: Multilingual Matters.

Chesterman, Andrew. 2004c. "Translation as an object of research". In *Übersetzung, Translation, Traduction*, H. Kittel, A. P. Frank and N. Greiner (eds), 93–100. Berlin: de Gruyter.

Chesterman, Andrew. 2005. "Problems with strategies". In *New Trends in Translation Studies. In Honour of Kinga Klaudy*, K. Károly and Á. Fóris (eds.), 17–28. Budapest: Akadémiai Kiadó.

Chesterman, Andrew. 2006a. "Interpreting the meaning of translation". In *A Man of Measure. Festschrift in Honour of Fred Karlsson on his 60th Birthday*, M. Suominen, A. Arppe, A. Airola, O. Heinämäki, M. Miestamo, U. Määttä, J. Niemi, K. K. Pitkänen and K. Sinnemäki (eds), 3–11. Turku: Linguistic Association of Finland. Also available at http://www.helsinki.fi/~chesterm/2006a.meaning.html.

Chesterman, Andrew. 2006b. "Questions in the sociology of translation". In *Translation Studies at the Interface of Disciplines*, J. Ferreira Duarte, A. Assis Rosa and T. Seruya (eds), 9–27. Amsterdam and Philadelphia: Benjamins, 9–27. doi: 10.1075/btl.68.03che

Chesterman, Andrew. 2007a. "Similarity analysis and the translation profile". *Belgian Journal of Linguistics* 21: 53–66. doi: 10.1075/bjl.21.05che

Chesterman, Andrew. 2007b. "What is a unique item?" In *Doubts and Directions in Translation Studies*, Y. Gambier, M. Shlesinger and R. Stolze (eds), 3–13. Amsterdam and Philadelphia: Benjamins. doi: 10.1075/btl.72.04che

Chesterman, Andrew. 2007c. "Bridge concepts in translation sociology". In *Constructing a sociology of translation*, M. Wolf and A. Fukari (eds), 171–183. Amsterdam and Philadelpia: Benjamins. doi: 10.1075/btl.74.12che

Chesterman, Andrew. 2008a. "The status of interpretive hypotheses". In *Efforts and Models in Interpreting and Translation Research*, G. Hansen, A. Chesterman and H. Gerzymisch-Arbogast (eds), 49–61. Amsterdam and Philadelphia: Benjamins.

Chesterman, Andrew. 2008b. "On explanation". In *Beyond Descriptive Translation Studies. Investigations in homage to Gideon Toury*, A. Pym, M. Shlesinger, and D. Simeoni (eds), 363–379. Amsterdam and Philadelphia: Benjamins. doi: 10.1075/btl.75.27che

Chesterman, Andrew. 2012. "The significance of hypotheses". *TTR* 24 (2): 65–86. doi: 10.7202/1013395ar

Chesterman, Andrew, and Rosemary Arrojo. 2000. "Shared ground in Translation Studies". *Target* 12 (1): 151–160. doi: 10.1075/target.12.1.08che

Chesterman, Andrew, and Mona Baker. 2008. "Ethics of renarration. An interview with Mona Baker". *Cultus* 1, 1: 10–33.

Chesterman, Andrew, Natividad Gallardo San Salvador, and Yves Gambier (eds). 2000. *Translation in Context*. Amsterdam and Philadelphia: Benjamins. doi: 10.1075/btl.39

Chesterman, Andrew, and Emma Wagner. 2002. *Can Theory Help Translators? A Dialogue between the Ivory Tower and the Wordface*. Manchester: St. Jerome Publishing.

Chevalier, Jean-Claude. 1995. "D'une figure de traduction : le changement de 'sujet'". In *L'Horlogerie de Saint Jérôme*, J-C. Chevalier and M-F. Delport, 27–44. Paris: L'Harmattan.

Cheyfitz, Eric. 1991. *The Poetics of Imperialism. Translation and Colonization from The Tempest to Tarzan*. Oxford: Oxford University Press.

Crisafulli, Edoardo. 2003. *The Vision of Dante. Cary's translation of The Divine Comedy*. Market Harborough: Troubador.

Croft, William. [1990] 2003. *Typology and Universals*. Cambridge: Cambridge University Press.

Cronin, Michael. 2000. *Across the Lines: Travel, Language and Translation*. Cork: Cork University Press.

Cross, Graham. 1998. "Review of Encyclopaedia of Translation Studies". *ITI Bulletin*, Feb. 27, 1998.

Cumps, Jan L. 1996. "The Impact of law students' language preference on translation". Paper read at the Transferre Necesse Est Second International Conference on Current Trends in Studies of Translation and Interpreting, 5–7 September 1996, Budapest.

Darwin, Charles. [1859] 1968. *The Origin of Species*. London: Penguin Books.

Dawkins, Richard. 1976. *The Selfish Gene*. Oxford: Oxford University Press.

Delabastita, Dirk. 1991. "A false opposition in Translation Studies: Theoretical versus/ and historical approaches". *Target* 3 (2): 137–152. doi: 10.1075/target.3.2.02del

Delabastita, Dirk. 2005. "Research in translation between paralysis and pretence". *Revista Canaria de Estudios Ingleses* 51: 33–49.

Delisle, Jean. 1993. *La traduction raisonnée*. Ottawa: Presses de l'Université d'Ottawa.

Delisle, Jean, Hannelore Lee-Jahnke, and Monique C. Cormier. 1999. *Terminologie de la traduction / Translation Terminology*. Amsterdam and Philadelphia: Benjamins. doi: 10.1075/fit.1

Delisle, Jean, and Judith Woodsworth (eds). 1995. *Translators through History*. Amsterdam and Philadelphia: Benjamins. doi: 10.1075/btl.13

Dennett, Daniel C. 1991. *Consciousness Explained*. London: Penguin.

Dennett, Daniel C. 1995. *Darwin's Dangerous Idea*. London: Penguin.

Devy, Ganesh. 1999. "Translation and literary history". In *Post-colonial Translation*, S. Bassnett and H. Trivedi (eds), 182–188. London: Routledge.

Diamond, Jared. 2005. *Collapse. How Societies Choose to Fail or Survive*. London: Allen Lane. (Penguin Books 2006.)

Diriker, Ebru. 2004. *De-/Re-contextualizing Conference Interpreting: Interpreters in the Ivory Tower?* Amsterdam and Philadelphia: Benjamins. doi: 10.1075/btl.53

Doherty, Monika (ed.). 1996. *Information Structure: a Key Concept for Translation Theory*. *Linguistics* 34 (3) (Special issue).

Dolet, Etienne. 1540. *La Manière de Bien Traduire d'une Langue en Aultre*. Paris: Marnef.

Dollerup, Cay. 1997. "Translation as imposition vs. translation as requisition". In *Translation as Intercultural Communication*, M. Snell-Hornby, Z. Jettmarová and K. Kaindl (eds), 45–56. Amsterdam and Philadelphia: Benjamins. doi: 10.1075/btl.20.06dol

Ehrensberger-Dow, Maureen, and Sharon O'Brien. 2015. "Ergonomics of the translation workplace: Potential for cognitive friction". *Translation Spaces* 4 (1): 98–118. doi: 10.1075/ts.4.1.05ehr

Englund Dimitrova, Birgitta. 1997. "Translation of dialect in fictional prose – Vilhelm Moberg in Russian and English as a case in point". In *Norm, Variation and Change in Language. Proceeedings of the centenary meeting of the Nyfilologiska sällskapet, Nedre Manilla 22–23 March, 1996*, 49–65. Stockholm: Almqvist and Wiksell.

Englund Dimitrova, Birgitta. 2005. *Expertise and Explicitation in the Translation Process*. Amsterdam and Philadelphia: Benjamins. doi: 10.1075/btl.64

Eriksson, Olof. 2004. "Entre traductologie et linguistique contrastive : La notion de 'Transposition'". In *Actes du 6e Colloque franco-finlandais de Linguistique Contrastive*, J. Härmä and U. Tuomarla (eds), 88–103. Helsinki: Département des Langues Romanes.

Even-Zohar, Itamar. 1990. *Polysystem Studies*. *Poetics Today* 11 (1).

Faerch, Claus, and Gabriele Kasper (eds) 1983. *Strategies in Interlanguage Communication*. London: Longman.

Fairclough, Norman. 1992. *Discourse and Social Change*. Cambridge: Polity Press.

Fawcett, Peter. 1997. *Translation and Language*. Manchester: St. Jerome Publishing.

Firth, John R. 1957. *Papers in Linguistics 1934–1951*. London: Oxford University Press.

Flotow, Luise von. 1991. "Feminist translation: Contexts, practices and theories". *TTR* 4 (2): 69–84. doi: 10.7202/037094ar

Flynn, Peter. 2004. "Skopos Theory: An ethnographic enquiry". *Perspectives* 12 (4): 270–285. doi: 10.1080/0907676X.2004.9961507

Føllesdal, Dagfinn. [1979] 1994. "Hermeneutics and the hypothetico-deductive method". *Dialectica* 33 (3–4): 319–336. Reprinted in M. Martin and L. C. McIntyre (eds), 1994, *Readings in the Philosophy of Social Science*, 233–245. Cambridge, Mass.: MIT Press.

Føllesdal, Dagfinn, Lars Walløe, and Jon Elster. 1984. *Argumentasjonsteori, Språk og Vitenskapsfilosofi*. Oslo: Universitetsforlaget.

Foot, Philippa, ed. 1967. *Theories of Ethics*. Oxford: Oxford University Press.

Footit, Hilary, and Michael Kelly (eds). 2012. *Languages at War. Policies and Practices of Language Contacts in Conflict*. London: Palgrave Macmillan.

Fortey, Richard. 2004. *The Earth. An Intimate History*. London: HarperCollins.

Frawley, William. 1984. "Prolegomenon to a theory of translation". In *Translation. Literary, Linguistic and Philosophical Perspectives*, W. Frawley (ed.), 159–175. Newark: University of Delaware Press.

Fuller, Steve. 2003. *Kuhn vs. Popper. The Struggle for the Soul of Science*. Cambridge: Icon Books.

Gambier, Yves. 1994. "La retraduction, tour et retour", *Meta* 39 (3): 413–417. doi:10.7202/002799ar

Gambier, Yves. 2008. "Stratégies et tactiques en traduction et interpretation". In *Efforts and Models in Interpreting and Translation Research*, G. Hansen, A. Chesterman and H. Gerzymisch-Arbogast (eds), 63–82. Amsterdam and Philadelphia: Benjamins.

García-Landa, Mariano. 1990. "A general theory of translation (and of language)". *Meta* 35 (3): 476–488. doi:10.7202/003392ar

Gerzymisch-Arbogast, Heidrun. 2001. "Equivalence parameters and evaluation". *Meta* 46 (2): 227–242. doi:10.7202/002886ar

Gile, Daniel. 2004a. "'Translation research versus interpreting research: Kinship, difference and prospects for partnership". In *Translation Research and Interpreting Research. Traditions, Gaps and Synergies*, C. Schäffner (ed.), 10–34. Clevedon: Multilingual Matters.

Gile, Daniel. 2004b. "Response to the invited papers". In *Translation Research and Interpreting Research. Traditions, Gaps and Synergies*, C. Schäffner (ed.), 124–127. Clevedon: Multilingual Matters.

Gile, Daniel. 2005a. "The liberal arts paradigm and the empirical science paradigm". Available at http://www.est-translationstudies.org/ > Research issues.

Gile, Daniel. 2005b. *La Traduction: la Comprendre, l'Apprendre*. Paris: Presses Universitaires de France. doi:10.3917/puf.gile.2005.01

Gile, Daniel. 2009. *Basic Concepts and Models for Interpreter and Translator Training*. Revised edition. Amsterdam and Philadelphia: Benjamins. doi:10.1075/btl.8

Glaser, Barney G., and Strauss, Anselm L. 1967. *The Discovery of Grounded Theory. Strategies for Qualitative Research*. New York: Aldine de Gruyter.

Gombrich, Ernst H. [1960] 1977. *Art and Illusion* (fifth edition). London: Phaidon.

González Núñez, Gabriel. 2016. "On translation policy". *Target* 28 (1): 87–109).

Goodman, Nelson. 1972. "Seven strictures on similarity". In *Problems and Projects*, N. Goodman, 437–447. Indianapolis, IN.: Bobbs-Merrill.

Göpferich, Susanne. 2009. "Towards a model of translation competence and its acquisition: the longitudinal study TransComp". In *Behind the Mind: Methods, Models and Results in Translation Process Research*, S. Göpferich, A. L. Jakobsen and I. M. Mees (eds), 11–37. Copenhagen: Samfundslitteratur.

Gouadec, Daniel. 1990. "Traduction signalétique". *Meta* 35 (2): 332–341. doi:10.7202/002945ar

Gouanvic, Jean-Marc. 1999. *Sociologie de la traduction*. Arras: Artois Presses Université.

Gouanvic, Jean-Marc. 2002. "The stakes of translation in literary fields". *Across Languages and Cultures* 3 (2): 159–168. doi:10.1556/Acr.3.2002.2.2

Gran, Laura, and John Dodds (eds). 1989. The Theoretical and Practical Aspects of Teaching Conference Interpretation. Udine: Campanotto.

Greimas, Algirdas J. 1983. *Du Sens*. Vol. 2. Paris: Seuil.

Grice, Paul. 1975. "Logic and conversation". In *Syntax and Semantics 3: Speech Acts*, P. Cole and J. L. Morgan (eds), 41–58. New York: Academic Press.

Gutt, Ernst-August. 1990. "A theoretical account of translation – without a translation theory". *Target* 2 (2): 135–164. doi: 10.1075/target.2.2.02gut
Gutt, Ernst-August. [1991] 2000. *Translation and Relevance. Cognition and Context*. Oxford: Blackwell. (Revised edition 2000. Manchester: St. Jerome Publishing.)
Güttinger, Fritz. 1963. *Zielsprache: Theorie und Technik des Übersetzens*. Zürich: Menesse Verlag.
Haddadian-Moghaddam, Esmaeil. 2014. *Literary Translation in Modern Iran. A Sociological Study*. Amsterdam and Philadelphia: Benjamins.
Halliday, Michael A. K. 1961. "Categories of the theory of grammar". *Word* 17 (3): 241–292. doi: 10.1080/00437956.1961.11659756
Halliday, Michael A. K. 1985. *An Introduction to Functional Grammar*. London: Arnold.
Halverson, Sandra. 1998a. *Concepts and Categories in Translation Studies*. Bergen: University of Bergen.
Halverson, Sandra. 1998b. "Translation Studies and representative corpora: Establishing links between translation corpora, theoretical/descriptive categories and a conception of the object of study". *Meta* 43 (4): 494–514. doi: 10.7202/003000ar
Halverson, Sandra. 2000. "Prototype effects in the 'translation' category". In *Translation in Context*, A. Chesterman, N. Gallardo and Y. Gambier (eds), 3–16. Amsterdam and Philadelphia: Benjamins. doi: 10.1075/btl.39.03hal
Halverson, Sandra. 2003. "The cognitive basis of translation universals". *Target* 15 (2): 197–241. doi: 10.1075/target.15.2.02hal
Halverson, Sandra. 2007. "Investigating gravitational pull in translation: The case of the English progressive construction". In *Texts, Process and Corpora: Research Inspired by Sonja Tirkkonen-Condit*, R. Jääskeläinen, T. Puurtinen and H. Stotesbury (eds), 175–195. Joensuu: Publications of the Savonlinna School of Translation Studies.
Hansen, Gyde (ed.). 1999. *Probing the Process in Translation: Methods and Results*, Copenhagen: Samfundslitteratur.
Hansen, Gyde. 2002. "Zeit und Qualität im Übersetzungsprozess". In *Empirical Translation Studies: process and product*, G. Hansen (ed.), 29–54. Copenhagen: Samfundslitteratur.
Hansen, Gyde. 2005. *Störquellen in Übersetzungsprozessen*. Copenhagen: CBS.
Harris, Brian. 1990. "Norms in interpretation". *Target* 2 (1): 115–119. doi: 10.1075/target.2.1.08har
Hatim, Basil, and Ian Mason. 1990. *Discourse and the Translator*. London: Longman.
Heat-Moon, William Least. 1984. *Blue Highways. A journey into America*. London: Picador/Pan Books.
Hebenstreit, Gernot. 2007. "Defining patterns in Translation Studies". *Target* 19 (2): 197–215. doi: 10.1075/target.19.2.03heb
Hekkanen, Raila. 2009. "Fields, networks and Finnish prose: A Comparison of Bourdieusian Field Theory and Actor-Network Theory in translation sociology". In *Selected Papers of the CETRA Research Seminar in Translation Studies 2008*, D. De Crom (ed.). Available at <https://www.arts.kuleuven.be/cetra/papers/files/hekkanen.pdf>.
Heidegger, Martin. 1962. *Being and Time*. (Translated by John Macquarrie and Edward Robinson.) New York: Harper and Row.
Heilbron, Johan. 2000. "Translation as a cultural world system". *Perspectives* 8 (1): 9–26. doi: 10.1080/0907676X.2000.9961369
Hempel, Carl G. 1952. *Fundamentals of Concept Formation in Empirical Sciences*. Chicago: University of Chicago Press.
Henry, Ronald. 1984. "Points of inquiry into total translation. A review of J. C. Catford's *A Linguistic Theory of Translation*". *Meta* 29 (2): 152–158. doi: 10.7202/003057ar

Hermans, Theo (ed.). 1985a. *The Manipulation of Literature*. London: Croom Helm.
Hermans, Theo. 1985b. "Introduction. Translation Studies and a new paradigm". In *The Manipulation of Literature. Studies in Literary Translation*, T. Hermans (ed.), 7–15. London. Croom Helm.
Hermans, Theo. 1985c. "Images of translation. Metaphor and imagery in the Renaissance discourse on translation". In *The Manipulation of Literature. Studies in Literary Translation*, T. Hermans (ed.), 103–136. London. Croom Helm.
Hermans, Theo. 1991. "Translational norms and correct translations". In *Translation Studies: The State of the Art*, K. van Leuven-Zwart and T. Naaijkens (eds), 155–169. Amsterdam: Rodopi.
Hermans, Theo. 1999. *Translation in Systems*. Manchester: St. Jerome Publishing.
Hermans, Theo. 2003. "Cross-cultural Translation Studies as thick translation". *Bulletin of the School of Oriental and African Studies, University of London*, 66 (3): 380–389. doi: 10.1017/S0041977X03000260
Hermans, Theo (ed.). 2006. *Translating Others*, vol. 1. Manchester: St. Jerome Publishing.
Hermans, Theo. 2007a. *The Conference of the Tongues*. Manchester: St. Jerome Publishing.
Hermans, Theo. 2007b. "Translation, irritation and resonance". In *Constructing a sociology of translation*, M. Wolf and A. Fukari (eds), 57–75. Amsterdam and Philadelphia: Benjamins. doi: 10.1075/btl.74.04her
Hickey, Leo (ed.). 1998. *The Pragmatics of Translation*. Clevedon: Multilingual Matters.
Hofstede, Geert. 1991. *Cultures and Organizations: Software of the Mind*. London: McGraw-Hill.
Holmes, James S. 1988a. *Translated! Papers on Literary Translation and Translation Studies*. Amsterdam: Rodopi.
Holmes, James S. [1988b] 2000. "The name and nature of Translation Studies". In J.S. Holmes, *Translated! Papers on Literary Translation and Translation Studies*. Amsterdam: Rodopi, 67–80. Reprinted e.g. in L. Venuti (ed.), 2000, *The Translation Studies Reader*, 172–185. London.
Holz-Mänttäri, Justa. 1984. *Translatorisches Handeln. Theorie und Methode*. Helsinki: Suomalainen Tiedeakatemia.
Hönig, Hans. 1995. *Konstruktives Übersetzen*. Tübingen: Stauffenberg.
Hönig, Hans G., and Paul Kußmaul. 1982. *Strategie der Übersetzung. Ein Lehr-und Arbeitsbuch*. Tübingen: Narr.
House, Juliane. 1981. *A Model for Translation Quality Assessment*. (Second edition.) Tübingen: Narr.
House, Juliane. 2008. "Beyond intervention. Universals in translation?" *trans-com* 1 (1): 6–19.
Ibrahim, Hasnah. 1994. "Translation assessment: a case for a spectral model". In *Teaching Translation and Interpreting* 2, C. Dollerup and A. Lindegaard (eds), 151–156. Amsterdam and Philadelphia: Benjamins. doi: 10.1075/btl.5.22ibr
Inghilleri, Moira (ed.). 2005. "Bourdieu and the sociology of translation and interpreting". Special issue of *The Translator*, 11 (2). doi: 10.1080/13556509.2005.10799195
Inghilleri, Moira. 2012. *Interpreting Justice. Ethics, Politics and Language*. London: Routledge.
Itkonen, Esa. 1983. *Causality in Linguistic Theory*. London: Croom Helm.
Ivir, Vladimir. 1981. "Formal correspondence vs. translation equivalence revisited". In *Theory of Translation and Intercultural Relations*, I. Even-Zohar and G. Toury (eds), 51–59. Tel Aviv: Porter Institute for Poetics and Semotics, Tel Aviv University [= *Poetics Today* 2:4].
Jääskeläinen, Riitta. 1993. "Investigating translation strategies". In *Recent Trends in Empirical Translation Research*, S. Tirkkonen-Condit and J. Laffling (eds), 99–119. Joensuu: University of Joensuu, Faculty of Arts.

Jääskeläinen, Riitta. 1999. *Tapping the Process: An Explorative Study of the Cognitive and Affective Factors Involved in Translating*. Joensuu: University of Joensuu.

Jääskeläinen, Riitta. 2002. "Think-aloud protocol studies into translation. An annotated bibliography". *Target* 14 (1): 107–136. doi: 10.1075/target.14.1.05jaa

Jääskeläinen, Riitta. 2004. "The fate of 'The Families of Medellín'. Tampering with a potential translation universal in the translation class". In *Translation Universals. Do they exist?*, A. Mauranen and P. Kujamäki (eds), 205–214. Amsterdam and Philadelphia: Benjamins. doi: 10.1075/btl.48.17jaa

Jakobsen, Arnt Lykke. 1999. "Logging target text production with Translog". In *Probing the Process in Translation: Methods and Results*, G. Hansen (ed.), 9–20. Copenhagen: Samfundslitteratur.

Jakobsen, Arnt Lykke. 2011. "Tracking translators' keystrokes and eye movements with Translog". In *Methods and Strategies of Process Research*, C. Alvstad, A. Hild and E. Tiselius (eds), 37–55. Amsterdam and Philadelphia: Benjamins. doi: 10.1075/btl.94.06jak

Jandl, Ernst. 1966. *Laut und Luise*. Kassel: Olten.

Jansen, Astrid, and Arnt Lykke Jakobsen. 2000. "Translating under time pressure". In *Translation in Context*, A. Chesterman, N. Gallardo San Salvador and Y. Gambier (eds), 105–116. Amsterdam and Philadelphia: Benjamins. doi: 10.1075/btl.39.13jen

Jantunen, Jarmo H. 2001. "Synonymity and lexical simplification in translations: A corpus-based approach". *Across Languages and Cultures* 2 (1): 97–112.

Jaworski, Adam. 1993. *The Power of Silence: Social and Pragmatic Perspectives*. Newbury Park, CA.: Sage. doi: 10.4135/9781483325460

Jerome, Eusebius. [395] 1997. *De optime genere interpretandi*. Translated by P. Carroll as "On the best kind of translator", in *Western Translation Theory from Herodotus to Nietzsche*, D. Robinson (ed.), 22–30. Manchester: St. Jerome Publishing.

Jodl, Friedrich. 1918. *Allgemeine Ethik*. Stuttgart and Berlin: J. G. Cotta'sche Buchhandlung Nachfolger.

Johansson, Stig. 2004. "Why change the subject? On changes in subject selection in translation from English into Norwegian". *Target* 16 (1): 29–52. doi: 10.1075/target.16.1.03joh

Jones, Francis R. 2011. *Poetry Translating as Expert Action: Processes, Priorities and Networks*. Amsterdam and Philadelphia: Benjamins. doi: 10.1075/btl.93

Kafka, Franz. [1926] 1935. *Das Schloß*. Berlin: Schocken Verlag. (First English translation by Edwin and Willa Muir as *The Castle*, 1930. New York: Knopf.)

Kalinowski, Isabelle. 2002. "La vocation au travail de traduction". *Actes de la recherche en sciences sociales* 144: 47–54. doi: 10.3917/arss.144.0047

Kaplan, Michael, and Ellen Kaplan. 2006. *Chances are… Adventures in Probability*. London: Viking Penguin.

Katan, David. 1999. *Translating Cultures*. Manchester: St. Jerome Publishing.

Kellerman, Eric. 1986. "An eye for an eye: Crosslinguistic constraints on the development of the L2 lexicon". In *Crosslinguistic Influence in Second Language Acquisition*, E. Kellerman and M. Sharwood Smith (eds), 35–48. New York: Pergamon Press.

Kelletat, Andreas. F. 1986. *Die Rückschritte der Übersetzungstheorie*. Vaasa: Vaasan korkeakoulu.

Kelly, Louis G. 1979. *The True Interpreter*. Oxford: Blackwell.

Kemble, Ian (ed.). 2005. *Translation Norms. What is 'Normal' in the Translation Profession?* Portsmouth: University of Portsmouth, School of Languages and Area Studies.

Kenny, Dorothy. 1998. "Creatures of habit? What translators usually do with words". *Meta* 43 (4): 515–523. doi: 10.7202/003302ar

Kinnunen, Tuija, and Kaisa Koskinen (eds). 2010. *Translators' Agency*. Tampere: Tampere University Press. Available at <http://urn.fi/urn:isbn:978-951-44-8082-9>.

Klaudy, Kinga. 1996. "Back-translation as a tool for detecting explicitation strategies in translation". In *Translation Studies in Hungary*, K. Klaudy, J. Lambert and A. Sohár (eds), 99–114. Budapest: Scholastica.

Klaudy, Kinga. 2003. *Languages in Translation*. Budapest: Scholastica.

Klein, Julie Thompson. 1990), *Interdisciplinarity: History, Theory and Practice*, Detroit, MI.: Wayne State University Press.

Kohlmayer, Rainer. 1988. "Der Literaturübersetzer zwischen Original und Markt. Eine Kritik funktionalistischer Übersetzungstheorien". *Lebende Sprachen* 33 (4): 145–156. doi: 10.1515/les.1988.33.4.145

Koller, Werner. 1979. *Einführung in die Übersetzungswissenschaft*. Heidelberg: Quelle und Meyer.

Koller, Werner. 1990. "Zum Gegenstand der Übersetzungswissenschaft". In *Übersetzungswissenschaft. Ergebnisse und Perspektiven, Festshcrift für Wolfram Wilss zum 65. Geburtstag*, R. Arntz and G. Thome (eds), 19–30. Tübingen: Narr.

Koller, Werner. 1995. "The concept of equivalence and the object of Translation Studies". *Target* 7 (2): 191–222. doi: 10.1075/target.7.2.02kol

Koskinen, Kaisa. 2000a. "Institutional illusions. Translating in the EU Commission". *The Translator* 6 (1): 49–65. doi: 10.1080/13556509.2000.10799055

Koskinen, Kaisa. 2000b. *Beyond Ambivalence. Postmodernity and the Ethics of Translation*. Tampere: University of Tampere.

Koskinen, Kaisa. 2008. *Translating Institutions. An Ethnographic Study of EU Translation*. Manchester: St. Jerome Publishing.

Koskinen, Kaisa, and Outi Paloposki. 2015. *Sata Kirjaa, Tuhat Suomennosta*. Helsinki: Suomen Kirjallisuuden Seura.

Kranach, Svenja. 2014. "Translations as a locus of language contact". In *Translation: A Multidisciplinary Approach*, J. House (ed.), 96–115. London: Palgrave Macmillan.

Krings, Hans P. 1986. *Was in den Köpfen von Übersetzern vorgeht: eine empirische Untersuchung zur Struktur des Übersetzungsprozesses an fortgeschrittenen Französischlernern*. Tübingen: Narr.

Kroeber, Alfred L., and Clyde Kluckhohn. 1952. *Cultures: A Critical Review of Concepts and Definitions*. [Peabody Museum Papers Vol. 47, no. 1.] Cambridge, MA.: Harvard University Press.

Krzeszowski, Tomasz P. 1990. *Contrasting Languages. The Scope of Contrastive Linguistics*. Berlin: Mouton de Gruyter. doi: 10.1515/9783110860146

Kuhn, Thomas S. [1962] 1970. *The Structure of Scientific Revolutions*. Second, enlarged edition. Chicago: University of Chicago Press.

Kujamäki, Pekka. 1998. *Deutsche Stimmen der Sieben Brüder*. Frankfurt am Main: Peter Lang.

Kujamäki, Pekka. 2001. "Finnish comet in German skies: Translation, retranslation and norms". *Target* 13 (1): 45–70. doi: 10.1075/target.13.1.04kuj

Kukkonen, Pirjo. 1993. *Kielen Silkki. Hiljaisuus ja rakkaus kielen ja kirjallisuuden kuvastimessa*. Helsinki: Yliopistopaino.

Kundera, Milan. 1993a. *Les Testaments Trahis*. Paris: Gallimard.

Kundera, Milan. 1993b. *Nesmrtelnost*. Brno: Atlantis.

Kundera, Milan. 1995. Interview in *Lidové Noviny*, Oct. 30.

Kundera, Milan. 2003. *L'ignorance*. Paris: Gallimard.

Künzli, Alexander, and Maureen Ehrensberger-Dow. 2011. "Innovative subtitling. A reception study". In *Methods and Strategies of Process Research*, C. Alvstad, A. Hild and E. Tiselius (eds), 187–200. Amsterdam and Philadelphia: Benjamins. doi:10.1075/btl.94.14kun

Kurz, Ingrid, and Klaus Kaindl (eds). 2005. *Wortklauber, Sinnverdreher, Brückenbauer? DolmetscherInnen und ÜbersetzerInnen als literarische Geschöpfe*. Vienna: Lit Verlag.

Kußmaul, Paul. 2007. *Verstehen und Übersetzen*. Tübingen: Gunter Narr.

Laaksovaara, Tuula H., and Gary Farell. 1992. "Position of silence in English and Finnish culture". *Erikoiskielet ja Käännösteoria / VAKKI-symposium* XII, 107–118.

Lado, Robert. 1957. *Linguistics across Cultures*. Ann Arbor: University of Michigan Press.

Lakatos, Imre. 1970. "Falsification and the methodology of scientific research programmes". In *Criticism and the Growth of Knowledge*, I. Lakatos and A. Musgrave (eds), 91–196. Cambridge: Cambridge University Press. doi:10.1017/CBO9781139171434.009

Lakoff, George. 1987. *Women, Fire, and Dangerous Things. What categories reveal about the mind*. Chicago: University of Chicago University Press. doi:10.7208/chicago/9780226471013.001.0001

Lakoff, George, and Mark Johnson. 1980. *Metaphors We Live By*. Chicago: University of Chicago Press.

Laland, Kevin N. and Gillian R. Brown. 2002. *Sense and Nonsense. Evolutionary perspectives on human behaviour*. Oxford: Oxford University Press.

Lambert, José. 1991. "Shifts, oppositions and goals in Translation Studies: Towards a Genealogy of Concepts". In *Translation Studies: The State of the Art*, K. van Leuven-Zwart and T. Naaijkens (eds), 25–37. Amsterdam: Rodopi.

Lambert, José. 1996. "Language and translation as general management problems". In *Teaching Translation and Interpreting 3: New Horizons*, C. Dollerup and V. Appel (eds), 271–293. Amsterdam and Philadelphia: Benjamins. doi:10.1075/btl.16.37lam

Lambert, José, and Hendrik van Gorp. 1985. "On describing translations". In *The Manipulation of Literature. Studies in Literary Translation*, T. Hermans (ed.), 42–53. London: Croom Helm.

Lane-Mercier, Gillian. 1997. "Translating the untranslatable: The translator's aesthetic, ideological and political responsibility". *Target* 9 (1): 43–68. doi:10.1075/target.9.1.04lan

Lang, George. 2000. "Translation from, to and within the Atlantic Creoles". *TTR* 8 (2): 11–28. doi:10.7202/037409ar

Lanstyák, István, and Pál Heltai. 2012. "Universals in language contact and translation". *Across Languages and Cultures* 13 (1): 99–121. doi:10.1556/Acr.13.2012.1.6

Lass, Roger. 1980. *On Explaining Language Change*. Cambridge: Cambridge University Press.

Laviosa-Braithwaite, Sara. 1996. *The English Comparable Corpus (ECC): A Resource and a Methodology for the Empirical Study of Translation*. Unpublished PhD thesis, UMIST, Manchester.

Law, John, and John Hassard (eds). 1998. *Actor Network Theory and After*. Oxford: Blackwell.

Lefevere, André. 1992a. *Translation, Rewriting and the Manipulation of Literary Fame*. London: Routledge.

Leech, Geoffrey N. 1983. *Principles of Pragmatics*, London: Longman.

Lefevere, André (ed.). 1992b. *Translation / History / Culture*. London: Routledge. doi:10.4324/9780203417607

Leppihalme, Ritva. 1997. *Culture Bumps. An empirical approach to the translation of allusions*. Clevedon: Multilingual Matters Ltd.

Leppihalme, Ritva. 2000a. "Foreignizing strategies in drama translation: the case of the Finnish Oleanna". In *Translation in Context*, A. Chesterman, N. Gallardo San Salvador and Y. Gambier (eds), 153–162. Amsterdam and Philadelphia: Benjamins. doi:10.1075/btl.39.18lep

Leppihalme, Ritva. 2000b. "Kulttuurisidonnaisuus kaunokirjallisuuden kääntämisessä". In *Käännöskirjallisuus ja sen Kritiikki*, O. Paloposki and H. Makkonen-Craig (eds), 89–105. Helsinki: AKO.

Leuven-Zwart, Kitty M. van. 1989/1990. "Translation and original. Similarities and dissimilarities, I and II". *Target* 1 (2): 151–181 and 2 (1): 69–95. doi:10.1075/target.1.2.03leu

Levenston, Edward A. 1971. "Over-indulgence and under-representation – Aspects of mother-tongue interference". In *Papers in Contrastive Linguistics*, G. Nickel (ed.), 115–121. Cambridge: Cambridge University Press.

Levinas, Emmanuel. 1982. *Éthique et Infini. Dialogues avec Philippe Nemo*. Paris: Fayard and Radio-France.

Levinas, Emmanuel. 1987. *Philosophy and the Idea of Infinity. Collected philosophical papers*. Translated by Alphonso Lingin. Dordrecht: Martinus Nijhoff. doi:10.1007/978-94-009-4364-3

Levý, Jiři. [1967] 1989. "Translation as a Decision Process". In *To Honor Roman Jakobson*, vol. II, 1171–1182. The Hague: Mouton de Gruyter. Reprinted in A. Chesterman (ed.), 1989, *Readings in Translation Theory*, 37–52. Helsinki: Finn Lectura.

Lewis, David K. 1969. *Convention: A Philosophical Study*. Cambridge, MA.: Harvard University Press.

Lewis, Philip E. 1985. "The measure of translation effects". In *Difference in Translation*, J. Graham (ed.), 31–62. Ithaca, NY: Cornell University Press

Lörscher, Wolfgang. 1989. "Models of the translation process: Claim and reality". *Target* 1 (1): 43–68. doi:10.1075/target.1.1.05lor

Lörscher, Wolfgang. 1991. *Translation Performance, Translation Process and Translation Strategies: A psycholinguistic investigation*. Tübingen: Narr.

Luhmann, Niklas. 1990. *Essays on Self-Reference*. New York: Columbia University Press.

MacIntyre, Alasdair. 1981. *After Virtue. A study in moral theory*. Notre Dame, Indiana: University of Notre Dame Press.

Maia, Belinda. 1998. "Word order and the first person singular in Portuguese and English". *Meta* 43 (4): 589–601. doi:10.7202/003539ar

Maier, Carol. 2006. "The Translator as Theôros: Thoughts on Cogitation, Figuration and Current Creative Writing". In *Translating Others*, vol. 1, Theo Hermans (ed.), 163–180. Manchester: St. Jerome Publishing.

Malblanc, Alfred. 1963. *Stylistique Comparée du Français et de l'Allemand*. 2nd edition. Paris: Didier.

Malmkjær, Kirsten. 1994. "Translating customer expectations into teaching". In *Quality-Assurance, Management and Control. ITI Conference 7, Proceedings*, C. Picken (ed.), 143–155. London: Institute of Translation and Interpreting.

Malmkjær, Kirsten. 2000. "Multidisciplinarity in process research". In *Tapping and Mapping the Processes of Translation and Interpreting*, Sonja Tirkkonen-Condit and Riittä Jääskeläinen (eds), 163–170. Amsterdam and Philadelphia: Benjamins. doi:10.1075/btl.37.16mal

Malmkjær, Kirsten. 2005. "Norms and nature in Translation Studies". *Synaps* (Norges Handelshøyskole, Bergen) 16: 13–19.

Malmkjær, Kirsten. 2007. "Norms and nature in translation studies". In *Incorporating Corpora – Corpora and the Translator*, G. Anderman and M. Rogers, (eds), 49–59. Clevedon: Multilingual Matters.

Malone, Joseph L. 1988. *The Science of Linguistics in the Art of Translation*. New York: State University of New York Press.

Martin, James R., and Peter R. R. White. 2005. *The Language of Evaluation. Appraisal in English.* London and New York: Palgrave Macmillan.

Martín de León, Celia. 2008. "Skopos and beyond. A critical study of functionalism". *Target* 20 (1): 1–28. doi:10.1075/target.20.1.02mar

Mason, Ian. 2000. "Audience design in translating". *The Translator* 6 (1): 1–22. doi:10.1080/13556509.2000.10799053

Matthiessen, Christian M. I. M. 2001. "The environment of translation". In *Exploring Translation and Multilingual Text Production*, E. Steiner and C. Yallop (eds), 41–124. Berlin and New York: Mouton de Gruyter. doi:10.1515/9783110866193.41

Mauranen, Anna. 2000. "Strange strings in translated language. A study on corpora". In *Intercultural Faultlines. Research Models in Translation Studies I. Textual and Cognitive Aspects*, M. Olohan (ed.), 119–141. Manchester: St. Jerome Publishing.

Mauranen, Anna, and Pekka Kujamäki (eds.). 2004. *Translation Universals. Do they exist?* Amsterdam and Philadelphia: Benjamins. doi:10.1075/btl.48

Mayoral Asensio, Roberto. 2000. "Parámetros sociales y traducción". *Trans: Revista de traductología* 4: 111–118.

McCarty, Willard. 1999. "Humanities computing as interdiscipline". Available at: <http://www.kcl.ac.uk/humanities/cch/wlm/essays/inter/>

McDonough Dolmaya, Julie. 2011a. "The ethics of crowdsourcing". *Linguistica Antverpiensia* 10: 97–111.

McDonough Dolmaya, Julie. 2011b. "Moral ambiguity: Some shortcomings of professional codes of ethics for translators". *JoSTrans* 15: 28–49.

Medin, Douglas L., and Robert L. Goldstone. 1995. "The predicates of similarity". In *Similarity in Language, Thought and Perception* [Semiotic and Cognitive Studies 1], C. Cacciari (ed.), 83–110. Turnhout: Brepols.

Melby, Alan K., with C. Terry Warner. 1995. *The Possibility of Language. A discussion of the nature of language, with implications for human and machine translation.* Amsterdam and Philadelphia: Benjamins. doi:10.1075/btl.14

Meylaerts, Reine. 2011. "Translation policy". In *Handbook of Translation Studies*, vol. 2, Y. Gambier and L. van Doorslaer (eds), 163–168. Amsterdam and Philadelphia: Benjamins. doi:10.1075/hts.2.tra10

Milton, John. 2001. "The figure of the factory translator". Paper presented at the Third EST Congress, Copenhagen, August 30 – September 1, 2001.

Misgeld, Dieter. 1991. "Modernity and hermeneutics: a critical-theoretical rejoinder". In *Gadamer and Hermeneutics*, H. J. Silverman (ed.), 163–177. London: Routledge.

Misgeld, Dieter, and Graeme Nicholson. 1992. "Writing and the living voice. Interview with Hans-Georg Gadamer". In *Hans-Georg Gadamer on Education, Poetry, and History*, D. Misgeld and G. Nicholson (eds), 63–71. Albany, N.Y.: State University of New York Press.

Molina, Lucía, and Amparo Hurtado Albir. 2002. "Translation techniques revisited: A dynamic and functionalist approach". *Meta* 47, 4, 498–512. doi:10.7202/008033ar

Mossop, Brian. 1998. "Four questions about the work habits of translators". Paper read at the EST Congress, Granada, 23–26.9.1998.

Mossop, Brian. 2000. "The workplace procedure of professional translators". In A. Chesterman, N. Gallardo San Salvador and Y. Gambier (eds), *Translation in Context*, 39–48. Amsterdam and Philadelphia: Benjamins. doi:10.1075/btl.39.07mos

Mossop, Brian. [2001] 2007. *Revising and Editing for Translators.* Manchester: St. Jerome Publishing.

Moster, Stefan. 2003. "Birthday blues". *Books from Finland* 2003 (1): 59–60. Also available at <http://www.finlit.fi/booksfromfinland/bff/103/moster.html>

Munday, Jeremy. 2001. *Introducing Translation Studies. Theories and Applications*. London: Routledge.

Munday, Jeremy (ed.). 2007. *Translation as Intervention*. London: Continuum.

Muñoz Martín, Ricardo. 2000. "Translation strategies. Somewhere over the rainbow". In *Investigating Translation*, A. Beeby, D. Ensinger and M. Presas (eds), 129–138. Amsterdam and Philadelphia: Benjamins. doi: 10.1075/btl.32.16mun

Muñoz Martín, Ricardo. 2016. "Processes of what models? On the cognitive indivisibility of translation acts and events". *Translation Spaces* 5 (1): 145–161. doi: 10.1075/ts.5.1.08mun

Murphy, Shirin. 2003. "Second language transfer during third language acquisition". *Teachers College, Columbia University Working Papers in TESOL & Applied Linguistics* 3 (2). (http://journals.tc-library.org/index.php/tesol/issue/view/6, 7 Jan. 2007)

Neubert, Albrecht. 2001. Review of Chesterman et al. (2000). *Target* 13 (2): 387–391. doi: 10.1075/target.13.2.24neu

Neubert, Albrecht, and Gregory M. Shreve. 1992. *Translation as Text*. Kent, Ohio: Kent State University Press.

Newmark, Peter. 1981. *Approaches to Translation*. Oxford: Pergamon Press.

Newmark, Peter. 1988. *A Textbook of Translation*. New York: Prentice Hall.

Nida, Eugene A. 1964. *Toward a Science of Translating*. Leiden: Brill.

Nida, Eugene A. [1969] 1989. "Science of translation". *Language* 45(3): 483–498. Reprinted in A. Chesterman (ed.), 1989, *Readings in Translation Theory*, 80–98. Helsinki: Finn Lectura.

Niiniluoto, Ilkka. 1983. *Tieteellinen Päättely ja Selittäminen*. Helsinki: Otava.

Norberg, Ulf. 2003. *Übersetzen mit Doppeltem Skopos*. Uppsala: Uppsala Universitet.

Nord, Christiane. 1988. *Textanalyse und Übersetzen. Theorie, Methode und didaktische Anwendung einer übersetzungsrelevanten Textanalyse*. Heidelberg: Groos.

Nord, Christiane. 1991a. *Text Analysis in Translation*. Amsterdam and Atlanta: Rodopi.

Nord, Christiane. 1991b. "Scopos, loyalty, and translational conventions". *Target* 3 (1): 91–109. doi: 10.1075/target.3.1.06nor

Nord, Christiane. 1997. *Translating as a Purposeful Activity*. Manchester: St. Jerome Publishing.

Nordman, Lieselott. 2009. *Lagöversättning som process och produkt*. Helsinki: Institutionen för nordiska språk och nordisk litteratur, Helsingfors universitet.

Odlin, Terence. 1991. "Irish English idioms and language transfer". *English World-Wide* 12 (2): 175–193. doi: 10.1075/eww.12.2.02odl

Olk, Harold. 2002. "Critical Discourse Analysis in translation". *The Translator* 8 (1): 101–116. doi: 10.1080/13556509.2002.10799118

Olohan, Maeve, and Mona Baker. 2000. "Reporting that in translated English. Evidence for subconscious processes of explicitation?" *Across Languages and Cultures* 1 (2): 141–158. doi: 10.1556/Acr.1.2000.2.1

Øverås, Linn. 1998. "In search of the third code: an investigation of norms in literary translation". *Meta* 43 (4): 571–588. doi: 10.7202/003775ar

Paasilinna, Arto. 1984. *Ukkosenjumalan poika*. Helsinki: WSOY.

Paasilinna, Arto. 1999. *Der Sohn des Donnergottes*. (Translation by S. Moster.) München: Ehrenwirth.

Paloposki, Outi. 1996. "Originality in translation". In *Aspectus varii translationis II* [Studia Translatologica, Ser. B., vol. 2.], R. Oittinen, O. Paloposki and J. Schopp (eds), 66–84. Tampere: Tampere University Publications.

Paloposki, Outi. 2009. "Limits of freedom. Agency, choice and constraints in the work of the translator". In *Agents of Translation*, J. Milton and P. Banda (eds), 189–208. Amsterdam and Philadelphia: Benjamins. doi: 10.1075/btl.81.09pal

Paloposki, Outi, and Kaisa Koskinen. 2004. "Thousand and one translations. Retranslation hypothesis revisited". In *Claims, Changes and Challenges in Translation Studies*, G. Hansen, K. Malmkjær and D. Gile (eds), 27–38. Amsterdam and Philadelphia: Benjamins. doi: 10.1075/btl.50.04pal

Pápai, Vilma. 2004. "Explicitation: a universal of translated text?" In *Translation Universals. Do they exist?*, A. Mauranen and P. Kujamäki (eds), 143–164. Amsterdam and Philadelphia: John Benjamins. doi: 10.1075/btl.48.12pap

Peeters, Jean. 1999. *La médiation de l'étranger. Une sociolinguistique de la traduction*. Arras: Artois Presses Université.

Pergnier, Maurice. [1978] 1993. *Les fondements sociolinguistiques de la traduction*. Lille: Presses Universitaires de Lille.

Phillips, Adam. 2007. "After Strachey". *London Review of Books*, 4.10.2007, 36–38.

Pike, Kenneth. L. 1959. "Language as particle, wave and field". *Texas Quarterly* 2 (2): 37–54.

Pöchhacker, Franz. 2004. *Introducing Interpreting Studies*. London: Routledge.

Pokorn, Nike K. 2000. "Translation into a non-mother tongue in translation theory: deconstruction of the traditional". In *Translation in Context*, A. Chesterman, N. Gallardo San Salvador and Y. Gambier (eds), 61–72. Amsterdam and Philadelphia: Benjamins. doi: 10.1075/btl.39.09pok

Polezzi, Loredana (ed.). 2006. *Translation, Travel, Migration*. Special issue of *The Translator*, 12 (2).

Poltermann, A. 1992. "Normen des literarischen Übersetzens im System der Literatur". In *Geschichte, System, Literarische Übersetzung. Histories, Systems, Literary Translation*, H. Kittel (ed.), 5–31. Berlin: Erich Schmidt.

Popovič, Anton. 1970. "The concept 'shift of expression' in translation analysis". In *The Nature of Translation*, J. S. Holmes, F. de Haan and A. Popovič (eds), 78–87. The Hague: Mouton.

Popper, Karl R. [1945] 1962. *The Open Society and its Enemies*. London: Routledge and Kegan Paul.

Popper, Karl R. 1959. *The Logic of Scientific Discovery*. London: Hutchinson.

Popper, Karl R. 1963. *Conjectures and Refutations: The Growth of Scientific Knowledge*. London: Routledge and Kegan Paul.

Popper, Karl R. 1972. *Objective Knowledge. An evolutionary approach*. Oxford: Clarendon Press.

Prunč, Erich. 1997a. "Versuch einer Skopostypologie". In *Text – Kultur – Kommunikation*, N. Grbic and M. Wolf (eds), 33–52. Tübingen: Stauffenburg.

Prunč, E. 1997b. "Translationskultur. Versuch einer konstruktiven Kritik des translatorischen Handels". *TEXTconTEXT* 11 (2): 99–127.

Putnam, Hilary. 2002. *The Collapse of the Fact/Value Dichotomy and Other Essays*. Cambridge, MA.: Harvard University Press.

Puurtinen, Tiina. 1995. *Linguistic Acceptability in Translated Children's Literature*. [University of Joensuu Publications in the Humanities 15.] Joensuu: University of Joensuu.

Pym, Anthony. 1992a. *Translation and Text Transfer*. Frankfurt am Main: Peter Lang.

Pym, Anthony. 1992b. "The relation between translation and material text transfer". *Target* 4 (2): 171–189. doi: 10.1075/target.4.2.03pym

Pym, Anthony. 1992c. "Translation error analysis and the interface with language teaching". In *Teaching Translation and Interpreting: Training, Talent and Experience*, C. Dollerup and A. Loddegaard (eds), 279–288. Amsterdam and Philadelphia: Benjamins. doi: 10.1075/z.56.42pym

Pym, Anthony. 1995. "European Translation Studies, une science qui dérange, and why equivalence needn't be a dirty word". *TTR* 8 (1): 153–176. doi:10.7202/037200ar
Pym, Anthony. [1997] 2012. *Pour une éthique du traducteur*. Arras Presses Université. (English translation 2012: *On Translator Ethics. Principles for mediation between cultures*. Amsterdam and Philadelphia: Benjamins.
Pym, Anthony. 1998. *Method in Translation History*. Manchester: St. Jerome Publishing.
Pym, Anthony. 1999. "Translation Studies beyond 2000". In *Translation and the (Re)Location of Meaning*, J. Vandaele (ed.), 443–448. Leuven: CETRA, Katholieke Universiteit Leuven.
Pym, Anthony. 2000. "On cooperation". In *Intercultural Faultlines. Research Models in Translation Studies I. Textual and Cognitive Apects*, M. Olohan (ed.), 181–192. Manchester: St. Jerome Publishing.
Pym, Anthony. 2004. *The Moving Text*. Amsterdam and Philadelphia: Benjamins. doi:10.1075/btl.49
Pym, Anthony. 2006. "On the social and the cultural in Translation Studies". In *Sociocultural Aspects of Translating and Interpreting*, A. Pym, M. Shlesinger and Z. Jettmarová (eds), 1–25. Amsterdam and Philadelphia: Benjamins. doi:10.1075/btl.67.02pym
Pym, Anthony. 2007a. "Natural and directional equivalence in theories of translation". *Target* 19(2): 271–294. doi:10.1075/target.19.2.07pym
Pym, Anthony. 2007b. "On history in formal conceptualizations of translation". *Across Languages and Cultures* 8 (2): 153–166. doi:10.1556/Acr.8.2007.2.1
Pym, Anthony. 2009. "Using process studies in translator training. Self-discovery through lousy experiments". In *Methodology, Technology and Innovation in Translation Process Research*, S. Göpferich, F. Alves & I. M. Mees (eds), 135–156. Copenhagen: Samfundslitteratur.
Pym, Anthony. 2010. *Exploring Translation Theories*. London and New York: Routledge.
Pym, Anthony. 2011. "Translation theory as historical problem-solving". *Intercultural Communication Review* 9: 49–61.
Pym, Anthony. 2016. *Translation Solutions for Many Languages – Histories of a Flawed Dream*. London: Bloomsbury Publishing.
Quine, Willard van O. 1960. *Word and Object*. Cambridge, MA.: MIT Press.
Raittila, Hannu. 2001. *Canal Grande*. Helsinki: WSOY.
Raz, Joseph. 1975. *Practical Reason and Norms*. London: Hutchinson University Library.
Reiß, Katharina. 1971. *Möglichkeiten und Grenzen der Übersetzungskritik*. München: Max Hueber.
Reiß, Katharina, and Hans J. Vermeer. 1984. *Grundlegung einer Allgemeinen Translationstheorie*. Tübingen: Niemeyer. doi:10.1515/9783111351919
Retsker, Ya. I. 1974. *Teoriya perevoda i perevodcheskaya praktika*. Moscow: Mezhdunarodnie otnosheniya.
Risku, Hanna. 1998. *Translatorische Kompetenz. Kognitive Grundlagen des Übersetzens als Expertentätigkeit*. Tübingen: Stauffenburg.
Risku, Hanna. 2002. "Situatedness in Translation Studies". *Cognitive Systems Research* 3 (3): 523–533. doi:10.1016/S1389-0417(02)00055-4
Risku, Hanna. 2010. "A cognitive scientific view of technical communication and translation. Do embodiment and situatedness really make a difference?" *Target* 22 (1): 94–111. doi:10.1075/target.22.1.06ris
Risku, Hanna, and Roland Freihoff. 2000. "Kooperative Textgestaltung im translatorischen Handlungsrahmen". In *Translation in Context*, A. Chesterman, N. Gallardo San Salvador and Y. Gambier (eds), 49–59. Amsterdam and Philadelphia: Benjamins. doi:10.1075/btl.39.08ris

Robinson, Douglas. 1991. *The Translator's Turn*. Baltimore: Johns Hopkins University Press.
Robinson, Douglas. 1997. *Becoming a Translator. An Accelerated Course*. London: Routledge.
Robinson, Douglas. 1999. "Nine theses about anecdotalism in the study of translation (With Special Reference to Sherry Simon, Ed., Culture in Transit)". *Meta* 44 (2): 402–408.
   doi: 10.7202/003966ar
Round, Nicholas G. 2005. "Translation and its metaphors: the (N+1) wise men and the elephant". *SKASE* 1 (1): 47–69.
Rudner, Richard. [1953] 1998. "The scientist qua scientist does make value judgements". *Philosophy of Science* 20, 1–6. Reprinted in E. D. Klemke, R. Hollinger and D. W. Rudge (eds), 1998, *Introductory Readings in the Philosophy of Science* (3rd edition), 492–498. Amherst, NY.: Prometheus Books.
Runciman, W. G. 1998. *The Social Animal*. London: Harper Collins.
Rushdie, Salman. 1992. *Imaginary Homelands*. London: Granta Books.
Sager, Juan C. 1994. *Language Engineering and Translation. Consequences of Automation*, Amsterdam and Philadelphia: Benjamins. doi: 10.1075/btl.1
Sager, Juan C. 1997. "Text types and translation". In *Text Typology and Translation*, A. Trosberg (ed.), 25–41. Amsterdam and Philadelphia: Benjamins. doi: 10.1075/btl.26.04sag
Salmon, Wesley C. 1998. *Causality and Explanation*. New York: OUP.
   doi: 10.1093/0195108647.001.0001
Savory, Theodore H. [1957] 1968. *The Art of Translation*. London: Cape.
Schäffner, Christina (ed.). 1998. *Translation and Quality*. Clevedon: Multilingual Matters.
Schäffner, Christina (ed.). 1999. *Translation and Norms*. Clevedon: Multilingual Matters.
Schiavi, Giuliana. 1996. "There is always a teller in a tale". *Target* 8 (1): 1–21.
   doi: 10.1075/target.8.1.02sch
Schleifer, Ronald. 1987. *A. J. Greimas and the Nature of Meaning: Linguistics, Semiotics and Discourse*. Beckenham: Croom Helm.
Schmidt, Morena Azbel. 2005. *"How Do You Do it Anyway?" A Longitudinal Study of three Translator Students Translating from Russian into Swedish*. Stockholm: Stockholm University. Available at <http://su.diva-portal.org/smash/record.jsf?pid=diva2:197703>
Schreiber, Michael. 1998. "Übersetzungstypen und Übersetzungsverfahren". In *Handbuch Translation*, M. Snell-Hornby, H. G. Hönig, P. Kußmaul and P. A. Schmitt (eds), 151–154. Tübingen: Stauffenburg.
Schulte, Rainer, and John Biguenet (eds). 1992. *Theories of Translation*. Chicago: University of Chicago Press.
Searle, John R. [1964] 1967. "How to derive 'ought' from 'is'". *Philosophical Review* 73: 43–58. Reprinted e.g. in P. Foot (ed.), 1967, *Theories of Ethics*, 101–114. Oxford: Oxford University Press.
Segerstråle, Ullica. 2000. *Defenders of the Truth. The battle for science in the sociobiology debate and beyond*. Oxford: Oxford University Press.
Séguinot, Candace. 1982. "The editing function of translation". *Bulletin of the Canadian Association of Applied Linguistics* 4 (1): 151–161.
Séguinot, Candace. 1989. "The translation process: an experimental study". In *The Translation Process*, C. Séguinot (ed.), 21–53. School of Translation, York University: H. G. Publications.
Seleskovitch, Danica, and Marianne Lederer 1984. *Interpréter pour traduire*. Paris: Didier.
Shlesinger, Miriam. 1989. "Extending the theory of translation to interpretation: Norms as a case in point". *Target* 1 (1): 111–115. doi: 10.1075/target.1.1.09shl

Shreve, Gregory M., Isabel Lacruz, and Erik Angelone. 2011. "Sight translation and speech disfluency: Performance analysis as a window to cognitive translation processes". In *Methods and Strategies of Process Research*, C. Alvstad, A. Hild and E. Tiselius (eds), 93–120. Amsterdam and Philadelphia: Benjamins. doi:10.1075/btl.94.09shr

Shuttleworth, Mark, and Moira Cowie. 1997. *Dictionary of Translation Studies*. Manchester: St. Jerome Publishing.

Siitonen, Arto. [1991] 1993. "Insinöörin etiikasta". In Airaksinen (ed.) [1991] 1993: 265–284.

Simeoni, Daniel. 1998. "The pivotal status of the translator's habitus". *Target* 10 (1): 1–39. doi:10.1075/target.10.1.02sim

Simmel, Georg. [1908] 1950. *Soziologie. Untersuchungen über die Forme der Gesellschaft*. Leipzig: Duncker and Humblot. Translated and edited by Kurt. H. Wolff. 1950) as *The Sociology of Georg Simmel*. New York: The Free Press. ("The stranger" is the title of Chapter 3, pp. 402–408.)

Sintonen, Matti. 1984. *The Pragmatics of Scientific Explanation*. Helsinki: Societas Philosophica Fennica.

Snell-Hornby, Mary. 1991. "Translation Studies – Art, science or utopia?" In *Translation Studies: The State of the Art*, K. van Leuven-Zwart and T. Naaijkens (eds), 13–23. Amsterdam: Rodopi.

Snell-Hornby, Mary. 2006. *The Turns of Translation Studies*. Amsterdam and Philadelphia: Benjamins. doi:10.1075/btl.66

Snell-Hornby, Mary, Franz Pöchhacker and Klaus Kaindl (eds). 1994. *Translation Studies. An Interdiscipline*. Amsterdam: Benjamins. doi:10.1075/btl.2

Sovran, Tamar. 1992. "Between similarity and sameness". *Journal of Pragmatics* 18 (4): 329–344. doi:10.1016/0378-2166(92)90093-Q

Sperber, Dan, and Deidre Wilson. 1986. *Relevance: Communication and Cognition*. Oxford: Blackwell.

Sprung, R. C. (ed.). 2000. *Translating into Success*. Amsterdam and Philadelphia: Benjamins. doi:10.1075/ata.xi

Stecconi, Ubaldo. 2004. "Interpretive semiotics and translation theory: the semiotic conditions to translation". *Semiotica* 150: 471–489.

Stetting, Karen. 1989. "Transediting – a new term for coping with a grey area between editing and translating". In *Proceedings from the Fourth Nordic Conference for English Studies*, G. D. Caie, K. Haastrup, A. L. Jakobsen, J. E. Nielsen, J. Sevaldsen, H. Specht and A. Zettersten (eds), 371–382. Copenhagen: Department of English, University of Copenhagen.

Sunwoo, Min. 2007. "Operationalizing the translation purpose (Skopos)". *MuTra conference proceedings: LSP Translation Scenarios*. Available at http://www.euroconferences.info/proceedings/2007_Proceedings/2007_Sunwoo_Min.pdf (Accessed 16.4.2009).

Susam-Sarajeva, Şebnem. 2001. "Is one case always enough?" *Perspectives* 9 (3): 167–176. doi:10.1080/0907676X.2001.9961415

Taivalkoski-Shilov, Kristiina. 2002. "Traduire la mixité formelle: l'exemple des premières (re)traductions de Fielding en France. *Faits de Langue* 19: 85–97.

Taivalkoski-Shilov, Kristiina. 2006. *La Tierce Main. Le discours rapporté dans les traductions françaises de Fielding au XVIIIe siècle*. Arras Cedex: Artois Presses Université.

Tannen, Deborah, and Muriel Saville-Troike (eds). 1985. *Perspectives on Silence*. Norwood, NJ: Ablex.

Tarasti, Eero. 1988. "Suomi semiootikon silmin". *Synteesi* 1–2: 12–19.

Tirkkonen-Condit, Sonja. 2000. "In search of translation universals: non-equivalence or 'unique' items in a corpus test". Paper presented at the UMIST/UCL Research Models in Translation Studies Conference, Manchester, 28–30 April 2000.

Tirkkonen-Condit, Sonja. 2002. "Translationese – a myth or an empirical fact?" *Target* 14 (2): 207–220. doi:10.1075/target.14.2.02tir

Tirkkonen-Condit, Sonja. 2004. "Unique items – over- or under-represented in translated language?" In *Translation Universals. Do they exist?*, A. Mauranen and P. Kujamäki (eds.), 177–184. Amsterdam and Philadelphia: John Benjamins. doi:10.1075/btl.48.14tir

Tirkkonen-Condit, Sonja. 2005. "The Monitor Model revisited: Evidence from process research". *Meta* 50 (2): 405–414. doi:10.7202/010990ar

Toury, Gideon. 1980. *In Search of a Theory of Translation*. Tel Aviv: Porter Institute for Poetics and Semiotics.

Toury, Gideon. 1985. "A rationale for Descriptive Translation Studies". In *The Manipulation of Literature: Studies in Literary Translation*, T. Hermans (ed.), 16–41. London: Croom Helm.

Toury, Gideon. 1991. "What are descriptive studies into translation likely to yield apart from isolated descriptions?" In *Translation Studies: The State of the Art. Proceedings of the First James S Holmes Symposium on Translation Studies*, K. van Leuven-Zwart and T. Naaijkens (eds), 179–192. Amsterdam and Atlanta, GA: Rodopi.

Toury, Gideon. [1995] 2012. *Descriptive Translation Studies and Beyond*. Amsterdam: Benjamins. (Revised edition 2012.) doi:10.1075/btl.4

Toury, Gideon. 1996. "In search of laws of translational behavior". In *Basic Issues in Translation Studies: Proceedings of the Fifth International Conference*, A. Neubert, G. M. Shreve, and K. Gommlich (eds), 45–56. Kent, OH.: Kent State University Press

Toury, Gideon. 2002. "What's the problem with 'translation problem'?" In *Translation and Meaning, Part 6*, B. Lewandowska-Tomaszczyk and M. Thelén (eds), 57–71. Maastricht: Hogeschool Zuyd, Maastricht School of Translation and Interpreting.

Toury, Gideon. 2004a. "Probabilistic explanations in Translation Studies: Universals – or a challenge to the very concept?" In *Claims, Changes and Challenges in Translation Studies*, G. Hansen, K. Malmkjær and D. Gile (eds), 15–25. Amsterdam and Philadelphia: Benjamins. doi:10.1075/btl.50.03tou

Toury, Gideon. 2004b. "Probabilistic explanations in translation studies. Welcome as they are, would they qualify as universals?" In *Translation Universals. Do they Exist?*, A. Mauranen and P. Kujamäki, (eds), 15–32. Amsterdam and Philadelphia: Benjamins. doi:10.1075/btl.48.03tou

Toury, Gideon. 2006. "Conducting research on a 'wish-to-understand' basis". In *Translation Studies at the Interface of Disciplines*, J. Ferreira Duarte, A. Assis Rosa and T. Seruya (eds), 55–66. Amsterdam and Philadelphia: Benjamins. doi:10.1075/btl.68.06tou

Trivedi, Harish. 2006. "In our own time, on our own terms: 'translation' in India". In *Translating Others*, Volume 1, T. Hermans (ed.), 102–119. Manchester: St. Jerome Publishing.

Tversky, Amos. 1977. "Features of similarity". *Psychological Review* 84: 327–352. doi:10.1037/0033-295X.84.4.327

Tymoczko, Maria. 1998. "Computerized corpora and the future of Translation Studies". *Meta* 43 (4): 652–659. doi:10.7202/004515ar

Tymoczko, Maria. 1999. *Translation in a Postcolonial Context*. Manchester: St. Jerome Publishing.

Tymoczko, Maria. 2000. "Translation and political engagement. Activism, social change and the role of translation in geopolitical shifts". *The Translator* 6 (1): 23–47.
doi: 10.1080/13556509.2000.10799054

Tymoczko, Maria. 2002. "Connecting the two infinite orders. Research methods in Translation Studies". In *Crosscultural Transgressions*, T. Hermans (ed.), 9–25. Manchester: St. Jerome Publishing.

Tymoczko, Maria. 2006. "Reconceptualizing translation theory. Integrating non-Western thought about translation". In *Translating Others*, Volume 1, T. Hermans (ed.), 13–32. Manchester: St. Jerome Publishing.

Tymoczko, Maria. 2007a. "Why European translators should want to de-Westernize Translation Studies". Plenary talk to the European Society for Translation Studies Conference, Ljubljana, September 2007. (See also http://videolectures.net/est07_tymoczko_wet/.)

Tymoczko, Maria. 2007b. *Enlarging Translation, Empowering Translators*. Manchester: St. Jerome Publishing.

Tymoczko, Maria, and Gentzler, Edwin (eds). 2002. *Translation and Power*. Amherst: University of Massachusetts Press.

Tytler, Alexander F. [1797] 1978. *Essay on the Principles of Translation*. Amsterdam and Philadelphia: Benjamins.

Ullmann-Margalit, Edna. 1977. *The Emergence of Norms*. Oxford: Oxford University Press.

Ulrych, Margherita. 2009. "Translating and editing as mediated discourse: focus on the recipient". In *Translators and Their Readers*. In *Homage to Eugene A. Nida*, R. Dimitriu and M. Shlesinger (eds), 219–234. Brussels: Editions du Hasard.

van Dam, Helle, and Karen K. Zethsen. 2008. "Translator status. A study of Danish company translators". *The Translator* 14 (1): 71–96. doi: 10.1080/13556509.2008.10799250

van Leuven-Zwart, Kitty M., and Ton Naaijkens (eds). 1991. *Translation Studies: The State of the Art. Proceedings of the First James S Holmes Symposium on Translation Studies*. Amsterdam and Atlanta, GA: Rodopi.

Vehmas-Lehto, Inkeri. 1989. *Quasi-correctness. A Critical Study of Finnish Translations of Russian Journalistic Texts*. Helsinki: Neuvostoliittoinstituutti.

Vehviläinen, Päivi. 2000. *Kerro, Kerro Kääntäjä. Kaunokirjallisuuden suomentajan identiteetti haastettelupuheessa*. Licentiate thesis, Department of Translation Studies, University of Tampere.

Venuti, Lawrence. 1995. *The Translator's Invisibility. A history of translation*. London: Routledge.
doi: 10.4324/9780203360064

Venuti, Lawrence. 1998. *The Scandals of Translation: towards an ethics of difference*. London: Routledge. doi: 10.4324/9780203269701

Venuti, Lawrence (ed.). 2000. *The Translation Studies Reader*. London: Routledge.
doi: 10.4324/9780203446621

Venuti, Lawrence. 2002. "The difference that translation makes: the translator's unconscious". In *Translation Studies: perspectives on an emerging discipline*, A. Riccardi (ed.), 214–241. Cambridge: Cambridge University Press.

Vermeer, Hans J. 1996. *A Skopos Theory of Translation. (Some arguments for and against.)* Heidelberg: TEXTconTEXT.

Vermeer, Hans J. 1997. "Translation and the 'meme'". *Target* 9 (1): 155–166.
doi: 10.1075/target.9.1.10ver

Vermeer, Hans J. 1998. "Starting to unask what translatology is all about". *Target* 10 (1): 41–68. doi: 10.1075/target.10.1.03ver

Viaggio, Sergio. 1994. "Theory and professional development: or admonishing translators to be good". In *Teaching Translation and Interpreting 2*, C. Dollerup and A, Lindegaard (eds), 97–105. Amsterdam and Philadelphia: Benjamins. doi: 10.1075/btl.5.16via

Vieira, Else R. P. 1994. "A postmodern translational aesthetics in Brazil". *Translation Studies: An Interdiscipline*, M. Snell-Hornby, F. Pöchhacker and K. Kaindl (eds), 65–72. Amsterdam and Philadelphia: Benjamins. doi: 10.1075/btl.2.09rib

Vinay, Jean-Paul, and Jean Darbelnet. 1958. *Stylistique comparée du français et de l'anglais*. Paris: Didier.

von Wright, Georg H. 1968. *An Essay in Deontic Logic and the General Theory of Action*. Amsterdam: North-Holland. [Acta Philosophica Fennica 21.]

von Wright, Georg H. 1971. *Explanation and Understanding*. Ithaca: Cornell University Press.

Wakabayashi, Judy, and Rita Kothari (eds). 2009. *Decentering Translation Studies. India and Beyond*. Amsterdam and Philadelphia: Benjamins. doi: 10.1075/btl.86

Williams, Jenny, and Andrew Chesterman. 2002. *The Map. A beginner's guide to doing research in Translation Studies*. Manchester: St. Jerome Publishing.

Wilson, Andrew. 2009. *Translators on Translating. Inside the invisible art*. Vancouver: CCSP Press.

Wilson, Edward O. 1998. *Consilience. The Unity of Knowledge*. London: Little, Brown and Company.

Wolf, Michaela, and Alexandra Fukari (eds). 2007. *Constructing a Sociology of Translation*. Amsterdam and Philadelphia: Benjamins. doi: 10.1075/btl.74

Zabalbeascoa, Patrick. 2000. "From techniques to types of solutions". In *Investigating Translation*, A. Beeby, D. Ensinger and M. Presas (eds), 117–127. Amsterdam and Philadelphia: Benjamins. doi: 10.1075/btl.32.15zab

Zalán, Peter. 1990. "Zur Problematik von Normen und Übersetzen". In *Übersetzungswissenschaft. Ergebnisse und Perspektiven: Festschrift für Wolfram Wilss zum 65. Geburtstag*, R. Arntz and G. Thome (eds), 55–58. Tübingen: Narr.

Name index

A
Abdallah 319, 345
Airaksinen 354
Alvstad 35, 237
Amman 70
Andreotti 64
Appiah 252
Aristotle 66, 108, 110, 112, 137, 144–145, 155, 157–158
Armstrong 5
Arrojo 1, 15, 17, 137, 148
Aunger 41
Austin 43, 75, 176

B
Bachleiter 326
Baker 27, 36, 59, 69, 89, 159, 260–261, 263, 278, 300, 308, 326, 345, 367–368
Bartsch 170–174, 180, 182, 186, 188–189
Bassnett 27, 36, 143, 307
Berglund 45, 98
Berman, A. 131, 257, 259–260, 285, 348
Berman, S. 345
Berthele 313
Biguenet 255
Blackmore 41
Blum-Kulka 13, 259–260, 263, 301
Bly 340–341
Boase-Beier 81–82, 88
Booth 4
Born 163
Bourdieu 305, 310–312, 314, 316
Brems 43
Brisset 312
Brooke-Rose 229
Brown 41
Brownlie 13, 66, 86, 161, 191, 321
Buzelin 319, 341

C
Campbell 266, 345
Carl 95, 338
Carlson 121
Catford v, 9, 31, 43, 71–79, 125–126, 202–203, 206–207, 238–240, 273, 278
Chalmers 15, 151
Chesterman 2, 4, 8–9, 15, 17, 23, 26, 35, 37–38, 41, 43, 48, 52, 58–59, 62–63, 67, 69–70, 84, 109, 111, 116, 121, 127–128, 148, 150, 152, 155, 161, 193, 199, 203, 206–207, 209, 224–225, 231, 235, 244, 251, 256, 298–299, 305, 307, 314, 316, 321, 324–329, 334, 350, 355, 359, 365, 367–368
Chevalier 263
Cheyfitz 143
Constable 82, 92
Cowie 100, 123, 238
Crisafulli 165
Croft 152, 163, 300
Cronin 229, 232
Cross 2, 46
Cumps 119

D
Darbelnet 9, 125, 127, 202–203, 206–207, 209, 238, 260–261, 277
Darwin 40–41, 159, 223
Dawkins 41
Delabastita 151, 170
Delisle 202, 312
Dennett 40–41
Devy 7, 360
Diamond 154
Diriker 326
Dodds 85
Doherty 261
Dolet 254
Dollerup 111

E
Ehrensberger-Dow 331, 341, 345
Englund Dimitrova 13, 25, 43, 237, 239, 243–247, 260, 331, 339, 341
Eriksson 209
Even-Zohar 38, 144

F
Faerch 275, 277
Fairclough 312
Farell 214
Fawcett 71, 203
Firth 72, 75
Flotow 27
Flynn 64
Føllesdal 95, 130, 228–229, 231–233, 235, 299
Foot 176
Footit 345
Fortey 164
Frawley 259
Fuller 223, 296–297

G
Gadamer 198, 226, 235
Gambier 50, 131, 185, 193, 269
García-Landa 126, 302
Gerzymisch-Arbogast 225, 285
Gile 1–2, 15, 121, 164, 225–226, 231, 324, 336, 342
Glaser 234
Goethe 50, 83, 92, 131
Goldstone 197
Gombrich 81–83
González Núñez 305
Goodman 196
Göpferich 342
Gouadec 100, 103–104
Gouanvic 310
Gran 85
Greimas 96, 137, 140

Grice 182, 265, 313, 353
Gutt 12, 52, 69–70, 79, 108, 117, 127, 139, 145, 156, 265, 320
Güttinger 270

H
Haddadian-Moghaddam 96
Halliday 71–72, 75, 78, 239
Halverson 152, 154, 187, 244, 251, 262, 301
Hansen 11, 13, 65, 127, 225, 318
Harris 174, 181
Hassard 319
Hatim 313
Heat-Moon 347
Hebenstreit 58
Hekkanen 305, 319
Heidegger 228, 284
Heilbron 310, 326
Heltai 301
Hempel 28, 43, 46–47, 54, 96, 154–155
Henry 72
Hermans 1, 8, 14, 36, 137, 143, 173, 175–176, 230, 252, 296–297, 310–311, 366
Hickey 313
Hofstede 309, 315
Hogarth 92–93
Holmes 28, 120, 305, 323–328
Holz-Mänttäri 60, 69, 144, 314, 340, 348
Hönig 206, 335
House 174, 281, 300
Hurtado Albir 39, 202–207, 209–210

I
Ibrahim 100
Inghilleri 326, 345
Itkonen 170, 178
Ivir 242–243

J
Jääskeläinen 13, 87, 156, 203, 205–206, 213, 321, 339
Jakobsen 243, 337–338
Jandl 169
Jansen 243
Jantunen 220
Jaworski 214
Jerome 254–256
Jodl 167, 176–177, 183
Johansson 4
Johnson 6
Jones 332, 341

K
Kafka 281, 283–288, 292
Kaindl 326
Kalinowski 311
Kaplan, E. 164
Kaplan, M. 164
Kasper 275, 277
Katan 308
Kellerman 275
Kelletat 58, 60, 63, 65
Kelly, L. 198
Kelly, M. 345
Kemble 185
Kenny 260
Kinnunen 91, 96, 333, 341
Klaudy 201–202, 204, 207, 260, 265
Klein 35–36
Kluckhohn 308
Kohlmayer 65
Koller 9, 58, 60, 62, 69, 281
Koskinen 1, 63, 84–85, 91, 96, 164, 326, 333, 341, 345, 348–349
Kothari 296
Kranach 224
Krings 127, 335, 337
Kroeber 308
Krzeszowski 239–240
Kuhn 32, 223, 231, 296
Kujamäki 5, 12–13, 87, 187, 238, 253, 297, 300
Kukkonen 214
Kundera vi, 252, 257, 281–294
Künzli 341
Kurz 326
Kußmaul 206, 336–337, 339

L
Laaksovaara 214
Lado 275
Lakatos 7, 14, 233
Lakoff 6–7
Laland 41
Lambert 163, 314, 324
Lane-Mercier 351
Lang 313
Lanstyák 301
Lass 153, 160
Laviosa (-Braithwaite) 90, 260, 263
Law 319
Lederer 31, 85, 243
Lefevere 8, 27, 36, 50, 111, 143, 230, 307, 310
Leech 353
Leppihalme 50, 118, 121, 164, 202, 205, 214, 336
Leuven-Zwart 131, 203, 206, 242
Levenston 274–275, 277
Levinas 349
Levý 178, 320, 335–336, 342
Lewis, D. K. 172
Lewis, P. E. 348
Lörscher 178, 205, 337, 339
Luhmann 311–312

M
MacIntyre 48, 316–317, 347, 353–355
Maia 261
Maier 16, 229, 232–233, 326
Malblanc 261
Malmkjær 36, 153, 165, 318
Malone 203, 206, 209
Martin 193
Martín de León 60, 68
Matthiessen 241
Mauranen 13, 87, 187, 220, 238, 253, 260–261, 297, 300
Mayoral Asensio 313
McCarty 35
McDonough Dolmaya 345
Medin 197
Melby 108, 112, 349
Meylaerts 305
Mills 345
Milton 261
Misgeld 226, 231
Molina 39, 202–207, 209–210
Mossop 37, 43, 54, 127, 245, 318, 327

Name index

Moster 88, 363–368
Munday 71, 230, 257, 326, 367
Muñoz Martín 205, 305
Murphy 243

N
Neubert 202, 307
Newmark 47, 51, 84, 202, 238, 277
Nicholson 226
Nida 10, 75, 123, 126–127, 144, 202, 204, 206, 243–244, 246, 248, 297, 313, 335, 363–364, 368
Niiniluoto 226, 235
Norberg 66, 331
Nord 10–11, 59, 66–68, 100, 116, 124, 126, 144, 172–174, 205, 271, 314, 335, 349
Nordman 64, 237, 247–248, 341

O
Odlin 275
Olk 313
Olohan 89, 123, 278
Øverås 260

P
Paasilinna 363–366
Paloposki 96, 111, 121
Pápai 88
Peeters 313–314
Pergnier 313
Phillips 226–227
Pike 4
Pöchhacker 13
Pokorn 266
Polezzi 229
Poltermann 311
Popovič 203
Popper 6, 95, 127, 148, 190, 223, 225, 227, 231, 233, 297, 329, 352
Prunč 67, 69
Putnam 165
Puurtinen 50, 114, 213
Pym 9, 16, 36, 66, 74, 83, 108, 116, 128, 143, 147, 155, 160–161, 163–164, 193, 207, 232, 236, 240, 247, 287, 291, 297, 303, 305, 308, 312, 324, 342, 345, 349, 357, 366

Q
Quine 112, 287

R
Raittila 81, 88
Ramos Pinto 43
Raz 171
Reiß 31, 55–56, 58–61, 64–65, 67, 70, 78, 83, 144, 270–271, 273, 314, 340, 368
Retsker 202
Risku 61, 314, 332
Robinson 137, 311
Round 229
Rudner 68–69
Runciman 316
Rushdie 92

S
Sager 10, 38, 100–101, 126, 340
Salmon 5, 148–149, 157, 159–160, 162, 234
Saville-Troike 214
Savory 254
Schäffner 36, 185, 258
Schiavi 126
Schleifer 140
Schmidt 342
Schreiber 193
Schulte 255
Searle 176
Segerstråle 40
Séguinot 206, 220
Seleskovitch 31, 85, 243
Shlesinger 147, 181, 269, 363
Shreve 202, 337
Shuttleworth 100, 123, 238
Siitonen 358
Simeoni 147, 311
Simmel 281, 290–291
Sintonen 148–149
Snell-Hornby 35, 71, 324
Sovran 195, 197–198
Sperber 117
Sprung 314
Stecconi 299
Stetting 101
Strauss 234
Sunwoo 59, 68
Susam-Sarajeva 154

T
Taivalkoski-Shilov 50, 260
Tannen 214
Tarasti 214
Tirkkonen-Condit 89, 213, 242–244, 260, 269–271, 273, 277, 279
Toury x, 1, 12–13, 28, 32, 37, 46–49, 60, 68, 74, 79, 95, 99, 106, 111–112, 127, 134, 144, 147, 149, 151–155, 157, 160–163, 165, 168–170, 185, 187, 198, 205, 230, 242–243, 251, 259–261, 263, 301, 305, 311, 324, 327, 331–332, 334–336, 350
Trivedi 226
Turner 83, 92
Tversky 195–197
Tymoczko 15, 36, 75, 137, 143, 251–252, 263, 296, 298, 301–302, 308, 347, 356, 358
Tytler 254

U
Ullmann-Margalit 173
Ulrych 301

V
Van Dam 326
Van Gorp 163
Vehmas-Lehto 220
Vehviläinen 318
Venuti 1, 27, 48, 50, 111, 137, 143, 226, 229, 255, 345, 348
Vermeer 11, 31, 41, 43, 52, 55–60, 62, 64, 66–70, 78, 83, 144, 156, 314, 340, 368
Viaggio 47–48
Vieira 86, 297
Vinay 9, 125, 127, 202–203, 206–207, 209, 238, 260–261, 277
Von Wright 95, 128, 148–149, 151, 157–160, 171

W
Wagner 2, 67, 84, 121, 262, 314
Wakabayashi 296
White 193
Williams 38
Wilson, A. 247

Wilson, D. 117
Wilson, E. O. 2, 40–41
Wolf 305, 326, 331
Wood 345
Woodsworth 312

Z
Zabalbeascoa 204, 211
Zalán 178
Zethsen 326

Subject index

A

Actor-network theory 305, 319–320, 341
Art (painting) 82–83, 92–93, 227

C

Category, categorization 2, 78, 162, 229–230, 244, 251
Causality 4–5, 11–12, 19–20, 37–40, 48–54, 65–67, 86, 105–121, 123–135, 137–146, 150, 155–164, 181–182, 185–186, 196–198
see also Explanation
Consilience 2, 16, 35, 40–41, 305
Contrastive analysis 9–10, 72–75, 108, 125, 195–198, 207, 213, 239, 274–276, 278
Corpus 9–10, 13–15, 38, 54, 220, 252, 259, 262–263, 266, 278, 297, 302
Correspondence 71, 73–75, 79, 203, 239–240, 242, 274

D

Definition 18, 22–23, 56–60, 71–74, 98–99, 113, 131, 168, 186, 202–205, 230–231, 239–241, 251–252, 271, 302, 308–309, 316, 323, 329, 332–333
Descriptive hypothesis 6, 13, 15, 22, 24, 123, 132–135, 234, 251, 253, 264, 266, 333
see also Universals
Deverbalization 31, 85, 201, 243–245

E

Effects 11–13, 20–22, 27–28, 30–33, 38–39, 48–54, 59, 86, 92, 97–98, 113–121, 127–129, 133–135, 139–140, 143–145, 265, 281, 341, 358–359
Equivalence 9, 31, 59–60, 73–76, 82–85, 91, 99–101, 125, 181–182, 195–199, 207, 211, 230, 239–240, 248, 258–259, 272–274, 284, 293, 297–299, 360
Ethics 21, 37, 48, 64, 68–69, 120, 165, 176–177, 182, 259, 316, 326–327, 345–361, 363–368
Explanation, explanatory hypothesis 4–6, 12–14, 22, 25, 28, 47, 49, 65–66, 95–96, 107, 132–133, 147–164, 170, 180–182, 187, 234–235, 244–245, 264–265, 278–279, 292, 334
Explicitation 13, 88–89, 246, 251, 257, 259–265

F

Fallacy 43, 114–115, 176, 253, 255, 295–296
Falsification 63, 65–66, 81, 95, 98, 107, 111, 114, 132, 160, 180, 223, 231, 233–235, 242, 251, 299, 339

G

Generalization 4–5, 28, 47, 57, 78, 81, 96, 106–107, 118, 139, 147, 151–155, 160, 162–163, 187, 196, 208, 251 256, 258, 260–263, 293, 295, 297–298, 301, 334, 343

H

Hermeneutic(s) 1–2, 25–27, 29, 46–47, 55, 91, 130, 137, 148–149, 155, 198, 225–235, 303
Hypothesis 6–7, 12–16, 21–24, 30, 48–52, 66–68, 83, 87, 95–96, 107, 114, 123, 130–135, 165, 185, 190–191, 223–249, 293, 296–298, 300–302
see also Descriptive hypothesis, Explanation, Interpretive hypothesis, Literal translation, Prediction, Unique items

I

Implicitation 89, 109, 251
Interdiscipline 35–36, 40, 266, 323–324
Interference 32, 48, 79, 111–112, 162, 188, 220, 243–244, 260, 274–275, 337
Interpretive hypothesis ix, 6–9, 14, 21, 23–24, 58, 63, 130–131, 149, 223, 225–235, 299

L

Law 13, 22, 24, 28, 30, 32, 47, 79, 82, 95, 111–115, 134–135, 138, 151–154, 157–159, 167–170, 178–180, 187, 251, 253, 260
Literal translation 13, 65, 86, 101, 191, 214, 219, 237–249, 255, 275, 277, 281, 340

M

Memetics 8, 41, 162
Metaphor 5–8, 16, 19, 30, 35, 51, 60–61, 75, 85–86, 98–99, 126, 130, 149–150, 162, 198–199, 229, 233–234, 283, 295, 298–299, 353, 360

Model   1, 3, 6, 9–12, 15–16, 37–38, 123–135, 158, 226, 242–244, 307, 309–315, 328–329, 331–343, 347–353, 366–367
Myth   5–8, 16, 255, 347

N
Norm   12, 20, 22, 24, 36, 38–39, 40, 46–48, 83, 85, 92–93, 108–109, 129, 138–139, 156, 158, 165–191, 247–248, 265, 285, 314, 350–353, 266–367

P
Polysystem   14, 31–32, 123, 127, 144, 156, 160, 284–285, 310
Prediction, predictive hypothesis   5–6, 13, 22, 24, 28, 47, 49–51, 62, 66, 95, 111, 119, 132–134, 151, 180, 253, 256, 262, 334–336, 339, 341, 343
Prescriptivism, prescriptive view   21–22, 24, 26, 28, 43, 45–54, 57, 61–62, 65, 70, 81, 84–85, 88, 97–98, 119–120, 128, 170, 176–179 186, 254–256, 335

Q
Quality   12–13, 19, 21, 25–27, 33, 46–47, 54, 102, 135, 182–183, 186, 256, 258, 266, 270, 314–318, 320–321
see also Ethics

R
Relevance theory   12, 69–70, 110, 117–118, 127, 139, 145, 150, 156, 265, 320
Repetition   13, 87, 90, 135, 187, 260, 284–285
Retranslation   13, 96, 123, 130–133, 227, 260, 263
Revision   10, 13, 43, 101–104, 131, 243, 245–249, 317–318, 327, 333, 340–341

S
Salience threshold   213–216, 219–221
Semiotics   103, 126, 137–146, 214, 226–227, 348
Shadow translation   4, 241
Shift   75, 153–154, 201–204, 206, 208, 210–211, 242, 273–274
Similarity   6, 59, 117, 125–126, 162, 169, 193, 195–199, 201, 211, 228–230, 235, 239, 246–248, 271–274
Skopos theory   10–11, 26, 31–32, 39, 43, 52, 55–70, 77–78, 83–84, 108, 110, 116, 124, 127, 135, 144, 150, 156, 161, 271, 297, 314, 326, 335, 340, 348, 366, 368
Sociology   10, 36–40, 87, 96, 110, 180, 290, 305–329, 331–333, 340–341
Standardization   32, 79, 111–112, 127–128, 151, 187, 193, 244, 260–264, 300–301
Stranger   290–293
Strategy   4, 39–40, 48–50, 53–54, 67–68, 89, 109–110, 121, 178–182, 193, 201–211, 238, 246, 275, 277, 320, 337

T
Telos   59, 326, 368
Terminology   2, 4, 26, 39, 64, 69, 152, 193, 202–203, 263–264, 302–303, 314
Theoros   3, 16, 229, 233
Theory   3–16, 17–24, 28, 31–33, 36, 45, 47, 57–58, 62, 66, 71–79, 81–88, 98, 121, 123–124, 140, 144, 154, 159, 161, 163, 170, 177, 180, 223, 227, 229, 255, 295–299, 303, 305, 311, 313, 325, 333
see also Actor-Network, Model, Norm, Polysystem, Relevance, Skopos

Translation act   49, 51, 128–129, 137, 188, 249, 325, 331–332, 334–335, 337–338, 340
Translation event   1, 37–38, 49, 51, 128–129, 137, 249, 311, 317, 325, 327, 331–333, 338, 340–341
Translation policy   33, 87, 305, 315, 324, 327
Translation process   10–13, 16, 19, 38, 61, 64, 108, 117–118, 126–127, 134, 150, 168–169, 173–174, 197–199, 203–204, 210, 241, 243–246, 248, 264, 276, 308–309, 314–315, 317–318, 320, 325–327, 331–343
see also Translation act, Translation event
Translog   11, 127, 150, 243, 337
Typology   4, 9, 26, 30–31, 49, 67, 72–74, 96–97, 99–104, 193, 201–211, 255–256, 258, 300

U
Unification   4–5, 16, 147, 159–160, 163, 234
Unique items   89, 238, 244, 269–279
Universals   4, 9, 13–14, 22, 38, 87–88, 90, 134–135, 145, 152, 165, 170, 238, 244–245, 251–294, 300–302